A Separate Canaan

A Separate Canaan

· · · · · · · · · · · · · · · · ·

The Making of an Afro-Moravian World

in North Carolina, 1763–1840

Jon F. Sensbach

Published for the Omohundro Institute of Early

American History and Culture, Williamsburg, Virginia,

by the University of North Carolina Press,

Chapel Hill and London

The Omohundro Institute of Early American History and Culture is
sponsored jointly by the College of William and Mary and the Colonial
Williamsburg Foundation. On November 15, 1996, the Institute adopted
the present name in honor of a bequest from Malvern H. Omohundro, Jr.

Library of Congress Cataloging-in-Publication Data
Sensbach, Jon F.
A separate Canaan : the making of an Afro-Moravian world in North
Carolina, 1763–1840 / Jon F. Sensbach.
p. cm. Includes bibliographical references (p.   ) and index.
ISBN 0-8078-2394-5 (cloth: alk. paper)
ISBN 0-8078-4698-8 (pbk.: alk. paper)
1. Afro-Americans—North Carolina—History—18th century. 2. Afro-
Americans—North Carolina—History—19th century. 3. Moravians—
North Carolina—History—18th century. 4. Moravians—North
Carolina—History—19th century. 5. North Carolina—Race relations.
I. Title.
E185.93.N6S46   1998   97-17726
975.6'00496073—dc21   CIP

This volume received indirect support from an unrestricted book
publication grant awarded to the Institute by the L. J. Skaggs and Mary C.
Skaggs Foundation of Oakland, California.

02 01 00 99 98   5 4 3 2 1

For Beverly

ACKNOWLEDGMENTS

. . . .

THIS STUDY WOULD NOT have been possible without the help and encouragement of many people—historians, archivists, museum professionals, friends, and family—who have absorbed me into a kind of extended-kin support network, much like the black and white Moravians who inhabit the following pages.

I am grateful to the Moravian Church, Southern Province, based in Winston-Salem, North Carolina, for granting me access to the splendid manuscript collections upon which this study rests. A survey by consultant Frank Myers suggested the wealth of records for a study of African-American Moravians. Moravian Archives director C. Daniel Crews and former director Thomas Haupert graciously met my requests to study many thousands of pages of documents. Assistants Richard Starbuck and Grace Robinson provided additional help and kindness that enriched my work there.

I am also indebted to the staffs of the Moravian Archives, Northern Province, in Bethlehem, Pennsylvania, the Archiv der Brüder-Unität in Herrnhut, Germany, the Library of Congress, the Duke University Manuscript Collection, the Southern Historical Collection at the University of North Carolina at Chapel Hill, the North Carolina Division of Archives and History, and the Stokes County Courthouse for making their manuscript collections available to me.

At Duke University, where this study emerged as a doctoral dissertation, Peter Wood diverted my interest in the twentieth-century civil rights movement into early American history—while making me understand how much those two eras have in common. Peter first pointed me in the direction of the Moravians, and his inspiring teaching and his creative penchant for devising fresh ways of viewing history have provided an intellectual guide that I am fortunate to have had. Julius Scott, Ray Gavins, and Leland Ferguson of the University of South Carolina also read this work as a dissertation and gave perceptive criticisms. Further thanks go to Leland for providing copies of his archaeological reports from summer excavations at the African-American graveyard in Salem, work that is literally unearthing new information about antebellum black Christians. I benefited from the encouragement and powerful intellectual examples of John Hope Franklin and C. Eric Lincoln. Though not directly involved in this project, Larry Goodwyn taught me much about the nature of American democracy. And at Duke's Office of Research Support, Judy Argon generously allowed me a flexible work schedule for extended research trips.

As this project took shape, I had the extraordinary good fortune to work for three years as an adviser to the "African-Americans in Salem" project at Old Salem, Inc., a living-history museum in the restored Moravian village where so many of the events described in this book took place. Strategically placed at the fertile intersection of academic and public history, I benefited enormously from working with a large and dedicated staff whose expertise helped shape this study. A generous grant from the Jessie Ball DuPont Fund made the program possible. Gene Capps and Carol Hall are due special thanks for their commitment to the project and for helping me in countless ways. Sally Gant graciously let me stay for several weeks in her wonderful eighteenth-century Moravian home in Old Salem during my first extended research trip. Among dozens of staff members past and present who helped in various ways, I also thank Karen Becker, Hobie Cawood, Tom Cowan, Malinda Crutchfield, Michael Hammond, John Larson, Paula Locklair, Jane Steele, Ken Zogry, and the late William Alderson. Also during my years in Winston-Salem, the Reverend Cedric Rodney introduced me to the Saint Philip's congregation and helped me better understand its marvelous legacy. William Rice and Melvin "Schoolboy" Oates revealed hidden aspects of the town's rich African-American past.

A postdoctoral fellowship from the Institute of Early American History and Culture, partly funded by the National Endowment for the Humanities, afforded me the rare luxury of time for research and writing. I am especially grateful for Director Ronald Hoffman's friendship, humor, and support in making my two years in Williamsburg enjoyable and productive. Sally Mason and Beverly Smith provided many kindnesses, and I was fortunate to be in residence with two other fellows, Kathy Brown and Darren Staloff, two outstanding scholars who became close friends.

The Institute also furnished the best criticism and direction of my project that I could have hoped for. Early in my tenure there, staff members and I took part in a morning's vigorous discussion that helped shape in many ways my subsequent work. I benefited from the thoughtful commentary, both oral and written, of Kathy Brown, Ron Hoffman, Sally Mason, Mike McGiffert, John Selby, Darren Staloff, and Fredrika Teute. Additional readers Ira Berlin and Mechal Sobel, whose work I have long admired and who also participated in that session, gave excellent advice on rethinking crucial points. Later, Gwendolyn Midlo Hall and Albert Raboteau provided adept critiques of a revised manuscript that helped me sharpen several arguments.

Editor Fredrika Teute took an interest in the story of the Moravians years ago and has supported this project ever since. Her detailed and relentlessly probing comments on several drafts have strengthened the book in many ways, not least of which was her insistence on connecting the Moravians to broader developments in America. Virginia Montijo Chew skillfully guided the manuscript through copyediting and production, improving it greatly along the way. I am grateful to both for their commitment, diligence, and insight.

Several others have contributed in meaningful ways to my understanding of Moraviana. Dan Thorp perceptively commented on several chapters and graciously shared important findings from his own research. His work on the early settlement of Wachovia provided me with a sturdy foundation. I have benefited from many discussions with two other historians, Elisabeth Sommer and Scott Rohrer, both of whom are helping to fill the still-large gap in our knowledge of Moravian culture.

Portions of this book have appeared in two previously published essays and are used here with the permission of their editors: "Interracial Sects: Religion, Race, and Gender among Early North Carolina Moravians," in Catherine Clinton and Michele Gillespie, eds., *The Devil's Lane: Sex and Race in the Early South* (New York, 1997), 154–167; and "Conflict and Culture in the Early Black Church: A Moravian Mission Congregation in Antebellum North Carolina," *North Carolina Historical Review*, LXXI (1994), 401–429.

At the University of Southern Mississippi, friends and colleagues in the History Department have provided a supportive environment for teaching and scholarship. Chair Orazio Ciccarelli has helped out with enthusiastic encouragement and travel funds and has worked hard to make my job easier. Shelia Nelson has supplied administrative assistance of many kinds with patience and good cheer.

My thanks go, as well, to other friends who have offered advice and support at various stages of this project, including Herman Bennett, Chuck Bolton, Peter Gunter, Woody Holton, Marjolein Kars, Johanna Miller Lewis, Doug Mackaman, and Ted Pearson.

My greatest debt is to my family. My parents, Werner and Gladys Sensbach, have always taken an active interest in my work and have assisted and supported me in many ways through the years; I appreciate my father's help in deciphering many a document in baffling German script. My mother, along with my parents-in-law, John and Nancy Schultz, stepped in to lend crucial help during a moment of need, allowing me to write when I urgently needed to. Ever the good fraternalist, my brother Steve has given steady encouragement and friendship. My wife, Beverly, has been a special source of inspiration for me and for the evolution of this work. Patiently putting up with my long hours of work and extended research trips away from home, she has contributed in countless ways to my ability to complete this book. Exemplifying the best Moravian traditions, her love and great generosity of spirit have been my best guide.

CONTENTS

. . . .

Contents

ILLUSTRATIONS

. . . .

· · · · · · · · · · · · · · · · ·

 RECORDS OF THE Moravian Church in Winston-Salem, North Carolina, form the basis of this study. An eleven-volume compilation of abstracts from these records edited by Adelaide L. Fries et al. is *Records of the Moravians in North Carolina* (Raleigh, N.C., 1922–1969). I have drawn heavily from those volumes. The translated passages in the *Records*, however, represent only a small portion of the diaries, church board minutes, memoirs, and personal journals in the Moravian Archives. Most of these sources were written in German script and remain untranslated. Over the years, various translation efforts have made several important bodies of records accessible to a broader readership, though they remain in typescript form in the archives. These include (with translator):

Aeltesten Conferenz, or Elders' Conference (abbreviated as Aelt. Conf.), 1765–1769, 1780–1823 (Frances Cumnock)

Aufseher Collegium, or Salem Board of Overseers (abbreviated as Auf. Col.), 1772–1856 (Erika Huber)

Gemein Rath, or Salem Congregational Council, 1772–1843 (Erika Huber)

Helfer Conferenz, or Helpers' Conference (abbreviated as Help. Conf.), intermittent years

Diary of the Small Negro Congregation in and around Salem (referred to as Negro Congregation Diary), 1822–1842 (Elizabeth Marx)

Translators of other assorted documents are credited by the initials EH (Erika Huber), EM (Elizabeth Marx), ES (Edmund Schwarze), and FC (Frances Cumnock). All other translations are my own. All citations of primary sources are from documents housed in the Moravian Archives, Southern Province, Winston-Salem, North Carolina, unless indicated otherwise.

German terms are italicized in the text only on their first use.

Other abbreviations:

AHR	*American Historical Review*
GHC	Grosse Helfer Conferenz
HCfG	Helfer Conferenz fürs Ganze (Helpers' Conference for Wachovia)
JAH	*Journal of American History*
JIH	*Journal of Interdisciplinary History*
JNH	*Journal of Negro History*
JSH	*Journal of Southern History*
LAC	Landarbeiter Conferenz (Conference of Country Congregation Ministers)
NCDAH	North Carolina Division of Archives and History
NCHR	*North Carolina Historical Review*
PAC	Provinzial Aeltesten Conferenz (Provincial Elders' Conference)
PHC	Provinzial Helfer Conferenz (Provincial Helpers' Conference)
PMHB	*Pennsylvania Magazine of History and Biography*
SAE	Societät zu Ausbreitung des Evangelii unter den Heiden in Nord-America (Society for the Propagation of the Gospel among the Heathen in North America)
SHC	Southern Historical Collection, Chapel Hill, N.C.
TMHS	Moravian Historical Society, *Transactions*
VMHB	*Virginia Magazine of History and Biography*
WMQ	*William and Mary Quarterly*

INTRODUCTION

. . . .

THIS WORK IS ABOUT A MOMENT of flickering hope in the maelstrom of American race relations. It is also the first sustained study of the meeting of Germans and Africans in early America. And it explores what happened in a place and time when the lives of black and white people commingled in an intimate embrace of oppression and fellowship, antagonism and respect, attraction and repulsion. This is a story about belonging and exclusion in America.

The events described here took place partly in Africa, in Europe, and in the Caribbean; but most of all, they unfolded in the red clay hills of Piedmont North Carolina. There, in the winter of 1753, a band of religious German-speaking immigrants planted a settlement on land so rich, spacious, and—as they saw it—uncluttered by human occupation that it seemed "reserved by the Lord" for them.[1] These settlers were members of the Renewed Unity of Brethren, more commonly known as the Moravian Church, an evangelical Protestant church from central Europe. They saw themselves as agents of God, and they meant their settlement in North Carolina to be an exclusive refuge from religious persecution where they would live in sanctified seclusion.

But soon they admitted outsiders into their midst—African and African-American people, all of whom were enslaved. The Moravian Brethren already had considerable experience with Africans, being among the first Protestant missionaries to preach to Africans in the West Indies, as early as the 1730s. Although they fervently believed in the inclusiveness of the Christian gospel, they hardly opposed human bondage themselves. In a period when slavery was expanding rapidly in the southern upcountry, the Moravians began buying slaves to help build and operate the farms, craft

---

1. August Spangenberg Diary, in Adelaide L. Fries et al., eds., *Records of the Moravians in North Carolina*, 11 vols. (Raleigh, N.C., 1922–1969), I, 59–60.

xvii

shops, and industries that would bring prosperity and acclaim to their North Carolina sanctuary. By the early nineteenth century, hundreds of African Americans had worked for the Brethren. And, because many of them were looking for a new faith at a time when the Moravians were offering one, dozens joined the Moravian Church and were received into full membership. In this mixed German and African enclave, free white and enslaved black Brethren worked and worshiped side by side. They were partners in the self-styled family of Christ.

The Moravian experiment takes us inside the social ferment of Revolutionary America, when some strains of radical evangelical religion and natural rights philosophy questioned the racist doctrine that had evolved in the enslavement of Africans in the Americas for more than two hundred years. By the late eighteenth century, strongholds of black and white Christians occupied much of the South, often to the dismay of the planters. For a time, the door to a more open society appeared to stand ajar. But how wide, and for how long? In an era of sometimes violent social change, black Moravian Brethren, like all African Americans, were wary of the ephemeral nature of white racial attitudes. The precariousness of their position was not lost on them.

THE WORLD OF black and white Moravians invites questions about the American drama—questions, for example, about American slavery, black culture, and American pluralism. For years, the study of African-American slavery was dominated by historians' fixation on its antebellum form—with the cotton plantation world of the Old South on the eve of the Civil War. This focus constricted the view of slavery to the last three decades of a seemingly unchanging institution that was in reality more than three centuries old in the Americas by 1861. Delving deeper into the eighteenth and seventeenth centuries, and looking to Africa itself, scholars have learned much more about the origins and development of racial slavery and African-American culture in early America. Portraits of African life in the South Carolina lowcountry, the Chesapeake, the Caribbean, and New England have revealed not only the prominence of Africans in colonial British America but also the complexities and variations of slave societies at different times and in different places. Historians have broadened their vision even further, beyond the scope of colonial Anglo-America, to African and African-American life in an array of settings from French Louisiana to Spanish

Florida, from coastal plantations to inland forests to the high seas, to the Dutch, French, Spanish, and Portuguese worlds of the West Indies and Latin America. Africans were central to the evolving colonial order of the Americas. Stereotypical images of slavery and African-American life as rooted timelessly in the antebellum cotton South stand forever altered.[2]

What, then, do we make of an unfamiliar place devised and shared by Germans and Africans in central North Carolina? After all, like African Americans, the place of German immigrants in early southern history has been equally ignored or misconstrued, though many thousands settled the region. The two groups are seldom mentioned together, though evidence suggests they had much more traffic with each other than historians have generally recognized. On one hand, the black presence in the Moravian settlement was far smaller than on the tobacco and rice plantations to the east, measured by scores and hundreds of people rather than by thousands. Yet, here was a world where African and African-American captives worked in craft shops and on communal farms with free white German immigrants, where black and white Moravians prayed and lived (sometimes in the same dormitory) together in a tightly structured Moravian Church family underpinned by the two poles of racial slavery and spiritual fellowship. In this place, many blacks spoke German better than English; though on a limited scale, the Moravian settlement contained the largest German-speaking black population known in the early South. Some African Americans wrote and read German and English, figured mathematics, and played classical instruments; here, they taught some Germans how to speak English. Measured against stock images of southern history, such a place seems strange and anomalous, and perhaps it was. But the convergence of Germans and

2. These historiographical developments are described in Peter H. Wood, " 'I Did the Best I Could for My Day': The Study of Early Black History during the Second Reconstruction, 1960 to 1976," *WMQ*, 3d Ser., XXXV (1978), 185–225; and Jon F. Sensbach, "Charting a Course in Early African-American History," *WMQ*, 3d Ser., L (1993), 394–405. As I explain in the latter essay, I do not mean to imply by these generalizations that earlier generations of historians entirely ignored the African presence in colonial America. A small group of determined scholars such as Carter G. Woodson, Luther P. Jackson, Lorenzo Greene, Melville Herskovits, and others pioneered research in the field. They were, however, largely ignored by the mainstream of the profession. Important overviews include Robin Blackburn, *The Making of New World Slavery: From the Baroque to the Modern, 1492–1800* (New York, 1997); John Thornton, *Africa and Africans in the Making of the Atlantic World, 1400–1680* (New York, 1992); Ira Berlin, "From Creole to African: Atlantic Creoles and the Origins of African-American Society in Mainland North America," *WMQ*, 3d Ser., LIII (1996), 251–288; and Stephan Palmié, *Slave Cultures and the Cultures of Slavery* (Knoxville, Tenn., 1996).

African Americans gives new dimensions to our understanding of the cultural diversity of the early South.[3]

And their experience raises questions about how black and white people have regarded each other, and themselves, during the long racial trauma handed down from one generation of Americans to another. There is no longer any doubt that the concept of "race" is a socially engineered idea that, although it has meant different things at different times, in American history has most often been deployed in support of white domination.[4] But the painful record of relations between white and black Americans has been punctuated by occasional attempts to forge a common language, whether social, economic, political, or religious. Stretching back in time from the Civil Rights movement of the 1950s and 1960s, to various labor struggles of the 1930s, to the Populist movement of the 1890s, to abolitionism, to the age of revolution in the late eighteenth century, and, especially, deep into the colonial period, before racial hierarchies became fixed, at least some blacks and some whites could look across—and even attempt to bridge—the chasm of racial identity and regard each other with a degree of mutual respect and common interest.

The Moravian social and spiritual experiment flourished in just such an era when the racial divide showed important signs of narrowing. Though scarcely a movement for political or economic equality, at least from the white perspective, the fellowship of the Brethren, like that of other evan-

3. Historians are filling the void regarding Germans in the early South. See, for example, A. G. Roeber, *Palatines, Liberty, and Property: German Lutherans in Colonial British America* (Baltimore, 1993); Daniel B. Thorp, *The Moravian Community in Colonial North Carolina: Pluralism on the Southern Frontier* (Knoxville, Tenn., 1989); Aaron Spencer Fogleman, *Hopeful Journeys: German Immigration, Settlement, and Political Culture in Colonial America* (Philadelphia, 1996); and George Fenwick Jones, *The Salzburger Saga* (Athens, Ga., 1984).

4. On the social construction of racial ideology, see Ivan Hannaford, *Race: The History of an Idea in the West* (Baltimore, 1996); Barbara Fields, "Ideology and Race in American History," in J. Morgan Kousser and James M. McPherson, eds., *Region, Race, and Reconstruction: Essays in Honor of C. Vann Woodward* (New York, 1982), 143–177; Kathleen M. Brown, *Good Wives, Nasty Wenches, and Anxious Patriarchs: Gender, Race, and Power in Colonial Virginia* (Chapel Hill, N.C., 1996); and a special issue of the *William and Mary Quarterly* called "Constructing Race: Differentiating Peoples in the Early Modern World," 3d Ser., LIV (1997), esp. Robin Blackburn, "The Old World Background to European Colonial Slavery," 65–102, Benjamin Braude, "The Sons of Noah and the Construction of Ethnic and Geographical Identities in the Medieval and Early Modern Periods," 103–142, James H. Sweet, "The Iberian Roots of American Racist Thought," 143–166, and Jennifer L. Morgan, " 'Some Could Suckle over Their Shoulder': Male Travelers, Female Bodies, and the Gendering of Racial Ideology, 1500–1700," 167–192.

gelical groups, nonetheless manifested an important first step—white acknowledgment of black humanity—that seemed to herald a sense of fluidity in the American caste system. In fact, during the second half of the eighteenth century, black and white people in America often encountered and influenced each other in ways that appear startling when viewed through the lens of hindsight that can narrow our focus to a bleak, seemingly undifferentiated historical sweep of racial oppression.[5]

Although African Americans have on occasion been cautiously receptive to cooperative efforts with whites, whether political or social, bitter experience has provided ample reminders that to bank survival on such overtures has consistently been a recipe for disappointment. Instead, black Americans have sought to develop distinctive institutions and cultural languages to lend more reliable support against a hostile world. Indeed, in the present context the image of a "separate Canaan" springs from the very different interpretations that black and white Christians attached to the gospel. European Christian immigrants (such as the Moravians) perceived America as a new Israel, a refuge from the spiritual and physical "wilderness" of Europe, and a biblical model for the moral regeneration of the world. For Afro-Christians, on the other hand, America, the land of captivity, represented the opposite image—Egypt, a wilderness of exile and bondage like that of the Israelites with whom they identified. In a metaphorical sense of separateness, then, black Moravians' search for a usable faith was an effort to sustain a vision of salvation, or Canaan, within the Moravian Church, yet distinct from that of white Brethren. In a literal sense, and with profound implications, that search was undertaken increasingly apart from whites and was intimately connected with black kinship practices. The interplay of these competing languages defined the making of an Afro-Moravian world.[6]

THIS STORY RESTS on a vast but little-known cache of documentary evidence left by the Moravian Church. Throughout American history, religious

5. The work of Mechal Sobel has been exemplary in exploring cross-cultural exchanges between Africans and Europeans in colonial America; see *The World They Made Together: Black and White Values in Eighteenth-Century Virginia* (Princeton, N.J., 1988), and "Whatever You Do, Treat People Right: Personal Ethics in a Slave Society," in Ted Ownby, ed., *Black and White Cultural Interaction in the Antebellum South* (Jackson, Miss., 1993), 55–82.

6. Vincent Harding, "The Uses of the Afro-American Past," in Donald R. Cutler, ed., *The Religious Situation: 1969* (Boston, Mass., 1969), 829–840. The point is echoed in Albert J.

groups out to regenerate the world have often left a long paper trail as a kind of accounting statement to God and as a blueprint to show others exactly how new Jerusalem was built. So, with exceptional thoroughness, Moravian ministers and diarists, like the Puritans and Mormons, to name two better-known examples, recorded the daily activities of the Brethren from the first moments of settlement. From mundane details about weather, harvests, and baptisms to major events like the American Revolution and the hasty as-sembly of militia following Nat Turner's rebellion, the diaries provide al-most an hour-by-hour account of life in what they, again like the Puritans, regarded as their city on a hill. In addition, the elaborate web of church governing boards that met weekly or monthly left many books of minutes, scrawled in archaic German script, bearing richly detailed insights into the workings of a culture. The result is a wealth of information giving a rare and often intimate window into the late colonial and early national period.[7]

African Americans emerge in often vivid detail from these documents. One most unusual source has been especially helpful in reconstructing the lives of black Moravians. Each member of the Moravian Church was re-quired to leave a *Lebenslauf* (literally, life course), a memoir or short autobi-ography describing a few details of the person's outward life and an account of his or her spiritual journey. Typically the memoirs depict a sequential process leading from an unredeemed life of sin to spiritual crisis, conversion, and a new life dedicated to Christ. After the person's death, a minister finished the memoir and read it aloud at the funeral. Thousands of these documents in the Moravian Archives form a great but virtually untapped source for southern history. Among the memoirs are dozens of accounts, usually a few pages long, written about black Moravians in the third person by ministers who based much of their narrative on testimony from the subject. The black Moravian biographies, though not first-person, are signif-icant because so few eighteenth-century sources provide accounts of African

---

Raboteau, *Slave Religion: The "Invisible Institution" in the Antebellum South* (New York, 1978), 251. See also Raboteau, "African-Americans, Exodus, and the American Israel," in Raboteau, *A Fire in the Bones: Reflections on African-American Religious History* (Boston, 1995), 17–36. W.E.B. Du Bois famously described what he called the "double-consciousness," or "twoness," of African Americans as the challenge of being "an American, a Negro; two souls, two thoughts, two unreconciled strivings; two warring ideals in one dark body, whose dogged strength alone keeps it from being torn asunder" (Du Bois, *The Souls of Black Folk* [1903; reprint, New York, 1961], 3). On this continuing challenge, see Gerald Early, ed., *Lure and Loathing: Essays on Race, Identity, and the Ambivalence of Assimilation* (New York, 1993).

7. Portions of these documents are extracted in Fries et al., eds., *Records*.

Americans. These documents provide much important information and together form a rare composite portrait of a people.[8]

The Moravian records vividly show how complex, changeable, and intimately interwoven the relationship of black to white could be in early America. That relationship contained the seeds of racial rapprochement, or what historian C. Vann Woodward described for a similar period in the late nineteenth century as "forgotten alternatives" to social orthodoxies. It may be that the most racially divided hour in the United States is still 11:00 A.M. on Sunday morning. That schism has not always been so. How we inherited it is another matter.[9]

8. For a published example of one firsthand Lebenslauf by a black Moravian in a different place, Bethlehem, Pennsylvania, see Daniel B. Thorp, "Chattel with a Soul: The Autobiography of a Moravian Slave," *PMHB*, CXII (1988), 433–451.

9. C. Vann Woodward, *The Strange Career of Jim Crow,* 3d ed. (New York, 1974); Robert L. Hall, "Commentary," in Ownby, ed., *Black and White,* 44.

A Separate Canaan

I do not ask who you are. . . . that is not important to me.
You can do nothing and be nothing but what I will
   infold you.

To a drudge of the cottonfields or emptier of privies
   I lean. . . . on his right cheek I put the family kiss,
And in my soul I swear I never will deny him.
   —Walt Whitman, "Song of Myself"

· · · · · · · · · · · · · · · · ·

A Rapid Motion
Agitating the Universe

An African Odyssey

THE SEA AND THE SHIP were behind him now—he had stumbled alive from the nautical coffin.

Not long ago, he had been a soldier from a powerful family in West Africa. His father's words could sway his countrymen to war or peace; they chose war. In battle, the son was captured by warriors from another African nation, sold to European slave traders, hustled aboard a slave ship, and chained in the hold for a voyage of no return. In America, he and a handful of fellow slaves traveled in shackles overland, nearly three hundred miles from the Chesapeake's worn tobacco fields to the farms and forested hills of the North Carolina upcountry. Now, on a strange continent in August 1771, this captive Mandingo found himself in a remote village whose lyrical Hebrew name contained a cruel irony: Bethabara, "house of passage."

He was called Sambo; his face was scarred by battle, and his African captors had clipped his ears. He limped from a toe infection caused by what Europeans called the Guinea worm. Indigenous to Africa, the worm burrowed into the bare foot, where it grew to great length, as thin as a silk thread, causing severe pain to the host. Only an operation of the greatest delicacy could purge the unwanted colonist. When the worm finally broke through the skin trying to find an exit, it was pulled out gradually over the course of several weeks, rolled up carefully around a quill feather. If the

1

worm broke, leaving any of its length embedded in the flesh, the foot became infected.

Sambo's limp caught the attention of the villagers in Bethabara, who
were German-speaking members of the Moravian Church. Looking for
slaves to power their growing settlement, they were interested in the African but regarded him as damaged property and thought the price of seventy
pounds too high. They offered his owner, Edmund Lyne, sixty-four pounds,
and the deal was struck. Bethabara, a religious refuge for Moravian immigrants, became the "house of passage" for this African in America.[1]

When Sambo arrived in North Carolina, slave ships had been carrying
human property from Africa to the Americas for more than two hundred
years. By the time the trade ended more than a century later, some eleven
million Africans, perhaps many more, had been spirited across the water.
We may never fully understand the enormity of the costs they paid during
the largest forced migration in history. But something of a recognizable
human scale can emerge from the story of one who survived. Few deported
Africans, in fact, ever had the opportunity to leave any formal record of
their lives. Sambo—who joined the Moravian Church and was christened
Abraham in 1780—was one of the exceptions.[2]

Upon Abraham's death in 1797, a Moravian minister wrote in German a
short account of his life based largely on oral testimony the African Moravian had supplied before he died. This *Lebenslauf,* or memoir, is a rare
document in the record of African experiences in America. Buttressed by
evidence from other sources, it permits us to reconstruct something of one
man's forced journey from freedom to slavery. Through Abraham and his
semi-autobiography, we have a lens, however fragmented, into the Atlantic
world of the eighteenth-century slave trade. Abraham's experiences did not
necessarily mirror those of all captive Africans, but they reveal ways in

1. This account is pieced together from the Memoir of Abraham (trans. EH); and Wachovia
Diary, Aug. 23–24, 1771. Identified as Edmund Lyne in a bill of sale from Aug. 24, 1771. See
Bills of Sale file, Slavery box. For descriptions of the Guinea worm, see C.G.A. Oldendorp,
*History of the Mission of the Evangelical Brethren on the Caribbean Islands of St. Thomas, St.
Croix, and St. John,* ed. and trans. Arnold R. Highfield and Vladimir Barac (1770; reprint, Ann
Arbor, Mich., 1987), 87; and Francis Moore, *Travels into the Inland Parts of Africa . . .* (London,
1738), 130.

2. The estimate is taken from James A. Rawley, *The Transatlantic Slave Trade: A History*
(New York, 1981), 428. Rawley's estimate exceeds by nearly two million that of Philip D.
Curtin, which had set the previous scholarly standard for measuring the extent of the slave
trade. See Curtin, *The Atlantic Slave Trade: A Census* (Madison, Wis., 1969).

which enslaved people, stripped from their homeland, tried to remake themselves on a distant shore. The chapters that follow track his and other Africans' new lives in America: their relations with masters and with each other, their work and families, and their participation in the Moravian Church. We shall explore the world Abraham helped shape and the one that evolved after his death. But we start in Africa, as he did.[3]

"OUR DEAR BROTHER ABRAHAM, otherwise called Sambo, a Negro from the Mandingo nation on the coast of African Guinea, was born about the year 1730." So begins the narrative of the life of Sambo, an African prisoner in the land of freedom. This opening statement raises immediate questions about its subject's identity. His name and ethnicity, for example, are open to interpretation. The name Sambo, or variations such as Samba, was common in West Africa, though it bore different meanings among various peoples. Sambo thus might well have clung stubbornly to his real name in America. Or the name might have been arbitrarily assigned by his new masters, although in the eighteenth century it carried none of the pejorative connotations given it by later generations of white Americans.[4]

Nor can Sambo's precise ethnic identity be determined, because of shifting and complex meanings of the term "Mandingo." The original inhabitants of some areas of West Africa subjugated by the Mandingoes intermarried with them or took their name. Furthermore, many enslaved Africans in

3. A number of Africans sold into American slavery, of course, wrote autobiographies, many of them far more detailed than Abraham's. Nonetheless, an account of even a few pages about one among the unnamed millions is a rare document indeed. A good overview of African slave narratives is William L. Andrews, *To Tell a Free Story: The First Century of Afro-American Autobiography, 1760–1865* (Urbana, Ill., 1986). Examples of accounts by individual Africans sold into American slavery include Philip D. Curtin, ed., *Africa Remembered: Narratives by West Africans from the Era of the Slave Trade* (Madison, Wis., 1967); "Autobiography of Omar ibn Said, Slave in North Carolina, 1831," *AHR*, XXX (1925), 787–795; and Daniel B. Thorp, "Chattel with a Soul: The Autobiography of a Moravian Slave," *PMHB*, CXII (1988), 433–451. In the last example, the narrator, known as Andrew the Moor, dictated his memoir in the first person, whereas Abraham's was written in the third person by a white Moravian minister on the basis of information supplied by Abraham. In the account that follows, all details of Sambo/Abraham's life are taken from his memoir, to which readers may refer in Appendix B. I call him Sambo until his baptism and christening in 1780, after which the name Abraham is used.

4. Memoir of Abraham; J. L. Dillard, *Black English: Its History and Usage in the United States* (New York, 1972), 130–132.

the New World deliberately misidentified themselves as Mandingo in an attempt to pass as members of that ruling elite. Whatever the case, Mandingo is the only identification we have for Sambo, and it is enough around which to build a plausible profile of him.[5]

The Mandingoes were spread throughout the region comprising present-day Senegal, Gambia, Guinea, and Sierra Leone. They were among a group of related peoples, together known as Mande, who had composed the kingdom of Mali on the upper Niger River, founded by a powerful general, Sundiata, in the thirteenth century. Over the course of the next century, traders from Mali spread Mande culture along vast trade networks throughout upper and lower Guinea, and, under emperor Mansa Musa, Mali became one of the world's great empires by the 1330s. Mali declined during the fifteenth century, but the Mandingoes had already won military superiority over other peoples, such as the Wolofs, Fulas, and Djolas, among whom they interspersed their settlements along the coast and upstream several hundred miles along the Gambia River.[6]

Richard Jobson, an English traveler to the region in 1620, called the Mandingoes "Lords, and Commaunders of this country . . . [who] professe themselves the naturall Inhabitants." To the Upper Guinea Coast the Mandingoes, along with other Mande peoples, brought a mastery of state building through the creation of administrative provinces ruled by governors subservient to the emperor of Mali. Mandingo was the lingua franca along the Gambia, and related tongues of the Mandekan family were spoken throughout the region.[7]

5. Walter Rodney, "Upper Guinea and the Significance of the Origins of Africans Enslaved in the New World," *JNH*, LIV (1969), 334–335; Michael A. Gomez, "Muslims in Early America," *JSH*, LX (1994), 685.

6. Basil Davidson, with F. K. Buah, *A History of West Africa: To the Nineteenth Century* (Garden City, N.J., 1966), 53–63.

7. Richard Jobson, quoted in Douglas Grant, *The Fortunate Slave: An Illustration of African Slavery in the Early Eighteenth Century* (London, 1968), 11; Walter Rodney, *History of the Upper Guinea Coast, 1545–1800* (Oxford, 1970), 25–26; Charles S. Bird, "The Development of Mandekan (Manding): A Study of the Role of Extra-Linguistic Factors in Linguistic Change," in David Dalby, ed., *Language and History in Africa: A Volume of Collected Papers Presented to the London Seminar on Language and History in Africa (Held at the School of Oriental and African Studies, 1967–69)* (New York, 1970), 146–159; John Thornton, *Africa and Africans in the Making of the Atlantic World, 1400–1680* (New York, 1992), 187–188. On the origins of one Mandingo state, see Donald R. Wright, *The Early History of Niumi: Settlement and Foundation of a Mandinka State on the Gambia River*, in *Papers in International Studies*, Africa Series, no. 32 (Athens, Ohio, 1977).

Like other peoples in Upper Guinea, the Mandingoes lived by a combination of agriculture, trade, and hunting. They cultivated corn, millet, tobacco, and rice and tended cattle and goats. Generally, women and slaves did most of the farming, and men helped out only at planting and harvesttimes. The Gambia and other rivers carried vessels laden with salt, hides, ivory, and gold between the coastal towns and the large inland states of Mali. The Mandingoes were also renowned for their ironwork and textiles, which they plied along all the trade routes of Guinea from Senegambia to the Ivory Coast. Moravian missionary C.G.A. Oldendorp, who met enslaved Mandingoes in the West Indies in the 1760s, noted that many "can not only read and write, but they can also do sums and are skilled in commerce. Likewise, various handicrafts are practiced among them, and the arts of spinning, sewing and weaving are all known to them."[8]

Europeans often remarked on the importance of dancing, wrestling, and drumming in Mandingo culture. "They are naturally very jocose and merry," wrote English trader Francis Moore in the 1730s, "and will dance to a drum or a Balafeu [xylophone] sometimes four and twenty Hours together, dancing now and then very regular, and at other times in very odd gestures, striving always to outdo one another in Nimbleness and Activity."[9]

Mandingoes followed the common West African practice of facial markings to designate ethnic and social status. They etched their faces with straight vertical lines, whereas other people used horizontal or circular incisions. Such markings, often quite ornate, could cover the face and torso. For clothing, Mandingo men wore a loose cotton frock and drawers reaching the knees, with sandals and white cotton caps. Women wore two pieces of cloth, one wrapped around the waist and hanging to the ankles, the other thrown over the shoulders. A cotton headdress topped off the ensemble.[10]

If Sambo led a typical Mandingo life, he would have grown up in a compact settlement of as many as three thousand inhabitants. They lived in

---

8. Grant, *Fortunate Slave*, 11–13; Robert Farris Thompson, *Flash of the Spirit: African and Afro-American Art and Philosophy* (New York, 1983), 195–222; Rodney, *Upper Guinea Coast*, 64–65; Oldendorp, *Caribbean Mission*, ed. and trans. Highfield and Barac, 181. On West African economic networks, see Thornton, *Africa and Africans in the Making of the Atlantic World*, chaps. 1–2.

9. Moore, *Travels*, 110; Grant, *The Fortunate Slave*, 14–15.

10. Oldendorp, *Caribbean Mission*, ed. and trans. Highfield and Barac, 169; Moore, *Travels*, 110. On facial markings as a sign of social initiation, see John S. Mbiti, *African Religions and Philosophy* (New York, 1969), 152.

houses one European described as "small and incommodious hovels" built of a "circular mud wall, about four feet high, upon which is placed a conical roof, composed of the bamboo cane, and thatched with grass." The simple design, although appearing "incommodious" to Europeans, not only ensured coolness and ventilation but also reflected the primary Mande philosophical and aesthetic value, the search for "the *kolo,* the kernel, the nucleus, the essential structure, [which] militated against ostentatious display or mindless presentations of one's wealth." This philosophy was further encoded in the spatial organization of houses in circular clusters or compounds by family lineage. A household was not one dwelling but an entire compound, in accordance with the Mande concept of the individual's place in an organic social sphere.[11]

The village leader, or alkali, was the senior descendant of the founder of the community. Though the alkali ruled with the advice of the village council, he "hath a great Power," wrote Francis Moore. "[He] appoints the Labour of all the People . . . and has the first Voice in all Conferences, concerning Things belonging to his Town." As the slave trade gathered momentum in the seventeenth and eighteenth centuries, the alkali wielded tremendous power, for European traders had to go through him to obtain slaves. He bargained with traders to supply them captives and prisoners of war and earned a custom per head on each slave sold. Sambo's father might have held such a position of power in the village, for, as Sambo's memoir reports, "it appears that his father was a respected man among his countrymen."[12]

In Mandingo society, as in West Africa generally, no line divided sacred from secular; the African universe was spiritual. Religion suffused and dominated every aspect of life, for the will of the divine was believed to lie behind every event. To live in such a culture was to be religious. Thus we learn that, in his youth, Sambo, "through diligent praying . . . established a religious way of thinking himself, though this was mixed with heathen superstition." This description says nothing about the substance of Sambo's

11. Mungo Park, *The Life and Travels of Mungo Park* (Edinburgh, 1864), 19–20 (orig. pub. in 1799 as *Travels in the Interior Districts of Africa*); Thompson, *Flash of the Spirit,* 196–197. See also Susan Denyer, *African Traditional Architecture: An Historical and Geographical Perspective* (New York, 1978), 71, 134, 160.

12. Charlotte A. Quinn, *Mandingo Kingdoms of the Senegambia: Traditionalism, Islam, and European Expansion* (Evanston, Ill., 1972), 11–14 (quotation on 13 n. 15); Nicholas S. Hopkins, "Mandinka Social Organization," in Carleton T. Hodge, ed., *Papers on the Manding* (Bloomington, Ind., 1971), 99–105; Memoir of Abraham.

beliefs, since his "religious way of thinking" might have been either traditional or Muslim, or—as his biographer perhaps hints—a combination of both. There is a good chance Sambo was Muslim, since many West African peoples worshiped Allah. Islam had penetrated the region by the twelfth century via Muslim traders from northern Africa, many of whom secured positions of honor at such royal courts as Ghana and Mali. During the fourteenth century, Islam spread from the west coast to the great trading cities of Timbuktu and Gao in the southern Sahara.[13]

A class of ascetic Muslim teachers, traders, and medicine men called Marabouts held tremendous prestige in Mandingo society. These traders played such a decisive role in the spread of Islam and Arabic literacy throughout the region that Europeans called all Muslims "Mandingo" until the end of the eighteenth century. A Mandingo slave in Jamaica, according to a planter, steadfastly remembered "the morning and evening prayer which his father taught him." "In proof of this assertion, he chants, in an audible and shrill tone, a sentence that I conceive to be a part of the Alcoran, *La illa, ill lilla!*, which he says they sing aloud at the first appearance of the new moon. I once had another Mandingo servant who could write with great beauty and exactness, the Arabic alphabet, and some passages from the Alcoran."[14]

Among the Mandingoes, adherents of traditional beliefs nonetheless outnumbered Muslims, and it may be significant that the Moravians did not note Sambo as Muslim. For one thing, Christian missionaries in the Americas often took special notice of Muslim slaves, whom they considered slightly more civilized than other Africans. Islam, to Europeans, at least held the Old Testament in common with Christianity, and African Muslims could not be accused of idolatry. Christians also accorded Muslims somewhat higher esteem for their tenacity of belief, which included shunning liquor and pork.[15]

13. Memoir of Abraham; Peter B. Clarke, *West Africa and Islam: A Study of Religious Development from the Eighth to the Twentieth Century* (New York, 1982); Gomez, "Muslims in Early America," *JSH*, LX (1994), 671–710. On the lives of three Muslim West Africans, see Grant, *Fortunate Slave*; Terry Alford, *Prince among Slaves* (New York, 1977); and "Autobiography of Omar ibn Said," *AHR*, XXX (1925), 787–795, esp. n. 25.

14. Rodney, *Upper Guinea Coast*, 231; Bryan Edwards, *The History, Civil and Commercial, of the British Colonies in the West Indies* (Dublin, 1793), II, 56–77, quoted in Roger D. Abrahams and John F. Szwed, *After Africa* (New Haven, Conn., 1983), 64–65. The chant means, "There is no God, but God." See also Quinn, *Mandingo Kingdoms*, 53–57.

15. For examples of Muslim slaves who impressed whites with their sobriety, see Grant, *Fortunate Slave*, 95–96; and Alford, *Prince among Slaves*, 64–65. Enslaved Africans in America

No one in America described Sambo as fasting or chanting Koranic verses; he was said only to have "stayed in his former heathen ways."[16] If, then, he was not Muslim but a follower of more traditional beliefs, what might they have been? The hundreds of African religions reflect the continent's diversity of peoples and environments. Yet all the captives sold into American slavery shared certain fundamental assumptions about the religious world. They held a belief in a supreme God who was commonly thought to be the creator of the world, omniscient and all-powerful, who was generally considered remote from daily affairs. God left the running of the world to a pantheon of subordinate gods or spirits who inhabited the natural world—plants and animals, earth, water and sky—and were held responsible for good fortune and calamity.

People therefore tried to stay in the spirits' favor through sacrifice and prayer and to manipulate them for good or evil purposes with the help of diviners and medicine men and through the use of spiritually charged amulets, charms, and potions. The actions of spirits, or their enlistment by humans to achieve certain ends, were widely seen as the chief agent of causation. Secret societies and cults, divided by sex, were among the chief social and religious institutions of a community. Sambo, like most West African men and women, as an adolescent would almost certainly have joined a secret society that steered him through a rigorous initiation process. Isolated in the woods for months, initiates communed with spirits and learned prayer, ritual, and a sacred sense of communal obligation. At the end of their training, they were considered to have died and been reborn as adults, and they received moral and religious supervision from these societies throughout their lifetime.[17]

In Sambo's universe, attitudes toward God could not be separated from beliefs about family, community, the physical world, and time. The quest for

---

were also sometimes appalled by what they regarded as whites' lack of religious faith. Omar ibn Said considered his master a "complete infidel" who had no fear of God; see "Autobiography of Omar ibn Said," *AHR*, XXX (1925), 793. See also Philip D. Morgan, "British Encounters with Africans and African-Americans, circa 1600–1780," in Bernard Bailyn and Philip D. Morgan, eds., *Strangers within the Realm: Cultural Margins of the First British Empire* (Chapel Hill, N.C., 1991), 200.

16. Memoir of Abraham.

17. Mbiti, *African Religions and Philosophy,* 37–96, 217–265; Dominique Zahan, *The Religion, Spirituality, and Thought of Traditional Africa* (Chicago, 1970), 6–35, 53–65, 81–107; W. T. Harris and Harry Sawyerr, *The Springs of Mende Belief and Conduct: A Discussion of the Influence of the Belief in the Supernatural among the Mende* (Freetown, Sierra Leone, 1968);

knowledge involved not only the web of living kin but the ancestors, whose memories were preserved in oral tradition and who were watching closely to safeguard communal values. Together, the living, the dead, and the hierarchy of divinities formed a sacred partnership with multiple interlocking connections. It was this world that was shattered forever for Sambo and the millions of other Africans sold into slavery in the Americas.[18]

THE MANDINGO EMPIRE had been built on commerce, on iron, gold, and textiles, and on military might. But by the eighteenth century, the complexion of Upper Guinea had changed. Mandingo rulers, though still formidable, no longer dominated the region from the inland empire of Mali to the coast, and the nature of trade had taken a different turn. The most important commodity was no longer cloth or metal, but slaves. Rulers shifted their energy away from administering their domains into the race to keep European traders working the Gambia River supplied with human merchandise for New World plantations. The slave trade became the dominant political and economic force in West Africa, and Sambo was pulled into its vortex.

Slavery was a crucial component of precolonial African societies. In contrast to Europe, where land was the principal source of revenue-producing property, in Africa land was held, not individually, but corporately. Slaves, as the only recognized private property of value, were an important source of investment. Victorious armies enslaved their prisoners of war, and indigent parents sometimes sold children or themselves into slavery. A well-developed slave trade, already in place by the fifteenth century, supplied regional and trans-African markets.

African slavery took many forms. Slaves served as soldiers and retainers in royal courts; slave labor in mines and on plantations generated the income that sparked commercial development for many rulers. In less-exploitative contexts, many slaves were regarded, not as disposable work machines, but as an extension of the master's household. Often incorporated into free families, they received protection from harsh treatment and sale. To Francis

---

K. L. Little, *The Mende of Sierra Leone,* 2d ed. (London, 1967), 115–132, 240–253. For a discussion of the possible role of secret societies in shaping African-American belief in the South Carolina Sea Islands, see Margaret Washington Creel, *"A Peculiar People": Slave Religion and Community-Culture among the Gullahs* (New York, 1988), 46–50, 181–182, 288–297.

18. Benjamin C. Ray, *African Religions: Symbol, Ritual, and Community* (Englewood Cliffs, N.J., 1976), 17; Mbiti, *African Religions and Philosophy,* 2–4, 87–100, 141.

Moore's unpracticed eye, house slaves "live so well and easy, that it is a very hard Matter to know the Slaves from their Masters or Mistresses."[19]

The Portuguese, in the fifteenth century, were the first Europeans to establish West African trading bases for buying slaves to work plantations in the Cape Verde Islands off the coast of Senegambia. Over the next two hundred years, as Spain, Britain, France, and Holland entered the slaving sweepstakes, the plundering of Africa's peoples accelerated in earnest. The immensity of the slave trade as a capitalistic enterprise—the sheer complexity of procuring and shipping captive people by the millions—consumed vast resources and generated enormous profits for European powers and their African trading partners.

Africans proved formidable military opponents in the early modern period, and Africa was a hostile disease environment for Europeans bent on imperial expansion. With the exception of the Portuguese conquest of Angola, Europeans therefore generally did not subjugate African peoples to acquire slaves during the first three centuries of the Atlantic trade. Instead, they tapped into existing African markets by negotiating to buy slaves from local rulers. These markets initially were capable of supplying European traders without disrupting African social and economic systems, but, as the trade intensified, rulers stepped up their efforts to meet European demands. African nations continually raided and fought each other in a spiral of "predatory incursions [that] depend so much on the demand for slaves," noted a European in 1789, "that if in any one year there be a greater concourse of European ships than usual, it is observed that a much greater number of captives from the interior parts of the country is brought to market the next." Climbing steadily through the eighteenth century, the number of slaves shipped to the New World peaked at about one hundred thousand annually by the 1780s.[20]

---

19. Moore, *Travels,* 110. My interpretation of African slavery draws heavily on the synthesis and analysis of Thornton, *Africa and Africans in the Making of the Atlantic World,* chap. 3. But see also Igor Kopytoff and Suzanne Miers, eds., *Slavery in Africa: Historical and Anthropological Perspectives* (Madison, Wis., 1977); Paul E. Lovejoy, *Transformations in Slavery: A History of Slavery in Africa* (New York, 1983); Patrick Manning, *Slavery and African Life: Occidental, Oriental, and African Slave Trades* (Cambridge, 1990).

20. Elizabeth Donnan, ed., *Documents Illustrative of the History of the Slave Trade to America,* 4 vols. (Washington, D.C., 1930–1935), II, 599. On the slave trade in Africa, see J. E. Inikori, ed., *Forced Migration: The Impact of the Export Slave Trade on African Societies* (New York, 1982); Joseph E. Inikori and Stanley L. Engerman, eds., *The Atlantic Slave Trade: Effects on Economies, Societies, and Peoples in Africa, the Americas, and Europe* (Durham, N.C., 1992);

In Upper Guinea, the trade was dominated by Mandingo kings. Each year, as early as the 1450s, their armies siphoned thousands of slaves from the hinterlands for sale to European traders on the Gambia. "The unhappy captives, many of whom are people of distinction, such as princes, priests and persons high in office, are conducted by Mandingoes in droves of twenty, thirty and forty, chained together" to slaving depots on the coast. Among their favorite victims were the Djolas, a traditional enemy, who raided and captured the Mandingoes in return, perpetuating a debilitating cycle of wars for many years.[21]

In one such campaign, against the Djolas or another people, Sambo was captured. Any number of scenarios is possible, but the year might have been between 1760 and 1770 when, if his estimated birth date was close, he would have been about thirty to forty years old. As his life account explains, Sambo was already an adult with several children when "he went to war like others in the frequent hostilities with the neighboring tribes. In one of those wars he was wounded severely in head and face and was taken prisoner, and then sent back to his father with mutilated ears."

His father, the narrative continues, "a respected man among his countrymen," was angered by his son's treatment and "stirred the inhabitants of the community to another war to get his revenge. They started at once, and Sambo, wounded though he was, did not let them keep him from following them." The Mandingo forces apparently absorbed another defeat, for Sambo was captured again. "Now he was taken prisoner a second time and sold to European slave traders." These traders were probably either French or English, who were bitterly contesting the Senegambian trade at the time.[22]

Through the testimony of other Africans sold into slavery, what un-

---

Philip D. Curtin, *Economic Change in Precolonial Africa: Senegambia in the Era of the Slave Trade* (Madison, Wis., 1975); Rawley, *Transatlantic Slave Trade*, chap. 11; Winston McGowan, "African Resistance to the Atlantic Slave Trade in Africa," *Slavery and Abolition*, XI (1990), 5–29. For an 18th-century account of the slave trade based at least partly on interviews with slaves in the Danish West Indies, see Oldendorp, *Caribbean Mission*, ed. and trans. Highfield and Barac, 207–211.

21. Rawley, *Transatlantic Slave Trade*, 429. For one African's classic account of being kidnapped at an early age and sold into slavery, see Olaudah Equiano, *The Interesting Narrative of the Life of Olaudah Equiano, or Gustavas Vassa, the African . . .* (1789; reprint, London, 1815), in Henry Louis Gates, Jr., ed., *The Classic Slave Narratives* (New York, 1987), 1–182.

22. Memoir of Abraham; Rodney, *Upper Guinea Coast*, 243; Rawley, *Transatlantic Slave Trade*, chap. 6; Gwendolyn Midlo Hall, *Africans in Colonial Louisiana: The Development of Afro-Creole Culture in the Eighteenth Century* (Baton Rouge, La., 1992), chaps. 2–3.

doubtedly happened next to Sambo, as to so many others, has become a familiar story: the long, forced march to the sea by scores or hundreds of manacled prisoners, the flesh searing under the brand, the captives huddling in barracoons to await an unknown fate, the packing of the human freight into the foul hold of a ship, and the months-long, agonizing voyage across the sea, filled with whippings, disease, and death.

But beyond the images of suffering and despair, the middle passage represented certain truths for all African prisoners. When they last gazed at the African coast before being dragged below deck, they were about to embark on a forced journey into a frightening abyss. Whatever lay ahead, they could never be the same people again. When they set foot in America to face the prodding and squeezing of their emaciated bodies by European hands and the sight of a plantation where they were to work out their days, these newly enslaved people could no longer think of themselves in exactly the same ways as before. The land had anchored them to family, community, and belief; but now the land was gone and, with it, the signposts that had given meaning to everyday life. No system of beliefs could survive such rupture intact. An enormous gulf separated what they had known and what they would come to know.[23]

Throughout the Americas, the task for enslaved Africans was to hunt out the familiar, to try to approximate, as far as the limits of slave society would allow, a recognizable code by which to live, and to adapt what they could salvage of the cultures they had left behind to new ways of surviving. Africans learned to redefine themselves under the cruelest of conditions.[24]

23. Despite the vast literature on the transatlantic slave trade, oddly enough the experiences of Africans themselves during the middle passage have yet to receive full study. Suggestive and sensitive treatments from the perspective of those enslaved include Vincent Harding, *There Is a River: The Black Struggle for Freedom in America* (New York, 1981), chap. 1; and Nathan Irvin Huggins, *Black Odyssey: The African-American Ordeal in Slavery* (New York, 1990), chap. 2. A still-important theoretical statement on the middle passage as a crucible of cultural change and formation is Sidney Mintz and Richard Price, *The Birth of African-American Culture: An Anthropological Perspective* (1976; reprint, Boston, 1992). See also Joseph C. Miller, *Way of Death: Merchant Capitalism and the Angolan Slave Trade, 1730–1830* (Madison, Wis., 1988).

24. The themes of dislocation and adaptation among Africans in the New World have dominated the writing of African-American history for several decades. On the challenges posed by this line of inquiry, see Mintz and Price, *Birth of African-American Culture;* Thornton, *Africa and Africans in the Making of the Atlantic World,* pt. II; and Ira Berlin, "From Creole to African: Atlantic Creoles and the Origins of African-American Society in Mainland North

In the eighteenth century, only about 6 percent of all captives shipped from Africa to the Americas landed in North America. Three-quarters went to Brazil or the Antilles, and among them was Sambo. After his capture, the European slave traders who purchased him "brought him to the West Indies and sold him on a French island." "He stayed there for several years." We know little more than this; yet it is possible to speculate on some of what he encountered and on how a newly enslaved person began to remake his life.[25]

One of the first steps in marshaling his psychological defenses was simply to find someone to talk to. Prisoners began building communication bridges between themselves early in their ordeal, long before they ever arrived in America. In each coffle making its way to the coast, in each slave barracoon and every ship leaving port, Africans from a galaxy of nations experimented with ways to surmount ethnic and language barriers. Olaudah Equiano, an Ibo sold into slavery in about 1755, later remembered that after his kidnapping: "I always found somebody that understood me till I came to the sea coast. The languages of different nations did not totally differ, nor were they so copious as those of the Europeans, particularly the English. They were therefore easily learned; and, while I was journeying thus through Africa, I acquired two or three different tongues." Such multilingualism was fairly common in West Africa, where the trade in slaves and other commodities created a cosmopolitan class of middlemen skilled in negotiating among diverse parties. Plying the ports and rivers were traders, often of mixed European and African descent, "who are very expert at reckoning and talking the different Languages of their own Country and those of the Europeans."[26]

On slaving ships, captives could further communicate through slave "linguisters" who interpreted between white crews and their black cargoes, receiving certain privileges in return, such as freedom from fetters. Thus, the ships, besides acting as cultural conduits between Africa and America, helped incubate attempts at linguistic exchange that fueled cooperation among prisoners. The trauma of the voyage could also instill lasting bonds of

America," *WMQ*, 3d Ser., LIII (1996), 251–288. "In terms of immigration alone," one historian reminds us, "America was an extension of Africa rather than Europe until late in the nineteenth century"; see David Eltis, "Free and Coerced Transatlantic Migrations: Some Comparisons," *AHR*, LXXXVIII (1983), 255.

25. Memoir of Abraham.

26. Equiano, *Narrative*, in Gates, ed., *Classic Slave Narratives*, 28; Donnan, ed., *Documents*, II, 598; Berlin, "From Creole to African," *WMQ*, 3d Ser., LIII (1996), 251–288.

companionship. Shipmate ties forged on board achieved quasi-kinship status that often endured on land. Helping to cushion the shock of enslavement, shipmates might represent the first threads of community in America.[27]

The exhausted Africans who survived the grueling journey of up to three months staggered from the ships with little idea of their fate. Many thought they would be eaten or boiled for oil. But in a colony where heavy African importation continued throughout the eighteenth century—in any Caribbean port, in fact—new arrivals could generally hear the welcome sound of familiar tongues. In the Danish West Indies, at an auction of newly arrived Africans, missionary Oldendorp saw "a ray of hope brighten the gloomy faces of the Negroes who were about to be offered for sale. The joy of being visited by their countrymen who were already established on the island had a great deal to do with their change in mood. As the result of quite lively conversations with the former, they no doubt acquired a better understanding of what lay ahead of them." Perhaps they learned tips from the veterans about how to salvage the best result from their impending sale. Alert to such chances, several Africans on the auction block, apparently perceiving Oldendorp to be a preacher, "let me know by friendly gestures and motions that they wished to be purchased by me." As such attempts to broker their own sale demonstrate, the middle passage might have honed rather than dulled many Africans' sense of survival.[28]

When money changed hands and captives were led away by their new masters, shipmate and kinship ties were often severed. Equiano remembered seeing several brothers sold apart and that "it was very moving . . . to see their distress and hear their cries at parting." On the plantation, masters assigned a pair of experienced slaves to socialize new arrivals into an un-

27. On language aboard ship, see Oldendorp, *Caribbean Mission*, ed. and trans. Highfield and Barac, 216–217; and Peter H. Wood, *Black Majority: Negroes in Colonial South Carolina from 1670 through the Stono Rebellion* (New York, 1974), 173–174. On shipmates, see Mintz and Price, *Birth of African-American Culture*, 22–23; Orlando Patterson, *The Sociology of Slavery: An Analysis of the Origins, Development, and Structure of Negro Slave Society in Jamaica* (London, 1967), 150; and Mary C. Karasch, *Slave Life in Rio de Janeiro, 1808–1850* (Princeton, N.J., 1987), 298.

28. Oldendorp, *Caribbean Mission*, ed. and trans. Highfield and Barac, 219. This is not to downplay the shock of forced uprooting; some slaves found it too great and took their own lives. See Patterson, *Sociology of Slavery*, 195, 264–265; and William D. Piersen, "White Cannibals, Black Martyrs: Fear, Depression, and Religious Faith as Causes of Suicide among New Slaves," *JNH*, LXII (1977), 147–159.

familiar and frightening world. They introduced them to backbreaking gang labor in sugar or indigo fields, helped them start a garden from which they would feed themselves, and taught them the patois of their new land. The student "respects them as he would his own parents." Such a mentoring system might have furnished a welcome reminder of the secret societies the captives had left in Africa.[29]

Sugar production in the Americas revolutionized the world, and it was to feed the French sugar industry's voracious appetite for slaves that Sambo found himself in the West Indies in the 1760s. "The labors of the people of these islands are the sole basis of the African trade," wrote a Frenchman. "They may be considered as the principal cause of the rapid motion which now agitates the universe." So profitable was the cultivation of sugarcane that planters found it easier and cheaper to work Africans to death within five or six years and simply buy new replacements than to keep workers alive as long as possible. Machete in hand, an African standing for the first time in an endless sea of cane under the tropical sun was gazing at an invitation to his or her own funeral.[30]

Numerical probability suggests that Sambo found himself on the island of Saint Domingue, which after a swift burst of development in the mid-eighteenth century was the largest single producer of both sugar and coffee in the world. Its sugar output nearly matched the entire total of the British West Indies. The slave labor force behind that kind of production was vast. After Brazil, Saint Domingue was the second largest importer of slaves in the Americas during the era of the transatlantic trade. About 20,000 Africans poured into the French islands annually during the 1760s, and that number doubled in the 1780s. Most of them ended up in Saint Domingue, where, on the eve of the revolution of 1791, Africans outnumbered whites 450,000 to 40,000.[31]

29. Equiano, *Narrative*, in Gates, ed., *Classic Slave Narratives*, 38; Oldendorp, *Caribbean Mission*, ed. and trans. Highfield and Barac, 220. It is also true, as Oldendorp pointed out, that patron/ward relationships could turn abusive when mentors forced their charges to work their ground to the neglect of the newcomers' own plot, forcing the latter to steal to survive.

30. Rawley, *Transatlantic Slave Trade*, 120. On sugar, see Sidney Mintz, *Sweetness and Power: The Place of Sugar in Modern History* (New York, 1985); and Philip D. Curtin, *The Rise and Fall of the Plantation Complex: Essays in Atlantic History* (New York, 1990).

31. Rawley, *Transatlantic Slave Trade*, 130; Curtin, *Rise and Fall of the Plantation Complex*, 161. See also C.L.R. James, *The Black Jacobins: Toussaint L'Ouverture and the San Domingo Revolution*, 2d ed. (New York, 1963); David Geggus, "Sugar and Coffee Cultivation in Saint

Sambo would have found much he recognized in such a place and much that was strange. West Africans of practically all ethnic groups lived in the French island colonies. By the mid-eighteenth century, the African immigrant also confronted a creole-born enslaved population whose language and religion comprised an amalgamation of African and French strands. We know only that Sambo stayed long enough in the Caribbean to pick up some knowledge of French. He might have taken part in *voudun*, or voodoo rituals, and perhaps would have known future rebels in the revolution that would lead to the creation of the hemisphere's first black-controlled nation, Haiti.

In any case, it was his luck to elude a life and probable death in the cane fields. Sambo's memoir tells us that within a few years he was taken to Virginia. We do not know in what year, nor how he came to be sold. Only limited trade—and illicit at that—flowed between the French West Indies and Virginia. Instead, he might have been sold to a British colony such as Barbados, from where "seasoned" slaves were shipped to Virginia throughout the eighteenth century. Another possibility is that he lived, not in Saint Domingue, but in Guadeloupe or Martinique—French islands occupied by the British during the Seven Years' War, whence slaves were traded to British North America.[32]

His life once more disrupted, Sambo was forced to adapt to strange new surroundings in Virginia. What French he had picked up would do him little good. And, although the population of the French West Indies was overwhelmingly black, only about 40 percent, or some one hundred thousand, of Virginia's inhabitants in 1750 were black. Their ethnicity and distribution also contrasted with what Sambo had seen in the Caribbean, where African cultures were reinvigorated by the many thousands of annual arrivals who were confined to sugar plantations in densely packed numbers. In the tobacco-driven Chesapeake, African imports declined after the 1730s as the black population grew naturally. This demographic change diluted African

---

Domingue and the Shaping of the Slave Labor Force," in Ira Berlin and Philip D. Morgan, eds., *Cultivation and Culture: Labor and the Shaping of Slave Life in the Americas* (Charlottesville, Va., 1993), 73–98; Carolyn E. Fick, *The Making of Haiti: The Saint Domingue Revolution from Below* (Knoxville, Tenn., 1990); and Michel-Rolph Trouillot, "Motion in the System: Coffee, Color, and Slavery in Eighteenth-Century Saint-Domingue," *Review, Fernand Braudel Center for the Study of Economies, Historical Systems, and Civilizations*, V (1982), 331–388.

32. Susan Westbury, "Slaves of Colonial Virginia: Where They Came From," *WMQ*, 3d Ser., XLII (1985), 228–237; Herbert S. Klein, "Slaves and Shipping in Eighteenth-Century Virginia," *JIH*, III (1974–1975), 383–412; Rawley, *Transatlantic Slave Trade*, 118–119, 332–333.

cultures while promoting an Afro-Virginian culture more influenced by contact with whites.[33]

Isolated and driven to rigorous labor in the tobacco fields, African immigrants stood less chance of connecting with each other. Yet they did encounter one another on occasion, when their command of languages worked to good purpose, and those opportunities could assume real and symbolic importance in sustaining a shared culture. In time, Sambo did make such a contact. At some point after his arrival in Virginia, he was bought by a white man, Edmund Lyne, who owned another African named Jupiter. The Moravians later described Jupiter as "by nature a very proud man . . . a true heathen, a king's son from Guinea." Whether Jupiter and Sambo arrived in Virginia on the same ship from the West Indies and were purchased together by Lyne is unknown. But like Sambo, Jupiter "had taken part in various battles in his homeland, from which his face was still noticeably marked with cuts and scars."[34]

Though we know little else about Jupiter, including his ethnicity, we may speculate on at least one aspect of his state of mind. Members of African royalty found it particularly hard to accept enslavement by whites who were often less lettered than themselves and whom they disdained as inferiors. One African woman in the West Indies refused to obey her mistress, saying: "I was much greater in Guinea than you are here. I had many more slaves in my service than you have. Now you expect me to be your slave? I would rather die of starvation." And so she did. Whites might have tried to beat such pride out of Africans, noble or otherwise, but many defiantly maintained their sense of identity, even if it meant death.[35]

Perhaps it was Jupiter's "proud" character, and Sambo's worm-infected foot, that made Lyne want to unload them. Or he might have simply been a slave trader working the southern Virginia and North Carolina circuit. Lyne probably brought the Africans along a trade route down through the Virginia Piedmont into the Moravian village of Bethabara. There, Sambo was

33. Allan Kulikoff, "The Origins of Afro-American Society in Tidewater Maryland and Virginia, 1700 to 1790," WMQ, 3d Ser., XXXV (1978), 226–259; Jean Butenhoff Lee, "The Problem of Slave Community in the Eighteenth-Century Chesapeake," WMQ, 3d Ser., XLIII (1986), 333–361.

34. SAE, November 1802, "Nachricht von den Negern in der Wachau," pt. B, sec. 1, "Hope."

35. Oldendorp, Caribbean Mission, ed. and trans. Highfield and Barac, 220. See also Alford, Prince among Slaves, 43–44, 61, 81; and William D. Piersen, Black Legacy: America's Hidden Heritage (Amherst, Mass., 1993), chap. 4, though its argument is overstated.

bought and sent to work in a tannery in the nearby Moravian town of Salem, whereas Jupiter ended up in a settlement a few miles away called Hope. For the two Africans, the experience of enduring the arduous journey from Virginia together apparently retained a special meaning, as though they had been shipmates during the terrifying transatlantic voyage. Years later, they would remember and verify that bond for all time by cementing their spiritual kinship formally through baptism into the Moravian Church.

Sambo's journey had taken him from Senegambia to the West Indies to Virginia to North Carolina. He had lived in a French colony, then an English one; now he found himself among still a third group of Europeans shouting at him in another incomprehensible tongue, German. Enslavement had thrust him into a splintered world of forced labor, of changing places and people, of the constant threat that tenuous ties could be snapped at the whim of a master.

Equally important, the Americas were peopled with millions like him—captives who had traveled thousands of miles, learned new languages, were often skilled at negotiating their way in hostile settings, and had an emerging sense of themselves as exploited members of a wider transatlantic African world. Wherever his unwilling voyages took him around the rim of that world in the 1760s, Sambo was bound to find threads of continuity with the land he had left behind. A recognizable tongue, a telltale set of ethnic markings, a familiar religious ritual—all these he could encounter with varying frequency in the European colonies of America. Such cultural shards offered fragments of his earlier life and helped preserve the vitality of his beliefs. His survival rested on the mental and physical dexterity to confront the immense barriers before him. His ability to adapt would be challenged every day for the rest of his life.

CHAPTER ONE

. . . .

From Serfs to Slaveholders

 AROUND THE TIME of Sambo's birth in West Africa in the 1730s, a small but fervent Protestant fellowship called the Renewed Unity of Brethren was aglow in spiritual revival far to the north in eastern Saxony. The spark of this resurgent piety would soon sweep the Brethren across the seas on an ambitious global mission. Through tropical forests, across frozen tundras, and onto sweltering sugar plantations, teams of earnest German evangelists relentlessly carried word of Christ's martyrdom to indigenous peoples on five continents and to enslaved Africans in the Americas. At the same time, larger bands of Brethren left Saxony to plant settlements in North America, where they covenanted to live by their understanding of Christ's word. By the mid-eighteenth century, this small group of Christian disciples, known by then in the English-speaking world as the Moravian Church, drew a strong sense of collective identity from what they considered their divine appointment as international ambassadors for evangelical Protestantism.

But even as the Moravian Brethren preached the gospel to the "heathen," they acquired some of them as slaves. The elect too need food and shelter, and Moravians reasoned they could serve God better if others helped to carry their earthly burden. Those others had black skin. The Brethren saw no contradiction between Christian doctrine and slaveholding. In their belief, subordination of some humans to others was natural and proper in the divine order. As they saw it, all people were—or should be—servants of Christ, the true authority of the only realm that really mattered, the soul. To own a slave or to be a slave—what did the Savior care, as long as both acknowledged him master? It was this bundle of views about Christian society—and about human bondage—that shaped the North Carolina Moravian world that the disinherited African Sambo entered in the summer of 1771.

The Moravians' ideology of slaveholding evolved and changed sharply over the course of three centuries. In fact, if ever a group of European immigrants to America should have been temperamentally equipped by ancient pedigree to abhor slavery, it was the Moravians. They had descended from a fifteenth-century group of Czech religious radicals, the *Unitas Fratrum*, or Unity of Brethren. The Brethren were part of a long genealogy of medieval church reformers who combined calls for spiritual renewal with progressive social doctrine. Long before the Lutheran Reformation of the sixteenth century, reform movements traced a trajectory across late-medieval Europe, nurtured by a simmering undercurrent of dissatisfaction with Rome. Bridging time and space, a rich cross-fertilization of ideas linked such reformers as the Waldensians in late-twelfth-century France, John Wyclif in fourteenth-century England, and John Hus in fifteenth-century Bohemia. All pushed for ethical cleansing of the clergy and greater participation in worship by the laity, including Communion. They also sought reforms in the medieval class structure to make the lives of the poor more bearable.[1]

The spiritual father of the Unity of Brethren was John Hus, a scholar and leader of the Czech reform movement who was condemned as a heretic by church fathers. After his death at the stake in 1415, his followers rose against the church in an armed rebellion known as the Hussite Revolution. A moderate wing of the Hussite movement was called the Utraquists. A more militant branch, the Taborites, sought to erect a socially equal kingdom of the elect in several heavily armed and fortified enclaves in Bohemia and Moravia.[2]

One disciple of the Hussites was a rural philosopher named Peter Chelcice, who had known Waldensians and Taborites during his youth in Moravia. The Hussite Revolution found its most radically egalitarian voice in Chelcice, for whom Christ's life and teachings provided the true model of spiritual and social regeneration. In 1457, Chelcice attracted a small group of

---

1. For an overview of the period, see Steven Ozment, *The Age of Reform, 1250–1550: An Intellectual and Religious History of Late Medieval and Reformation Europe* (New Haven, Conn., 1980).

2. Ibid., 170. On the Hussite period, see the following works by Howard Kaminsky: "The Religion of Hussite Tabor," in Miloslav Rechcigl, ed., *The Czechoslovak Contribution to World Culture* (The Hague, 1964), 210–223; "Chiliasm and the Hussite Revolution," *Church History,* XXVI (1957), 43–71; and *A History of the Hussite Revolution* (Berkeley, Calif., 1967).

followers to the village of Kunwald, north of Prague in northeast Bohemia, to start a separatist biblical community. This act marks the birth of the Unitas Fratrum. Within a few years, the Brethren formed an independent church based more on spiritual renewal and moral discipline than on theological rigor.[3]

For Chelcice, taking Christ seriously meant renouncing wealth and holding property in common. He considered all forms of worldly authority corrupt, especially the trappings of state power such as oaths, judicial systems, and armies. Only Christian love offered a valid basis for social organization. Unlike the Taborites, he considered violence, including self-defense and capital punishment, ungodly. Although oppression of any kind was evil, it must not be resisted but borne with patient humility. Chelcice's teachings also drew on the Taborite tradition of moral protest against social injustice and exalted the common man in the spirit of the Scriptures. To this Christian visionary, the class inequalities of feudal society defied divine law.

In this regard, Chelcice surpassed all his predecessors in the Hussite Revolution, none of whom (except the Taborites for a brief period in 1420 while they expected the imminent millennium) had advocated the complete overthrow of social hierarchies. He denounced wealth and privilege as false, since they had been stolen and maintained by violence; the nobility were "useless drones" living on corrupt gains, "quite unable to show any passages from God's scriptures why, apart from their superior descent, they are any different from other people." As for serfdom, if the nobility's "forefathers bought human beings together with their hereditary rights to the property, then they bought something that was not theirs to buy and sell." The clergy, too, lived easy lives of luxury at the expense of the poor. Chelcice needed to invent no earthly blueprint to construct a society without class, violence, or oppression. It was all in the New Testament.

Chelcice's condemnation of worldly authority startlingly reversed nearly a millennium and a half of Christian doctrine on the relationship of spirit to body. From Paul to Thomas Aquinas and beyond, church theorists conceived of bonded servitude as a fixture in the divine hierarchy of the universe.

---

3. Chelcice's name is variously spelled Chelciky or Chelcicky. This paragraph and the next two are drawn from Peter Brock, *The Political and Social Doctrines of the Unity of Czech Brethren in the Fifteenth and Early Sixteenth Centuries* (London, 1957), 25–69 (quotations on 64); Murray L. Wagner, *Petr Chelčický, a Radical Separatist in Hussite Bohemia* (Scottdale, Pa., 1983); Howard Kaminsky, "Peter Chelciky: Treatises on Christianity and the Social Order," *Studies in Medieval and Renaissance History*, I (1964), 107–179.

Slavery and serfdom were deserved consequences of sin, ordained by God and unalterable. Slaves could find spiritual freedom in the eternal salvation offered by Christ but must remain in their earthly station.[4]

In the village of Kunwald, membership in the Unitas Fratrum swelled during the 1460s and 1470s with Bohemian peasants and small craftsmen drawn to Chelcice's vision of a Christian order grounded in spiritual rebirth and fellowship. Like their mentor, the Brethren believed social inequality to be based on "fear, cruelty, beating, fighting, killing, reviling, violence, imprisonment, cutting-off of limbs, murder, and other physical torments." They maintained close contact with other dissenting groups in Bohemia, such as the Anabaptists, who likewise condemned worldly power and aspired to sanctified lives.[5]

By the late fifteenth century, though, the Brethren abandoned their most radical social doctrines in the face of persecution and internal crisis. When Utraquist government officials arrested and harassed the Brethren in the 1460s and 1470s for their refusal to bear arms, they sought refuge on the estates of noblemen who appreciated their submissiveness and found them good tenants. By the 1490s, many Brethren, asking how much punishment they should be expected to withstand for their faith, reevaluated their relationship to the world and the state. Much of the shift in belief came when the Unity, which originally had an overwhelmingly agrarian appeal, began to draw urban folk in search of a heartfelt religion. Many newcomers had little use for a life of pastoral withdrawal and viewed wealth, not as a disgrace, but as a sign of God's blessing. As elder leaders died, few young defenders of the original values took their places. Overriding the bitter objections of the remaining old guard, spokesmen for change began to dominate debate in the church.[6]

---

4. David Brion Davis, *The Problem of Slavery in Western Culture* (Ithaca, N.Y., 1966), 83–106. For a reexamination of early Christian thought on slavery, see Dale B. Martin, *Slavery as Salvation: The Metaphor of Slavery in Pauline Christianity* (New Haven, Conn., 1990).

5. Brock, *Political and Social Doctrines*, 70–102 (quotation on 90); Marianka S. Fousek, "The Perfectionism of the Early Unitas Fratum," *Church History*, XXX (1961), 396–413; Claus-Peter Clasen, *Anabaptism: A Social History, 1525–1618* (Ithaca, N.Y., 1972); Jarold Knox Zeman, *The Anabaptists and the Czech Brethren in Moravia, 1526–1628: A Study of Origins and Contacts* (The Hague, 1969).

6. This paragraph and subsequent discussion are based on Brock, *Political and Social Doctrines*, 153–240 (quotation on 228); Marianka S. Fousek, "Spiritual Direction and Discipline: A Key to the Flowering and Decay of the Sixteenth Century Unitas Fratrum," *Archive for Reformation History*, LXII (1971), 207–224; Fousek, "On Secular Authority and Military

New decrees devalued or discredited Chelcice's writings, the spiritual wellspring of the old Unity. From the new leaders emerged an accommodating attitude toward authority. Far from being a corrupt, man-made abomination of divine law, the social order, including the nobility, was now seen as the instrument of God's will. Hence, courts of law must be obeyed, and Brethren could swear civil oaths and participate in legal proceedings. Capital punishment became acceptable (though the sword stroke must be administered with Christian love), and Brethren could take up arms in a righteous cause.

For their part, the poor must forget whatever nonsense they had learned from Chelcice. They must "realize that the world order is ordained by God for their own good; they should know their place, and that the servants of the world [authorities] are set up for their good also and to preserve them from evil. The poor should be obedient . . . [and] never exercise authority not properly entrusted to them but rather endure suffering. . . . They should refrain from striving after equality." The voice of protest that first inspired the Brethren just thirty years earlier had been rooted out and replaced by the time-honored justification of the social order.

A formal schism split the Unity in 1495, when the outnumbered defenders of the old doctrines withdrew to form a separate sect. That group dwindled and disappeared by the middle of the next century. The Unity, meanwhile, attracting rich and influential supporters, prospered during the Reformation, numbering some two hundred thousand members, four hundred worship sites, and three seminaries by the early sixteenth century. The faith survived occasional persecution and the dispersal of members by Catholic rulers. A new era of toleration began when the Czech Confession of 1575 guaranteed freedom of worship to Protestants. By the early seventeenth century, more than half of all Protestants in Bohemia and Moravia were members of the Unity.

The Thirty Years' War, however, negated the gains the Unity and Protestantism in general had made in Bohemia. With the defeat of the Protestant elector in 1620 and Habsburg dominance restored in Bohemia, religious liberty ended and the Brethren were forced underground. For the next century, they survived and worshiped secretly or lived in exile in Poland and

Service among the Bohemian Brethren in the Sixteenth and Early Seventeenth Centuries," in Bela K. Kiraly, ed., *Tolerance and Movements of Religious Dissent in Eastern Europe* (New York, 1975), 53–64; and Gillian Lindt Gollin, *Moravians in Two Worlds: A Study of Changing Communities* (New York, 1967), 9–10.

various German states, kept alive by their strong sense of Christian community, devotion to lay participation in worship, and a strict code of ethical conduct. By 1722, a few remnants of the church, led by a Moravian-born carpenter named Christian David, lived in eastern Saxony and maintained secret ties with small communities of Brethren in Moravia and Austria. Looking for a refuge where they could worship in peace, David met a young German count, Nikolaus Ludwig von Zinzendorf, who granted them asylum on his estate in Berthelsdorf, about fifty miles east of Dresden.[7]

This group of Moravian Brethren was, not Czech, but the descendants of German Waldensians who had migrated to Moravia and joined the Unity in 1480. They thus constituted the historical link between the old Unitas Fratrum and what would soon become, under Zinzendorf's patronage, the Renewed Unity of Brethren. In retreat from the world, these few persecuted carriers of the faith built a new settlement on the count's estate. They called it Herrnhut—"in the care of the Lord."[8]

More than any other person, Count Zinzendorf was responsible for refashioning a band of harried Moravian stragglers into an aggressive proselytizing force that within a few years was sending missionaries to non-Christians over an extraordinary geographic range, from Greenland to Africa to the Americas. Zinzendorf, one of the dominant figures of the eighteenth-century Protestant revival movement known as Pietism, left a heavy spiritual imprint on the Moravians through his forceful personality and powerful position as both feudal lord and benefactor. Originally, he had offered them shelter with the apparent aim of converting them to his own religion, Lutheranism. But soon, intrigued by their legacy of a simple, heartfelt faith and high ethical standards, Zinzendorf instead decided to revive the ancient Unity, an event marked by a special Holy Communion in 1727. From that date, the distinctive faith of the Renewed Unitas Fratrum began to evolve, based on a blend of traditional Moravian doctrine and Zinzendorf's Lutheran Pietism, eventually making them the most influential of all the Pietist groups.

The count's own religious training emphasized many of the same goals as the Moravian refugees he now harbored. Born in 1700, Zinzendorf was

7. Robert Bireley, *Religion and Politics in the Age of the Counterreformation: Emperor Ferdinand II, William Lamormaini, S. J., and the Formation of Imperial Policy* (Chapel Hill, N.C., 1981), 3–4; Gollin, *Moravians in Two Worlds*, 4–5.

8. The German ethnicity of these Brethren is discussed in Zeman, *Anabaptists and Czech Brethren*, 72.

raised in the tradition of the seventeenth-century Pietist movement founded by his godfather, Philip Jakob Spener. Zinzendorf had learned the principles of the faith as a youth at the famous Pietist academy in Halle. Pietism was in essence a reformation of the Reformation, a reaction against the formalism of the Lutheran scholastics. For the Pietists, faith had nothing to do with a codified set of pre-determined rules that governed one's relationship to God. "As soon as truth becomes a system," said Zinzendorf, "one does not possess it." Instead, religion was utterly personal, a matter of emotionally "experiencing" God with the heart, rather than thinking or making rational judgments about God. Humans could never begin to comprehend divine ways, but could only stand in awe before God's self-revelation, Jesus Christ. For Zinzendorf, in the words of one student, Christ "is the known God in his totality. Christ is God the Creator and Sustainer of the universe, God the Lord of history, as well as God the Redeemer." Christ's sacrifice gave people joyful knowledge of salvation, as long as they rejected the old life and embraced a "new birth" grounded in that faith.[9]

This brief summary simplifies the complexities of the Halle school of Pietism and of the philosophy of Count Zinzendorf. What concerns us here is how his theology shaped the emergence of the Unity of Brethren as a cadre of God's self-styled chosen people. Zinzendorf tested many of his ideas in Herrnhut, the community of Brethren on his estate, which flourished as new migrants, all religious enthusiasts of different stripes, streamed in from Bohemia, Austria, and Saxony. By May 1725, some ninety people lived in Herrnhut. An orphanage, a school, and a meetinghouse were built. The count as yet played little part in the daily functioning of the community, and factional squabbling soon threatened to dissolve it.

To end the bickering, the count in 1727 drew up a list of forty-two statutes regulating residents' conduct in social, religious, family, and economic life under his own patronage. Brethren covenanted to "judge none, enter into no disputes with any, nor behave themselves unseemly towards any; but rather seek to maintain among themselves the pure evangelical

9. This summary of Pietism is drawn from F. Ernest Stoeffler, *German Pietism during the Eighteenth Century* (Leiden, 1973), 140–147 (quotations on 143, 146); Kenneth G. Hamilton and J. Taylor Hamilton, *History of the Moravian Church: The Renewed Unitas Fratrum, 1722–1957* (Bethlehem, Pa., 1967), 16–22; A. G. Roeber, *Palatines, Liberty, and Property: German Lutherans in Colonial British America* (Baltimore, 1993), chap. 3. An overview that evaluates the Renewed Unity in the context of 18th-century Protestant revivalism is W. R. Ward, *The Protestant Evangelical Awakening* (Cambridge, 1992), esp. chap. 2.

doctrine, simplicity and grace." A council of twelve elders was appointed to supervise spiritual activities, admonish backsliders, and assert hierarchical social control. Contact between single people of opposite sexes was restricted, and all marriages needed the elders' approval. Those wishing to start a trade likewise required community consent, and any adopting "an open course of levity and sin" would be "excluded from . . . Brotherly fellowship." These principles reflected the count's view that the saved—or in Calvinist terms the "aristocracy of the elect"—should organize into communities pursuing a single common goal, to serve Christ. These "conventicles," without formally leaving the church, would live apart from the world in emulation of the ancient Christians.[10]

Accordingly, the distinctive features of Moravian worship and social organization emerged in the following years. The use of the lot in community decision making, for example, became the Moravians' device for determining God's will in important church matters in which no clear answer or consensus seemed to exist. Generally, three answers were put in a bowl from which one was drawn and taken as the Savior's wish: either a "yes," a "no," or a blank, which usually meant the question was submitted again at the elders' discretion. Questions put to the lot generally concerned a candidate's admission to Communion, a suitor's permission to marry, and matters of importance to the entire community. As the instrument of divine guidance, the lot assumed high purpose in reaffirming the Moravians' notion of themselves as God's appointees.

Another mark of Herrnhut and of later Moravian communities was the division of brothers and sisters into separate groups called choirs, according to age, sex, and marital status. Choir members worshiped and studied together, and some choirs—most notably the Single Brothers and many of the Single Sisters—lived in dormitory-style quarters. Such groupings were intended to enrich congregants' religious life through spiritual affinity, help them concentrate on the goals of the community, and minimize contact between single men and women. Choirs also absorbed some of the traditional childrearing functions of the family and helped socialize children.[11]

In many respects, the statutes of 1727 echoed precepts laid down by the

---

10. Hamilton and Hamilton, *History*, 31–32; "Statutes of the Congregation at Herrnhut, in the year 1727," *The Memorial Days of the Renewed Church of the Brethren* (Ashton-under-Lyne, 1822), 106–109 (quotations on 106, 109).

11. On the lot and the choir system, see Gollin, *Moravians in Two Worlds*, 50–63, 67–109.

Figure 1. Central Europe in the Mid-Eighteenth Century.
Drawn by Richard Stinely

early Unitas Fratrum. But they also reflected a heavy dose of Zinzendorfian theory about class relationships. As a Pietist, and as master of a large estate in Saxony where serfdom and seigneurial privilege were still far more strongly entrenched than in western Europe, Zinzendorf stood squarely in both the feudal and the Lutheran traditions. The Pietists, following in Luther's footsteps, believed that social hierarchy had been divinely ordained. Although striving to bring all classes together in worship, they rejected formal social equality and preached submission to authority.[12]

12. Koppel S. Pinson, *Pietism as a Factor in the Rise of German Nationalism* (New York, 1934), 104–111; Ernst Troeltsch, *The Social Teaching of the Christian Churches*, 2 vols., trans. Olive Wyon (New York, 1931), II, 547–576, 714–721; John G. Gagliardo, *From Pariah to Patriot: The Changing Image of the German Peasant, 1770–1840* (Lexington, Ky., 1969), 81–85; Mary Fulbrook, *Piety and Politics: Religion and the Rise of Absolutism in England, Württemberg,*

As far as Zinzendorf was concerned, social class in any case was nothing more than an outer badge, a "messenger-sign" or "daily burden" of the flesh. Social standing meant nothing beside the knowledge of God carried in the heart. To Moravian church father August Gottlieb Spangenberg, the poor, lacking "artful deceits" or self-deluded pride in wealth and luxury, were far closer to God. With a flourish of Pietist logic, Spangenberg concluded that "many thousands have reason to bless God for their having been poor in the world." Citing a battery of New Testament injunctions counseling slaves to work hard and remain obedient, he drew the lesson: "The apostles did not abolish the diversity of stations in life. They let masters remain masters, and servants, servants. . . . They call the service of a poor slave, even though it be done for an heathen master, a service of God." In short, like the old Unitas in the early fifteenth century, the renewed brotherhood again invoked apostolic teachings to defend worldly power.[13]

Accordingly, Brethren agreed to regard "human regulations and customs . . . in a spirit of meekness, love and obedience, till the Lord himself brings about a change." Herrnhut was to be an undemocratic union of believers, each fulfilling a God-prescribed duty. "No business carried on among us," they resolved, "is to be looked upon as in itself mean and despicable." Most of the Moravians were craftsmen, unskilled workers, tradesmen, or domestic workers, but a sizable upper class of aristocrats and their servants lived there as well. There were apparently no unfree workers, although some of the Moravian refugees had been serfs elsewhere. In 1770, a "Brotherly Agreement" expressed the spirit of class division in Herrnhut: "Just as the abrogation or even intermingling of social classes is contrary to the arrangement of human society established by God, so in our own community of faith and equality of the inner calling, the divine regulation of the

and Prussia (New York, 1983), 43. On the wider currents of medieval, Reformation, and early modern thought concerning servitude and the social order, see Davis, The Problem of Slavery in Western Culture, chap. 4. The manorial traditions that nurtured hierarchical views of the social order held by aristocrats such as Zinzendorf are discussed in Jerome Blum, The End of the Old Order in Rural Europe (Princeton, N.J., 1978); Robert M. Berdahl, The Politics of the Prussian Nobility: The Development of a Conservative Ideology, 1770–1848 (Princeton, N.J., 1988). Also useful, though its focus is primarily on the 19th century, is Shearer Davis Bowman, Masters and Lords: Mid-Nineteenth Century U.S. Planters and Prussian Junkers (New York, 1993).

13. Gerhard Kaiser, Pietismus und Patriotismus im literarischen Deutschland . . . (Wiesbaden, 1961), 86–87; August Gottlieb Spangenberg, An Exposition of Christian Doctrine as Taught in the Protestant Church of the United Brethren or Unitas Fratrum, ed. and trans. J. Kenneth Pfohl and Edmund Schwarze (1778; reprint, Winston-Salem, N.C., 1959), 65–66, 325.

social differentiation of classes shall not be lost sight of, even in our own congregation."[14]

In covenanting together, the Renewed Unity of Brethren restated an old theme of longing for a simple Christian life. Like many before them and many to follow, the Moravians believed they had found the key to righteousness in the communal celebration of Christ's sacrifice. When they took Communion, exchanged the kiss of greeting, or laid on hands, they were recreating a primal moment in Christian fellowship. In their version of Eden reclaimed, it was the devotion of believers that mattered, not their temporal position. They filled the place God had carved for them. By the end of the eighteenth century, the Moravians' appeal to emotion and feeling, which included an exaltation of female spirituality, attracted the attention of writers and philosophers across the Continent and left a formative influence on German romanticism. Restored by new birth though the Moravians might be, however, they had long forgotten the radical social doctrines of an obscure agrarian philosopher, Peter Chelcice.

THE MORAVIANS' ATTITUDES about Christ, power, and community soon intersected with another category of human experience relatively new to them—physical difference. Within a few years after the Brethren codified their principles of godly conduct, they had what might have been their first contact with Africans, an encounter that was to change the church forever. While visiting the royal court of Denmark in 1731, Zinzendorf and a Moravian carpenter, David Nitschmann, met a black, Dutch-speaking Christian named Anthony, the servant of a nobleman who was a director of the Danish West India Company. Anthony, also known as Anton Ulrich, was born a slave on the Danish West Indian colony of Saint Thomas in about 1715. "He used to sit alone on the seashore," he told Zinzendorf, "longing for a more immediate manifestation of the presence of God, and prayed to God to enlighten him concerning the doctrine that was often spoken about, but

14. "Statutes," *Memorial Days*, 108, 110; Gollin, *Moravians in Two Worlds*, 146–147. See also Pinson, *Pietism as a Factor in German Nationalism*, 68; Otto Uttendörfer, *Zinzendorfs Weltbetrachtung: eine systematische Darstellung der Gedankenwelt des Begrunders der Brüdergemeine* (Berlin, 1929), 304–315. These principles did not spring without precedent from the philosophy of Zinzendorf and the Brethren but drew from a complex web of early modern social and religious traditions. See R. Po-Chia Hsia, *Social Discipline in the Reformation: Central Europe, 1550–1750* (London, 1989).

hardly ever practiced by the Christians." His master took Anthony to Copenhagen, where he received instruction in Christianity and was baptized. Anthony told Zinzendorf about the plight of African slaves in the West Indies, including his brother Abraham and sister Anna, "who shared his longing to come to know about God. However, she was deprived of both the time and the opportunity to do so, owing to her condition as a slave." Anthony told Zinzendorf that the slaves urgently needed to hear of Christ and assured him many would convert. This was what the count wanted to hear, because, as he interpreted Anthony's story, the slaves' tragedy was, not their bondage, but their lack of exposure to Christianity.[15]

The count must have had a complex reaction to this bilingual Afro–West Indian. It is not clear, for example, how Zinzendorf perceived Anthony's skin color. The count wrote practically nothing about the physical qualities of Africans, because he took little interest in abstract or applied notions of racial difference. At one level, he was no original theorist on race, subscribing as he did to the commonly held European belief that Africans' blackness was divine punishment for the long-ago sins of Ham, a view invoked to defend the slave trade. Zinzendorf evidently found it difficult to step outside the long and often contradictory medieval and early modern legacy of attitudes about blackness and Africans derived from popular culture, church doctrine, and limited personal contact. For centuries, and in a web of evolving guises, Africans appeared in literature, drama, and iconography as demons, witches, and torturers; as kings, Christian saints, and martyrs; and as exotic objects of revulsion and fascination. Germanic peoples, no less than the English or Iberians, had formed opinions about things African and in some cases had received direct exposure to African images and people.

Zinzendorf must surely have known of the northern European cult of the black saint Maurice, who had a shrine in Halle, where the count spent his formative school years. Because of his close connection with the Danish

15. The story of Anthony's momentous meeting with Zinzendorf is recounted in many works. See Hans Werner Debrunner, *Presence and Prestige, Africans in Europe: A History of Africans in Europe before 1918* (Basel, 1979), 105–106; Hamilton and Hamilton, *History,* 41–46; and C.G.A. Oldendorp, *History of the Mission of the Evangelical Brethren on the Caribbean Islands of St. Thomas, St. Croix, and St. John,* ed. and trans. Arnold R. Highfield and Vladimir Barac (1770; reprint, Ann Arbor, Mich., 1987), 270–273 (quotations). New editorial efforts to restore the full text of this heavily edited but exceptionally important document are described in Gudrun Meier, "Preliminary Remarks on the Oldendorp Manuscripts and Their History," in Stephan Palmié, ed., *Slave Cultures and the Cultures of Slavery* (Knoxville, Tenn., 1996), 67–77.

court, he was well aware of Danish slave trading from Africa to the Danish sugar islands, though his notion of Africans toiling on faraway plantations apparently remained vague until he heard Anthony's description. Perhaps he knew that German-speaking people had also trafficked in slaves between 1682 and 1717 through the Brandenburg African Company. By the early eighteenth century, hundreds of Africans served at various courts throughout Europe, and Zinzendorf could scarcely have been unaware of Ghana-born Anton Wilhelm Amo, a philosopher on the faculty at the University of Halle in the 1730s. So the count was hardly a blank slate on the question of Africans at the time of his encounter with Anthony, though the precise nature of his thinking is difficult to know.[16]

In any case, Anthony's story convinced him that the Danish West Indies were fertile ground for the missionary work he believed God had chosen the Moravians to perform. In what would come to be a characteristic stamp of Zinzendorf and Moravianism, the count was primarily interested in the potential salvation of souls, regardless of racial or ethnic identity. He had been impressed by the Pietist Halle school's mission to the Malabar Islands near Ceylon in the early eighteenth century and believed strongly that Christianity needed to be broadcast to the world. He also reasoned that evangelical work would fortify the Moravians' self-perception as a people of destiny, thus cementing the renewal of the Unity in 1727.

Seeing his opportunity, Zinzendorf took Anthony with him back to

16. A superb overview of changing European attitudes toward blackness and Africans is Ladislas Bugner, ed., *The Image of the Black in Western Art*, 4 vols. (Lausanne and Cambridge, Mass., 1979–1989). See esp. II, *From the Early Christian Era to the "Age of Discovery,"* pt. 1, Jean Devisse, *From the Demonic Threat to the Incarnation of Sainthood*, trans. William Granger Ryan (1979), and II, pt. 2, Jean Devisse and Michel Mollat, *Africans in the Christian Ordinance of the World (Fourteenth to Sixteenth Century)*, trans. Ryan (1979). For a description of a German's views of Africa, see the latter volume, 246, 297 nn. 208–212. See also Benjamin Braude, "The Sons of Noah and the Construction of Ethnic and Geographical Identities in the Medieval and Early Modern Periods," *WMQ*, 3d Ser., LIV (1997), 103–142; Winthrop D. Jordan, *White over Black: American Attitudes toward the Negro, 1550–1812* (Chapel Hill, N.C., 1968), chap. 1; and Debrunner, *Presence and Prestige*. On Germanic attitudes in particular, see Francis B. Gummere, "On the Symbolic Use of the Colors Black and White in Germanic Tradition," *Haverford College Studies*, I (1889), 112–162; Beverly Harris-Schenz, *Black Images in Eighteenth-Century German Literature* (Stuttgart, 1981); Sander L. Gilman, *On Blackness without Blacks: Essays on the Image of the Black in Germany* (Boston, 1982), chaps. 2–3; and Peter Martin, *Schwarze Teufel, edle Mohren* (Hamburg, 1993). On Danish and German slave trading, see James A. Rawley, *The Transatlantic Slave Trade: A History* (New York, 1981), chap. 4. On Anton Wilhelm Amo, see W. E. Abraham, "The Life and Times of Anton Wilhelm Amo," Historical Society of Ghana, *Transactions*, VII (1964), 60–81.

Herrnhut in July 1731, where he repeated his tale to the congregation, be-seeching them to carry the gospel to the slaves. Explaining the difficulties of doing so, given the slaves' exhaustion and lack of time, Anthony suggested the only way the missionaries could get close to them was to become slaves themselves. Undaunted by that prospect, two Brethren, David Nitschmann and Leonard Dober, were so inspired by Anthony's plea that they left Herrn-hut to preach the gospel, arriving in Saint Thomas in December 1732. They carried a letter written in Dutch from Anthony to his brother and sister. Finding the two on a Danish sugar plantation, the Brethren read them the letter that introduced the missionaries and quoted John 17:3, "And this is life eternal, that they might know thee, the only true God, and Jesus Christ, whom thou has sent." Anna was reportedly moved, and, although the family "later disappointed the missionaries," the first mission by the Brethren had begun.[17]

Dober and Nitschmann found lodging on the estate of a planter who helped support them (despite their willingness to become slaves, the mis-sionaries were forbidden by Danish law to do so). There they began holding religious meetings for slaves. After a slow start, they soon attracted converts as well as the unkind scrutiny of Danish authorities. The Moravians had unwittingly arrived at a time of increasing restiveness among the enslaved population of Saint Thomas, Saint Croix, and Saint John. Africans had inhabited the islands since slave imports there had begun in the late seven-teenth century. By 1715, enslaved workers on the Danish sugar and indigo plantations of Saint Thomas outnumbered whites 3,042 to 555. Beyond the harsh treatment the slaves ordinarily received, the chief catalyst for their rebelliousness was a long famine between the mid-1720s and the early 1730s caused by overcultivation of staples. Drought and hurricanes devas-tated the few food crops, and hundreds of slaves starved to death. In 1733, an

17. Hamilton and Hamilton, *History,* 53–46; Debrunner, *Presence and Prestige,* 106. "Anton Ulrich's narrative to Nitschmann and Zinzendorf attained great fame with the Moravian community as the 'divine indication' that the Virgin Islands should become the first Moravian Mission field," Debrunner writes. "Curiously enough, the personality of Anton Ulrich re-mains shadowy in spite of the importance given to the incident (but perhaps, not to the person of Anton Ulrich). Historians of the Moravian Mission and of Protestant Mission work in general seldom omit the touching encounter of the Moravians and Anton Ulrich." It is worth adding that the story retains equally powerful stature among black Moravians in the Carib-bean today as a sort of mythical origins tradition, according to Cedric Rodney, Guyanese-born pastor of St. Philip's Moravian Church in Winston-Salem, North Carolina (Rodney, interview with author, Apr. 4, 1990).

enormous uprising finally erupted on Saint John in which Africans killed many whites and captured most of the island. The rebellion was not suppressed until three months later by a combined force from Saint Thomas, Saint Croix, and the French colony of Martinique. By some accounts, 300 slaves committed suicide rather than surrender.[18]

In the midst of this warfare, authorities and planters regarded the Moravian missionaries as an unwelcome annoyance at best and at worst as outright subversives. Zinzendorf taught that non-Christians already believed in God; they just needed to hear and accept that Christ's death redeemed them. That seemed close to blasphemy to Lutheran or Reformed Danes who believed that blacks had been created by the devil and therefore could not be saved. Whites also feared that Christianity would make slaves even more rebellious. It had been common practice in the West Indies, including the Danish islands, to free converted slaves, "and even though that practice was abandoned," wrote missionary C.G.A. Oldendorp, "it was still to be feared that converted slaves might become too clever, too similar to the Whites, and therefore more inclined to rebellion."[19]

Early results of Moravian preaching gave weight to such fears. One enslaved follower of the Brethren on Saint Thomas, for example, "asserted on the authority of his teacher that black men were no less creatures of God and beneficiaries of the promise of eternal salvation, bought by the blood of Jesus Christ, than were the Whites." Another man, questioned by authorities whether the Moravians had taught that black would rule white on Judgment Day, answered, "After death, we will be with God, and there we will all be equal." Such testimony quickly earned the Moravians a reputation for subversive preaching. Slaves who attended Moravian meetings

18. On Africans in the Danish West Indies, see N.A.T. Hall, "Maritime Maroons: *Grand Marronage* from the Danish West Indies," *WMQ*, 3d Ser., XLII (1985), 476–498 (demographic figures on 476–478); Karen Fog Olwig, *Cultural Adaptation and Resistance on St. John: Three Centuries of Afro-Caribbean Life* (Gainesville, Fla., 1985), and "African Cultural Principles in Caribbean Slave Societies: A View from the Danish West Indies," in Palmié, ed., *Slave Cultures and the Cultures of Slavery*, 23–39; Waldemar Westergaard, *The Danish West Indies under Company Rule, 1671–1754* (New York, 1917), 157–178. Westergaard disputes reports of the mass suicide, contending that lists made in 1734 show that 146 slaves participated in the uprising (176).

19. Zinzendorf's views on non-Christians are set forth in a series of treatises and instructions for missionaries; see Nikolaus Ludwig von Zinzendorf, *Texte zur Mission* (1748; reprint, Hamburg, 1979). See also John R. Weinlick, *Count Zinzendorf* (New York, 1956), 99; Oldendorp, *Caribbean Mission*, ed. and trans. Highfield and Barac, 322.

were frequently beaten and forbidden to leave their plantations. "A certain master indulged in the cruel pleasure of setting his slaves' reading texts afire and then beating them in the face with the flaming pages until the fire was extinguished in that way," reported Oldendorp. "Others resorted to a variety of violent means, with the objective of intimidating the Negroes and preventing them from visiting their teacher." In 1739, more than thirty planters petitioned the government to have the preaching stopped and the Brethren expelled from the island. The Moravian message was simply too great a threat to a white colonial society under siege.[20]

The Brethren protested that they had no intention of challenging slavery. They insisted that Christianity "tended to convert formerly rebellious, disobedient, and wild slaves into benevolent, faithful, and genuinely devoted people." Zinzendorf himself addressed these issues on a visit to Saint Thomas in January 1739. Danish hostility had crested several months earlier when several missionaries were jailed on trumped-up robbery charges. The count arrived on Saint Thomas unexpectedly, unaware of their plight, and, when he learned of it, began lobbying the governor for their release. Both to calm white authorities' fears and to remind slaves of their "place," Zinzendorf called a gathering of several hundred blacks who regularly attended Moravian services and addressed them in Dutch creole. God, he told them, had "made everything himself—kings, masters, servants, and slaves. And as long as we live in this world, everyone must gladly endure the state into which God has placed him." Showing minimal empathy for the enslaved Africans' temporal state, the Saxon count told them that slavery was God's punishment for the "first Negroes" (a reference to the story of Ham), and their recognition of Christ as Savior, although not freeing them from earthly chains, removed "all evil thoughts, deceit, laziness, faithlessness, and everything that makes your condition of slavery burdensome." He exhorted them to follow Christ's "example to all other laborers" through hard work and obedience.[21]

Whatever the assembled Africans' reaction to Zinzendorf's words, the speech failed to mollify white opponents of the mission, who pressed for stronger patrols, rules forbidding slaves to leave their plantations after sun-

---

20. Oldendorp, *Caribbean Mission*, ed. and trans. Highfield and Barac, 322, 354, 356, 359–360. For other examples of repression, see 367–368, 420, 489.

21. Ibid., 335, 363.

Figure 2. *Baptism of the Negroes.* Engraving by Johann Jakob Bossart, 1757. Courtesy, Archiv der Brüder-Unität, Herrnhut, Germany

down, and limits on the size of religious meetings. Persecution of black Christians continued, though in time most planters grudgingly conceded that the Moravian message might actually provide a vital ideological tool for slave control. Writing years later, Bishop Spangenberg remembered the initial planter hostility on Saint Thomas, but, "as they saw from our practice that we urged our Negroes to be faithful and friendly to their masters, and to remain slaves willingly for the sake of the Savior, if he called them in that situation, then they asked to help us in it."[22]

But Zinzendorf's appeal to the slaves may also be seen in another light. The Moravian message exemplified a tension in European attitudes toward the enslavement of non-Christians that had been present in dialogues concerning the New World since the sixteenth-century Spanish debates about Indians. On one hand, the Moravian stance was firmly rooted in traditional

22. August Spangenberg to Samuel Isles, June 27, 1756, quoted in Vernon H. Nelson, "Samuel Isles, First Moravian Missionary on Antigua," *TMHS*, XXI (1966), 3–27. See also Oliver W. Furley, "Moravian Missionaries and Slaves in the West Indies," *Caribbean Studies*, V, no. 2 (July 1965), 3–16, esp. 15.

feudal doctrine that urged slaves to observe the divine hierarchy. The Moravians held other Europeans' repugnance for African ways, a belief that "heathenism" was synonymous with evil, and an assurance that theirs was the only proper religion. Zinzendorf told slaves that "a heathen is accustomed to evil since his youth and has not learned anything better." Oldendorp directly connected skin color with depravity: "There is not much good to say about a people for whom Paul's expression in Ephesians 5:8 *For ye were sometimes darkness* has to be applied in the literal sense."[23]

On the other hand, in the Moravians an urgent tone now tempered the self-righteous sense of election with which many northern Europeans viewed themselves. Anglicans and Puritans in North America, of course, had admitted blacks into their congregations, but in small numbers, for the complexity of the catechisms, the hostility of both planters and slaves, and the inability of missionaries to communicate with Africans all conspired against black conversion. Yet the Moravians brought to their evangelizing a sense that *all* people were chosen by God and that acknowledgment of Christ's martyrdom was the only qualification for conversion. This inclusiveness did not diminish the racial bias of the Moravians' denunciation of African culture; if anything, their Christocentric lens intensified their jaundiced view of "heathenism." But the Brethren's belief that conversion brought spiritual equality to Africans inspired the intensity of their mission.[24]

This vision made the Moravians something of a new force in the world of Protestant evangelism, surpassing the Puritans and the Anglican missionaries of the Society for the Propagation of the Gospel in their zeal to win converts. They were determined to preach in the face of obstacles, even eager to suffer persecution if necessary to spread the gospel. They harnessed enthusiasm to a highly coordinated and effective system of mission organization aided by innovative use of evangelical methods that put them near the forefront of Protestant mission work. One tactic was a willingness to learn Dutch creole to talk to slaves. Bishop August Spangenberg, on his visit to Saint Thomas in 1736, was the first to preach in creole, and the practice

23. Oldendorp, *Caribbean Mission*, ed. and trans. Highfield and Barac, 246, 362. For overviews of the role of Christianity in the development of racialized Western thought, see Jordan, *White over Black*, chap. 4; Forrest G. Wood, *The Arrogance of Faith: Christianity and Race in America from the Colonial Era to the Twentieth Century* (New York, 1990), chap. 1; and Braude, "Sons of Noah," *WMQ*, 3d Ser., LIV (1997), 103–142.

24. On early Protestant missionary efforts in British North America, see Jordan, *White over Black*, 205–212.

quickly became standard. The Brethren gained further ground by translating German texts and hymns into creole.[25]

Another innovation was the use of reports to inform officials in Europe and preachers in the field of the progress of multiple missions. Between the 1730s and 1760s, the Unity expanded its evangelizing efforts throughout the West Indies, to Saint John and Saint Croix, then to Jamaica, Antigua, and other islands. They also extended their worldwide reach to Greenland, South Africa, the Gold Coast, Algeria, Surinam, Ceylon, and Arctic Russia. In the Danish West Indies alone, they baptized more than forty-five hundred slaves by the late 1760s. In all of these places, missionaries filed reports describing in precise detail their techniques, triumphs and failures, and numbers of converts won. Reports were sent to Herrnhut, collected with those from other mission outposts and congregations, printed as *Gemein Nachrichten* (Unity news), and distributed to all missionaries. The growing Moravian evangelical empire was thereby encapsulated in a newspaper from which missionaries could learn how their Brethren around the world were faring.[26]

Most dramatically, black converts were crucial to the spread of the gospel at a time when planters throughout slave societies in the Americas feared the articulation of any kind of black longing or rhetorical power. During the Great Awakening in the North American British colonies in the 1740s and thereafter, black preachers gained repute for their ability to captivate an audience. On Saint Thomas, black exhorters helped the Moravians reach Africans as early as 1736. Missionaries understood—or discovered—that their message carried more credibility when relayed by a black preacher. Missionary Friedrich Martin, for example, was often accompanied on "ex-

25. On Moravian use of creole, see Oldendorp, *Caribbean Mission*, ed. and trans. Highfield and Barac, 322, 371. See 251–260 for a fascinating discussion of the language, including an account of missionaries' efforts to translate German texts into creole. See also Meier, "Preliminary Remarks on the Oldendorp Manuscripts," in Palmié, ed., *Slave Cultures and the Cultures of Slavery*, 70–71.

26. Hamilton and Hamilton, *History*, 52–59; Oldendorp, *Caribbean Mission*, ed. and trans. Highfield and Barac, 626. An old but still useful account of Moravian missions is J. Taylor Hamilton, *A History of the Missions of the Moravian Church during the Eighteenth and Nineteenth Centuries* (Bethlehem, Pa., 1901). An excellent treatment of the Unity mission in Surinam in the 1750s is Richard Price, *Alabi's World* (Baltimore, 1990). Many Afro-Moravian congregations founded during the mid-18th century form the ancestral nucleus for the thriving Moravian Church in the Caribbean today. The full story of the birth of those congregations cannot be told here and awaits separate study.

Figure 3. *First Fruits.* By Valentin Haidt, 1749. The painting depicts the first
converts from worldwide Moravian missions that began in 1732.
Courtesy, Archiv der Brüder-Unität, Herrnhut, Germany

hausting trips to the country" by baptized slaves who were "particularly
useful and important, insofar as his message to the Negroes could be confirmed by a believer from their own nation." One such preacher, a free
mulatto named Rebekka, even married a missionary, Matthaeus Freundlich,
in 1738. Another well-known slave preacher, Abraham, "had the advantage
over his white coworkers of completely understanding the language of the
Negroes, an ability in which his white brethren were still lagging behind. In
addition, he was also more intimately acquainted than they with the super-
stitions, customs and practices of his fellow Blacks." Abraham delivered
exhortations "charged with a special force that swept his listeners along with
him. His preachings were not only attended by numerous Blacks, but even
quite a few Whites came to hear him. They listened to him in amazement.
In one discourse at the burial of a Negro in town in the year 1744, the entire
assembly of his listeners was powerfully moved." Black preachers sometimes incurred brutal retribution. In 1739, six armed whites raided a prayer
meeting where they "seized, severely beat and bound" Abraham and beat
the other slaves with whips and swords. Christianity nonetheless continued

to move swiftly through the quarters of Saint Thomas largely through the persistence and dynamism of black preachers.[27]

Afro-Moravian evangelical work among other blacks reached a high level of systematic organization when missionaries installed a network of "national helpers," in effect assistant preachers or elders. Helpers were baptized slaves charged with supervising the spiritual progress of small sex-segregated groups of five to ten slaves organized roughly according to African ethnicity. The groups "came together once a week under the tutelage of a missionary or his aides, in order to discuss their inner growth in the knowledge of Jesus Christ, to exchange confidences about their individual problems, to encourage one another, and to ask forgiveness for one another." Such groups helped novices cohere around the gospel in cultural and linguistic terms they could understand. By appropriating the efficiency of Moravian evangelical methods, Africans made the spread of Christianity a spiritual and social movement for each other.[28]

Soon their organizing spanned the ocean. Within a few years, as the Moravian mission network spread through the Caribbean, increasing numbers of African and African-American people converted to the faith. Some of them traveled with the Brethren to the new congregation town of Bethlehem, Pennsylvania, and many black Moravians even made their way to Europe. Joshua, a young boy who was missionary Friedrich Martin's first convert on Saint Thomas, returned with Martin to Herrnhut and joined the congregation. Another Saint Thomas convert, Maria, journeyed to Europe to live in the Moravian congregation town of Herrnhaag. An important black missionary was Christian Protten, a native of the Gold Coast in Africa and the son of a Danish father and a Ga mother who had been sent to Denmark to be educated in 1726. He joined the Moravian Church in 1735 and returned to his native land to preach periodically over the next twenty

27. All citations from Oldendorp, *Caribbean Mission,* ed. and trans. Highfield and Barac. On Friedrich Martin, see 328. On Rebekka and her marriage to missionary Matthaeus Freundlich, see 318, 338–339. Abraham's fiery sermon is recounted on 418–419, and his beating on 367–368.

28. The system of national helpers is discussed ibid., 333 (quotation), esp. 481–482, 541–543. On the comparable importance of converted Moravian Indians to the Unity's native American missions in Pennsylvania and Ohio between 1740 and 1780, see Edwin A. Sawyer, "The Religious Experience of the Colonial American Moravians," *TMHS,* XVIII (1961), 158–199. See also Jane T. Merritt, "Kinship, Community, and Practicing Culture: Indians and the Colonial Encounter in Pennsylvania, 1700–1763" (Ph.D. diss., University of Washington, 1995).

Figure 4. *Maria, the Mooress from St. Thomas.* By Valentin Haidt. Having converted to the Moravian faith in Saint Thomas, Maria was a member of the Herrnhaag congregation in Germany when this portrait was completed shortly before
her death in 1749. Courtesy, Archiv der Brüder-Unität, Herrnhut, Germany

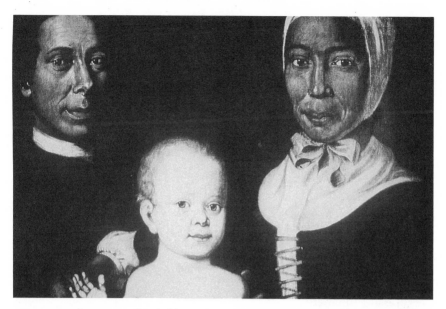

Figure 5. *Christian and Rebekka Protten*. By Abraham Brandt, circa 1740–1741. Saint Thomas convert Rebekka Freundlich and Afro-Dane Christian Protten married at Herrnhut in 1740. The child is Rebekka's from her previous marriage to a Moravian missionary. Courtesy, Archiv der Brüder-Unität, Herrnhut, Germany

years. In 1740, he married Rebekka Freundlich, the free mulatto widow of Saint Thomas missionary Matthaeus Freundlich, who had moved back to Herrnhut with him. Thus, by the mid-eighteenth century, black women and men were finding in the Moravian Church a sanctioned, transatlantic forum in which to express and preach their spirituality from Africa to Europe to the Caribbean to North America. Black Moravians staged the first international black Protestant movement.[29]

The message and the methods of the Moravians had broad implications. In their insistence on new birth as the only important requisite for salvation, they anticipated other evangelicals. Moravian missionaries, while traveling to Georgia with John Wesley, impressed him with their emphasis on religion of the heart, an influence that left an unmistakable imprint on Methodism. The New Light itinerants who began combing the North American colonies

29. On Christian Protten, Rebekka, and other black Moravians in North America and Europe, see Debrunner, *Presence and Prestige*, 82–83; Oldendorp, *Caribbean Mission*, ed. and trans. Highfield and Barac, 402, 679–680, 689, pt. 2, bk. 2, sec. 1, n. 1. Joshua's grave may still be seen in the Herrnhut congregational graveyard.

in the 1740s continued to spread the word that salvation was guaranteed for all, not for a select few. Some even suggested that equality ought to extend to this life and that human bondage was an affront to God.[30]

The last idea already far exceeded the limits of white Moravians' interpretation of Christian freedom. At the same time they were converting thousands of blacks and as enslaved Africans took an ever greater part in organizing their own Christian communities, white Brethren in the West Indies began buying slaves themselves, as if to confirm their willing acceptance of prevailing social hierarchies. In 1737, they bought a plantation and thirty to forty slaves on Saint Thomas to support their livelihood. In the following years, Moravian missionaries in Jamaica, Antigua, and other Caribbean colonies followed a similar course, finding it easier to join the plantation economy than to live on its fringes, dependent on handouts from Europe. They might also have reasoned that ownership of plantations and slaves would earn them favor with authorities.[31]

Expressing momentary uneasiness over these developments, August Spangenberg wrote in 1760: "I know of course that in the beginning we had none [slaves] and yet our dear Saviour provided for our needs. But the Brethren and Sisters tell me circumstances have changed since then and that the work could no longer be carried on as formerly." If Moravians were to own slaves, they must at least follow certain rules. "We cannot indeed apply literally the commandments given by God to the Jews regarding the treatment of their bond servants to the Negroes," the bishop cautioned. "But the divine purpose in such laws, the deep interest of our Master in heaven, the

30. See Clifford W. Towlson, *Moravian and Methodist: Relationships and Influences in the Eighteenth Century* (London, 1957); Leon Hynson, "John Wesley and the Unitas Fratrum: A Theological Analysis," *Methodist History,* XVIII (1979), 26–60; and, on the Methodist-Moravian relationship, F. Ernest Stoeffler, "Religious Roots of the Early Moravians and Methodist Movements," Warren Thomas Smith, "Eighteenth Century Encounters: Methodist-Moravian," David A. Schattschneider, "Moravianism as an American Denomination," Kenneth E. Rowe, "From Eighteenth Century Encounter to Nineteenth Century Estrangement: Images of Moravians in the Thought of Methodist Bishops Asbury and Simpson," and Barbara J. Strauss, "The Methodist/Moravian Legacy of Hymns," all in *Methodist History,* XXIV (1986), 132–140, 141–156, 157–170, 171–178, 179–190. On the Moravian influence on broader 18th-century evangelical currents, see Susan O'Brien, "A Transatlantic Community of Saints: The Great Awakening and the First Evangelical Network, 1735–1755," *AHR,* XCI (1986), 825–826.

31. Hamilton and Hamilton, *History,* 48, 251; Oldendorp, *Caribbean Mission,* ed. and trans. Highfield and Barac, 339–341; Furley, "Moravian Missionaries and Slaves," *Caribbean Studies,* V, no. 2 (July 1965), 4–5.

fundamental schema of love toward our neighbor, that must still hold and even to a much greater degree; for we are under the new covenant." In other words, although the Moravians were under no obligation to free slaves every seven years, incorporate them into their households, or permit them to own property as the ancient Hebrews had done, they must treat them with human dignity.[32]

The Brethren were hardly the first to use Christianity to humanize and legitimize slavery simultaneously. But later generations of white Brethren would regret their forerunners' ownership of slaves. "We grieve over it, and believe the Lord winked at those times of ignorance," lamented a missionary in Jamaica in 1854.[33]

As the mission spread, the Unity also dispatched bands of Brethren to various points in America and Europe to plant small communities insulated from the corruption of the outside world. Settlements flourished in Holland, England, and Germany. In 1735, the Brethren negotiated with James Ogle-thorpe to found a settlement and school in Savannah, Georgia, for native Americans. But when Georgia authorities asked them to bear arms against the Spanish attack on the colony in 1740, the Moravians migrated to Penn-sylvania, where they founded two new settlements, Nazareth and Bethle-hem. The latter became the church's American headquarters and a base for new missions to Indians.[34]

An additional impetus forced the Brethren to seek land for more settle-ments in the late 1740s. The Unity came under fire in Europe for what critics considered a bizarrely intense form of worship during the so-called sifting period. Between 1743 and 1750, many Moravian hymns, prayers, and cate-chisms took the emphasis on Christ's martyrdom to a highly emotional

---

32. Spangenberg, quoted in Hamilton and Hamilton, *History,* 662 n. 79. On Hebrew slave-holding practices, see David Brion Davis, *Slavery and Human Progress* (New York, 1984), 82–86.

33. J. H. Buchner, *The Moravians in Jamaica: History of the Mission of the United Brethren's Church to the Negroes in the Island of Jamaica, from the Year 1754 to 1854* (London, 1854), 22. The reference is to Acts 17:30, "The times of ignorance therefore God overlooked; but now he commandeth men that they should all everywhere repent." On early Moravian slaveholding, see also S. U. Hastings and B. L. MacLeavy, *Seedtime and Harvest: A Brief History of the Moravian Church in Jamaica, 1754–1979* (Bridgetown, Barbados, 1979), 32–37.

34. Hamilton and Hamilton, *History,* 76–86. On the short-lived Moravian settlement in Georgia, see also Adelaide L. Fries, *The Moravians in Georgia, 1735–40* (Raleigh, N.C., 1905).

level, glorifying the blood and wounds of Christ in vivid—or as some authors have charged, psychosexual—imagery. In some of the goriest of these
images, Moravians announced their desire to swim in the blood of Jesus,
crawl like worms into his side-wound, and drink the sweat of his agony like
bees. High church and state authorities condemned this gruesome "blood
and wounds" theology as heretical and reviled Zinzendorf as a charlatan.
Even their former allies, the Methodists, denounced the Brethren in England, and Moravian preachers were sometimes attacked, imprisoned, and
barred from preaching. In 1749, at the height of the sifting period, some
three thousand Moravians were evicted from Herrnhaag and Marienborn,
two settlements in the German principality of Wetteravia, after refusing
their landlord's order to join the state church.[35]

Searching for a refuge for these displaced people, the Moravians received
an offer of land from John Carteret, earl of Granville, lord proprietor of the
northern part of North Carolina. Granville was heir to one of eight lords
proprietor who had received land grants in North Carolina from Charles II
in 1663. Heirs to seven of the grants had sold their shares to the crown in
1728, but Granville kept his, a tract bounded only by the Virginia border on
the north and a line through the middle part of the colony in the south and
stretching on, in theory, to the end of the continent. In hope of developing
this enormous domain, Granville and his agents were looking for colonists
to settle the fertile stretches of the Piedmont where, by 1745, fewer than one
hundred white male immigrants lived.[36]

Granville had known Zinzendorf and the Moravians in England during
their successful quest for parliamentary recognition as a Protestant church,
which they hoped would dispel rumors that they were secretly papist supporters of the Stuarts. Aware of their reputation for diligence and faithful-
ness, Granville believed the Moravians would make ideal settlers. The population in eastern North Carolina was growing rapidly, and available land was
becoming scarce. In the west, however, vast stretches of land were still
relatively free of European settlers. There the Moravians could find a tract
for a settlement that they specified should be suitably removed from other
colonists to prevent their interference, yet close enough to trade with them.

35. Hamilton and Hamilton, *History*, 100–106. On the sifting period, see also Jacob John
Sessler, *Communal Pietism among Early American Moravians* (New York, 1933), 156–181.

36. A[rthur] Roger Ekirch, *"Poor Carolina": Politics and Society in Colonial North Carolina,
1729–1776* (Chapel Hill, N.C., 1981), 127–143 (western population figure on 129); Hugh T.
Lefler and William S. Powell, *Colonial North Carolina: A History* (New York, 1973), 81–112.

Negotiations between Granville and the Moravians began in 1749 and concluded in late 1751, when Zinzendorf agreed to buy one hundred thousand acres from the earl. The location of the tract had yet to be determined, for the great reaches of western territory in what was known as Anson County were largely uncharted. In August 1752, Bishop Spangenberg, leader of the Moravian Church in America and probably the Unity's second most important leader after Zinzendorf, set out on horseback with four others from Bethlehem for Edenton, North Carolina, to find and stake out the land that would become the Moravian refuge.[37]

In Edenton, the Moravians met with Granville's agent in North Carolina, Francis Corbin, who was to help them find a suitable tract of land. Unable to pinpoint a precise location where they might find the large piece they wanted, Corbin could only suggest that Spangenberg's party head for the unsurveyed stretches toward the mountains in the "Back of the Colony." In his journal, Spangenberg noted with dismay the "unbelievable confusion" of land matters in the colony. Officials maintained no comprehensive map or listing of landholdings, and it was therefore impossible to judge what land was vacant. Corbin "cannot now give a [land] Patent without fearing that when the tract is settled another man will come and say 'That is my land.' " Finally, the bishop and his party headed west accompanied by guides and Granville's chief surveyor, William Churton.[38]

As the party moved across eastern North Carolina and into the Piedmont, Spangenberg kept a perceptive, if critical and at times ethnocentric, eye trained on the colony that would hold the new Moravian outpost. North Carolina appeared raw and undeveloped to him. "Trade and business are poor," he reported to Zinzendorf and other Moravian leaders in Germany. "With no navigable rivers there is little shipping; with no export trade of importance the towns are few and small." The main economic staples seemed to

37. Hamilton and Hamilton, *History*, 107–118; Daniel B. Thorp, *The Moravian Community in Colonial North Carolina: Pluralism on the Southern Frontier* (Knoxville, Tenn., 1989), 22–29. Thorp points out that, in contrast to other Moravian ventures in America, the missionary impulse played little part in the founding of the North Carolina settlement (24). Rather, church leaders were more concerned about building a sanctuary where Brethren could worship freely and earn a profit for the Unity.

38. Spangenberg's account of the journey is contained in "Short Account of the Journey of Br. Joseph and His Party to Carolina," and the Spangenberg Diary, in Adelaide L. Fries et al., eds., *Records of the Moravians in North Carolina*, 11 vols. (Raleigh, N.C., 1922–1969), I, 28–62 (quotations on 32, 33). On controversies surrounding land policies in the Granville District, see Ekirch, *"Poor Carolina,"* 127–143.

bring in little revenue. Tobacco, cattle, and hogs were all taken to be sold in Virginia, whose merchants reaped the profits. Apparently absent were the skilled workers needed to keep an economy operating smoothly. "Of handicrafts I have seen practically nothing in the 150 miles we have traveled across this Province," he wrote. "Almost nobody has a trade. In Edenton I saw one smith, one cobbler, and one tailor at work, and no more; whether there are others I do not know. In 140 miles I saw not one wagon or plough, nor any sign of one." In the eastern counties, "one can ride for three hours without seeing anything except Pine Barrens, that is white sand grown up in pine trees, which will hardly produce anything else." There the people made tar, pitch, and turpentine. But beyond corn and hogs the farmland seemed unproductive, and "the work is poorly done." Clearly, as the bishop saw it, Moravian diligence and skill were sorely needed in this wasteland.[39]

Spangenberg could not restrain his contempt for the colony's white population. Native-born Carolinians, he noted, bore the climate well but were lazy. Recent immigrants from the British Isles were, in his view, little more than a collection of impoverished debtors, criminals, and "horse thieves"; "crowds of Irish" had moved in because they had mistakenly heard that their stock did not need to be fed in winter but could forage for themselves. But Spangenberg's bleak view was tempered by hope, for "I am told that a different type of settler is now coming in,—sturdy Germans." As for the Indians, Spangenberg found them "in a bad way." The eastern nations, the Chowan, the Tuscarora, and the Meherrin, were decimated and "oppressed by the whites." Further west, however, he reported that the Catawbas, Cherokees, and Senecas, resentful of white encroachment, were still apt to attack settlers on isolated farms.[40]

Traveling southwest away from European settlements, the group came in late November to the Catawba River in the southwest part of the colony, which they followed north to its headwaters. Surveyor Churton measured

---

39. Spangenberg Diary, in Fries et al., eds., *Records,* I, 38, 39. On the geography, economics, and population of the colony, see Lefler and Powell, *Colonial North Carolina;* and H. Roy Merrens, *Colonial North Carolina in the Eighteenth Century: A Study in Historical Geography* (Chapel Hill, N.C., 1964).

40. Spangenberg Diary, in Fries et al., eds., *Records,* I, 34, 36 (quotation), 40–41 (quotations), 48; Theda Perdue, *Native Carolinians: The Indians of North Carolina* (Raleigh, N.C., 1985); James H. Merrell, *The Indians' New World: Catawbas and Their Neighbors from European Contact through the Era of Removal* (Chapel Hill, N.C., 1989). Spangenberg made only passing reference to Africans but noted with care several laws regarding slaveholding.

several pieces of land that Spangenberg judged to be good farm land with ample water, but each was only several thousand acres—nowhere near the one hundred thousand acres the Moravians desired. All the same, this Moravian bishop who had traveled, preached, and organized settlements from Georgia to the Caribbean to Pennsylvania was filled with awe at what he saw in the North Carolina backcountry. "We are here in a region that has perhaps been seldom visited since the creation of the world," he reported. "We are some 70 or 80 miles from the last settlement in North Carolina, and have come over terrible mountains, and often through very dangerous ways."[41]

Uncertain where they were going, and led by a hunter who lost his way, the explorers headed west and scaled the Blue Ridge. "When we reached the top we saw mountains to right and to left, before and behind us, many hundreds of mountains, rising like great waves in a storm." Battling snow and wind and suffering from a lack of food, the party turned north until they came to the New River, far to the west of where they had intended to be. Turning southeast, the travelers in early January at last found what they were looking for—a large unclaimed tract of about one hundred thousand acres that framed the three forks of Muddy Creek, a tributary of the Yadkin River, in newly formed Rowan County. The native Saponi and Tutelo Indians had withdrawn from the northwest frontier of the colony, and the land was still virtually empty of Europeans. With plentiful meadowland, many creeks and streams (though none navigable), lowland for crops, and stones for building, the tract struck Spangenberg as ideal. He could only conclude: "The land on which we are now encamped seemed to me to have been reserved by the Lord for the Brethren."[42]

With the land staked out, Spangenberg and his party returned to Bethlehem and then traveled to London where, in August 1753, he signed the purchase contract with Granville for 500 pounds plus a yearly rent of about 148 pounds. The tract was named Wachau, or Wachovia, after an ancestral estate of the Zinzendorf family. Late in 1753, a band of fifteen Brethren came south from Bethlehem to begin building Bethabara, the first settlement of the new refuge. Here the Moravians would live in the service of the Lord—and African slaves would soon labor in the service of the Brethren.

41. Spangenberg Diary, in Fries et al., eds., *Records,* I, 54.

42. Ibid., I, 59–60; Thorp, *Moravian Community,* 30. See also Robert W. Ramsey, *Carolina Cradle: Settlement of the Northwest Carolina Frontier, 1747–1762* (Chapel Hill, N.C., 1964).

CHAPTER TWO

By the Drawing of Lots

Slavery and Divine Will

 THE MORAVIAN BRETHREN arrived in the North Carolina upcountry in 1753 untroubled by the concept of human bondage. In their missions throughout the slave societies of the Americas, they assured nervous authorities their goal was simply to spread the gospel, not to challenge slavery. As if to emphasize the point, they themselves bought African slaves in the West Indies. Yet the blueprint for their new colony-within-a-colony in Carolina contained no provisions for African slavery. Wachovia was to be an exclusive, self-sufficient Moravian sanctuary, sustained by the labors of godly brothers and sisters.

Yet this fertile land—earmarked by God for the Brethren, as they saw it—would not surrender its abundant riches without the work of many hands, more than the Moravians could muster. The Lord had not said who would supply the difference. As the heavy demands of building a new frontier settlement mounted, church leaders were forced to look beyond their own boundaries for help. A dilemma lay ahead: whether to use African slave labor in this refuge of the sanctified.

The question of slaveownership by the Moravians was embedded not only in their congregational philosophy but in the larger context of German slaveholding in America. Despite their uniqueness as a religious fellowship, the Brethren shared certain cultural assumptions and values with the thousands of other Germans who took part in the great eighteenth-century transatlantic voyages to America. Although the extent of German slaveholding in eighteenth-century America has yet to receive thorough scrutiny, the Moravian Brethren's views of African slavery reflected a continuing debate about the institution among German-speaking immigrants.[1]

As their English, French, and Spanish counterparts in North America busied themselves wringing huge profits from the labor of fettered Africans, most German colonists shied away from the practice, at least during their early years in America. A modest desire for self-sufficiency motivated the typical German immigrant, according to an enduring historical tradition that has some merit. Refugees from religious warfare or from economic strangulation in the service of some feudal lord, the great majority of Germans in America craved the independence of winning a livelihood in their own shop or on their own land by skill and hard work.[2] Many Germans feared that racial slavery, at least the large-scale holdings favored by English

---

1. For overviews of German immigration to America and early German-American historiography, see the following works by A. G. Roeber: *Palatines, Liberty, and Property: German Lutherans in Colonial British America* (Baltimore, 1993); "In German Ways? Problems and Potentials of Eighteenth-Century German Social and Emigration History," *WMQ*, 3d Ser., LXIV (1987), 750–774; and " 'The Origin of Whatever Is Not English among Us': The Dutch-speaking and German-speaking Peoples of Colonial British America," in Bernard Bailyn and Philip D. Morgan, eds., *Strangers within the Realm: Cultural Margins of the First British Empire* (Chapel Hill, N.C., 1991), 220–283. See also Aaron Spencer Fogleman, *Hopeful Journeys: German Immigration, Settlement, and Political Culture in Colonial America, 1717–1775* (Philadelphia, 1996); Frank Trommler and Joseph McVeigh, eds., *America and the Germans: An Assessment of a Three-Hundred-Year History,* 2 vols. (Philadelphia, 1985), esp. Hermann Wellenreuther, "Image and Counterimage, Tradition and Expectation: The German Immigrants in English Colonial Society in Pennsylvania, 1700–1765," I, 85–105, and Marianne Wokeck, "German Immigration to Colonial America: Prototype of a Transatlantic Mass Migration," I, 3–13; Wokeck, "Harnessing the Lure of the 'Best Poor Man's Country': The Dynamics of German-Speaking Immigration to British North America, 1683–1783," in Ida Altman and James Horn, eds., *"To Make America": European Emigration in the Early Modern Period* (Berkeley, Calif., 1991), 204–243; and Rosalind J. Beiler, "The Transatlantic World of Caspar Wistar: From Germany to America in the Eighteenth Century" (Ph.D. diss., University of Pennsylvania, 1994).

2. Walter M. Kollmorgen, "The Pennsylvania German Farmer," in Ralph Wood, ed., *The Pennsylvania Germans* (Princeton, N.J., 1942), 33; Richard H. Shryock, "British versus German Traditions in Colonial Agriculture," *Mississippi Valley Historical Review,* XXVI (1939–1940), 39–54; Edward Raymond Turner, *The Negro in Pennsylvania: Slavery-Servitude-Freedom, 1639–1861* (Philadelphia, 1911). Many Germans no doubt shared the reverence for land expressed by the English Digger, Gerrard Winstanley, in the mid-1600s. "True religion and undefiled," he wrote, "is to let everyone quietly have earth to manure"; see Christopher Hill, *The World Turned Upside Down: Radical Ideas during the English Revolution* (New York, 1972), 130. On German spiritual connections to the soil, for example, see Stevenson Whitcomb Fletcher, *Pennsylvania Agriculture and Country Life, 1640–1840* (Harrisburg, Pa., 1971), 50–51.

planters, would put white settlers of more modest means at a disadvantage against wealthy slaveowners. They argued that success could readily be seized without the use of slave labor.[3]

One well-known group of antislavery advocates was the Salzburgers, Pietist Lutheran immigrants in Georgia who vigorously supported the new colony's ban on slavery in the 1730s. Not only would runaway and rebellious slaves pose a physical threat to whites, they contended, but slave craftsmen would take work away from whites and lower their wages, as the Salzburgers pointed out had happened in Charleston. Pastor Johann Martin Bolzius held up the Salzburgers' own plentiful harvests as evidence that enslaved Africans were not needed to turn a profit and that, once whites adjusted to the hot climate of the subtropical lowcountry, they could work just as well as blacks. Similarly, farmers in Rowan County, North Carolina, home to numerous Germans, complained in 1774 that "the African Trade is injurious to this Colony, obstructs the Population of it by freemen, prevents manufacturers, and other Useful Emigrants from Europe from settling among us."[4]

Based on his travels through the colonies, Lutheran minister Henry Melchior Muhlenberg opposed slavery on similar grounds. In 1774, he praised the example of a German family in South Carolina who "cultivate[d] the place themselves in the sweat of their brows and prove[d] thereby that a man can live and find food and clothing without the use of black slaves, if he be godly and contented and does not desire to take more out of the world than he brought into it." Such sentiments had a limited impact in curtailing the growth of the plantation system in the eighteenth century. But they did articulate an important philosophical alternative to slavery that anticipated the core of free-soil Republican thought in the 1850s.[5]

3. See, for example, Fletcher, *Pennsylvania Agriculture and Country Life*, 116–119. Overviews of the little-studied relations between Germans and African Americans include Randall M. Miller, ed., *States of Progress: Germans and Blacks in America over Three Hundred Years* (Philadelphia, 1989); and Leroy T. Hopkins, "The Germantown Protest and Afro-German Relations in Pennsylvania and Maryland before the Civil War," in *The Report: A Journal of German-American History*, IV (1990), 23–31.

4. Betty Wood, *Slavery in Colonial Georgia, 1730–1775* (Athens, Ga., 1984), 60–73; and William L. Withuhn, "Salzburgers and Slavery: A Problem of *Mentalité*," *Georgia Historical Quarterly*, LXVIII (1984), 173–192; William L. Saunders, ed., *The Colonial Records of North Carolina*, 10 vols. (Raleigh, N.C., 1886–1890), IX, 1026.

5. Henry Melchior Muhlenberg, *The Journals of Henry Melchior Muhlenberg*, 3 vols., trans. Theodore G. Tappert and John W. Doberstein (Philadelphia, 1942–1958), II, 586. This is not to

It was the economics, not the ethics, of slavery that rankled these opponents. Except for some Quakers, Mennonites, Dunkards, and other quietist sects who opposed slavery on religious grounds, few Germans found moral fault with the idea of human bondage. Since most came from Lutheran or Reformed traditions, their views probably matched those of Muhlenberg, who wrote of a God-ordained hierarchy in the natural world and the human social order, in which African slaves ranked "only a little higher than cattle." And for many of these new residents of America, the ability to acquire personal property in the form of land and slaves represented a proclamation of their own newfound freedom from oppression in Europe.[6]

As the eighteenth century progressed, this combination of a stratified, racially chauvinistic social ethos and a desire to acquire property helped many Germans reconcile small-scale slavery with their belief in the freeholder's independence. More and more came to believe that, though the plantation slavery practiced in the eastern Carolinas and the Chesapeake would always threaten the yeoman, there was nothing wrong in owning a few bondpersons to help on the farm or in the shop. For some Germans, the change in attitude stemmed from dissatisfaction with indentured servants and their annoying habit of running away. In addition, Germans were discovering that, as Benjamin Franklin bluntly explained, slaves "may be kept as long as a Man pleases, or has Occasion for their Labour while hired men are continually leaving their Master (often in the midst of his Business) and setting up for themselves."[7]

Dunkard newspaper editor Christopher Sauer of Germantown, Pennsylvania, also noticed that the Seven Years' War had cut the supply of German

---

argue that German antislavery thought was unique or that free soilers traced their origins exclusively to Germans. Rather, Germans were among the growing number of Europeans who shared this emerging body of protest thought against slavery.

6. Ibid., 674. The famous Germantown protest of 1688 by German, Swiss, and Dutch Quakers is widely regarded as the first formal antislavery protest on moral grounds in North America; see Thomas E. Drake, *Quakers and Slavery in America* (New Haven, Conn., 1950), 11–13. George Fox's antislavery statements of 1657 and 1671–1672 might have been the first in America. Antislavery Quakers, however, were a minority within their own church. See also Leroy T. Hopkins, "The Germantown Protest: Origins of Abolitionism among the German Residents of Southeastern Pennsylvania," *Yearbook of German-American Studies*, XXIII (1988), 19–29. The connection between German notions of liberty and propertyholding is made in Roeber, *Palatines, Liberty, and Property*, with particular reference to slaveholding on 207.

7. Leonard W. Labaree et al., eds., *The Papers of Benjamin Franklin* (New Haven, Conn., 1959), IV, 230, quoted in Sharon V. Salinger, *"To Serve Well and Faithfully": Labor and Indentured Servitude in Pennsylvania, 1682–1800* (New York, 1987), 73.

immigrants, exacerbating the labor shortage. The consequences seemed ominous to Sauer. "Now also the Germans start out on the negro traffic because they cannot get German servants anymore, and although they make much money themselves do not want to pay a living wage to a free man or girl for help." Imports into Philadelphia, mostly from the West Indies, swelled between 1755 and 1765. The enslaved population in Pennsylvania remained relatively low through the end of the colonial period—about ten thousand, or 3 percent of the colony's total in 1775. But Sauer's fears about the rising use of slave labor by Pennsylvania Germans were well-founded. Germans owned more slaves than did other whites in predominantly Quaker Bucks County; in Lancaster County, Germans owned about 10 percent of the slaves in 1780. In the German-majority town of Lancaster lived blacks who spoke German, received baptism and Christian instruction, and worked as craftsmen with German masters.[8]

The Moravians in Bethlehem, Pennsylvania, provide a good example of Germans who turned readily to slavery in the mid-eighteenth century. Bethlehem, founded in 1741, was a church-controlled congregation town that operated on a communal *Oeconomy*, or general economy, during its first twenty years. The Brethren, who wanted to eliminate dependence on outsiders, would rather have done without non-Moravian workers. But because they heavily emphasized skilled or professional labor among their own ranks—at least among males—they often brought in non-Moravian workers for unskilled jobs. In Bethlehem by the early 1740s, both hired white hands and enslaved blacks served the Oeconomy. Some of the whites might have been indentured servants, but most were hired on short-term contracts. In 1742, contemplating a switch from free to unfree non-Moravian workers, town directors outlined the advantages of slaves over hired whites. "It was proposed to get rid of our white hired hands, because to the

8. Christopher Sauer, cited in Otto Pollak, "German Immigrant Problems in Eighteenth Century Pennsylvania as Reflected in Trouble Advertisements," *American Sociological Review*, VIII (1943), 679; Salinger, *"To Serve Well and Faithfully,"* 71–75; Darold D. Wax, "Quaker Merchants and the Slave Trade in Colonial Pennsylvania," *PMHB*, LXXXVI (1962), 150; Wax, "Negro Imports into Pennsylvania, 1720–1766," *Pennsylvania History*, XXXII (1965), 254–287; Wax, "Africans on the Delaware: The Pennsylvania Slave Trade, 1759–1765," *Pennsylvania History*, L (1983), 38–49; Owen S. Ireland, "Germans against Abolition: A Minority's View of Slavery in Revolutionary Pennsylvania," *JIH*, III (1972–1973), 694; Jerome H. Wood, Jr., "The Negro in Early Pennsylvania: The Lancaster Experience, 1730–90," in Elinor Miller and Eugene D. Genovese, eds., *Plantation, Town, and County: Essays on the Local History of American Slave Society* (Urbana, Ill., 1974), 442–452.

present they have behaved too arrogantly and insolently. And should we be compelled to keep hired hands, it would be preferable to buy Negroes from Saint Thomas and employ them as regular servants who would receive wages, to show Pennsylvania and a conscientious author, who in his writing opposed slavekeeping, how one could treat even Negroes."[9]

During the next two decades, the Moravians bought perhaps three dozen or more enslaved laborers to supplement their work force in Bethlehem and in the nearby Moravian settlements of Nazareth and Gnadenthal. Many were Africans shipped from Saint Thomas, Saint Vincent, or Jamaica to Philadelphia or New York. Blacks, roughly two-thirds of whom were men, worked as butchers, tanners, oil millers, farmers, and tavern servants and in many other occupations. At least some even received wages. More than two dozen blacks converted, and several became full communicants.[10]

German slaveholding increased as settlers streamed down from Pennsylvania to new homes in Maryland, Virginia, and the Carolinas during the great southern migrations that quickened after midcentury. The relentless demands of clearing land, building farms, and operating industries often outstripped the Germans' own prodigious capacity for work. To compensate, many bought or rented slaves to secure steady help that was often hard to find on the frontier. Most slaveholding Germans were small farmers who owned fewer than five slaves, but occasionally a master acquired as many as thirty or forty.[11]

9. Kenneth G. Hamilton, ed. and trans., *The Bethlehem Diary*, I, *1742–1744* (Bethlehem, Pa., 1971), 105–106. The identity of the "conscientious author" is unknown. On Bethlehem's early history, see Joseph Mortimer Levering, *A History of Bethlehem, Pennsylvania, 1741–1892, with Some Account of Its Founders and Their Early Activity* (Bethlehem, Pa., 1903), chaps. 2–10; Jacob Sessler, *Communal Pietism among Early American Moravians* (New York, 1933); and Gillian Lindt Gollin, *Moravians in Two Worlds: A Study of Changing Communities* (New York, 1967).

10. For an account of the life of one African-born Moravian brother in Bethlehem, see Daniel B. Thorp, "Chattel with a Soul: The Autobiography of a Moravian Slave," *PMHB*, CXII (1988), 433–451. Other data about black Moravians in Pennsylvania are contained in the Bethlehem and Nazareth church registers and diaries, the minute books of the Bethlehem Aeltesten Conferenz and Aufseher Collegium, the records of the Bethlehem Single Brothers' and Single Sisters' Houses, and the church memoir file, all in the Moravian Archives, Northern Province, Bethlehem.

11. For example, see Elizabeth A. Kessel, "Germans on the Maryland Frontier: A Social History of Frederick County, Maryland, 1730–1800" (Ph.D. diss., Rice University, 1981), 169–181; Klaus Wust, *The Virginia Germans* (Charlottesville, Va., 1969), 121–128, esp. the case of Isaac Hite in the Shenandoah Valley, who owned 38 slaves in 1782; William H. Gehrke, "Negro Slavery among the Germans in North Carolina," *NCHR*, XIV (1937), 307–324; Albert

Even the Lutheran Salzburgers, having lost their fight to keep slavery out of Georgia by the late 1740s, had given in and, like other white Georgians, started buying slaves to produce silk and lumber for export. "Negroes are reliable, cheap, and industrious labor," acknowledged a minister in 1754, admitting: "We dare not drive [white servants] harshly for fear of losing them. We have tried everything in our power to make do with white people. Had we succeeded, we would have been able to dispense with Negroes in our town; but this will not be possible until this country is full of people." The lament for a failed vision was touching, but the Salzburgers wasted no further time making up lost ground. By 1774, Pastor Christian Rabenhorst owned thirty slaves on the church-owned "Minister's Plantation."[12]

These developments did not go unnoticed by Henry Muhlenberg, who traveled the eastern seaboard for the better part of five decades and kept up a running commentary throughout his journals on slaveholding Germans and the economic folly of slaveownership.[13] But Germans continued to enmesh themselves in the slaveholding system. During the last quarter of the century, German slaveholding throughout the Carolina and Virginia upland increased, even dramatically in some areas. "Almost all" of the German families in Lincoln County, North Carolina, were said to own slaves in 1802. By 1820, a visitor to the German-dominated Valley of Virginia could write that almost every white family owned and worked alongside at least one slave.[14]

Bernhardt Faust, *The German Element in the United States . . .* , 2 vols. (New York, 1927), I, 182; Otto Niemeyer, "Deutsche Sklavenhalter und Germanisierte Neger," *Deutsche Pioneer*, II (1870–1871), 280–284.

12. Diary entry, Feb. 20, 1754, in George Fenwick Jones, ed., *Detailed Reports on the Salzburger Emigrants Who Settled in America . . . Edited by Samuel Urlsperger*, 17 vols., trans. Hermann J. Lacher (Athens, Ga., 1968–), XVI, 164–165. On Salzburgers' use of slave labor, see also Jones, "The Salzburger Mills: Georgia's First Successful Enterprises," *Yearbook of German-American Studies*, XXIII (1988), 105–117, and *The Salzburger Saga: Religious Exiles and other Germans along the Savannah* (Athens, Ga., 1984), 104.

13. For example: "It is a burdensome, expensive, and hardly profitable business managing a place with Negro slaves, especially when one tries to maintain them in a Christian or at least humane manner, as Mr. R[abenhorst] does. . . . His Negro slaves have not yet made him wealthy, and he can consider himself lucky when they earn their own food and clothing"; see Muhlenburg, *Journals*, trans. Tappert and Doberstein, II, 637. For other examples of Muhlenberg's sometimes caustic commentary on slaveholding Germans, see I, 342, 494, 721, II, 189, 515, 649, III, 120, 203, 552.

14. Gehrke, "Negro Slavery among the Germans in North Carolina," *NCHR*, XIV (1937), 308; Wust, *The Virginia Germans*, 122. See also G. D. Bernheim, *History of the German Settlements and of the Lutheran Church in North and South Carolina* (1872; reprint, Baltimore, 1975), 148.

Such impressions temper the prevailing stereotype of the hardy, industrious German farmer or craftsman who preferred to earn his bread by skill and hard work, disdaining those who lived by slave labor. Though attractive, the image is probably more accurate for the middle decades of the eighteenth century than for a generation later. In many cases, the need for labor on the frontier simply overwhelmed a vital strain of German antislavery thought. German slaveownership by no means matched the scale of Anglo-American holdings, but it had become an important source of labor in many German-American communities.[15]

The fifteen Brethren who left Bethlehem to build the new settlement in North Carolina in October 1753—men such as physician Martin Kalberlahn, minister Bernard Adam Grube, and choir supervisor Jacob Loesch—carried with them a history of slaveholding as well as the experience of living and worshiping intimately with Africans. Symbolic of that connection were the conch shells the Moravians blew for alarm or to summon their members together. They learned that method from Africans in the West Indies who called each other to prayer with a conch, which they called a tutu. Yet what role, if any, Africans might play in the Moravians' new home was by no means clear.[16]

COUNT ZINZENDORF and his advisers, architects of the Wachovia development project, sought foremost to secure the settlement's economic, social, and religious independence from the world beyond its boundaries. Total

15. "By habit and training," according to a standard history of North Carolina, "the German—Moravian, Lutheran or Reformed—was industrious, thrifty and law-abiding. Unaccustomed to slavery and unacquainted with Negroes, he [relied] on his own labor." See Hugh Talmage Lefler and Albert Ray Newsome, *North Carolina: The History of a Southern State* (Chapel Hill, N.C., 1954), 81. The Moravians had enslaved blacks since the 1730s and were therefore well "acquainted" with them. The authors even claim that the Quakers and Moravians "seem to have been the only religious groups to oppose slavery openly" (121). Similar interpretations of German self-reliance are contained in Hugh T. Lefler and William S. Powell, *Colonial North Carolina: A History* (New York, 1973), 100–108; Carl Bridenbaugh, *Myths and Realities: Societies of the Colonial South* (New York, 1963), 151–152; and H. Roy Merrens, *Colonial North Carolina in the Eighteenth Century: A Study in Historical Geography* (Chapel Hill, N.C., 1964), 11–19. One exception is Gehrke, "Negro Slavery among the Germans in North Carolina," *NCHR*, XIV (1937), 307–324, which has been largely overlooked by historians of early North Carolina.

16. C.G.A. Oldendorp, *History of the Mission of the Evangelical Brethren on the Caribbean Islands of St. Thomas, St. Croix, and St. John*, ed. and trans. Arnold R. Highfield and Vladimir

exclusion from the outside world was hardly their goal. In contrast to such plain German immigrants as the Amish and Mennonites who craved isolation and solitude, the Moravians envisioned an active, expansive trade network with arms spread widely through the colonial economy. Wachovia was conceived as an axis for the expanding Piedmont economy with links to surrounding communities and larger regional trading centers. These commercial tendrils would provide outlets for Moravian crafts, tanned skins, and agricultural goods, bringing in crucial revenue for settlers.[17]

At the same time, every aspect of community organization—from the physical layout of the settlement to internal government and religious life— was designed to regulate contact with the outside, ensuring Moravian autonomy and spiritual resolve. "We dont want extraordinary Priviledges," wrote Spangenberg, "if only we can live together as Brethren, without interfering with others and without being disturbed by them; and if only we can keep our Children from being hurt by wicked Examples, and our young people from following the foolish and sinful ways of the World."[18]

The Brethren worked hard to lay a firm economic foundation in agriculture and basic crafts in their first town, Bethabara, located on a northern branch of Muddy Creek some six miles inside Wachovia's boundaries. The pioneers spent the first few years clearing land, planting crops, tending livestock, building houses, workshops, and industries. More settlers, including women, arrived periodically from Pennsylvania to reinforce the tiny band. Church life and discipline reinforced group solidarity and a sense of apartness from outsiders. Married and single people lived in separate choir dwellings and worked for the communal system, or Oeconomy, in which settlers owned no land and as employees of the Unity performed labor in return for food and housing, but no wages.[19]

The effort of building the new settlement dominated daily life. In one

Barac (1770; reprint, Ann Arbor, Mich., 1987), 92, 226; Kenneth G. Hamilton and J. Taylor Hamilton, *History of the Moravian Church: The Renewed Unitas Fratrum, 1722–1957* (Bethlehem, Pa., 1967), 48, 655 n. 15. On the series of Moravian migrations to North Carolina that began in 1753, see Fogleman, *Hopeful Journeys,* chap. 4.

17. Daniel B. Thorp, *The Moravian Community in Colonial North Carolina: Pluralism on the Southern Frontier* (Knoxville, Tenn., 1989), chap. 1, esp. 17.

18. Ibid., 24.

19. For more on the Oeconomy, see Adelaide L. Fries et al., eds., *Records of the Moravians in North Carolina,* 11 vols. (Raleigh, N.C., 1922–1969), I, 241 n. 2; Thorp, *Moravian Community,* 40–41, 69–70; and W. Thomas Mainwaring, "Communal Ideals, Worldly Concerns, and the Moravians of North Carolina," *Journal of Communal Societies,* VI (1986), 138–142.

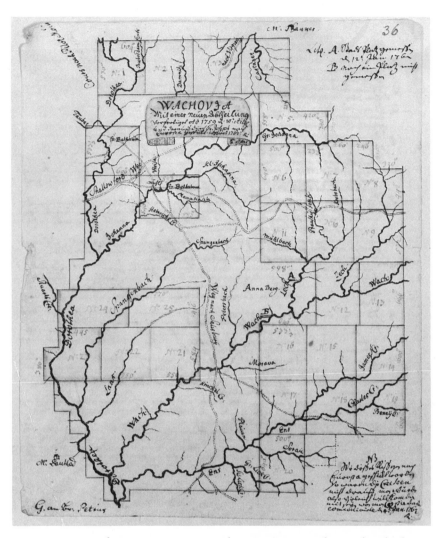

Figure 6. Wachovia, 1759. *Engraving by P.C.G. Reuter. The one-hundred-thousand-acre Moravian tract, showing Bethabara (north-central), founded in 1753, and Bethania (northwest), founded in 1759. Courtesy, Archiv der Brüder-Unität, Herrnhut, Germany*

early year, 1756, Brethren built a congregation meeting hall, pottery, tailor's and joiner's shops, and washhouse, cleared twenty-six acres of land, planted sixty acres of rye, wheat, oats, corn, hemp, flax, turnips, and other crops, cleared roads, and built bridges, cowpens, stables, and mills. By 1759, more than a dozen craftsmen were able to furnish the products the settlement needed to achieve greater independence, such as ironwork, tanned goods, and pottery. The Moravians quickly gained a regional reputation for their crafts, drawing buyers and traders from many miles throughout the Piedmont.[20]

By 1756, the Bethabara congregation had increased to sixty-five, two-thirds of them Single Brothers; three years later, the population swelled to seventy-three in Bethabara and thirty in Bethania, another village founded in 1759 three miles to the northwest. Wachovia's first planned community, Bethania was designed to absorb Bethabara's surplus population as well as some non-Moravian refugees who sought protection under the Brethren during the Seven Years' War and desired closer association with them.[21]

Despite the Moravian settlement's growth, the endless tasks of building, planting, chopping, and cooking provoked complaints from overworked Brethren that the Unity expected too much of their few numbers. Sometimes critical tasks went undone. "We ate the last of our potatoes," reported a diarist in December 1754. "We have had them hardly three months, but more than 20 bushels rotted because we could not dig them at the right time, being too busy with other things. Dec. 23rd we had the last of the pumpkins. They also would have lasted longer if we had been able to bring them in at the right time, but still we have had them for five months."[22]

The shortage of labor, a universal complaint along the ever-shifting frontier of colonial America, proved troublesome enough as Moravians confronted the daily demands of building and maintaining a community. But the Seven Years' War intensified the strain. The settlement was under constant threat of Cherokee attack, and a palisade was quickly thrown up

20. Wachovia Memorabilia, 1756, Bethabara Memorabilia, 1759, in Fries et al., eds., *Records*, I, 156, 208. Moravian crafts and craftsmen are discussed in the context of economic development in the North Carolina Piedmont in Johanna Miller Lewis, *Artisans in the North Carolina Backcountry* (Lexington, Ky., 1995), chap. 5.

21. Wachovia Memorabilia, 1756, Bethabara Memorabilia, 1759, and "F. W. Marshall's Notes concerning Wachovia," Feb. 1, 1764, in Fries et al., eds., *Records*, I, 156, 208, 293–294. On the origins of Bethania, see Daniel B. Thorp, "Assimilation in North Carolina's Moravian Community," *JSH*, LII (1986), 28–32.

22. Bethabara Diary, Dec. 18, 1754, in Fries et al., eds., *Records*, I, 112–113. On the other hand, the Moravians realized they could support only a limited number of new hands before the settlement was firmly on its feet. In 1755, Bethlehem was prepared to send 30 new settlers to North Carolina, but Brethren there protested they could house and feed only 8. Unity leaders recognized that reinforcements would have to be added gradually, lengthening the original timetable for the development of Wachovia; see Daniel B. Thorp, "Moravian Colonization of Wachovia, 1753–1772: The Maintenance of Community in Late Colonial North Carolina" (Ph.D. diss., Johns Hopkins University, 1982), 145.

around Bethabara in 1756. As the largest town for miles, Bethabara drew scores, sometimes hundreds of non-Moravian refugees from neighboring farms who streamed into the stockade periodically during the war. The task of feeding and caring for these multitudes stretched Moravian supplies and resourcefulness to the limit.

The war's end in 1763 brought some relief to the settlement, but the need for hands continued. Administrators complained that trade was languishing for lack of Brethren and put out urgent requests to Bethlehem for reinforcements. An overseer's departure left the stockyard in disarray, the store and tavern managers bungled their duties, and a shortage of teachers, teamsters, and weavers plagued the settlement. Other kinds of workers were urgently needed. The Moravians began hiring day laborers from the area to help with farming and construction as early as 1755, and they relied increasingly on such hired help. In late 1762, fifteen outside laborers were hired in Bethabara; a year later, the Brethren took on thirty-six outsiders for the fall harvest.[23]

Church leaders complained continually about the high cost of hired labor, but they had little choice. A decade after the first settlement, the population of Wachovia was far lower than hoped. The Seven Years' War hindered the passage of new settlers from Europe, and even after the war the Unity still owed large debts and could not afford to send many new colonists to America. And Bethlehem, which had supplied the bulk of North Carolina's early settlers, could no longer bear the drain of experienced manpower to the new settlement. Infusions of newcomers dwindled. Although the Unity had hoped to have about four hundred people living in Wachovia by 1759, the population did not reach that level until 1771, a dozen years later than planned.[24]

By the 1760s, moreover, the Moravians' needs and ambitions had grown. They had long since secured self-sufficiency in agriculture and many commodities and had started a profitable export trade in skins, flour, and butter with Charleston, Wilmington, and other coastal towns. They also expanded their frontier trade in lumber, meal, pottery, and liquor. Lying athwart the Great Wagon Road, Wachovia was an important station for travelers and

---

23. Johann Ettwein to Conference in Bethlehem, May 3, 1764, microfilm of correspondence in Moravian Archives, Northern Province, reel 1, no. 186; Ettwein to Christian Seidel, Dec. 6, 1762, reel 1, no. 160; Abraham von Gammern to Seidel, Oct. 9, 1763, reel 1, no. 180.

24. Thorp, *Moravian Community*, chap. 2, describes the forces that shaped the demography of early Wachovia.

Figure 7. *A View of Bethabara.* By Nicholas Garrison, 1757. Watercolor on paper.
Courtesy, Moravian Archives, Herrnhut, Germany

settlers on the north-south conduit. As its planners had hoped, the Moravian colony, a decade after its founding, had become one of the largest
commercial centers in the Carolina Piedmont.[25]

To help drive these prosperous ventures, the Brethren began hiring slaves
from non-Moravian neighbors. The first came in August 1763, when "from
James Blackborn, on the Town Fork" a few miles north of Bethabara, "Br.
Gammern . . . has hired a Negro woman, to serve as maid in the Tavern for
three years." The tavern brought in much-needed revenue from traders and
travelers, but town leaders wanted domestic service there performed by
a non-Moravian rather than risk exposing a Moravian woman to fights,
drunkenness, and coarse language. "The people of this land are rude, and if
the Sisters were placed where strangers came to trade they would be exposed
to insolence by day and night," wrote the Wachovia administrator, Frederic
Marshall, in 1769. Of the hired African-American woman, Franke, little else
was recorded during her service in Bethabara. In 1765, she asked John Ettwein for baptism, though there is no record the service was performed. In
December 1766, she complained of rheumatism and was unable to perform

25. On Wachovia's burgeoning importance to North Carolina's colonial commerce, see
Merrens, *Colonial North Carolina*, 114–115, 164–166, 175; and Charles Christopher Crittenden, *Commerce of North Carolina, 1763–1789* (New Haven, Conn., 1936), 85–95.

her work. Since she was nearing the end of her contracted term, the Moravians asked her master if her daughter could finish it out but were turned down. She was replaced in March 1767 by a young slave, Cate, who was rented for three years as payment of a debt her master owed the Moravians.[26]

Brethren probably hired no slaves before the 1760s, because the black population in the Carolina upcountry was still tiny. Through the mid-eighteenth century, enslaved African Americans remained heavily concentrated in eastern North Carolina, where they worked on tobacco and rice plantations, in forest and maritime industries, and on thousands of small farms. Although the number of slaves did not match that of the Chesapeake or South Carolina, slaves constituted between 40 and 80 percent of the population in most eastern North Carolina counties by 1767. In the Piedmont and western sections of the colony, however, slaveholding played but a slight role in the small-farm economy. "As you penetrate into the Country few Blacks are employed," noted Governor William Tryon in 1765. The region's population was little more than 2 to 3 percent black.[27]

Yet the complexion of the backcountry was changing rapidly. As English settlers pushed west from the sand plains and as Germans and Scots-Irish streamed south from Pennsylvania, the Piedmont's European population grew rapidly. The number of whites in Rowan County, site of Wachovia, grew from 4,576 in 1755 to 12,797 in 1767; similar increases held true in

26. Bethabara Diary, Aug. 22, 1763, Marshall's Report to Unity Elders' Conference, Aug. 31, 1769, in Fries et al., eds., *Records,* I, 274, II, 674; Bethabara Diary, May 11, 1765; Aelt. Conf., Dec. 6, 1766; Bethabara Diary, Mar. 13, Oct. 22, 1767; Bill of Rental for Cate, in Bills of Sale folder, Negro box. The practice of hiring slaves was common during the slavery period. A slave's labor would be hired out by his or her master to a buyer for a contracted term and fee. Rarely did the hired slaves themselves receive payment for their labor. For a broader discussion of taverns in the area, see Daniel B. Thorp, "Taverns and Tavern Culture on the Southern Colonial Frontier: Rowan County, North Carolina, 1753–1776," *JSH,* LXII (1996), 661–688.

27. Marvin L. Michael Kay and Lorin Lee Cary, "A Demographic Analysis of Colonial North Carolina, with Special Emphasis upon the Slave and Black Populations," in Jeffrey J. Crow and Flora J. Hatley, eds., *Black Americans in North Carolina and the South* (Chapel Hill, N.C., 1984), 71–121; Kay and Cary, *Slavery in North Carolina, 1748–1775* (Chapel Hill, N.C., 1995), 10–51; Jeffrey J. Crow, *The Black Experience in Revolutionary North Carolina* (Raleigh, N.C., 1977); Merrens, *Colonial North Carolina,* 75–79; William S. Powell, ed., "Tryon's 'Book' on North Carolina," *NCHR,* XXXIV (1957), 411 (quotation). For overviews of the development of African-American cultures in colonial British America, see Ira Berlin, "Time, Space, and the Evolution of Afro-American Society on British Mainland North America," *AHR,* LXXXV (1980), 44–78; and Philip D. Morgan, "British Encounters with Africans and African-Americans, circa 1600–1780," in Bailyn and Morgan, eds., *Strangers within the Realm,* 157–219.

other Piedmont counties. The black population swelled as well, from 102 to 719 in Rowan County during the same twelve-year period and on average nearly six-fold for the region as a whole. Blacks still constituted a relatively low proportion of the population, but Moravians traded and dealt more frequently with neighbors who owned slaves.[28]

Hired slave labor proved attractive and cheap for the Brethren. Although white day laborers in the mid-1760s earned as much as two shillings, four pence a day, the Moravians could rent a slave for thirty shillings a month, or less than half as much. Because Bethabara's economy was communal, Moravian leaders prevented individual congregants from hiring slaves. Instead, the church rented slaves on behalf of the community and assigned them to the tavern, farm, or stockyard under the supervision of church-appointed managers. In October 1764, "Br[other] Gammern rented Mr. Blackborn's Negro for six months in our stockyard." The man was transferred to the tavern for another six months but was replaced by a hired German youth when the tavernkeeper detected "traces of disloyalty" in him. More slaves were rented during that period—a man to help unload store supplies, another woman for the tavern, and, in late 1765, their most important addition, a young man named Sam, from William Ridge of Uwharrie, about forty miles southeast of Wachovia, to work in the stockyard.[29]

Sam's arrival coincided with—or perhaps was intended to solve—a potential crisis at the stockyard. Cattle raising had been an important component of the Bethabara economy since the earliest days of the settlement. A few years after arriving in North Carolina, the Brethren abandoned the traditional German practice of penning livestock and let them roam through the bush, as other Carolina settlers did. By the mid-1760s, however, Moravian leaders' emphasis on developing Wachovia's commercial base had produced an adult male population long on artisanal and trade skills but short on agricultural and husbandry know-how. Consequently, though the cattle herd in

---

28. Kay and Cary, "A Demographic Analysis," in Crow and Hatley, eds., *Black Americans in North Carolina,* 77, 82–84, 87–88. On the growing European and African presence in the North Carolina Piedmont, see Robert Ramsey, *Carolina Cradle: Settlement of the Northwest Carolina Frontier, 1747–1762* (Chapel Hill, N.C., 1964), esp. 176–177, on black population; Lefler and Powell, *Colonial North Carolina,* 96–112; and Merrens, *Colonial North Carolina,* 53–81.

29. Bethabara Diacony Ledger, 1764–1772 (I am grateful to Daniel Thorp for this reference); Helf. Conf., Apr. 1, Nov. 25, 1765, Mar. 31, 1766; Bethabara Diary, Oct. 11, 1764, Nov. 26, 1765; Diacony Journal, May 31, 1764; Bethabara Diacony Ledger, May 31, 1768. Thorp, *Moravian Community,* 55–56, discusses some of these early hirings.

Bethabara had grown to nearly two hundred head by 1765, the stockyard was foundering for lack of experienced workers and managers.[30]

Born in Rowan County in 1750, Sam might have learned open-country herding techniques from the Moravians, or he might already have possessed these abilities when he arrived in Wachovia. Since cattle herding in colonial America evolved from both African and European roots, it is possible Sam learned the skill from either Euro-American farmers or from Rowan's small African and African-American population. In any case, he quickly impressed the Moravians. Just a few months after his hiring, the overseer of the stockyard was fired for negligence and mistreatment of the animals, and Sam, along with a hired white hand, received temporary responsibility for managing the stockyard. Later, under the new manager, Sam assumed supervision of the cattle, and the white hand took charge of the calves. A diary notation gives a glimpse of his duties: "The Negro Samuel fetched our cows from Benner for some of our Sisters to milk at night." Sam, who shared a small cabin near the stockyard with the white hand, soon earned more responsibilities. In 1768, he was appointed wagoner for an expedition to Pennsylvania, and he kept the position of teamster for many years.[31]

These early slave hirings suggest that the Moravians drew few distinctions between white and black hired hands, but for the important difference that whites received pay and blacks did not. At least some black and white hands shared accommodations and meals and worked alongside each other. Black and white non-Moravians, or "strangers," also must certainly have rubbed elbows with Brethren despite the church's efforts to minimize such contact. The harsh frontier environment at times evoked a rough social parity between black and white settlers, strangers, and Brethren.[32]

30. Thorp, "Assimilation," *JSH*, LII (1986), 38–41; "Catalogue of the Inhabitants of Bethabara in Wachovia," in Fries et al., eds., *Records,* I, 343–345. For a description of Moravian herding techniques, see Bethabara Diary, Aug. 14, 1754, in Fries et al., eds., *Records,* I, 104, II, 532.

31. Bethabara Diary, Apr. 21, 30, May 24, 1766, July 8, Aug. 13, 1768. On European and African origins of cattle herding in early America, see Peter H. Wood, *Black Majority: Negroes in South Carolina from 1670 through the Stono Rebellion* (New York, 1974), 30–31; and John Solomon Otto, "Livestock-Raising in Early South Carolina, 1670–1700: Prelude to the Rice Plantation Economy," *Agricultural History,* LXI (1987), 13–24.

32. For other examples of frontier racial flexibility, see Wood, *Black Majority,* 97; Edmund S. Morgan, *American Slavery, American Freedom: The Ordeal of Colonial Virginia* (New York, 1975), 154–157; David Barry Gaspar, *Bondmen and Rebels: A Study of Master-Slave Relations in Antigua, with Implications for Colonial British America* (Baltimore, 1985), 36; and Salinger, "To Serve Well and Faithfully," 20.

Any equality begotten by the leveling influence of shared toil and living conditions could also create tensions. In one case, a few angry Brethren viewed Sam as a rival when he was chosen as wagoner, apparently ahead of them; one even quit the stockyard in protest. Perhaps leaders elevated Sam to wagoner as a ploy to goad or inspire younger Brethren to work harder in the hope of greater rewards. The slackening ways of Moravian youth were a favorite theme among pastors even as early as the 1760s. Still, Moravians preferred one of their own for a job whenever possible. Sam's selection as driver suggests that his skills overrode the offended sentiments of other Brethren. Churchmen were thus willing to forego community solidarity for more immediate pragmatic concerns. Indeed, Count Zinzendorf had insisted that early settlers should be chosen more for their practical skills than for their piety.[33]

Hiring slaves was perhaps an inevitable prelude to the possibility of owning them. That step, however, was by no means automatic, for it generated uncertainty among the Brethren about their direction. The issue arose in 1769 when Sam, who had worked for the Moravians for more than three years, expressed an interest in converting to Christianity, and his master offered to sell him to the Brethren. The *Aeltesten Conferenz*, or Elders' Conference, the board directing the settlement's religious affairs, agreed he was "worth the price."[34]

Yet they worried that slavery threatened the diligence, thrift, and sobriety they sought to instill in the faithful. After visiting a German settlement in South Carolina, John Ettwein, minister and administrator of Wachovia in the 1760s, wrote to planter Henry Laurens: "I wish their Children may turn out a good Race but am afraid the Negroes have too much Influence upon them and I have observ'd that often where a Man has Slaves his Children become lazy and indolent etc."[35]

Ettwein's concern—that the evil of slavery was the harm it inflicted on whites—was voiced often by many eighteenth-century antislavery spokesmen. On the other hand, the Brethren already owned slaves in Pennsylvania and the West Indies. They apparently accepted the limited use of slave labor

33. Bethabara Diary, Aug. 13, 1768; Thorp, *Moravian Community*, 41–42.

34. Aelt. Conf., Apr. 24, 1769, microfilm.

35. Ettwein to Laurens, Mar. 2, 1763, in Philip M. Hamer et al., eds., *The Papers of Henry Laurens*, 14 vols. (Columbia, S.C., 1968–), III, 356.

if it supplemented, but did not replace, the toil of white Moravian hands. If congregants worked hard, glorifying Christ by their labors, they might be permitted collectively to own or hire slaves. The distinction was critical, for it defined the terms under which slave labor could be used without threatening members' purity. Indeed, Bethlehem's leaders regarded the switch from white day laborers to enslaved African Americans in 1742 as an ideal way to solve labor shortages while preserving community morals.

In North Carolina, the elders could reach no consensus that Sam should be bought, so they sought guidance from the lot. The lot, the Moravian court of last resort, was a direct appeal to God's mediation, to be used "only in extraordinary cases where there is no clear certainty in the heart or the matter cannot be decided through discussion." The question of buying a slave therefore posed a major, perhaps divisive, dilemma. No record of the elders' deliberation has survived. One can only conjecture that some councillors argued that slavery could be woven into the fabric of the Moravian polity without damaging the cloth. The chance to nurture Sam's desire for Christianity was further reason to buy him—perhaps the main reason, it might have been argued, since conversion would bring him into the community.[36]

Whatever the debate, the elders asked the Lord to break the deadlock and drew a positive lot. God had assented. A bill of sale for human property was drawn up. "You will have heard that Sam the Negro is now our property for 120 pounds N.C.," wrote Bishop Johann Graff to Ettwein in Pennsylvania. "We hope he will also become the property of the Saviour, who has made him worth so much at such a young age." But another report reflected the ambivalence the transaction had aroused. Sam, it noted, had been bought "even though it is certainly not our way to buy men."[37]

The Lord himself had given his blessing to slavery in Wachovia. The decision was momentous. Slavery had pulled the Brethren in opposite directions. In 1769, the real question, anxiously posed, was not simply, "Should we buy Sam?" but rather, "Does slavery fit with our purpose here?" Had the lot said no, it is conceivable the Brethren would have bought no bondper-

36. Thorp, *Moravian Community,* 87. On the lot, see also Gollin, *Moravians in Two Worlds,* 50–63. John Ettwein, who had articulated fears against slavery, had been transferred to Pennsylvania in 1768 and took no part in discussions about Sam.

37. Graff to Ettwein, July 31, 1769, microfilm of Wachovia-Bethlehem Correspondence, reel 1, no. 28; Helf. Conf., Aug. 14, 1769. I am grateful to Daniel Thorp for directing me to the latter reference.

sons and slavery would never have become entrenched in Moravian life. Equally possible, given the Moravians' ability to manipulate the lot by repeated use, is that they would have kept asking until the Lord relented. In any case, the watershed had been reached. Elders never again asked divine permission to buy slaves for the balance of the eighteenth century.

DESPITE GOD'S CLEARANCE to begin stockpiling bondpersons, prohibitive costs held the Moravians back. "It is a recognized fact that in America there is no profit in a farm run with hired help," wrote Frederic Marshall in 1770. "Therefore the laying out of a great estate is not advantageous in America; and the man who has a larger farm than he can work with the aid of wife and children cannot expect to profit by it. Under such circumstances other people buy slaves, but to purchase ten or twelve would require an outlay of more than 1000 pounds: (the one we have cost 120 pounds, and was considered cheap), and not many of our Brethren or Sisters have the gift of handling slaves, without spoiling them." Given the high price of slaves, Marshall implied, slave labor might not be profitable as long as Moravians treated them humanely.[38]

Nonetheless, Brethren by now needed more laborers than ever, because since the mid-1760s they had been hard at work building the new town that would replace Bethabara as the spiritual, economic, and administrative heart of the settlement. Bethabara was never intended to be the hub of Wachovia but rather the midwife to a larger, more centrally located *Gemein Ort*, or congregation town, controlled by the church. Here would be based most of the church boards and the important crafts and industries, many of which would be moved from Bethabara. The Brethren had delayed building the town until Bethabara was firmly on its feet. Indeed, Bethabara was so well developed by the early 1760s that some wanted to abandon the idea of a new town. Nonetheless, a site was chosen on the middle fork of Muddy Creek near the center of the Wachovia tract in 1764. The town would be called Salem. Work began in 1766. Many of Bethabara's best craftsmen and builders redirected their efforts toward the construction of new homes, craft shops, and church buildings. The job was monumental for the Moravians' limited resources. "The present building of Salem is an extraordinary affair, which I would not have undertaken had not the Saviour Himself ordered it,"

38. Marshall's Report to Unity, Aug. 3, 1770, in Fries et al., eds., *Records*, II, 614.

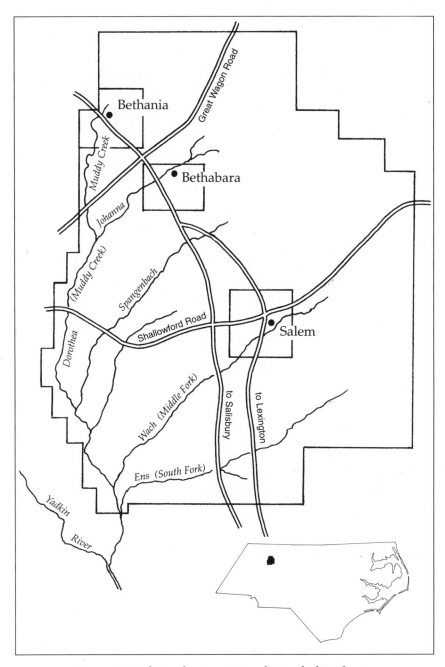

Figure 8. North Carolina in 1766, with Detail of Wachovia.
Drawn by Richard Stinely

remarked Marshall. The Brethren hired outside carpenters, brickmakers, masons, road builders, and other craftsmen and workers amid further grumbling from administrators about the high cost of labor.[39]

Hired slaves worked as construction laborers and teamsters in this great workforce. The Moravians also bought slaves. From William Gilbert of Rowan County they acquired Frank, an African whom they described as a "hardworking and useful Negro," in October 1771, to help as a mason's assistant in Salem. Frank was "born in Guinea and as a small boy was brought to a ship by a relative and sold, and taken to South Carolina to [serve] different masters," his biography later reported. How Gilbert came to acquire Frank is not clear, but, when he sold Frank to the Brethren, they estimated the African's age at about twenty. After working at construction in Salem for several months, he was transferred to the Bethabara horse stall in 1772. Meanwhile, the Salem tanner, Heinrich Herbst, "disappointed time and again" with his hired white help, "thinks of buying a Negro." So, from a passing slave trader the church bought another African with clipped ears and an infected foot, noting that he "seemed to be of good Humor, and could perhaps be won for the Lord." Thus Sambo, survivor of the African slaving wars and the middle passage, arrived at his home for the next twenty-six years.[40]

The multiplying demands of building Salem created a ripple effect in labor shortages for the rest of Wachovia. Bethabara turned to slave labor to bolster its undermanned workforce at home. "The more Salem grows, the more

39. References to Salem are in Helf. Conf., Mar. 31, Aug. 19, 1766, May 11, 1767; Marshall's Report to Unity, 1768, 1771, in Fries et al., eds., *Records,* II, 606, 618 (quotation). See also Thorp, *Moravian Community,* chap. 1, esp. 33. A detailed description of Bethabara in 1768 indicates why some Brethren were loathe to build a new town. Dozens of crafts and industries would have to be dismantled and moved; see Marshall's Report to Unity, 1768, in Fries et al., eds., *Records,* II, 605.

40. On hired slave labor, see Aelt. Conf., June 5, 1770, Wachovia Diary, Sept. 20–21, 1771. On Frank, see Wachovia Diary, Mar. 9, May 1, Oct. 11, 1771; Memoir of Christian (Frank), in Bethabara Church Book; Bethabara Diary, Feb. 21, 1772. On Sambo, see Aelt. Conf., Apr. 23, 1771; Wachovia Diary, Aug. 23–25, 1771; Memoir of Abraham (Sambo) (trans. EH). It is tempting to suggest that Herbst wanted Sambo because the latter already had some knowledge of tanning. West Africans were well acquainted with the craft. The Mandingoes, reported an Englishman, "make also Bridles and Saddles, of which I have seene some very neat, hardly to be bettered heere: whereby it seems they have skill to dress and dye their Deeres skins and Goats skins." Although any such connection between Sambo and Herbst is speculative, Sambo would certainly have been familiar with tanned products and perhaps tanning processes; see Richard Jobson, *The Golden Trade; or, A Discovery of the River Gambia, and the Golden Trade of the Aethiopians* (London, 1623), quoted in Basil Davidson, *The African Past* (Boston, 1964), 202.

difficulty we have in Bethabara to accomplish the necessary work," complained Marshall in 1771, "and as the inn already has a hired man-servant but cannot function without female help, so we found ourselves compelled to buy an elderly Negress, who has an alert little girl of about 9 years and we hope that the work will be done in this way." At least half a dozen hired slaves worked for varying intervals in Bethabara. In 1771, for example, one Shepherd "picked up his Negro, who served this winter in the cowstall, and for his remaining debt promised to bring a wagon full of fish here." When Salem officially became the chief congregation town in April 1772, only a fragmentary population of about fifty was left behind in Bethabara. By then the survival of Wachovia's first town depended largely on slave labor.[41]

African slavery became entrenched, as well, on the farms being cleared throughout Wachovia by new migrants from Europe and the colonies. This forested land was plentiful and fertile, but the Brethren dithered for years on what to do with it. Originally they thought it would hold a constellation of thirty-five farming "villages of the Lord," clustered around the central town. Bethania, founded in 1759, was to be the first. Planners also considered the possibility of slave-worked plantations owned by wealthy investors in the European-based group that backed the settlement, the North Carolina Land and Colony Establishment. These plantations would be managed by small enclaves of Moravians. In 1755, August Spangenberg suggested that investors situate two or three married couples of Brethren with a "gang of negroes" on their tracts. On a variation on the idea, the bishop proposed four years later that each investor settle half his two thousand acres with Brethren and on the other half establish a son "with a pair of negroes to do his work." To another Unity director in the mid-1750s, the idea of "mixing Negroes in the Establishment" is "something new." Still, he concluded, "I have nothing against Negroes if the Savior does not forbid it."[42]

41. Marshall Report to Unity Elders' Conference, Apr. 20, 1771 (trans. EM, first quotation); Wachovia Diary, May 4, 1774 (second quotation). Other examples of slave hirings may be found in Aelt. Conf., Mar. 20, 1770; Bethabara Diary, July 22, 1772, Mar. 2, May 4, 1774; and Bethabara Diacony A Ledger, 3.

42. Spangenberg to Jonas Paulus Weiss, Oct. 13, 1755; Spangenberg to Cornelius van Laer, Jan. 27, 1759; Jonas Paulus Weiss, "Mein Gedanken über br. Spangenberg's Vortrag wegen der Wachau," Library of Congress, Manuscripts Division, European Photostats, Germany, Herrnhut, Archiv der Brüder-Unität, R.14, Ba. Nr. 2b, Nr. 2c, 265–272, Nr. 2d, 157–166. On early plans for Wachovia, see Thorp, "Assimilation," *JSH*, LII (1986), 22–32, and "Buying Men and Saving Souls: the Moravians' Response to Slavery in Eighteenth-Century North Carolina" (unpublished paper, n.d.).

But the plan to introduce plantation slavery fell through when the Moravians changed their ideas about land development and settlement in the 1760s. Few people had proven willing to move to Wachovia and either settle on leased land, as in Bethania, or work for someone else. Frederic Marshall noted that redemptioners might resent the hard work required to pay off their voyage when they could be working their own land. Slave labor, moreover, required an enormous initial cost of the investor, and "either he is bankrupt, or he lives alone in the bush with his Negroes and has to be their *Bomba* [driver]." Large plantations thus were not yet financially viable. Eager to attract more settlers to ensure Wachovia's economic success, the Moravians elected instead to put land up for sale. As Marshall explained, "One could entice people who are already living in America with easy conditions until the undertaking gets a good name and everyone crowds to take advantage of Paradise, and then one increases the terms and the crowd decreases." The Moravians put out the word that cheap land could be had in their part of North Carolina.[43]

The strategy worked. Heeding the call, settlers flocked to Wachovia from odd corners of British America. Most of them had known Moravians elsewhere and, though they were not required to join the church, came to North Carolina expecting to do so. Three farming settlements composed of such migrants sprouted along the southern rim of Wachovia as early as the 1750s. Eventually known as Friedberg, Friedland, and Hope, these were, not compact, regulated communities such as Bethabara and Bethania, but rather dispersed groupings of farms loosely centered around a meetinghouse and school. Eventually they were organized into "societies," or religious communities affiliated with the Brethren and served by a Moravian minister. This arrangement enabled the church to control the spiritual affairs of the farming settlements though their members often lived far apart. Within a few years, after they demonstrated proper commitment to Unity ideals, all the societies became full Moravian congregations.

The diverse origins of these communities illustrate how far Moravian evangelism extended in eighteenth-century America. Friedberg's first set-

---

43. Marshall, Memorandum regarding Wachovia, Feb. 1, 1764, Vault Correspondence, folder 7, item 1, 2 (part of this letter is translated in Fries et al., eds., *Records,* I, 293–294). A bomba was a slave driver who worked under the supervision of a white overseer. The term was used widely in the Danish West Indies, and Marshall's use of it no doubt reflected his reading of missionary reports that referred often to bombas; see Oldendorp, *Caribbean Mission,* ed. and trans. Highfield and Barac, 654 n. 11.

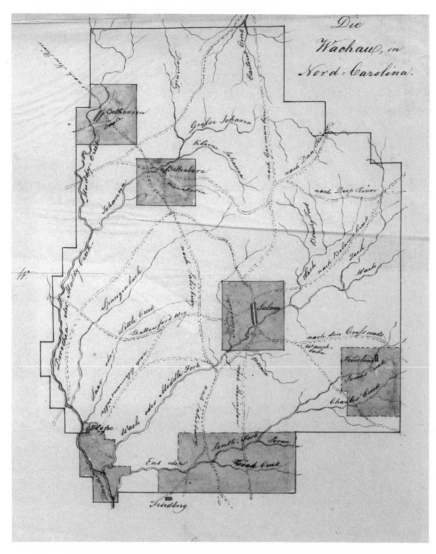

Figure 9. Wachovia, Late Eighteenth Century. *Shows the location of the three southern* Landgemeinen, *or country congregations, of (west to east) Hope, Friedberg, and Friedland. Courtesy, Archiv der Brüder-Unität, Herrnhut, Germany*

tler, for example, was Adam Spach, an Alsatian who had heard Moravian preaching in Manakosy, Maryland, and moved to the southern branch of Muddy Creek in 1753, soon to be joined by more Germans who had heard Moravian preaching in Pennsylvania. The southwest corner of Wachovia was settled in the 1750s by Irish and Germans who had known Moravians in

Maryland. Over the next two decades, English Moravian families moved to the area from Maryland. They occasionally attended services in Bethabara until they organized the Hope society under their own pastor in 1780. Hope remained Wachovia's only predominantly English-speaking Moravian settlement until the mid-nineteenth century. Friedland, in the southeast corner of the tract, was settled by Germans who had emigrated from the Palatinate to Broadbay, Maine, in the 1760s. There they were visited by George Soelle, a Danish-born Moravian minister who organized them into a society; in 1769, at the church's invitation, they began moving to Wachovia.[44]

Though plans for plantation-style slavery in the countryside fell through, small numbers of slaves worked in these burgeoning farm communities. They constructed buildings, harvested grain, and tended herds. In Friedberg, "a mulatto who was splitting rocks at the new mill sacrificed a hand to this work." African-born Jupiter, who arrived with Sambo in 1771, was bought by John Douthit in the English-speaking Moravian sector. Several English settlers brought slaves with them from Maryland, such as Priscilla and Esther, two women who accompanied the Peddycoard family to Wachovia in 1775.[45]

The character of the Moravian territory was taking shape—small craft-based towns, small farms, small-scale slaveholding. "Two men from Virginia spent the day here, and looked about with wonder and pleasure," reported a Bethabara diarist in 1773. "Among other questions they asked how many negroes we had? Answer, two. They were the more surprised to find that white people had done so much work." No doubt flattered, the Moravians could justly take pride in their accomplishments of only twenty years. In claiming they owned only two slaves, however, they revealed only part of the truth. The church owned only two slaves in Bethabara. Of larger significance was the work of hired slaves throughout Wachovia. The Breth-

44. On the settlement of these farming communities, see Thorp, "Assimilation," *JSH*, LII (1986), 34–37; three articles in *Three Forks of Muddy Creek*, 14 vols. (Winston-Salem, N.C., 1974–): Hunter James, "Friedberg: The Early Years," III (1976), 11–24, Frances Griffin, "Land of Peace," VII (1980), 1–12, Griffin, "The English Settlement," VI (1979), 1–12; and S. Scott Rohrer, "Assimilation in the Southern Backcountry: The Case of Hope, North Carolina, 1773–1815" (paper presented at the annual conference of the Omohundro Institute of Early American History and Culture, Winston-Salem, N.C., June 1997).

45. Marshall Report to the Unity Helper Department, Dec. 20, 1771 (trans. EM); Memoir of Abraham; Hope Church Register A, list of communicants (Priscilla) and death register, no. 25 (Esther). Other examples of bondpersons in southern Wachovia are cited in Marshall's Report to the Unity, Apr. 9, 1774 (trans. EM); and Joseph Powell to Marshall, July 26, 1772, in Fries et al., eds., *Records*, II, 720.

ren also neglected to tell the visitors they were buying more slaves all the time—in Salem, Hope, and Friedberg. By the early 1770s, Africans and African Americans lived beside Germans and English in the Moravian land. They were relatively few—perhaps no more than twenty-five. Yet they— and slavery itself—were firmly embedded in the young settlement.[46]

The Brethren, emigrating to America in search of religious freedom, had found it relatively simple to modify and transfer their notions of power and servitude to a new continent and a different people. As was so often the case in the European conquest of the Americas, an attempt to establish a luminous example of a new godly order came partly at the expense of others. White Moravians could see no paradox in this outcome, for God, speaking through the lot, had shown them that bonded servitude could help prop up his earthly kingdom. How masters and slaves were to live together in this rough backcountry outpost had not been settled, for they were still taking the measure of each other. Almost as soon as this mutual scrutiny began, war disrupted the negotiations.

46. Bethabara Diary, Sept. 20, 1773, in Fries et al., eds., *Records,* II, 780. The resiliency of the myth of Moravian antislavery is confirmed by its persistence in subsequent scholarship. See Sylvia R. Frey, *Water from the Rock: Black Resistance in a Revolutionary Age* (Princeton, N.J., 1991), 8; and Victoria Bynum, *Unruly Women: The Politics of Social and Sexual Control in the Old South* (Chapel Hill, N.C., 1992), 137.

· · · · · · · · · · · · · · · ·

CHAPTER THREE

A "Turbulent Spirit"

 THE LARGE GATHERING in the Salem prayer hall on November 13, 1771, celebrated two momentous events in the young Moravian settlement. Hundreds of people, black and white, had come to witness the consecration of the new hall facing the town square. For this affirmation of their work to erect a godly community, the Brethren also awaited a special service: the baptism of Sam, their first African-American slave, "into whose heart He had placed the longing to be washed from his sins in the blood of Jesus."[1] The ceremony would complete Sam's determined two-year campaign to become a Moravian brother.

The unadorned, whitewashed room was still as worshipers waited on wooden benches facing a plain altar. "The baptismal water was brought in by two Brethren," reported a witness, "then the candidate Sam was led into the Saal [assembly room] by the Brn. Herbst and Zillmann, and after he had answered the questions, and had received absolution in Jesus' name, he was baptized into the death of Jesus, receiving the name Johannes Samuel." The emotion of the moment, though quietly expressed, crowded the room. "The presence of the Saviour was deeply felt by the congregation, including the many friends and a few negroes; many said that the impression made upon them would never be forgotten." Johannes Samuel now entered the Bethabara Single Brothers' Choir as the first black Moravian in North Carolina.[2]

Johannes (more commonly known as Johann) Samuel was only one of a growing multitude of African Americans throughout the colonies to em-

1. Salem Diary, Nov. 13, 1771, in Adelaide L. Fries et al., eds., *Records of the Moravians in North Carolina*, 11 vols. (Raleigh, N.C., 1922–1969), I, 446.
2. Ibid.

brace Christianity in one form or another during the waning years of the colonial period. Redefining themselves for the first time through the lens of the gospel, thousands found spiritual release in Baptist revivals, Methodist camp meetings, Presbyterian churches, and secret meetings unobserved by white eyes. Fusing diverse strands of African and Christian beliefs, black Americans created new faiths that provided powerful religious and political sustenance in their struggle to survive racial oppression.[3]

The evangelical message of universal salvation gave the era an experimental air as black and white Christians tested the meaning of spiritual and temporal freedom in their relationships to each other and to the larger slave society. Evangelical communities across the South were nurseries of an emerging biracial culture based on spiritual equality. Surprising numbers of Christians sought to create a new language that would guarantee recognition of humanity for all. But what were the limits of this new language? After white and black cried hallelujah together, did their fellowship carry beyond the prayer hall? And how did Afro-Christians link spiritual renewal with resistance to slavery?

Such issues gathered urgency in the fermenting climate of revolution. By the early 1770s, freedom—defining it, winning it, or limiting it—was hotly debated throughout the colonies and in the Moravian settlement itself, and African Americans injected themselves vigorously in the discussion. Freedom of the body, freedom of the spirit: slaves drew inspiration from both the ringing political rhetoric around them and the liberating idiom of Afro-Christianity. Many saw the impending war over American independence as a war for their own freedom even as some sought to enter the Moravian Church. Engulfed by war, Wachovia seethed with a multisided struggle over the boundaries of Christian freedom and authority.

LIKE OTHER MESSIANIC immigrants before and after them, the Moravians came to America with the self-imposed weight of destiny on their shoulders. Their identity came from Christ's martyrdom. His pain was their freedom

3. The development of Afro-Christianity in 18th-century North America is effectively explored in, among many others, Albert J. Raboteau, *Slave Religion: The "Invisible Institution" in the Antebellum South* (New York, 1978); Mechal Sobel, *Trabelin' On: The Slave Journey to an Afro-Baptist Faith* (Westport, Conn., 1979); Margaret Washington Creel, *"A Peculiar People": Slave Religion and Community-Culture among the Gullahs* (New York, 1988); Sylvia R. Frey, "Shaking the Dry Bones: The Dialectic of Conversion," in Ted Ownby, ed., *Black and White*

and their shield; his work was their work. "Be commended to the lamb of God; his death, the nail prints—so red—the wounded side, the sweat in his agony, keep you from everything that might harm you," Bishop August Gottlieb Spangenberg reminded the faithful in words not far removed from the most vivid imagery of the "sifting period" a few years earlier. The Brethren considered themselves God's chosen carriers of the spores of grace from which human society would regenerate itself. Wachovia was to be more than a refuge for a select few; it embodied a chance to create a model community of apostolic purity for the world to emulate. Whereas their more famous predecessors, the Puritans, had crossed the ocean in the name of a loving but stern and selective God, the Moravians carried a message of all-embracing Christian love. Yet the vision fueling the Moravian and Puritan self-image as agents of divinity was the same. In a striking reverberation of words used by the Puritans 126 years earlier, Bishop Spangenberg wrote to the North Carolina Brethren in 1756: "The Saviour's heart will be blessed by you and your light will be seen far and wide, for you are a city built upon a hill."[4]

By 1772, Moravian eyes had turned to Salem for the fulfillment of that vision. That year, Salem finally assumed its place as the settlement's showcase New Testament congregation town. A Moravian congregation town, composed of the Lord's chosen people, was designated with a "peculiar grace" that lifted it above the ordinary. "A Congregation-Town," explained leader Frederic Marshall in 1765, "differs from other Congregations in that it is more like one family, where the religious and material condition of each member is known in detail, where each person receives the appropriate Choir oversight, and also assistance in consecrating the daily life." To live in Salem, one had to "feel that he has had a special call from the Lord to live in that place, and that the Lord has brought him to this people."[5]

Cultural Interaction in the Antebellum South (Jackson, Miss., 1993), 23–54; Frey, " 'The Year of Jubilee Is Come': Black Christianity in the Plantation South in Post-Revolutionary America," in Ronald Hoffman and Peter J. Albert, eds., *Religion in a Revolutionary Age* (Charlottesville, Va., 1994), 87–124.

4. Spangenberg to the Wachovia congregation, June 20, 1758 (first quotation), Feb. 27, 1756 (second quotation), vault 3, box 1, nos. 6, 20 (trans. EM). On the Puritan sense of destiny, see Perry Miller, *Errand into the Wilderness* (1956; reprint, New York, 1964), 1–15. See also Arthur Bestor, *Backwoods Utopias: The Sectarian Origins and the Owenite Phase of Communitarian Socialism in America, 1663–1829* (Philadelphia, 1950), 1–37.

5. Marshall, "Remarks concerning the Laying Out of the New Congregation Town in the Center of Wachovia," July 1765, and GHC, Nov. 30, 1772, in Fries et al., eds., *Records*, I, 313, II,

This sanctuary of the elect was still little more than a village of 120 in 1772: 38 married people, 2 widows, 43 single men and boys, 22 single women and older girls, and 15 children. The town's rectilinear design embodied its planners' vision of divine order. In the heart of town astride a gentle ridge lay a central square, faced on one side by the *Gemein Haus*, or meeting hall, across from the large Single Brothers' House and farm complex on the other (a third major building on the square, the Single Sisters' House, was built in 1786). Private homes and shops fronted the main street and adjoining lanes. Just south of town was a tavern, and downhill to the west in the industrial district along Salem Creek stood a slaughterhouse, tannery, and brewery / distillery, all operated by the church. A ring of farm and garden plots formed an outer shell around the town.[6]

Life in such a place was framed by the Unity's views on liberty and subordination, which were largely the legacy of Count Zinzendorf. The count had died in 1760, but his philosophy on the proper Christian life lingered in many aspects of Moravian practice. Zinzendorf held that a life in Christ was free—morally free, that is, since the Savior's death had liberated mankind from the shackles of sin, transforming the Old Testament's "thou shalt" to the New Testament's "I am allowed." Regenerate believers had the freedom to give themselves voluntarily to Christ and tap into the "peculiar grace" of a congregation town, but that freedom did not mean individual license to do whatever one pleased. On the contrary, freedom meant submitting to Christ's higher law and to church authority. Individual desires must be subordinated to the greater good of the congregation.[7]

These precepts meant that the church controlled virtually every aspect

---

725; Aelt. Conf., Mar. 28, 1781. On the notion of "peculiar grace," see Elisabeth Sommer, "A Different Kind of Freedom? Order and Discipline among the Moravian Brethren in Germany and Salem, North Carolina, 1771–1801," *Church History*, LXIII (1994), 224.

6. On Salem's town design, see Daniel B. Thorp, "The City That Never Was: Count von Zinzendorf's Original Plan for Salem," *NCHR*, LXI (1984), 36–58; William Hinman, "Philip Gottlieb Reuter, First Surveyor of Wachovia" (master's thesis, Wake Forest University, 1987); congregation figures in Fries et al., eds., *Records*, II, 658–666. The German word *Gemein* can be translated as either community or congregation, but the term is best left untranslated in the Moravians' usage because it combined both meanings. In this context, *Gemein Haus* (or *Gemeinhaus*) also has no satisfactory translation, since it served as more than a church or meetinghouse, being the pastor's home as well.

7. Sommer, "A Different Kind of Freedom?" *Church History*, LXIII (1994), 224. This view had much in common with the philosophy of the Hallensian school of Lutheran Pietism, with which Zinzendorf and the Brethren had strong links. See A. G. Roeber, *Palatines, Liberty, and Property: German Lutherans in Colonial British America* (Baltimore, 1993).

Figure 10. *A View of Salem in North Carolina 1787*. By Gottfried von Redeken. Watercolor on paper. Courtesy, Collection of the Wachovia Historical Society, Winston-Salem, North Carolina

of life in Salem. The town was not strictly communal in the sense that property and wealth were shared equally. Rather, the church owned all property and leased private homes and businesses to individuals. Congregants expected a high degree of regulation in daily life. Although a Brotherly Agreement outlined rules for conduct in each of Wachovia's six congregations, Salem's was easily the most restrictive and far-reaching. The church, through the binding power of the covenant and in consultation with congregation members, told them what work they could do, where they could live, whom they could marry, and how to raise their children. The collective integrity of the Moravians' mission depended on adherence to the code. "He who acts in accordance with the laws does so for his own benefit, for Jesus and the community," insisted church leaders. "He who acts against the laws and order does only harm to himself."[8]

8. Auf. Col., Nov. 7, 1772. The 1773 "Brotherly Agreement of the Evangelical *Gemeine* of Brethren at Salem" is as thorough a blueprint for an 18th-century Christian community as one is likely to find. For a similar, though less extensive, compact, see the 1780 Bethania Brotherly Agreement in Fries et al., eds., *Records*, IV, 1498–1508. See also Jerry L. Surratt, "The Role of Dissent in Community Evolution among Moravians in Salem, 1772–1860," *NCHR*, LII (1975), 235–255. Community statutes are discussed in Elisabeth W. Sommer, "Serving Two Masters: Authority, Faith, and Community among the Moravian Brethren in

An elaborate bureaucracy managed the vast job of ensuring conformity. The *Aeltesten Conferenz*, or Elders' Conference, the principal governing body of Wachovia, consisted of ordained ministers and their wives from Salem, Bethabara, and Bethania as well as officials of the Salem Single Brothers' and Single Sisters' Choirs. Although final authority on all matters rested with the elders, they spent most of their energy directing religious life. The *Aufseher Collegium*, or Board of Overseers, regulated secular affairs, including prices, wages, businesses, employment, and land transactions. The *Gemein Rath*, or Congregational Council, also deliberated policy matters. And, as the ultimate authority, Christ himself was considered Chief Elder, whose judgment through the lot resolved questions of supreme importance.[9]

This sacred and tightly knit vision of social discipline governed the Brethren's view of slavery in Salem. They regarded slavery as a legitimate supplement to their labor force, but it had to be carefully controlled by a set of regulations unique in the eighteenth-century South to preserve the "peculiar grace" of the town. Although the church permitted private slaveholding in most outlying congregations, Brethren in Salem were forbidden to buy slaves. The church feared that individual slaveholding would promote idleness among whites, thus infusing the virus of ungodly indolence into the community while replacing free white Moravian workers with enslaved black ones, leading to unemployment. Slaveowners would earn more money to buy more slaves to earn more money—a selfish display at the expense of the community. And African Americans, apparently either slave or free, like any non-Moravian, were outsiders, by definition untrustworthy. "No Journeyman, Prentice, Servant, Maid or Negro shall be received into any Family, without the Privity and Approbation of the Committee. And every Housekeeper shall put away all such as soon as they become Seducers," said a 1759 statute in the Moravian town of Lititz, Pennsylvania, that might just as well have been written in Salem.[10]

Germany and North Carolina in the Eighteenth Century" (Ph.D. diss., University of Virginia, 1991); and Sommer, "A Different Kind of Freedom?" *Church History,* LXIII (1994), 221–234.

9. Salem Diary, Nov. 11, 1777, in Fries et al., eds., *Records,* III, 1168. These boards represented only part of the intricate managerial apparatus of Wachovia. Besides Salem, each of the other five congregations was also governed by one or more committees, although generally to a lesser extent than Salem. Various additional boards of ministers and other officials, often with overlapping membership, helped supervise individual congregations as well as Wachovia as a whole. For an overview of this system, see III, 1330–1331. On Christ as Chief Elder, see Sommer, "A Different Kind of Freedom?" *Church History,* LXIII (1994), 225.

10. These provisions are sketched out in Philip Africa, "Slaveholding in the Salem Commu-

To forestall any of this, the church itself bought and owned any slaves it deemed necessary for the community's labor needs. These were then leased to tradesmen and proprietors, mostly of church-owned businesses like the tavern, tannery, and pottery. Craftsmen and other Brethren who needed additional labor might also get permission to hire slaves from outside the settlement.

So two seemingly contradictory things were happening. The Brethren needed slaves, but, fearing their presence as "Seducers," they sought to limit and control them. The solution to the quandary? Encourage slaves to convert. If these strangers were baptized into the Moravian fellowship, they would no longer threaten it. They would, in fact, share the exclusive covenant of the chosen people. By absorbing bondservants into their fellowship, white Brethren hoped to dissolve the distance between themselves and a separate, potentially rebellious, workforce. They would create a new identity for those they called at once "Brother" or "Sister" and "slave," an identity fused with and submerged in that of the collective. Because Brethren looked at the world in spiritual terms, this equation meant, at least theoretically, that an enslaved black Moravian would be treated with more esteem than a free white non-Moravian.

The Moravian stance varied sharply with a longstanding tradition in Anglican-dominated southern slave society. Many planters feared that not only would Christianity give slaves an elevated opinion of themselves; it would undermine a key philosophical justification for slavery. As historian Winthrop D. Jordan has written, "slavery could survive *only* if the Negro were a man set apart; he simply had to be different if slavery was to exist at all." White Brethren saw no tension whatever between spiritual freedom and temporal bondage in their fellowship. Rather, they saw a seamless web wherein slave and free, black and white, were bound together in a higher calling.[11]

Like all slave masters, white Moravians demanded obedience. They appre-

---

nity, 1771–1851," *NCHR,* LIV (1977), 271–307; Herbert H. Beck, "Town Regulations of Lititz, 1759," *TMHS,* XI (1936), 167.

11. On the racial ideology of exclusion, see Winthrop D. Jordan, *White over Black: American Attitudes toward the Negro, 1550–1812* (Chapel Hill, N.C., 1968), 94–96, 179–212 (quotation on 184). Perhaps typical of Anglican planter mentality was Virginian Landon Carter's comment that blacks "are devils, and to make them otherwise than slaves will be to set devils free"; see Jack P. Greene, ed., *The Diary of Colonel Landon Carter of Sabine Hall, 1752–1778,* 2 vols. (Charlottesville, Va., 1965), II, 1148–1149.

ciated the coercive power of colonial slave laws in ensuring the subjugation of slaves. But they clothed their expectations in religious garb to emphasize what they understood to be reciprocal obligations among congregants. Enslaved Moravians, according to the church fathers, had just as much freedom as legally free white Moravians—freedom in Christ, the only kind of freedom that really mattered. Still, some practical guide was needed for regulating relations with slaves in daily affairs. Drawing inspiration from Paul's letter to the Ephesians (6:5–9), the Moravians essentially offered slaves a trade: what they considered humane treatment in return for obedience. The exchange was especially aimed at enslaved Christians who were bound by a duty proceeding "from motives that are independent of the character of the master and his conduct toward his servants, be it harsh or generous." Slaves owed masters "the same fidelity and submissiveness" they gave Christ. By the same token, masters must "restrain themselves in the exercise of their authority over their slaves." In so doing, they would "lighten the slaves' condition" and make them "obedient, willing, and loyal." The proof of the formula was that masters of Christian slaves "are almost generally convinced that their interests are best served when their Negroes give their hearts to Christ." The Brethren thus counted themselves among a handful of slaveowners in the late eighteenth century who invoked a paternalist logic of interdependence between masters and slaves.[12]

White Brethren had clearly spelled out their side of the equation. On the other side, the idea of joining a Moravian congregation might have held a certain attractiveness for some enslaved African Americans. Those hungering for spiritual nourishment might find an inclusive message of salvation and a vehicle for religious awakening. An itinerant Danish Moravian preacher named George Soelle, who spread the gospel throughout the Yadkin River basin area around Wachovia, noted the eagerness with which blacks attended his words. In the South Fork settlement some five miles

12. C.G.A. Oldendorp, *History of the Mission of the Evangelical Brethren on the Caribbean Islands of St. Thomas, St. Croix, and St. John,* ed. and trans. Arnold R. Highfield and Vladimir Barac (1770; reprint, Ann Arbor, Mich., 1987), 229–230. Lest his readers mistake him for a sentimentalist, Oldendorp concluded his discussion of masters' authority by endorsing the virtues of amputating runaways' feet and flogging other offenders, even to death, as he witnessed in the West Indies. On the reciprocity of paternalism, see Eugene D. Genovese, *Roll, Jordan, Roll: The World the Slaves Made* (New York, 1974), esp. 3–7; and Allan Gallay, "The Origins of Slaveholders' Paternalism: George Whitefield, the Bryan Family, and the Great Awakening in the South," *JSH,* LIII (1987), 369–394.

south of Salem, which became the Moravian society of Friedberg, he found the slave of Valentine Frey "ready to listen and to accept." He "becomes softened and appears not unsuited for the Kingdom of God." At a meeting across the Smith River in Virginia in 1772, the slave of a Baptist preacher "bawled so loudly during the sermon that I could hardly hear my own words." At John Kimbrough's near the Uwharrie River, a fifteen-year-old boy saddling Soelle's horse told the Danish minister of his desire to be baptized. "He said this had come over him several weeks ago since his arrival from Virginia. He said he could not read much but liked to read in the Old Testament." Through his travels, Soelle noted the presence of blacks and whites summoning grace together at prayer meetings. On another trip to Virginia, he observed "many souls here among whites and blacks who give real promise, if only they would have proper care. As it is, they carry on and act the way they themselves think best. I spoke out frankly about the noise in their meeting . . . [saying] that it would hinder rather than further the gracious ministry of the Holy Spirit in their hearts." Though the minister disapproved of the rough emotionalism of these seekers, their yearning for a religion of the heart was obvious. Both outside and inside the Moravian settlement, blacks turned to the Brethren to fill the spiritual void.[13]

In an eighteenth-century America characterized by enforced black subordination, here too was perhaps a rare chance to gain certain privileges and a modicum of respect. For the small handful of enslaved people in the Moravian communities in the early 1770s, Moravian fellowship represented an opportunity to salvage something positive from their predicament. Unconverted, they remained outcasts. Incorporating themselves into the slaveholders' own society, on the other hand, was a way to break down social, religious, and racial barriers; to claim, if not freedom of the body, then at least freedom of the soul and in doing so secure a measure of defense against the vagaries of slavery.

Of course, it is all but impossible to judge why people sought conversion; we can only project some combination of spiritual and secular motives. Some might well have regarded servitude and church membership in Wachovia as a radical alternative to the harsh treatment and violence that non-Moravian masters regularly visited on them. In all the colonies, slave codes

13. George Soelle's *Lebenslauf* and a summary of his journals are contained in Fries et al., eds., *Records*, II, 784–807. All quotations, however, are taken from the manuscript of the journals (trans. Kenneth J. Hamilton), Mar. 30, 1771, May 10, Aug. 3, Sept. 25, 1772.

provided for practically unrestricted punishment of slaves, and such cruelty occurred frighteningly close at hand. West of the Yadkin River near Wachovia, the Moravian minister Soelle consoled a remorseful slaveowner in 1771 who had whipped a Negro girl to death. Not until 1774 was the killing of a slave considered homicide in North Carolina. Keen awareness of such realities informed black assessment of the world around them, including the world the Moravians offered.[14]

For whatever reasons, Sam, the first slave bought by the Brethren, asked the Brethren in late 1769 for instruction in reading German, apparently to study the Bible. They encouraged him, seeing a chance to gain their first black convert in North Carolina. Wanting him to be well versed in the faith, they intensified Sam's instruction in March 1771, counseling him to "remain in his external circumstances, obedient and faithful." He studied with Moravian boys in the Bethabara school; in May, he became a "candidate for baptism" and, the elders claimed, would be "treated as such" from then on. Lessons continued until November, when the elders, finally judging his learning sufficient, asked the lot whether Sam should be baptized and received an affirmative answer. Six possible Christian names for Sam were submitted to the lot—Johannes, Abraham, Christian, Thomas, Joseph, and Friedrich—from which the first was pulled. Ten days later, in the powerful ceremony at Salem, he was christened Johann Samuel.[15]

Now judged to have died and been born again, and having participated in an emotional induction into the church, Johann Samuel joined the Bethabara congregation. Armed with a new name and a new identity, he was no longer called "the Negro" but "the Single Brother Johann Samuel," the skilled teamster and driver who shuttled church officials and visitors throughout Wachovia and beyond. In church he sat with white Single Brothers: "In the afternoon the *Jünger's* [Zinzendorf's] Sermon to the Received was read, the three who have recently been received sitting on the front bench, and with them Johann Samuel, who has been baptized within the year." After-

14. Journal of George Soelle, July 18, 1771, 15. Examples of barbaric treatment of slaves are cited in Ellen Gibson Wilson, *The Loyal Blacks* (New York, 1976), 23–24; Jeffrey J. Crow, *The Black Experience in Revolutionary North Carolina* (Raleigh, N.C., 1977), 21. On colonial slave codes, see A. Leon Higginbotham, Jr., *In the Matter of Color: Race and the American Legal Process, the Colonial Period* (New York, 1978); Ernest James Clark, Jr., "Aspects of the North Carolina Slave Code, 1715–1860," *NCHR*, XXXIX (1962), 148–164.

15. Aelt. Conf., Apr. 24, 1769, Mar. 30, May 28, Nov. 3, 1771; Wachovia Diary, Mar. 30, 1771.

ward, in their choir house, the brothers celebrated with a lovefeast, a simple Moravian fellowship meal of coffee and bread. In August 1774, the Elders' Conference reported that Johann Samuel was making satisfactory spiritual progress, and two months later a drawing of lots revealed God's approval of his candidacy for Communion. Pending his admission to that important ritual, Johann Samuel was entitled to participate in all other church functions. He was now considered—and considered himself—not an outsider, but a brother.[16]

As Johann Samuel had done, other African Americans who were hired out to the Moravians lobbied their temporary masters to buy them—a decidedly active way to affect their enslavement for the better, as they apparently hoped. Ben, a hired hand in Bethabara for four years, in 1774 "pleaded with tears that the Brethren might purchase him from his master, who wishes to sell him." His plea was rejected, either because the Brethren did not need or could not afford him or because he had neglected to mention a crucial condition—a desire for salvation. A slave named Jacob who was working in the Salem tavern adopted a different and more perceptive tactic. Approaching Frederic Marshall in the tavern one day in 1775, he "told him with tears in his eyes that there are only two days left that somebody in the community could buy him," after which "his master would sell him God knows where." Perhaps sensing that the Moravians liked and needed to connect slaveholding with their spiritual mission, Jacob compared the uncertainty and peril of his bleak future with his alternative hope. "He asked fervently that somebody should buy him because he would like to stay with the Brethren and wants to become a son of Christ." Whether sincere in his professed desire or not, Jacob made his case convincingly. Seeing a chance to gain extra hands and another soul, the Brethren assented and bought him.[17]

Other blacks pressed the Moravians for spiritual nourishment. One was Cathy, a young girl bought by the church with her mother, Susy, to serve in the Bethabara tavern in 1771. In February 1772, when tavernkeepers Jacob and Catharina Meyer moved from Bethabara to assume direction of the new Salem tavern, Cathy and Susy moved with them. The next year, Cathy "begged to attend the Lovefeast" of the Moravian girls, who "were told to

16. Salem Diary, Apr. 26, 1772, in Fries et al., eds., *Records*, II, 678–679 (quotation); Aelt. Conf., Aug. 28, Nov. 12, 1774; Bethania Diary, Sept. 4, 1774. Elders occasionally lapsed and again referred to Johann Samuel as "our Negro"; see Salem Diary, Nov. 13, 1774, in Fries et al., eds., *Records*, II, 821.

17. PHC, Mar. 22, 1774; Auf. Col., Jan. 14, Mar. 15, 1775.

speak a good word for Cathy to the Saviour." Another was a tavern worker named Franke. Whether she was the same woman first hired by the Brethren in 1767 is unclear, but, when the church mission collection box was passed around in 1774, she "heard of it, told two others, and all three asked that their little gifts might also be accepted. That evening she came into the Saal, dressed in white; and since then it appears that the Holy Spirit is working within her heart." A few months later, Franke asked to be admitted into the Salem congregation, but the elders drew a blank lot, stalling her request, and she never got another chance.[18]

The Brethren were gaining something of a favorable reputation among blacks in the region, who were lobbying to be bought by them. Yet whites on the outside regarded the reverberations of racial spiritual equality coming from Moravian prayer halls as ominous. Uninformed of Moravian attitudes and suspicious of their motives, some accused the Brethren in 1773 of harboring runaway slaves. Whether the Brethren responded to the charge directly is not known, but they could have given impressive evidence that they had no intention of hiding runaways or undermining slavery any other way. Black spiritual liberation, yes; but bodily servitude forever.[19]

THROUGHOUT THE British North American colonies, African Americans confronted the 1770s with rising expectations tempered by hard choices. For, if independence occupied the thoughts and words of white colonists, it held intense interest for blacks as well. As tensions between whigs and tories mounted, enslaved Americans sought to capitalize on the rift among whites through bold efforts to seize or expand their freedom. They ran away in greater numbers, committed more acts of sabotage, and rose in armed insurrection more often. Whites viewed this rising rebelliousness with alarm. Rumors of uprisings circulated rapidly as the British assessed the possibility of arming slaves to help put down insurgent patriots. As white Revolutionaries in turn resorted to harsh treatment to cow bondpersons, the years 1774 and 1775 saw a pattern of increasing black activity, mounting white fears, and reprisals against slaves.[20]

18. Salem Diary, Jan. 6, 1774, in Fries et al., eds., *Records,* II, 814; Aelt. Conf., Apr. 13, 1774.
19. Bagge Manuscript, 1773, in Fries et al., eds., *Records,* II, 754.
20. The classic work on African Americans in the age of Revolution is Benjamin Quarles, *The Negro in the American Revolution* (1961; reprint, Chapel Hill, N.C., 1996). The following works are among the most important examinations of the subject: Crow, *The Black Experience*

Despite Moravian leaders' ardent desire to be left in peace and avoid the Revolutionary conflicts swirling around them, Wachovia could not but be inundated by the struggle. Authority broke down throughout the Carolina backcountry as antagonism against white elites by blacks and poor whites rose to a bitter crescendo. In 1774, the Brethren noted with uneasiness the fracturing of the social order they knew: "Even as the fields te[e]m with thieving creatures so it goes among men, for there is robbery, murder, stealing of horses and swine, and the counterfeiting of both paper and hard money. . . . The present unrest permits the turbulent spirit to increase greatly."[21]

Emboldened by the changing political and social climate, blacks in Wachovia became infected with the "turbulent spirit." In March 1774, a hired mulatto was discharged from the Bethabara tavern for "bad conduct." That same month, John Schaub of Bethabara discovered his female slave on a night excursion to visit Johann Samuel. Unauthorized liaisons between the sexes, especially involving congregation members, were strictly forbidden, and a church committee decreed that henceforth "our Negroes and Negresses should not leave their homes at night, but should stay where they work." Brother though he was, Johann Samuel's church membership meant little in such a situation: he was once again "our Negro."[22]

Blacks expressed growing rebelliousness through more dramatic acts as well. In 1772, a slave girl or woman belonging to Friedberg tavernkeeper Christian Frey ran away. Brethren quickly recaptured her, but her mutiny was not quelled. In April 1774, Frey "had the misfortune that his own Negro

---

in *Revolutionary North Carolina*; Ira Berlin and Ronald Hoffman, eds., *Slavery and Freedom in the Age of the American Revolution* (Charlottesville, Va., 1983); Sylvia R. Frey, *Water from the Rock: Black Resistance in a Revolutionary Age* (Princeton, N.J., 1991); and Peter H. Wood, " 'Liberty Is Sweet': African American Freedom Struggles in the Years before White Independence," in Alfred F. Young, ed., *Beyond the American Revolution: Explorations in the History of American Radicalism* (DeKalb, Ill., 1993), 149–184.

21. Salem Diary, Sept. 1, 1774, in Fries et al., eds., *Records*, II, 818; Marvin L. Michael Kay and Lorin Lee Cary, "Class, Mobility, and Conflict in North Carolina on the Eve of the Revolution," in Jeffrey J. Crow and Larry E. Tise, eds., *The Southern Experience in the American Revolution* (Chapel Hill, N.C., 1978), 109–151; Ronald Hoffman, "The 'Disaffected' in the Revolutionary South," in Alfred F. Young, ed., *The American Revolution: Explorations in the History of American Radicalism* (DeKalb, Ill., 1976), 275–316; and Jeffrey J. Crow, "Liberty Men and Loyalists: Disorder and Disaffection in the North Carolina Backcountry," in Ronald Hoffman, Thad W. Tate, and Peter J. Albert, eds., *An Uncivil War: The Southern Backcountry in the American Revolution* (Charlottesville, Va., 1985), 125–178.

22. Bethabara Diary, Mar. 2, 10, 1774; Bethabara Committee, Mar. 6, 1774.

girl, in order to spare herself the work with the cattle, set a fire through which his stable, barn and all his supplies were lost, at a value of over 280 pounds." The enslaved African, Sambo, committed "all sorts of excesses," and the elders considered selling him, "the sooner the better." Even Johann Samuel, a candidate for Communion by late 1774, showed such lack of submissiveness that the ministers questioned the sincerity of his conversion: "Matters are forthcoming regarding our Negro John Samuel, which, if they are actually the case and he does not honestly leave them off, advises us that brotherliness works very doubtfully with him."[23]

African Americans pried narrow cracks in the wall of constraint through illicit trading—with whites eager to bypass rules or to stave off economic hardship. Ministers could complain in more than one sense about a black market. Emphasizing a theme they would echo often in subsequent years, they clamped down in October 1774: "Since the Negroes practice all kinds of blackmarketing and disorder with their selling and buying in the community, we shall call together the community representatives and announce that from now on nobody will buy anything anymore from such a man, if he does not have permission from his master" to sell. Furthermore, "there should be less conversation with the Negroes, because it will lower social order." Black efforts to expand a zone of personal autonomy and movement collided with church leaders' desire to protect their flock from people whose race and religious status made them suspect.[24]

In early 1775, as the colonies moved toward war, racial tension climbed higher outside and inside Wachovia. News reached Salem of a suppressed slave rebellion in Georgia in which four whites were killed and the rebels were burned alive in retribution. Then, in April, as the British and Americans fired shots at Lexington and Concord, dramatic rumors spread throughout the South that Lord Dunmore, governor of Virginia, had threatened to free and arm any slaves of American Revolutionaries who would help sup-

23. Friedberg Diary, June 15, 1772; Marshall Report to Unity, Apr. 9, 1774 (trans. EM); PHC, Nov. 21, 1774.

24. Auf. Col., Oct. 11, 1774. Other southern towns passed similar restrictions. See, for example, James H. Brewer, "Legislation Designed to Control Slavery in Wilmington and Fayetteville," *NCHR*, XXX (1953), 155–166; Clark, "Aspects of the North Carolina Slave Code," *NCHR*, XXXIX (1962), 154–156; Philip D. Morgan, "Black Life in Eighteenth-Century Charleston," *Perspectives in American History*, N.S., I (1984), 206–207. On "black marketing" by African Americans, see Peter H. Wood, " 'Taking Care of Business' in Revolutionary South Carolina: Republicanism and the Slave Society," in Jeffrey J. Crow and Larry E. Tise, eds., *The Southern Experience in the American Revolution* (Chapel Hill, N.C., 1978), 275.

press the uprising. Inspired by the rumor (which would, in fact, not become reality for another six months), slaves throughout the upper South fled by the hundreds, perhaps even thousands, to try to reach Dunmore. Frightened elites took steps to prevent black uprisings. In May, the Committee of New Bern declared that "there is much Reason to fear, in these Times of general Tumult and Confusion, that the Slaves may be instigated and encouraged by our inveterate Enemies to an Insurrection, which in our present defenceless State might have the most dreadful Consequences." The Committee urged whites to form companies to "patrol and search the Negro Houses." In July, patrollers uncovered slave conspiracies in several eastern counties.[25]

The Moravians looked at the growing black resistance with alarm, unsure about the loyalty of their own slaves and wary of the threat posed by the huge black population to the east. In May, a runaway slave attacked five people near Bethabara in three separate incidents before being captured. "Although all the witnesses of his deeds were present he would admit nothing; he was therefore whipped, and sent to his master, John Marell." Salem officials, fully sensing the danger of the times, took precautions for self-defense that revealed their attitude about the use of military force in slave control. They had invoked "freedom of conscience" as a way of preserving the exemption from bearing arms that had been granted them in the 1750s. Yet they were not entirely pacifist; now faced with the threat of slave revolt they were quick to arm themselves, though circumspectly. "It would be good if in these critical times Brother Wallis [the Salem administrator] had a supply of approximately 15 to 20 pounds of powder, because we do not know whether the Negroes may try to rise in rebellion," declared officials in June 1775. Acutely aware of the political awkwardness of bearing arms for self-defense while claiming exemption from military service, the Brethren quietly resolved to hide weapons: "We must not have ammunition and guns on account of our conscience." Yet they thought it entirely appropriate to arm themselves against possible slave revolt.[26]

25. Salem Diary, Feb. 4, 1775, and "In the Committee at Newbern," May 31, 1775, in Fries et al., eds., *Records*, II, 864, 929; Jeffrey J. Crow, "Slave Rebelliousness and Social Conflict in North Carolina, 1775 to 1802," *WMQ*, 3d Ser., XXXVII (1980), 83–86.

26. Salem Diary, May 28–30, 1775, and the Brethren's "freedom of conscience" claim, in Fries et al., eds., *Records*, II, 841, 851, 873–874; Auf. Col., June 28, Aug. 17, 1775. The Moravians' problem was identified by abolitionist Quakers in Germantown, Pennsylvania, in their famous antislavery manifesto of 1688. What would pacifists do, they asked, if slaves should "joint themselves, fight for freedom, and handle their masters and mistresses as they

Whereas fear of insurrection obsessed slaveholders, including the Moravians, in the months before and after the outbreak of war, the times filled many African Americans with hope. The possibility of overthrowing, or at least escaping, slavery undoubtedly had never seemed so plausible. In Pennsylvania, minister Henry Melchior Muhlenberg heard the spirit of the times in the words of two black servants of an English family fleeing Philadelphia in September 1777. "They secretly wished that the British army might win," he noted, "for then all Negro slaves will gain their freedom. It is said that this sentiment is almost universal among the Negroes in America."[27]

At the height of the tense summer of 1775, two Moravian-owned slaves decided conditions were tumultuous enough to attempt escape. One was Sambo, who by then had lived in Salem for nearly four years and must have been profoundly alone and unhappy. He spoke little German or English and no doubt found communication difficult with either whites or blacks. He probably had few opportunities to see the other two Africans in the Moravian settlement, Frank in Bethabara and Jupiter in Hope.

Sambo finally saw a chance to flee in June. He might have been inspired by rumors of rebellion further east or by the possibility of reaching Dunmore; another catalyst might have been new information that reached Salem from a fortuitous source. In late June, the Moravians were visited by an Antiguan planter named Fearnly, who had known Moravian missionaries in Antigua. Fearnly had bought a plantation on the Dan River in southern Virginia and transported one hundred slaves there from Antigua. When the planter left Salem on July 2, Sambo and a slave belonging to Valentine Frey of Friedberg ran away the same day. Perhaps tories induced them to flee, for it was rumored that "a white man may have tempted them both." But Sambo might have been lured by the news that one hundred slaves from Antigua now lived near the Dan River only a few days away. The chance to find his way there and connect with other Africans could have provided a powerful temptation.[28]

If the plantation by the Dan was his destination, he never reached it; in

---

did handle them [slaves] before. Will the masters and mistresses take the sword at hand and war against the poor slaves? Or have these Negroes not as much right to fight for their freedom as you have to keep them slaves?" See Thomas E. Drake, *Quakers and Slavery in America* (New Haven, Conn., 1950), 12.

27. Henry Melchior Muhlenberg, *The Journals of Henry Melchior Muhlenberg*, 3 vols., trans. Theodore G. Tappert and John W. Doberstein (Philadelphia, 1942–1958), III, 78.

28. Salem Diary, June 29–July 3, 1775, in Fries et al., eds., *Records*, II, 876–877.

fact, he had ventured in the opposite direction. After less than three weeks, he was brought back to Salem by a white man from the Catawba River far to the south. "He was very miserable and hungry, has lived most of the time on berries he found in the woods, and will probably not be so eager to run away again," noted a diarist with a touch of smugness. A magistrate "sentenced the Negro Sambo to the punishment he deserved for running away, and it was administered by young Volp; he bore it patiently and meekly." Another score with an unruly slave was settled at the same time, for "Bro. Bagge had his negress punished also; he has hitherto done it himself, but seemed to be tired."[29]

Sambo's three weeks of freedom had ended in the bitterness of captivity again. Moravian leaders viewed his escape as a convincing reason to distance the restive black population, keeping them socially isolated. Addressing the Salem congregation on the evening of Sambo's return, town administrator John Wallis "gave earnest warning against too familiar intercourse with the Negroes." Wallis implied that Sambo had got information from conversations with whites that aided his escape. The episode also showed that Moravians were willing to abandon any lenient treatment that might have characterized their practices a scant two or three years earlier. The lash underscored that slaves' captivity ultimately rested on a bedrock of force. Whippings were white Moravians' way of restating the choice they, like all slaveholders, offered slaves: submit, be punished, or be sold.[30]

For the moment, some slaves chose defiance and took the consequences. Undeterred after his failed escape, Sambo again aroused the Moravians' wrath when in May 1776 he "went without permission to Baumgarten's

---

29. Salem Diary, July 21–22, 1775, ibid., II, 877–878. On runaways, see Marvin L. Michael Kay and Lorin Lee Cary, "Slave Runaways in Colonial North Carolina, 1748–1775," *NCHR*, LXIII (1986), 1–39. On the judicial system of slave trials and punishment, see Alan D. Watson, "North Carolina Slave Courts, 1715–1785," *NCHR*, LX (1983), 34–36. Though they sought to remain socially isolated from the world outside Wachovia, Brethren did have representation in the North Carolina judicial system. The magistrate who sentenced Sambo was Jacob Bonn, a Moravian physician appointed by the governor who held authority to hear small debt cases and try petty offenses, even those concerning non-Moravians in Wachovia. On the Brethren's relationship to county and colonial/state civil authority, see Thorp, *Moravian Community*, 163–168.

30. White Brethren were not averse to administering corporal punishment to miscreant whites as well. Two apprentices who fled Bethabara in 1769 were whipped, as was an apprentice who in 1782 "incited a younger boy to impudence toward his master"; see Wachovia Diary, Jan. 2, 1769, and Minutes of Salem Boards, 1782, in Fries et al., eds., *Records*, I, 387, IV, 1799.

house and frightened them with his impudence, for which he must be flogged." The tavern servant Franke, who just two years earlier had been a candidate for baptism, no longer found obedience useful and, in 1776, "because of her bad behaviour, was sold to a stranger." And in June 1779, a Bethabara diarist reported that "as the Negro Caesar had behaved very badly he was whipped and sent away from the tavern." These scattered acts of disobedience were not universal among blacks and scarcely signified a sustained threat by a hopelessly outnumbered enslaved population. But they occurred frequently enough to indicate that slaves were far less willing to submit patiently to the coercion of bondage. White Brethren could read the signs plainly enough.[31]

AFRICAN-AMERICAN DISCONTENT was only one among a web of problems confronting Moravian leaders during the war years. Severe economic, social, and political stresses drove wedges between congregants, and ministers found their authority questioned from many sides. One of the church's major concerns was to stay out of the fighting that raged around them for more than six years while preserving their military exemption. During the early months of the war in 1775, both the English and the rebels vied for Moravian loyalty. On May 31, the New Bern Committee sent the Brethren a circular urging patriots to unite against the king. At the same time, loyalist agents asked the Moravians to sign the Oath of Allegiance to the crown, and some nearly did, stopped only by their aversion to oath taking. The Moravians viewed the Revolutionaries as hotheads, as they had regarded the North Carolina Regulators a few years earlier. Their inclination was to support the king but to avoid taking sides openly or, if sides must be taken, to be as inconspicuous about it as possible.[32]

31. Aelt. Conf., May 21, 1776; Salem Memorabilia, 1776, Bethabara Diary, June 1, 1779, in Fries et al., eds., Records, III, 1042, 1334.

32. The Moravians' position is explained in Bagge Manuscript, and Graff to Unity Elder's Conference, June 27, 1775, in Fries et al., eds., Records, II, 847, 849, 876. The Regulators had organized heavily in and around Wachovia, and many were embittered by the Moravians' failure to support their cause. The Brethren's loyalty to the crown earned them high praise from Governor William Tryon during his six-day visit to Wachovia in June 1771, less than a month after his forces had defeated the Regulators at Alamance. See Daniel B. Thorp, The Moravian Community in Colonial North Carolina: Pluralism on the Southern Frontier (Knoxville, Tenn., 1989), 180–182; and, among several studies of the Regulators, Marvin L. Michael

In July 1775, when the Congress in Philadelphia called a "Day of Fasting and Prayer," the Moravians ignored the call. Instead, they drafted in English a "Declaration" announcing to the North Carolina convention their intent to "remain faithfull and loyal subjects to our Sovereign Lord King George the Third, and bear due Allegiance to him." Calling themselves "a quiet conscientious People," the Brethren avowed their love for "the Province of North Carolina in which we are settled" and pledged to "promote its Welfare at all times." But they pleaded that they could not "burthen" their "Consciences with bearing arms in the present calamitous Circumstances of North America." Stout words they were, but the message may never have reached its intended audience. Storekeeper Traugott Bagge, who later wrote his own memoir of the Revolution in the Moravian settlement, admitted: "Whether this *Declaration* was sent to any one, or to whom, I do not now remember." The Brethren continued to shun whig overtures. Revolutionaries invited the Moravians to send delegates to the Hillsborough Convention in August, where militias of minutemen were organized, but again the Moravians did not respond.[33]

Their public stance of neutrality pleased no one. Both sides accused them of helping the other. When whigs demanded their presence at muster, the Brethren asked to pay a tax instead. When a company of soldiers passed through Friedberg, "practically all the young men and boys, and some of the men, were in hiding in the woods." But a turning point came in early 1776. In February, after the whigs gained control of North Carolina with their defeat of the loyalists at Moore's Creek Bridge, they absolved the Moravians from bearing arms. When the Declaration of Independence was drafted in July, the Moravians decided that "the name of King George III should be omitted from the Liturgy, and that the prayers should be simply for the rulers of our land." The change reflected a tacit recognition of the Continental Congress as the new authority. In 1779, the Brethren declared allegiance to the state assembly, agreeing to pay a triple tax in return for military exemption. By the following year, their loyalties had switched completely: "Our Brethren shall not permit themselves to be called *Tories*,

---

Kay, "The North Carolina Regulation, 1766–1776: A Class Conflict," in Young, ed., *The American Revolution*, 71–123.

33. Salem Diary, July 29, Sept. 4, 1775, "To the Honourable the House of Delegates Appointed for a General Convention in the Province of North Carolina," August 1775, in Fries et al., eds., *Records*, II, 877, 883, 944.

which slanders them. We must put quite away from us the idea that we will be in danger from the English if we are not Tories."[34]

Throughout the war, a continual stream of troops from both sides traipsed through Wachovia demanding food, shelter, clothing, horses, iron, and leather. Under huge pressure and in no position to refuse any demand, the Moravians tried to meet them all. When General Horatio Gates demanded one thousand pairs of shoes or the equivalent quantity of leather in 1780, Brethren hustled to fill the order, only to be told the American army did not really need the leather but simply wanted to test their loyalty. Sometimes armies paid for goods in worthless paper money, but more often they did not pay at all. Struggling Salem craftsmen, in violation of town ordinances, raised prices above authorized levels. Wages could not keep up with prices. The town board tried to compensate by raising wages and artificially revaluing currency, but inflation outraced both measures.[35]

Thus, by the mid-1770s, African Americans were not alone in their chafing. Disgruntled Moravian workmen and artisans flouted rules openly. Even during the calmest of times, officials spent much energy disciplining congregants for endless infractions—excessive drinking, adultery, slander, quarreling, laziness, worldliness, and other sins. During the Revolutionary years, the intensity of their censures, repeated like incantations, betrayed a growing anxiety that the divine experiment was being gnawed away from within. Moravian youth seemed infected with the rhetoric of liberty loose in the colonies, which was not at all the kind of liberty the church fathers wanted for God's elect.

In April 1778, the conflict over wages culminated in a strike by about a dozen Single Brothers protesting their raises. "It seemed as though an evil spirit had taken possession of them, particularly of the younger Brethren born and brought up in the Unity," lamented the elders. Strikers' "godless

34. Friedberg Diary, Feb. 21–22, 1776, Bethabara Diary, Aug. 9, 1776, Salem Memorabilia, 1779, and Congregational Council, July 3, 1780, in Fries et al., eds., *Records*, III, 1100, 1110, 1285, IV, 1591–1592. See also Hunter James, *The Quiet People of the Land: A Story of the North Carolina Moravians in Revolutionary Times* (Chapel Hill, N.C., 1976); and Ruth Blackwelder, "The Attitude of the North Carolina Moravians toward the American Revolution," *NCHR*, IX (1932), 1–21.

35. Salem Diary, Oct. 3–4, 1780, and Bagge Manuscript, 1778, in Fries et al., eds., *Records*, III, 1212, IV, 1570. On war-related economic distress in the Carolina backcountry, see Crow, "Liberty Men and Loyalists," in Hoffman, Tate, and Albert, eds., *An Uncivil War*, 148.

intention" was to "force a larger increase in their wages, and to make the officials dance to their piping." The brothers returned to work the next day but were suspended from church services to ponder the folly of their "audacious combination." Though the uprising had quickly collapsed, signs of youthful impatience were unmistakable. Ministers noted anxiously in 1780: "Members are beginning to feel the spirit of freedom in the land, and to think that as soon as the children attain their majority they are at liberty to do as they please, and no longer give their parents respect or obedience."[36]

Restlessness by Moravian youth and African Americans was of a piece in the elders' minds, which perhaps explains why they put great emphasis on stopping friendships between the two groups. It was not easy to separate black from white in a setting where they lived and worked side by side. Some blacks tried to exploit not only younger whites' discontent but their curiosity about exotic outsiders. Secretly socializing with younger whites restless for freedom and adventure, slaves might have hoped to gain advantages such as greater mobility, perhaps even companionship. Elders feared that blacks—or at least black non-Moravians—would expose whites to temptation. In 1775, the Collegium reprimanded two Single Brothers who, along with a black, were "reported to have gone over the bridge last Sunday evening, where a party of Negroes has been gathering." The Bethabara Congregational Council decreed that "when on Sundays any Brother leaves town accompanied by a Negro, he must notify the Negro's master first and must return him in an orderly fashion."[37]

For blacks, cross-racial friendships represented both an opportunity and a risk. As Sambo discovered, whites sometimes forgot they were supposed to treat slaves humanely. "Our Brethren are too friendly with the Negroes and afterwards they are amazed at their freshness," complained the board. "The main fault with our Brethren is that they are always with the Negroes in jokes and fun, and the next day they beat them like dogs. Poor Sambo is said to be in a very poor state and unable to work right now because of the beating he has received. He has to be under the care of a doctor." Although deploring Sambo's beating, ministers also fretted that hobnobbing with

36. Salem Diary, Apr. 1–2, 1778, Aelt. Conf., Apr. 3, 1778, and LAC, Nov. 14, 1780, in Fries et al., eds., *Records*, III, 1225–1226, 1259, IV, 1609. Strains within Moravian society during this period are also discussed in Norma Taylor Mitchell, "Freedom and Authority in the Moravian Community of North Carolina, 1753–1837 . . ." (master's thesis, Duke University, 1961), chap. 3.

37. Auf. Col., Feb. 7, 1775; Bethabara Diary, Dec. 26, 1777.

whites made him "fresh." As they saw it, African Americans, given their disdain for authority, scarcely needed further encouragement.[38]

Sambo learned that whites could take his "jokes and fun" the wrong way. In again showing their distinction between the chosen few and the excluded many, some Brethren could be brutal indeed. The African nonetheless continued to explore ways to challenge captivity.

THE CONNECTIONS BETWEEN Christianity and black liberation during the war years represented a tangle of hopes, frustrations, and conflicting impulses. No one in the Moravian settlement better embodied those tensions than the tavern worker Jacob, who with "tears in his eyes" persuaded the Brethren to buy him in 1775. Given an entrée into the closed community, Jacob did not assimilate placidly.

At first, he made himself an important figure in the tavern. He attained a fairly high degree of responsibility, holding a position something like an assistant to tavernkeeper Jacob Meyer, as a sort of hostler-barkeeper. Since the post involved daily contact with non-Moravian strangers, the Brethren might have wanted it done by another outsider. It is also likely, though, that Jacob's own talents played some part in his appointment. Jacob's first tongue was English, so he could communicate with English-speaking guests more readily than most Moravian men, few of whom yet spoke the language. Jacob also seems to have picked up German fairly quickly, for documents show him conversing on many occasions with Moravians. Thus, his linguistic ability allowed him to move easily between English guests and their German hosts, both of whom depended on him. He became an unusual variant of what historians have termed "cultural brokers," or multilingual interpreters who mediated between the many European, African, and Indian cultures in early America.[39]

38. Auf. Col., Apr. 10, 1776.

39. Evidence of Jacob's linguistic importance rests on deliberations by the elders in March 1778, when they considered moving him into another position. The board "thought of taking the Negro Jacob out of the tavern and putting him to the team and having Brother [Johann] Walther in the Tavern. The latter, however, cannot speak English, and Brother Meyer is much concerned about this." Walther's possible appointment as Jacob's replacement was referred to as his becoming Meyer's "assistant." Therefore, Jacob must have been something like an assistant tavernkeeper. Tavernkeeper Meyer also spoke English, but his many duties probably kept him from dealing with every customer, making the role of the hostler-barkeeper an important one. See Aelt. Conf., Mar. 31, Apr. 3, 1778; Salem Diary, Apr. 2, 1778, in Fries et al.,

There is even some indication Jacob was paid for his work. Although no record of wages has been found in account books, other Moravian-owned slaves sometimes received pay, and the Collegium discussed in 1775 how they could "manage to give [Jacob] clothing, food and salary." Jacob's job on the cultural front line of dealing with the non-Moravian public could at times even be dangerous, particularly during the tumultuous 1770s. On one occasion, a "shabby fellow" who had stayed at the tavern left wearing Meyer's slops, or shoes, as his own shoes were being repaired. "Jacob was sent after him, with his shoes, and when he received them he returned the slops; but when he was asked to pay for the mending of the shoes he drew his sword and drove the Negro away." Another time while fetching the tavern's cows from the country, he was attacked by a man wielding a club who struck him, demanding his clothes. After a tussle, Jacob escaped.[40]

In other ways, however, Jacob's actions displayed an undercurrent of protest against his forced servitude. Soon after granting his request to buy him in 1775, the elders complained that he showed insufficient gratitude. Salem administrator John Wallis reprimanded Jacob: "He has been bought by the mercy of the Collegium, but he shows no thankfulness. On the contrary, he is as mean and insolent as can be." For Moravian as well as non-Moravian masters, the notion of gratitude was an important psychological ingredient in the slaveholding relationship, because it fed their sense of paternal kindness. Good masters expected bondpersons to properly acknowledge the favor of being bought by a benevolent owner. If they did not, they violated the code of reciprocal obligation so dear to masters. For white Brethren, the notion of thankfulness took on added significance, since all believers in the redeemed community were required to show profound gratitude toward Christ. Jacob's failure to do so surprised and displeased the authorities. They griped, furthermore, about his attempts to seek companions among Moravian youth. Complaining that Jacob "tries to find friends among the young

eds., *Records*, III, 1226. On cultural brokers, see A. G. Roeber, " 'The Origin of Whatever Is Not English among Us': The Dutch-speaking and the German-speaking Peoples of Colonial British America," in Bernard Bailyn and Philip D. Morgan, eds., *Strangers within the Realm: Cultural Margins of the First British Empire* (Chapel Hill, N.C., 1991), 255. To be sure, the Moravian community had its share of more formal brokers. Enormous pressure was placed on storekeeper Traugott Bagge, for example, as an intermediary during the American Revolution. See James, *The Quiet People of the Land*.

40. Auf. Col., Mar. 15, 1775; Salem Diary, Aug. 30, 1776, June 3, 1777, in Fries et al., eds., *Records*, III, 1075, 1152.

people in the Single Brothers House," the overseers threatened to sell him unless he stopped visiting the house.[41]

Evidently taking the warning to heart, Jacob must have amended his behavior and sought religious instruction, for a year later, in July 1776, he applied for admission into the Salem congregation. His request impressed the Aeltesten Conferenz. Minister Gottfried Pretzel "spoke of the negro Jacob and his Reception into the congregation, giving him a good reputation." "We asked, with two lots, 'Shall we ask about this today?' 'Yes.' With three lots [yes, no, and blank], 'Can he be received next Sunday?' 'Yes.'" The new convert was expected to hew to approved interpretations of liberty and forget any hope of emancipation. Pretzel carefully explained to Jacob (perhaps after an inquiry by the latter) that baptism "does not mean that he becomes free and the equal of his master." The ceremony took place, and Jacob was now a brother. But as the ministers learned, Jacob remained unconvinced about the links between conversion and freedom, as though baptism, far from slowing his private impulse to rebel, actually ratified it.[42]

Restless under the restraints of brotherhood, Jacob secretly became a financial wheeler-dealer, accumulating a considerable stash through wages or side deals. In 1776, he used his savings to buy a watch from a white brother, Charles Holder, paying with gold and silver, then he traded it to another Moravian, Matthew Oesterlein, for a second watch. Whether he valued the watch for its own sake or whether he regarded it as a tradable investment is unknown. But the Collegium was furious when it learned of the deal and made all three participants return the items, even enforcing a certain notion of fairness and property rights by directing Holder to "return his money to the Negro, even if he cannot pay it all at once." Of far greater concern was the threat to order the deal posed, which the board hammered home to congregants: "Since it is indecent to deal with the Negro without the permission of his master, we have announced openly that Brethren shall not communicate nor deal with the Negroes in any way." The measure put Jacob in a kind of social limbo. Though a brother in the Unity, he was to be virtually shunned. To the authorities, Jacob's actions made his racial identity and enslaved social status supersede his spiritual regeneration. Having

41. Auf. Col., June 28, 1775. On Moravian expectations of gratitude by all believers, see Sommer, "A Different Kind of Freedom?" *Church History*, LXIII (1994), 224. On the notion of gratitude in the wider spectrum of paternalist thought, see Genovese, *Roll, Jordan, Roll*, 144.

42. Aelt. Conf., July 2, 1776, in Fries et al., eds., *Records*, III, 1085.

crossed the line, he was now lumped together with *all* blacks, including non-Moravians, as off-limits. Officials left no doubt about their message: Jacob was first an enslaved black, and only second a brother.[43]

Perhaps spurred on by the incident, Jacob continued to whittle at the limits of the allowable. In 1777, he was reported to have "stolen some money from Brother Meyer and on the whole does not behave as desired." The Collegium ruled that "he cannot stay any longer in the tavern." Tavern-keeper Meyer was instructed to confiscate Jacob's money and other valuables and "to punish him for his unfaithfulness." The elders offered another view—that Jacob had been "misled" and was not entirely to blame. "To this many Brethren have contributed by being too familiar with him, borrowing money from him, selling him things, etc. Jacob must be punished, but it remains to be seen whether this will have a salutary effect on him or whether we shall have to take other measures." Ministers again lectured white congregants that "in future all Brethren who offend in this way will be dealt with according to congregation discipline." They advised Meyer to "be more careful with the Negro so that he does not pretend to take authority upon himself." Officials finally moved Jacob out of the tavern to serve as teamster for the Single Brothers, apparently to increase supervision over him. The tactic seemed to produce the desired result. Perhaps Jacob found the comradeship he sought, away from the stresses of tavern service, for a year after his transfer he was reportedly "behaving very nicely with the Single Brothers."[44]

But, in 1779, Jacob struck back with rejuvenated boldness. He might have decided that membership in such a community was no great bargain, and it is perhaps possible to pin his assertiveness on developments in the war. Shifting their military focus to the South, the British won quick victories in Georgia, South Carolina, and Virginia in 1779. In June, British commander Henry Clinton renewed the offer of freedom to any rebel's slave who would help suppress the Americans, and again hundreds of slaves tried to escape to the British.[45]

In the middle of these events, Jacob began a frontal assault on Moravian

43. Auf. Col., Dec. 31, 1776.

44. Ibid., Dec. 31, 1777, Jan. 7, 1778, Feb. 8, 1779; Aelt. Conf., Dec. 30, 1777, Jan. 20, 1778; Salem Diary, Apr. 2, 1778, in Fries et al., eds., *Records,* III, 1226.

45. Salem Diary, May 18, 20, 1779, in Fries et al., eds., *Records,* III, 1303, 1304. On this phase of the southern campaign, see Don Higginbotham, *The War of American Independence: Military Attitudes, Policies, and Practice, 1763–1789* (New York, 1971), 353–356.

authority. He might very well have known about developments in the war, because reports filtered into Salem regularly. An American officer who had fled Charleston ahead of British siege forces and passed through Salem "could scarcely find words strong enough to describe the distress in that city." Whether Jacob's rising defiance can be attributed to such news is speculative, but his challenge to the Brethren was part of a torrent of heightened African-American resistance across the South. In May, the Salem diarist reported the theft of clothes and material from three places in Salem: "From the stable Wageman lost a silk neckerchief and a handkerchief, Sister Reuter lost twenty-eight skeins of cotton yarn, and from the Sisters House garden some stockings, gloves, etc. are missing." And, in July, George Stockburger reported a quarter crock of butter missing from his dairy. All the thefts were attributed to outsiders. In early August, however, Jacob "ran away . . . to escape punishment for his bad conduct of various kinds." He was captured in Bethabara and returned to Salem, where "he took his punishment without trying to beg off, and admitted that he was the thief who stole the things last Whitsuntide."[46]

The next day, "Jacob was whipped again, for he admitted that he had poisoned the Brothers' fine horse which died suddenly yesterday." He also admitted taking the clothes in May, but gave conflicting answers where he had hidden them, finally saying he had given them to Valentine Frey's slave in Friedberg. When questioned, that man (the same one who had run away with Sambo in the summer of 1775 and who evidently had been recaptured) "denied everything that Jacob had said about him, though Herbst's Negro, Sambo, declared there had been secret trading between the two." Jacob, the diarist concluded, was "full of wickedness and malice" and would be sold at the first opportunity "as far away as possible, for there is danger that he will do something worse out of spite."[47]

In September, Jacob was finally sold to Robert Lanier, a state assemblyman from Rowan County. "We have been hoping for signs of true repentance on the part of the negro, but he shows none, so it is better to sell him than to risk further damage from him." Jacob, it appears, had decided to end the charade of good behavior and contrition demanded by the Brethren.

---

46. Salem Diary, Mar. 23, Aug. 3–6, 1779, in Fries et al., eds., *Records*, III, 1296, 1311. On African-American reaction to military developments in the South, see Frey, *Water from the Rock*, chaps. 3–5.

47. Salem Diary, Aug. 4–6, 1779, in Fries et al., eds., *Records*, III, 1311.

Perhaps, from his vantage point, the winds of liberation were rising too fast to do otherwise. To their mutual relief, Jacob and the Moravians parted ways. He offended them by returning briefly to Salem in January 1780 to fetch some clothes. They "sent [him] away empty-handed, for in the first place they did not belong to him, and in the second place he had done much damage here." But that was not the last they heard of him. In December 1780, word reached Salem that Jacob still had not given up. He had run away from Robert Lanier.[48]

Jacob might have wanted to make his way to Cornwallis's army advancing north through the Carolina backcountry in pursuit of the Continental army. During the winter of 1780–1781, a steady stream of soldiers swarmed through the Moravian settlement, first American militia and cavalry, followed closely by Cornwallis's two-thousand-man army, which camped in Bethania on February 9. Sagging under the strain of these unwanted visits, Bethabara and Bethania were virtually ransacked for food. Refugees passed through just ahead of the armies, such as a family that "came in flight from Georgia, bringing about twenty Negroes; like those who preceded them they camped in the woods opposite the Tavern, and the place looked like a Negro village." Wherever the British army went, enslaved African Americans escaped to their lines, though the records are silent whether any blacks in Wachovia tried to flee with Cornwallis at this crucial juncture.[49]

After the two armies fought to a standoff at Guilford Courthouse just twenty-five miles east of Salem in March 1781, Cornwallis began the long trek to the coast that led him north to Yorktown and defeat in October. Bottled up in Yorktown, the British evicted the black soldiers and refugees who had followed and supported them, a betrayal that cut them loose to face the wrath of the Continental army and slaveowners. From behind their redoubts before their own surrender, the British could gaze out across a

48. Salem Diary, Sept. 15, 1779, Jan. 16, Dec. 30, 1780, in Fries et al., eds., *Records*, III, 1313, IV, 1522, 1580.

49. In 1780, elders reported that "the Bethabara wagon and two-horse team have been pressed and it is doubtful whether Johann Samuel should be sent with them." Perhaps they were afraid he would escape or be abducted—if the former, it was a sign they still did not trust him. See Salem Diary, June 14, 1780, Aelt. Conf., Aug. 7, 1780, in Fries et al., eds., *Records*, IV, 1546, 1595. On this stage of the war, see Higginbotham, *War of American Independence*, 352–368; Frey, *Water from the Rock*, 129–142; and Crow, "Liberty Men and Loyalists," in Hoffman, Tate, and Albert, eds., *An Uncivil War*, 125–178.

desolate battlefield strewn with black victims of smallpox and gunfire. For the great majority of African Americans, the dream of liberation that held such promise during the war ended dismally on the bluffs of Yorktown.[50]

MORAVIAN BRETHREN gathered in the Salem square on July 4, 1783, to give thanks and prayers for deliverance from the hostilities that had buffeted them for eight years. The occasion marked the first celebration of the war's end anywhere in the new nation. But the prayers masked unresolved stresses generated by the war for American Independence. White Moravians, particularly the young, had already begun stretching the sanctioned definition of freedom in America. And African Americans watching the ceremony could scarcely hail the end of a war that finished their own immediate hopes for freedom.[51]

The war left white Moravians' grip secure, but it had touched off a chain of events that challenged their connection between slavery and Christian social ethics. The war created unprecedented opportunities for the enslaved to contest their role in a turbulent world. African Americans knew a safe choice was open to them. Baptism would bring them into the exclusive Moravian society as members of the Christian family. Though acquiescence to the Moravian moral order was the price of inclusion, the covenant offered a seductive attraction for people looking to secure themselves in a perilous world.

Others refused the quid pro quo offered by the Moravians. Some no doubt did so out of dislike for Moravian culture, an unwillingness to adopt the faith, or as a form of muted resistance. For others, the liberating potential of the Revolutionary decade made assimilation into the masters' culture unpalatable. A powerful quest for freedom—a "black Declaration of Independence," in the words of one historian—inspired thousands of slaves in the 1770s. Some in Wachovia linked rejection of slavery and things Moravian with a radical consciousness that must be viewed in the context of the wider political and social crisis of the times. Whereas the Moravian ethos emphasized stability, order, and social hierarchy, African Americans sought

50. On black participation in the final phases of the war and its aftermath, see Frey, *Water from the Rock*, chaps. 5–6; Quarles, *Negro in the American Revolution*, 158–181; Wilson, *The Loyal Blacks*, 141–161.

51. See Adelaide L. Fries, "An Early Fourth of July Celebration," *JAH*, IX (1915), 469–474.

to destabilize their allotted place in that arrangement and create their own order based on alternative notions of liberty.[52]

It was Jacob, finally, whose struggle magnified the tension between freedom and obedience in the cosmos of white Moravians. First embracing the spiritual inclusiveness of that vision, he ultimately found it severely limiting, and whites could not use it to control him. Jacob's thinking and motivations cannot fully be known. His rejection of the Brethren might have stemmed as much from disgust with Christianity itself as with slavery. But it is equally possible he viewed himself as even more of a brother in the Christian family than whites, drawing inspiration for his rebellion from a prophetic vision of Christ the emancipator of souls *and* bodies. Who, he might have asked along with thousands of the enslaved, were the real chosen people?[53]

52. Benjamin Quarles, "The Revolutionary War as a Black Declaration of Independence," in Berlin and Hoffman, eds., *Slavery and Freedom,* 283–301.

53. On millenarian elements of Afro-Christianity, see Frey, "Shaking the Dry Bones," in Ownby, ed., *Black and White Cultural Interaction,* 25–28.

. . . .

CHAPTER FOUR

To Drink of One Spirit

For in one Spirit were we all baptized into one body,
whether Jews or Greeks, whether bond or free; and were
all made to drink of one Spirit.—I Cor. 12:13

 QUARANTINED ON THE margins of Moravian society, African Americans in 1780 might have been furtive friends among themselves, but they remained *Fremden*—strangers—to the white majority. Scattered in small numbers across the breadth of Wachovia, granted little chance for social contact, they could not easily build families or sustain comradeship. But as their numbers grew and as they gained greater dexterity with the German language, some of the enslaved again sought both a new faith and a sense of community within the Moravian Church. As black conversion accelerated into a new stage after the Revolution, the Moravian fellowship resembled scores of flourishing evangelical congregations across the South that fostered intense interracial spiritual bonding. To be sure, not all blacks received the hand of fellowship from white Moravians, and others turned it down outright. But a visible minority of black converts fused themselves into Moravian congregations, where they were invited to drink of one spirit with white Brethren. The church provided an unusual vehicle for intimate social and spiritual contact between German-speaking black and white Christians.[1]

An eighteenth-century brother or sister lived in a complex social world of

---

1. The Brethren cited the injunction "to drink of one Spirit" as inspiration for the inclusiveness of their church. August Gottlieb Spangenberg, *An Exposition of Christian Doctrine as Taught in the Protestant Church of the United Brethren or Unitas Fratrum*, ed. and trans. J. Kenneth Pfohl and Edmund Schwarze (1778; reprint, Winston-Salem, N.C., 1959), 406.

overlapping religious, family, and community bonds. Just as the body was the earthly vessel of the soul, so the social organization of the Moravian congregational polity housed its religious faith. A person could not simply exist independently for six days and then show up in church for a weekly dose of preaching on Sunday. One's identity was shaped every hour of every day by family, coworkers, and fellow choir members. All of these reinforced—or were supposed to reinforce—the principles that would ensure the Unity's survival. In this net of relationships was encoded a believer's place in the world. That place was never static. As a person aged, entered a new choir, trained at a skill, joined the workforce, and started a family, he or she negotiated each new step with church elders. Tension between individual desires and the church's needs was bound to occur, and the minutes of the boards reflect their daily struggle to reconcile the two. The Unity was only as strong as the faith and commitment of its adherents. In the span of years between birth and burial, the church tried to channel every fiber of a person's being toward service to Christ. A Moravian belonged to an extended church family.[2]

Black converts were absorbed—and absorbed themselves—into this intricate web of social relations as thoroughly as any white person. Mutual obligations bound them to other church members. Their subordinate legal status as slaves, moreover, did not always dictate a similar social standing. On the contrary, in many cases they enjoyed the same rights and privileges and were hedged in by the same constraints as whites. Church leaders were hardly color-blind; it would be implausible to argue that Moravian congregational life constituted any sort of golden age in eighteenth-century race relations. But equally important in mediating racial identity were other

2. For a paradigm of the Christian community as corporate family in late medieval and early modern Europe, see John Bossy, *Christianity in the West, 1400–1700* (New York, 1985); and for an equally penetrating exploration of the same theme at the community level, see David Sabean, *Power in the Blood: Popular Culture and Village Discourse in Early Modern Germany* (New York, 1984). Historians have long sought to understand the Puritan communities of New England as extended religious families with multiple layers of mutual obligation and supervision. The literature on this theme for the 18th-century South is much less extensive. Examples include Mechal Sobel, *The World They Made Together: Black and White Values in Eighteenth-Century Virginia* (Princeton, N.J., 1988); Rachel N. Klein, *Unification of a Slave State: The Rise of the Planter Class in the South Carolina Backcountry, 1760–1808* (Chapel Hill, N.C., 1990), chap. 9; Daniel B. Thorp, *The Moravian Community in Colonial North Carolina: Pluralism on the Southern Frontier* (Knoxville, Tenn., 1989); and Rhys Isaac, *The Transformation of Virginia, 1740–1790* (Chapel Hill, N.C., 1982).

characteristics that measured one's station in life, such as age, gender, and marital status. At some profound level, slave and master became brother and brother, sister and sister.

The irony was that to black Brethren the church represented both oppressor and ally. If they shared spiritual regeneration with whites, as church doctrine proclaimed, where did that equality end and worldly subjugation begin in a community where secular and spiritual concerns blurred so freely? How much was black desire for self-determination sacrificed by possible advantages of church membership? And how could Afro-Moravians maintain a sense of personal identity in a religious union designed to submerge the individual within the whole?

THAT BLACKS WOULD JOIN the Unity of Brethren in significant numbers might have seemed unlikely in the early 1780s. Johann Samuel was the first African American to join the North Carolina branch of the Unity in 1771; nine years later, after the banishment of Jacob, Samuel again remained as the only black brother. A gulf of hostility separated white Moravians from most African Americans. But the experiences of Sambo, Jacob, and others had proven the futility of direct resistance against the Moravians. And any prospect of black liberation by the British remained uncertain at best and was indeed erased by 1781.

In this tense climate, the strategic advantages of church membership might have again beckoned to slaves. Black adoption of the Moravian faith appears partly grounded on a deliberate decision to confront slavery in a less overtly hostile but equally direct way. By laying claim to the masters' covenant, slaves would undercut the supposed differences between them, chipping away at the rock of racism on which slavery rested. They could, in effect, challenge slavery at its brute core—the negation of their humanity.

A desire for worship also must have been a motivation. The middle passage had sundered Africans from the cords of human experience that defined their identities. Now, perhaps, black longing for spiritual anchoring could find satisfaction in certain parts of the Moravian message reinterpreted through the lens of racial slavery. The universality of sin and salvation could resonate with liberating clarity to the enslaved, involving, in a minister's words, a "recognition of our profound corruption, whereby a person must be thoroughly convinced that he is no better than the most godless person under the sun." The proposition that masters were as sinful as themselves appealed to slaves. Black Christians, moreover—and nothing suggests Afro-Moravians were any different—took the offer of Christ's martyrdom a step further than whites, personalizing and identifying with it as their own. Mankind had been granted a blanket pardon, but Christ loved *them* and had died especially to save them, the enslaved and dispossessed, not in spite of their disinheritedness, but because of it.[3]

No concept of predestination drove the Brethren, no belief that some people had been born to eternal damnation. There was not even a formal theology to be mastered. One merely had to feel a direct flood of Christian love in the heart. In this way, noted Lutheran minister Henry Melchior Muhlenberg with some scorn, "a missionary could perhaps bring about a certain feeling in the hearts of the Negroes without instruction." This absence of formal doctrine appealed to one Georgia slaveowner in 1775 whose goal was "to help him and his Negroes to see the Lord without sanctification," a desire "compatible with the new, so-called Moravian system, because it is something that can be felt." Or as one slave in Georgia said in a sly satire of European theological hairsplitting, "He would rather belong to the Moravian Brethren than to the High Church because the latter was always preaching about work and labor, whereas the former preached faith without works, and he was tired of working." Ministers of course wanted black disciples to know something of the faith they were adopting, and aspiring converts received religious lessons. But they did not have to learn a catechism.[4]

In any case, African Americans again began to court the Moravian Church. Three joined in 1780, followed by four more in 1783 and another in 1786. Small though these numbers were, they nonetheless represented the kernels of a germinating black Moravian community. One convert was a young woman named Ida, who had been bought for the Salem tavern in July 1778 under an unusual arrangement that promised her freedom in seventeen years. In March 1780, the elders noted hopefully: Ida "asks very urgently for baptism. A genuine grasping may be sensed in her and Brother

3. C.G.A. Oldendorp, *History of the Mission of the Evangelical Brethren on the Caribbean Islands of St. Thomas, St. Croix, and St. John,* ed. and trans. Arnold R. Highfield and Vladimir Barac (1770; reprint, Ann Arbor, Mich., 1987), 514; Howard Thurman, *Jesus and the Disinherited,* 2d ed. (Richmond, Ind., 1976); Albert Raboteau, *Slave Religion: The "Invisible Institution" in the Antebellum South* (New York, 1978); Lawrence W. Levine, *Black Culture and Black Consciousness: Afro-American Folk Thought from Slavery to Freedom* (New York, 1977), chap. 1.

4. Henry Melchior Muhlenberg, *The Journals of Henry Melchior Muhlenberg,* 3 vols., trans. Theodore G. Tappert and John W. Doberstein (Philadelphia, 1942–1958), II, 638, 683, 684.

and Sister Meyer gave her a good witness. The Saviour was therefore asked, May we regard the Negro woman Ida as a candidate for baptism?" They drew a "no" lot, indicating the decision of Christ, the Chief Elder, that she would have to wait.[5]

Though initially rebuffed, Ida continued pressing for baptism along with two others—Africans Sambo and Frank, who had lived as slaves of the Moravians since 1771. Cast adrift in America with little chance for communication, the pair must have felt strongly isolated, and both were initially hostile toward Christianity. For a long time, Sambo "stayed in his former heathen ways and mores." "We could not give him the right instruction," his memoir later reported, "because he understood only his native language and a little French."[6] German was at least the third European language to which Sambo had been exposed, and his refusal to learn it quickly was apparently a form of defiance. During the 1770s, he had run away and expressed his hatred of enslavement in other ways, drawing lashes from the Moravians in response.

But not long thereafter, according to his memoir, "he started to think about the status of his soul, attended diligently the Congregation meetings, and was eager to learn German and verses." Proficiency in a new language was an important first step in Sambo's acculturation, as it was for all displaced Africans in the Americas. The close connections between language and religion indicated how blacks began to assimilate into this Germanic culture. With at least a passing grasp of some German, Sambo soon "learned to see himself as the poorest sinner and to realize this evil." In December 1779: "Sambo has already expressed at various times his desire for baptism. Although he cannot express himself very understandably either in German or English, we nevertheless have noted meaningful signs of grace working in his heart." He applied for baptism, and though they drew a "no" lot, the elders resolved to "accept him" more than they had previously and "seek thereby to bring about in him the correct comprehension." In March, he and Ida were permitted to attend an important lovefeast, or *Liebesmahl*.[7]

5. Salem Diary, June 19, 1780, in Adelaide L. Fries et al., eds., *Records of the Moravians in North Carolina*, 11 vols. (Raleigh, N.C., 1922–1969), III, 1236; Auf. Col., July 22, 29, 1779; Aelt. Conf., Mar. 8, 1780.

6. Memoir of Abraham (trans. EH).

7. Memoir of Abraham; Aelt. Conf., Dec. 22, 1779, Mar. 22, 1780. On linguistic acculturation among Africans in the Americas, see Sidney Mintz and Richard Price, *The Birth of African-American Culture: An Anthropological Perspective* (1976; reprint, Boston, 1992); John

Meanwhile, Frank, who lived in Bethabara, also indicated "through his broken words that he stood in close communion with the Saviour." Affirmative lots were drawn for both his and Ida's admission into the church, and the two were baptized within a fortnight of each other in August 1780. Ida was christened Maria, and Frank received the name Christian. Sambo, meanwhile, traveled a more difficult path to baptism. The elders consulted the lot several more times, but it denied him on each occasion. His frustration grew at repeated rejection by the whimsy of the lot (or, as the Moravians would have it, the will of the Lord). "Sambo, who is extremely perplexed about his long-delayed baptism, should remain in our prayers at Christmas," the elders remarked. Finally, in late December 1780, they drew an affirmative lot, and the rite was performed. At the age of about fifty, the African warrior received a new name: Abraham.[8]

Others followed these converts into the Moravian Church, though sometimes through different processes of linguistic and cultural adaptation. Another African-born slave called Patty, who served in the Salem tavern, was described in 1783 as "very troubled about Holy Baptism and has urgently requested it." Patty, whom the Brethren had bought from a slaveowner in Salisbury, North Carolina, understood a little English, and so rather than trying to teach her German right away the Moravians proceeded in English. "The necessary instruction in the redeeming truths and in Holy Baptism will be imparted to her beforehand by Brother Friz in the English language, which she understands best." In late December, the church arranged her marriage to Christian, and three weeks later she was christened Anna and joined the Salem congregation. In time, Anna learned German as well, indicating a bilingualism or even multilingualism among Afro-Moravians that permitted flexible access to the white religious community as well as to non–German-speakers both within and outside Wachovia.[9]

Another black Moravian contingent took root in the rural Hope commu-

---

Thornton, *Africa and Africans in the Making of the Atlantic World, 1400–1680* (New York, 1992), 211–218; Peter H. Wood, *Black Majority: Negroes in Colonial South Carolina from 1670 through the Stono Rebellion* (New York, 1974), chap. 6; and Philip D. Morgan, "British Encounters with Africans and African-Americans, circa 1600 to 1780," in Bernard Bailyn and Philip D. Morgan, eds., *Strangers within the Realm: Cultural Margins of the First British Empire* (Chapel Hill, N.C., 1991), 203–207.

8. Memoir of Christian; Aelt. Conf., Aug. 12, 23, Dec. 13, 20, 1780.

9. Aelt. Conf., Dec. 11, 1782, July 23, 1783. On German-speaking African Americans in North Carolina, see William H. Gehrke, "Negro Slavery among the Germans in North Carolina," *NCHR*, XIV (1937), 311.

nity south of Salem. These worshipers, however, spoke English better than German, for they lived among the English-speaking Moravian emigrants from Maryland. One was Jupiter, the African-born king's son and former traveling companion of Abraham / Sambo during their forced journey from Virginia in 1771. Little is known about his activities during the subsequent decade, but he was evidently exposed to Moravian teachings in the Hope meetinghouse or by his master, John Douthit. "This man, very proud by nature, was first softened by the gospel and converted to Jesus," a church report noted. "In half Guinea language and half English he stammered his desire to belong to the flock of believers." By December 1781, the elders reported: "The Negro Jupiter in Hope has diligently attended instruction under Br. Fritz and now declares a longing for Holy Baptism, so that he thereby might become a Society member." A first lot drawn in December was negative, but another turned up positive in May, and the elders appointed three other black Moravian men—Johann Samuel, Christian, and Abraham—baptismal sponsors or witnesses for Jupiter. On a Sunday in May, the three traveled the five miles from Salem to the Hope meetinghouse to watch as Jupiter, clothed in white, was baptized and christened Paul. Another to join the Hope Society was a woman named Priscilla, a "widow and property of our Sr. Peddycort," who was born in Maryland in 1748 and "baptized in the English church." She moved south with the Peddycord (also spelled variously as Peddycort or Peddycoard) family and other English Moravians who settled in Hope in the 1770s. "She was taken into the congregation in 1783 and admitted in the following year to Holy Communion," remaining for years the only African-American communicant in Hope. The Afro-Moravian web was beginning to spread to the distant corners of Wachovia.[10]

One black worker, Oliver, pressed the Brethren with unusual aggressiveness to become Moravian. Born in King and Queen County, Virginia, in 1766, Oliver came to Wachovia from southern Virginia, where he evidently was living by the 1780s. His master was William Blackburne of Halifax

---

10. SAE, November 1802, "Nachricht von den Negern in der Wachau," pt. B, sec. 1, "Hope"; Aelt. Conf., May 15, Dec. 31, 1782. The familiar image of southern "born again" Christians, black and white, wading into shallow baptism ponds clothed in white bears some similarity to Moravian tradition. Although the Brethren did not believe in baptism by immersion and hence did not conduct the ceremony in a pond or pool, the candidate wore white clothing. As the elders arranged for Jupiter's baptism, they decided that "robes will not be used just now in connection with the baptism of adults in the country congregations, but that the baptismal candidates can appear in other kinds of white clothing" (Aelt. Conf., May 15, 1782).

County, Virginia, some eighty miles northeast of Salem. Oliver was first reported in the Moravian records in August 1784, working as a hired laborer in Bethania. The eighteen-year-old youth professed a longing for Christianity and sought to convince the Brethren of his desire to join their community. "The Negro Oliver in Bethania insists he would like for us to buy him," reported the elders. "His lease comes to an end at the beginning of January, and he has an inclination toward the Gemeine."[11]

Blackburne would not sell Oliver, but he refused to give up. "As his master in the year 1785 wanted to take him away from here and sell him to another master," his memoir later explained, "this put him in the greatest perplexity and sadness." In what was by now a familiar scene, "he begged us earnestly with tears that the Brothers should have consideration for him and buy him." In July 1785, Oliver was transferred to service in the Single Brothers' House in Salem, and, in February 1786, finally bowing to his "ardent and almost fierce perseverance," church officials bought him for one hundred dollars "in the hope that his soul may be saved." After several months of Bible lessons, a positive lot gave the elders permission to baptize him. They drew "Peter" from among several choices for Christian names, and his old name became a new surname. On November 12, 1786, Oliver was christened Peter Oliver and joined the Single Brothers' Choir. His quest showed how insistently some African Americans sought an intense personal relationship with God, the comfort of spiritual fellowship, the security of church membership, or all of these goals.[12]

Like all who joined the church, blacks were required to redefine themselves in Christian terms through the conversion experience. The Moravian theory of conversion, as expressed by Count Zinzendorf, was that "one must become a sinner, then one is given grace, and with that everything is accomplished." God would work quietly and gradually on the soul, without a long emotional struggle, until faith came miraculously and with it the assurance of salvation. Such an approach contrasted with that of other evan-

11. Peter Oliver, Bill of Sale, 1786; Aelt. Conf., Aug. 15, 1784.

12. Aelt. Conf., Feb. 12, 1786; Oliver, Bill of Sale, 1786; Memoir of Peter Oliver; Single Brothers' Diary, July 7, 1785, Feb. 18, 1786. Some also made emotional deathbed conversions, such as Kathy (or Cathy), the young tavern servant in Salem, Esther in Hope, and Rachel in Bethania. The last two were described as having spent a lifetime avoiding the gospel but after illness and acceptance of Christ were buried in the congregational graveyards. See Salem Diary, Sept. 22, 1777, in Fries et al., eds., *Records*, III, 1163; Death Notice of Esther, Nov. 23, 1790, in Hope Church A, Deaths; Death Notice of Rachel, Bethania Diary, Sept. 27, 1782.

gelicals such as the Methodists, who considered the soul a battleground for intense struggle between good and evil that threw many into long periods of self-torment about whether they had really been saved.[13]

Though the Moravian conversion experience was supposed to be smoother, it could also prove painful. That spiritual odyssey, documented in thousands of Moravian memoirs, followed a fairly formulaic progression. Typically, memoirists reported living an early life of abandon with no regard for salvation. This reckless indulgence in sinfulness gave way to doubt, fear, and guilt. Paralyzed by feelings of depravity and mortality, the wayward came to understand they were helpless and lost unless they acknowledged Christ's ransom. The revelation of knowledge flowing from that crisis-turned-catharsis inevitably ended in conversion and a sanctified life in the church.[14]

Because most black memoirs were written in the third person by ministers, they probably combine the subject's own oral testimony and the writer's idealized interpretation of what he believed to have happened. Behind their rigid emphasis on prescribed behavior, however, the memoirs reveal glimpses of the restless searching for faith by black converts. They spoke of enduring protracted anguish before joining the Moravian fellowship, much as black Baptists and Methodists spoke of spirit "travels" that transported them to revelation through dreams, prayers, and visions.[15]

In one rare black first-person memoir, Andrew, an African Moravian in Bethlehem, Pennsylvania, described himself as bedeviled by near-suicidal anguish. Taken from West Africa as a boy of about twelve in 1741, he was bought by a Moravian, Thomas Noble of New York, who sent him to school. Soon he was reading the New Testament and praying with the Noble family. "I was very anxious about my salvation and attempted to receive it through my own power," he wrote. But he was haunted with deadly visions and the sense of a monumental struggle within him. "There often came over me through prayer in my room such fear that I thought the devil was standing

13. Clarke Garrett, *Spirit Possession and Popular Religion: From the Camisards to the Shakers* (Baltimore, 1987), 102.

14. Beverly Prior Smaby, *The Transformation of Moravian Bethlehem: From Communal Mission to Family Economy* (Philadelphia, 1988), 145–180.

15. On the conversion experiences of other black Christians, see Mechal Sobel, *Trabelin' On: The Slave Journey to an Afro-Baptist Faith*, 2d ed. (Princeton, N.J., 1988), 90–97, 108–122; Raboteau, *Slave Religion*, chap. 3, 266–271; Clifton H. Johnson, eds., *God Struck Me Dead: Religious Conversion Experiences of Negro Ex-Slaves* (Philadelphia, 1969).

behind me. Once when I perceived this hard and troublesome road to salvation completely and saw no possibility to reach my goal, I resolved to throw
myself out of a window and thus make an end to my sinful life. I was already
standing in the opening and wanted to make the leap. Then it was as if
someone pulled me back. In the process I returned to my senses and with a
thousand tears begged forgiveness of the Savior." Rescued from the abyss,
Andrew came to "recognize my unworthiness and powerlessness daily, and
the Savior's love and mercy and his selfless passion and death made such an
impression on my heart that I wished nothing so much as to become a
genuine black offering to Jesus and a member of the congregation."[16]

Similarly, although less dramatically, Abraham in Salem was reported to
have endured a long quest before at last coming "to the thorough perception of his lost condition, and admitted openheartedly and repentantly to a
Brother what a slave of sin he had been up to now and how much he would
like to be saved and become happy." As portrayed in these accounts, both
men gained redemptive grace through a gentle flooding of divine love rather
than from the ecstatic moment of rapture or a concussive jolt of divine
power felt by many black evangelicals.[17]

It is difficult to know how sincerely these "genuine black offering[s] to
Jesus" considered themselves to have shed their former selves and been
"born again," or whether they simply gave a convincing impression of doing
so. African-born initiates could hardly have forgotten or rejected all their
beliefs, despite their professed acceptance of Christ. Outwardly, they gave
much evidence they had cast aside their former lives, which meant abandon-
ing African cultural and spiritual expressions likely to offend white Moravian sensibilities. Abraham, who had clung to his "former heathen ways and
mores" for many years, after conversion "used opportunities to announce to
other Negroes the truths of the Gospel," though he "could hardly express
himself in matters concerning his soul." Before his conversion, Frank could
be seen on the streets of Bethabara trying to earn money by dancing, or, in
the words of his memoir, "his peculiar turns of the body that no one could
imitate." Frank's movements signified a desire to preserve the cultural memory of African dance customs and even bring in some cash. Such a display
must have seemed incongruous in the austere Moravian community, and,

16. Daniel B. Thorp, "Chattel with a Soul: The Autobiography of a Moravian Slave," *PMHB*,
CXII (1988), 449–450.
17. Memoir of Abraham.

indeed, to white Brethren, a whirling African in their midst represented licentious idolatry. They were pleased that, after gaining "self-knowledge about his lost condition, [Frank's] whole way of walking changed, he spoke few words, and when one talked to him about his spiritual state one could clearly tell from his broken words that he stood in close communion with the Saviour." Yet his decision to forego dance and redirect his cultural expression into Christian fellowship could not have been easy. His conversion might well have been shadowed by a sense of loss, possibly emotional anguish, over familiar ways sacrificed.[18]

For these early black inductees, the passage from the old life to the new was symbolized by the baptismal ceremony. To Africans, the ritual bore some resemblance to initiation ceremonies they had already passed. Candidates for African secret societies entered the bush as adolescents and left as young adults. To formalize their rebirth, they were washed in a stream and dressed in fine clothes for their final return to the village. Christian baptism was really no different. Witness the baptism of Frank in Bethabara in August 1780:

> Brother Reichel . . . said we must walk with Jesus into a new life. He spoke especially to the candidate, and told him he would be cleansed of his sins through Holy Baptism. The congregation stood up and the baptismal water was brought into the room by two brothers. The candidate kneeled again; Brother Reichel asked the Saviour to cleanse this poor sinner and absolved him of all his sins with the laying on of hands. Brother Reichel asked the congregation: How are you baptised, who are baptised into Jesus Christ? Into his death. Into his death I baptise you Christian, in the name of the Father, Son and Holy Ghost. He placed his hand on the candidate's head and the congregation said amen. The water was taken away and the baptized fell on his face and prayed as several verses were sung. He stood up; Brother Reichel blessed him

18. Memoir of Abraham; Memoir of Christian; Oldendorp, *Caribbean Mission*, ed. and trans. Highfield and Barac, 249. See also the many passages on African and African-American dance in Roger D. Abrahams and John F. Szwed, eds., *After Africa: Extracts from British Travel Accounts and Journals of the Seventeenth, Eighteenth, and Nineteenth Centuries concerning the Slaves, Their Manners, and Customs in the British West Indies* (New Haven, Conn., 1983). One author calls African Americans' acceptance of certain kinds of Christian religious and social privileges at the expense of renouncing "heathen" ways "truly a Faustian bargain, the willingness to sell their own souls"; see Richard Price, *Alabi's World* (Baltimore, 1990), 67–68, 297 n. 15.

with the laying on of hands. The two brothers who had brought him into the room kissed him, and took him out of the room.

The elaborate ritual was grounded in the metaphors of death and rebirth found in the New Testament: the conferral of new life through water, the laying on of hands, and the kiss of peace. To the Brethren, such gestures signified far more than self-conscious attempts to emulate the first Christians. They represented a strict code handed down by the apostles to reaffirm the living, almost tangible, presence of Christ among his latter-day disciples. Ritual in the Moravian Church was not merely symbolic but a visceral communion with the Savior in God's earthly kingdom.[19]

The kiss of peace merits special attention as an emblem of the relationship of African Americans to the Moravian Church. The Unity placed strong emphasis on the kiss as a transmitter of the Holy Spirit. With deep roots in both Judaic and Hellenistic tradition, the kiss had been a key component of early Christian ritual. As a mystic symbol of holy grace, it had many purposes: a form of greeting, an act of reconciliation and reunion, a vehicle for initiating neophytes into the Christian brotherhood, a preface to the taking of Communion. "Salute one another with an holy kiss," Paul had advised (Rom. 16:16). In this nonerotic context, the kiss was passed from lips to lips rather than lips to cheek (at least in the early Christian church), since the mouth was believed to be the passageway to the soul and the conveyor of breath containing the spirit. "The Holy Spirit has made us temples of Christ," according to the ancient Greek church. "Therefore when we kiss each other's mouths, we are kissing the entrance of the temple."[20]

Moravians used the kiss as a gesture of affirmation from the earliest days of the renewed Unity in Herrnhut in the 1720s. Perhaps because of Count Zinzendorf's awareness of the potential erotic connotations of the act, the kiss was exchanged only by members of the same sex and probably on the

19. Bethabara Diary, Aug. 27, 1780. Bishop August Gottlieb Spangenberg was clear about the Unity's aim of erecting an ethics based on the New Testament. See Spangenberg, *An Exposition of Christian Doctrine*, ed. and trans. Pfohl and Schwarze, esp. 397–454. See also John S. Mbiti, *African Religions and Philosophy* (New York, 1969), 158–159, 231.

20. This discussion draws from Nicolas James Nicolas Perella's excellent study, *The Kiss Sacred and Profane: An Interpretive History of Kiss Symbolism and Related Religio-Erotic Themes* (Berkeley, Calif., 1969), chap. 1 (quotation on 27, from ancient baptism instructions). See also Willem Frijhoff, "The Kiss Sacred and Profane: Reflections on a Cross-Cultural Confrontation," in Jan N. Bremmer and Herman Roodenburg, eds., *A Cultural History of Gesture* (Ithaca, N.Y., 1992), 210–236.

cheek. An eighteenth-century engraving depicts two rows each of men and of women in Herrnhut exchanging kisses, although whether on the cheek or on the mouth is unclear. In any case, the spirit of the act remained the same as in the early Christian churches, signaling a transcendent moment of joyous union with Christ.[21]

For enslaved inductees into the Unity, the baptism ceremony climaxed by a kiss held powerful significance. It meant welcome and inclusion, a spiritual leveling, the acceptance of all into the fellowship of Christ. The kiss portended something of a dismantling, or at least a tempering, of the edifice of white domination. African Americans were recognized to carry the spark of divinity—to be, in effect, as much an extension of Christ as any white brother or sister. Moravian missionaries ushered slaves into black West Indian congregations in the 1730s with the kiss of peace, and the practice remained central to the incorporation of blacks into North Carolina congregations. The kiss embodied a quiet moment of high drama in a world where most Euro-Americans regarded Africans with a contempt often sliding easily into outright demonization.[22]

Yet to white Moravians, as to other slave masters across time and space, these acts of initiation also symbolized the erasure of the slave's former existence. The ritual of induction signified not only spiritual fellowship with Christ but the affirmation of power over the slave. No more direct statement of the rebirth of the initiate could be found than in the change of his or her name. If a name was an exterior badge of identity, then to replace it with a name of the master's choosing meant a symbolic retooling of the slave's

21. Kenneth G. Hamilton and J. Taylor Hamilton, *History of the Moravian Church: The Renewed Unitas Fratrum, 1722–1957* (Bethlehem, Pa., 1967), 38. For another example of the kiss in Moravian services, see Friedberg Diary, Apr. 4, 1773, in Fries et al., eds., *Records,* III, 781. Moravian Bishop August Spangenberg discusses the important role of the kiss in the early churches in *An Exposition of Christian Doctrine,* ed. and trans. Pfohl and Schwarze, 452–453. The engraving of the kiss in early Unity practice is reproduced in Jacob John Sessler, *Communal Pietism among Early American Moravians* (New York, 1933), opposite 134. Early Christian leaders also warned against the dangers of the "impure" kiss; see Perella, *The Kiss Sacred and Profane,* 29–31. In an entirely different context, Count Zinzendorf, "when he officiated at the wedding of a Christian Negress in St. Thomas, in accordance with the custom, kissed the bride"; see Arthur James Lewis, *Zinzendorf, the Ecumenical Pioneer: A Study in the Moravian Contribution to Christian Mission and Unity* (Philadelphia, 1962), 92.

22. Use of the kiss on Saint Thomas is cited in Oldendorp, *Caribbean Mission,* ed. and trans. Highfield and Barac, 332. Baptismal procedures for converts, climaxed by the kiss, are detailed in "At the Baptism of Adults from among the Heathen," *Liturgic Hymns of the United Brethren* (London, 1793), 115–120.

persona in the master's image. And the ultimate master in the case was presumed to be Christ. Just as the men who became Paul and Christian in the 1780s had been stripped of their African names upon arrival in America and redefined as Jupiter and Frank, so too their new Christian names were intended to submerge their new identities into the communal body. Freedom and submission in Christ were inseparable. But as an unmistakable mark of enslavement, the absence of a surname (the notable exceptions being Johann Samuel, Peter Oliver, and, a few years later, a man named John Immanuel) encoded the differences separating black Brethren from white.[23]

Though whites believed a "new birth" signified the transformation of the soul, the term might have couched another metaphorical meaning for the enslaved. If we accept Orlando Patterson's premise that slavery entailed the ultimate form of ostracism, or "social death," then absorption into the Moravian fellowship heralded social resurrection. A sense of the value attached by both whites and blacks to baptism—no doubt for different reasons—may be seen in a similar context in Brazil, where unbaptized slaves "are not considered as members of society, but rather as brute animals, until they can lawfully go to mass, confess their sins, and receive the sacrament." In much the same way, perhaps the most important thing the Unity offered black Brethren was a sense of belonging and recognition.[24]

Of course, membership in a Moravian congregation could not replace or duplicate the circle of gods and ancestors that African Moravians had left behind. The fundamental differences between Protestant Christianity and African traditional religions have been amply documented. Against a complex array of spirits and deities in the African world was set Christ the Redeemer. Africans, furthermore, had no equivalent theological understanding of original sin. Struggling to explain the concept to Africans in the West Indies, missionary C.G.A. Oldendorp "found it necessary to suggest 'uncleanliness,' 'evil,' or 'bad things' as terms to be used in its place." Even though memoirs described black converts as aware of their sinful natures, they probably understood that idea differently from white Brethren.[25]

23. Patterson, *Slavery and Social Death*, 54–55. On Moravian slave names, see Thorp, "Chattel with a Soul," *PMHB*, CXII (1988), 444.

24. Henry Koster, *Travels in Brazil* (London, 1817), in Robert E. Conrad, ed., *Children of God's Fire: A Documentary History of Black Slavery in Brazil* (Princeton, N.J., 1983), 187.

25. Oldendorp, *Caribbean Mission*, ed. and trans. Highfield and Barac, 200. On the comparison of African and Christian notions of sin, see Eugene D. Genovese, *Roll, Jordan, Roll: The*

Yet for Africans, as for white Brethren, there was no distinction between sacred and secular realms; everything had religious meaning. Religion was a corporate endeavor through which one's place in the world and relationship to God were defined. In this sense, perhaps the tightly knit congregations of the Brethren, which collapsed the spiritual and the social, appealed to Africans and African Americans alike. To be "born again" signified reentry into the world of the living. Perhaps that was why a group of slaves from Bethania asked permission in 1805 to hold a special observance on the second anniversary of the baptism of a black brother, John Immanuel. According to a minister, the delegation "asked to celebrate the baptismal-day—or as they call it—the birthday of the Negro John Immanuel."[26]

The crucial question of why some African Americans sought to join the church, however, is poised against the reality that the majority did not. The black population of the Moravian territory rose steadily after 1780. By 1790, white Brethren owned thirty-five slaves; by 1802, they owned seventy-three slaves, while free blacks and hired slaves pushed the black population to one hundred or more, some 7 or 8 percent of Wachovia's total. Yet, in the early nineteenth century, only fifteen African Americans called themselves Moravian—at most one fifth of the black population.

Part of the reason for these relatively low numbers is that whites did not view all blacks as potential converts. The settlement was always intended more as a moneymaking venture and as a refuge for European Brethren than as a mission base. Whites consequently never seriously attempted to evangelize to blacks in their own communities during the eighteenth century. The ministers preferred to wait for African Americans to show interest, then cultivate their curiosity. They were content to promote conversion on that small scale. Ministers also felt less inclination to win souls in rural areas where so many more blacks lived. Unlike Salem or Bethabara, where the need for social and congregational cohesion was paramount, life in the hinterland was less strictly monitored by the church, and parishioners were held to a lower standard of godliness. As a result, the impetus to convert blacks to minimize their contamination of the holy community was less

---

World the Slaves Made (New York, 1974), 246–247. Forrest G. Wood has likened African traditional religions and Christianity to "square pegs and round holes"; see Wood, *The Arrogance of Faith: Christianity and Race in America from the Colonial Era to the Twentieth Century* (New York, 1990), chap. 5.

26. Protocoll der Committee in Bethania, Nov. 18, 1805.

pressing. And since virtually all slaves in the Moravian countryside were owned by private individuals rather than the church, some masters even opposed mission work among bondpersons, like many slaveowners throughout the South.

Many African Americans themselves doubtless wanted no part of the ministers. The records tell little about those who remained unconverted, since scribes naturally focused on the success stories. Some simply rejected the whites' religion out of hand, whereas others might have thought that church membership entailed too much sacrifice of personal autonomy or too much association with whites. Blacks in rural Wachovia also had greater opportunity to form social and familial links; hence, they might have felt less need to erase their marginality by assimilating into the masters' culture.

Speculating on why most slaves remained unconverted, a Moravian mission society admitted: "There would be great obstacles to working among them, partly on account of their masters and partly on account of them. Many examples have shown, especially with such Negroes who live in the *Gemeinen,* how hard it is for the Gospel to find admittance among them. One cause may be found in their connections and dealings with whites, since one also observes this among Indians who have lived among whites." The last observation is unclear. Perhaps the ministers meant that slaves did not want to join the religion of their masters, or that they were put off by whites who themselves were poor Christians, or even that some masters opposed slave conversion.[27]

Despite growing numbers of black brothers and sisters, Moravian fellowship by no means held universal appeal for African Americans. The region's people remained split three ways by race and spiritual status: white Moravians, black Moravians, and black non-Moravians, each group representing a different perspective on black Christianity at a different time.

BLACK BRETHREN UNDERSTOOD they would share their lives intimately with white people. That bond was framed by the church's sense of identity as a large family bound together by the blood of Christ.

Under Count Zinzendorf's influence, the church, according to one scholar,

27. SAE, November 1793.

"came to be thought of as the bride of Jesus, and the believers were referred to as the family of God."[28] A person's relationship to this organic web of spiritual kin was complex, for the "family" of brothers and sisters could take on many layers of meaning, both literal and metaphorical, from nuclear family to choir to congregation to worldwide Unity. Cooperation and friction marked the daily routines of work, worship, and trade, for the interests of a community of two or three hundred meshed with and rubbed against the specific interests of each member. The success of the Moravian vision rested on the lure of inclusion in that group and the threat of exclusion from it. The nurture of the church family had to be made so attractive that to be shut off from it would be harsh punishment indeed.

This sense of group solidarity hinged on a ceaseless succession of church services, prayer meetings, and festivities. Sundays were devoted entirely to worship. In the morning, the faithful attended three services—the litany, the sermon, and the public reading of the *Nachrichten*, the Unity mission report. After a Bible reading in the afternoon came a *Singstunde*, or singing service, and prayer in the evening. Choir meetings throughout the week sustained further discussion of the gospel. In addition, at least one congregational meeting was held every evening during the week in Salem, Bethabara, Bethania, and Friedland. The *Losungen*, or daily Scripture texts, formed the core of these meetings. The texts were a collection of scriptural extracts, one for each day of the year, compiled in Germany and distributed in various languages to all congregations and mission outposts. Every day Brethren worldwide contemplated the same text—a crucial organizational and spiritual device.

Other rituals expanded the worship cycle. In the gender-segregated *Pedilavium*, or foot washing, Brethren reenacted the symbolic washing away of sin performed on the disciples by Christ in John 13. Beyond this normal routine, the yearly calendar was studded with special celebrations, such as a week-long series of Easter services culminating in a dramatic Easter morning sunrise service in God's Acre. Once a year, worshipers gathered for *Gemeintag*, or congregation day, for a reading of the Memorabilia, a written account of the previous year. Special observances of Christmas and the August 13 commemoration of the renewal of the Unity added further emo-

---

28. Gillian Lindt Gollin, *Moravians in Two Worlds: A Study of Changing Communities* (New York, 1967), 14.

tional impact to the cycle of consecration in the body of Christ. Ritual smoothed life's rough social edges. The discord normal in any small community often frayed relations among parishioners. If emotions ran too hot, a lovefeast could restore a sense of shared purpose.[29]

Within this close-knit community, so dependent on adherence to well-defined roles and deference to authority, relations between black and white Brethren might be characterized as "fraternalistic." The term is of course an offspring of the paternalism identified by some historians as an important feature of master-slave relations in the antebellum South. Paternalism is usually described as an ideology of social relations developed by planters to reconcile the contradiction between the brutality of slavery and their need to recognize the humanity of slaves. Claiming a sense of "responsibility" and "duty" toward their captives, slaveowners sought to preserve what they regarded as the moral and legal legitimacy of slavery while making the institution more humane. In turn, masters expected subservience and obligation from slaves, thus developing an immutable bond of dependency between ruler and ruled.[30]

Fraternalism incorporated many of these elements but differed in some key respects. Whereas paternalism describes an ethos underlying a master's view toward a slave or group of slaves, fraternalism characterizes the corporate relationship among black and white Moravians who, as nominal spiritual equals, owed allegiance to a higher authority, Christ. In this closed society, particularly in Salem and Bethabara, where most enslaved Brethren were owned communally and few whites were masters, it was the church and its custodians, the elders, who regulated social and spiritual life. Their job was to preserve unequal power relations among congregants while

29. The foregoing description is based on Fries et al., eds., *Records*, I, 418–424; Thorp, *Moravian Community*, 17–18; Sessler, *Communal Pietism among Early American Moravians*, 106–133; and Gollin, *Moravians in Two Worlds*, 20–22. Examples of lovefeasts held as conciliatory occasions may be found in Auf. Col., May 26, 1779; and Aelt. Conf., June 18, 1783.

30. Genovese, *Roll, Jordan, Roll*, esp. 3–7, 75–86; Alan Gallay, "The Origins of Slaveholders' Paternalism: George Whitefield, the Bryan Family, and the Great Awakening in the South," *JSH*, LIII (1987), 369–394. On the Gramscian constructions of hegemony and consent that have so influenced discussion of paternalism, see T. J. Jackson Lears, "The Concept of Cultural Hegemony: Problems and Possibilities," *AHR*, XC (1985), 567–593. For critiques of the concept of paternalism, see James Oakes, *The Ruling Race: A History of American Slaveholders* (New York, 1982); and Michael Tadman, *Speculators and Slaves: Masters, Traders, and Slaves in the Old South* (Madison, Wis., 1989).

smoothing over racial differences and promoting harmony based on spiritual kinship.[31]

This principle was carefully described by Bishop August Spangenberg, who, writing of black Moravians in Pennsylvania, explained: "Because of our love to them we do not free them, for they would be in a worse condition if they got free as if we kept them. Actually they are not slaves with us, and there is no difference between them and other Brothers and Sisters. They dress as we do, they eat what we eat, they work when we work, they rest when we rest, and they enjoy quite naturally what other Brothers and Sisters enjoy." Enslaved Brethren surely questioned the bishop's glowing contention that there was "no difference" between them and white Brethren. Nonetheless, the description offers a way to probe their lives inside this select circle.[32]

Foremost, fraternalism shaped spiritual relations between black and white Brethren. In church, blacks participated fully as members of the self-styled chosen people. Each of the six congregations had a meetinghouse. The Gemeinhaus in Bethabara, for example, was built in 1788 to supplant the original meetinghouse of the 1750s. Much like a Quaker meetinghouse, it employed a functional economy of style meant to embody the simple and quiet emotion of a regenerative faith. Whitewashed walls and oak floors in the square chapel expressed a plain aesthetics that directed the worshiper toward inner harmony and communion with the divine. Hymns from a hand-pumped organ in the back loft filled the room. Sitting at a small table in the front, the minister faced the congregation. The faithful sat on backless benches, men on one side of the aisle, women on the other, divided further into choir groupings. Here is where Johann Samuel and his family, Anna and Christian, Peter Oliver, and other blacks worshiped side by side on the same benches with Württembergers, Saxons, and Danes. Here black and white Brethren washed each other's feet in wooden tubs. Here—albeit for different reasons—they groped toward the chance that a common faith would replace the whip as the currency of interracial discourse.

31. I use the term "fraternalism" to describe relations among brothers *and* sisters because it reflects male hegemony in a group that collectively called itself the Unity of Brethren or *Brüdergemeine*, the Brothers' Congregation, a term encompassing men and women.

32. Memorandum of August Spangenberg, Jan. 8, 1760, quoted in Susan Lenius, "Slavery and the Moravian Church in North Carolina" (honors thesis, Moravian College, 1974), 108. See also Thorp, "Chattel with a Soul," *PMHB*, CXII (1988), 433–451 (quotation on 445).

Daily congregational routine was designed to achieve this possibility. *Abendmahl,* or Communion, reaffirmed the believer's pact with God, and Moravians took care to preserve that bond. When Johann Samuel lay ill with smallpox in 1781, the Bethabara minister took Samuel's portion to his home and administered it on his sickbed. Black Brethren took part, too, in the *Stundengebet,* or Hourly Intercession, a ritual requiring a team of brothers and sisters to maintain around-the-clock prayer for up to eight weeks. A man and a woman served one-hour shifts throughout the day and night, praying, reading, and singing hymns separately in their own rooms. The elders drew lots to select the group from a cross section of the adult choirs. In 1784, they drew five names from the Single Brothers' Choir, including Abraham's. Dubious about his spiritual state, perhaps because of some infraction, the elders asked the lot regarding the "doubt that had arisen concerning the Negro Abraham" and drew an affirmative answer. With God's approval, Abraham took his place in the *Stundenbetergesell-schaft,* or Hourly Intercession Society.[33]

Fragmentary evidence indicates that black Brethren were not simply going through the motions in church ritual but saw the devotional cycle as a vital way to affirm their relationship to God and their place in the community. Paul (previously Jupiter), for instance, was sold to another master in Rowan County, some twenty miles away, in the early nineteenth century but continued to return to Hope each year for the special Easter celebration. John Immanuel, baptized in 1804, as late as the 1830s still invited Moravian children—evidently both black and white—to an annual lovefeast on the anniversary of his baptism.[34]

Records also hint that black worshipers imbued certain practices with a distinctively Afro-Moravian meaning. Abraham, for example, derived special significance from the reading of the Unity *Nachrichten.* "He enjoyed the news from our missions in the West Indies very much, thought of it daily, and contributed his part." Perhaps he felt an affinity with blacks in the

33. Aelt. Conf., Feb. 4, 1784. Other instances of blacks being chosen for the *Stunden-betergesellschaft* are recorded in the same minutes, June 9, 1784, Jan. 17, 1787, Dec. 19, 1789, and June 5, 1790. All-black Moravian congregations in the West Indies also followed the practice. See Oldendorp, *Caribbean Mission,* ed. and trans. Highfield and Barac, 364. A description of the Hourly Intercession may be found in Adelaide L. Fries, "Moravian Customs: Our Inheritance," *TMHS,* XI, pt. 3 (1936), 248.

34. SAE, November 1802, "Nachricht von den Negern," pt. B, sec. 1, "Hope"; death notice of John Immanuel, Negro Congregation Diary, Aug. 25, 1835.

Figure 11. Bethabara Gemeinhaus. *Photograph, nineteenth century.*
Courtesy, Collection of Old Salem, Winston-Salem, North Carolina

West Indies, where he had lived before coming to North Carolina. He seems
to have seen himself as a member of a larger black Christian network, which
he tried to extend by his "contributions" and his teaching. Despite his lack of
fluency in either German or English, his memoir lauded his willingness to
"announce to other Negroes the truths of the Gospel." Abraham, in effect,
acted as a preacher, translating his own experience into terms relevant to
other blacks. Such commitment suggests that black brothers and sisters actively—sometimes aggressively—used European Moravian cultural forms
to express African sensibilities.[35]

Music played an important and well-known part in Moravian worship.
The Unity's musical heritage was steeped in the classical traditions of central Europe. Moravian composers on both sides of the Atlantic turned out a
rich and sophisticated abundance of chamber and choral works, including
some of the first classical music composed in America. Moravian ensembles
performed the complete works of Bach's sons. Every service was laced with
selections from the more than twenty-three hundred hymns written or
collected by the Brethren. Especially acclaimed by outside observers was
the Singstunde, a series of stanzas strung together from various hymns to

35. Memoir of Abraham. On slave preachers, see Raboteau, *Slave Religion*, 133–143; Genovese, *Roll, Jordan, Roll*, 255–279.

form a musical sermon. Music accompanied the rhythm of life outside the church. Night watchmen sang hymns on their rounds; harvesters sang in the fields. All Moravian children learned music in school.[36]

Music held no less sacred power for black converts. From the earliest days of slavery, the adaptation of African musical traditions to African-American needs and conditions was a long and complex process. One of the most important factors in this musical journey was the growing black acceptance of Christianity after the middle of the eighteenth century. Colonial ministers often ascribed a celestial quality to the singing of Christian music by African Americans. Black Brethren adapted likewise to Moravian music. During services, blacks and whites sang together—in German. Black children educated in Moravian schools developed advanced singing and instrumental capability on flute and violin in the classical tradition of the Unity—vivid evidence of their thorough absorption of elements of Germanic culture. In 1817, a minister from Salem, Peter Wolle, described in somewhat less-glowing terms the mingling of voices during a service he led in a Friedberg home:

> Soon I had to step behind the table and preach. About 20 Negroes were present, and also a bench full of [white] young men and 3 women. All of those present, the Negroes, and especially John Spach sang in a loud voice the Methodist melody (short meter) d / g a h a / g e d etc. I will always remember the first verse because of the horrible dissonances that appeared in it, because the women sang in nothing but pure fifths. In order to correct this mistake, I succeeded in the second verse to hit their tone, so that I could at least unite the two parts.

Even if the singing sounded dissonant to this trained musician, it helped break down the wall of racial slavery that divided black from white, if only for the duration of the service.[37]

---

36. Thorp, *Moravian Community*, 18–19; Maurer Maurer, "Music in Wachovia, 1753–1800," *WMQ*, 3d Ser., VIII (1951), 214–227; Jeannine S. Ingram, "Music in American Moravian Communities: Transplanted Traditions in Indigenous Practices," *Communal Societies*, II (1982), 39–52; Alice M. Caldwell, "Liturgical and Social Change in Moravian Communities, 1750–1823," *Communal Societies*, IX (1989), 23–38.

37. Death notice of Christian Samuel, in Negro Congregation Diary, Mar. 20, 1826; Diary of Peter Wolle, Nov. 2, 1817. Blacks were singing in German elsewhere in 18th- and 19th-century America as well. See, for example, the entry of Dec. 11, 1778, in Muhlenberg, *Journals*, trans. Tappert and Doberstein, III, 203. On early African-American music, see Dena J. Epstein, *Sinful Tunes and Spirituals: Black Folk Music to the Civil War* (Urbana, Ill., 1977); Eileen Southern, *Music of Black Americans: A History* (New York, 1971).

Like whites, black Brethren were carefully groomed to identify with their choirs, perhaps the most important vehicle for instilling and reaffirming Moravian values from childhood until death. A brother or sister passed from one choir to the next at each subsequent stage of life, drawing spiritual sustenance from affinities of gender, age, and marital status with other congregants who became fictive kin. Congregations were thus divided into eleven choirs: Infants, Young Boys, Young Girls, Older Boys, Older Girls, Single Brothers, Single Sisters, Married Men, Married Women, Widows and Widowers. Although all choirs worshiped together, only a few shared living quarters. But those few accommodations were important to choir members and the community. The most prominent examples of such group-ings were the Single Brothers' and Single Sisters' Houses in Salem. Mora-vian children in Salem attended school between the ages of five and thirteen, then left home to live at one of the houses with either the Older Boys' or Older Girls' Choir. There they apprenticed at a craft, learned a skill, or, as young women sometimes did, hired themselves out as domestics. And there they lived until they married or died.[38]

Choirs gathered in the evenings for prayer in the *Saal*, or meeting room. They worshiped together in church. Choir leaders held interviews called *Sprechen* (speakings) with their charges each month and before Commu-nion to determine their spiritual condition. Records of house conferences from the Single Brothers' Choir reveal how leaders handled the brothers with a mix of gentle counseling and forceful discipline. To rein in signs of straying devotion, the house *Vorsteher*, or supervisor, harangued them to make their beds, clean their rooms, avoid soldiers, shun the tavern, stop urinating in front of the house, and quit tormenting the house cats.[39]

At least three men—Jacob, Abraham, and Peter Oliver—were members of the Single Brothers' Choir in Salem at various times between 1775 and 1788. The choir preserved many of the communal ideals of the early Wa-chovia settlement. Brothers shared literally every aspect of their lives in the large four-story building on Salem's central square. They ate in the common mess hall, slept in the dormitory, worshiped in the Saal, toiled in the work-shops, and sometimes boisterously enjoyed products from their distillery

38. The origins and development of the choir system remain a source of debate among historians. For a summary of competing views, see Thorp, *Moravian Community*, 60–62.

39. Protocoll der Haus-Conferenz der led. Brn. in Salem, 1774–1782 [Minutes of the House-Conference of the Single Brothers in Salem], May 25, 1774; Single Sisters' Diary.

far into the night. It is not known for certain whether blacks lived in the house; however, Afro-Moravians lived in the brothers' and sisters' houses in Bethlehem, and nothing suggests they did not in Salem as well, since virtually every other phase of congregational life was racially integrated.

Jacob worked as house teamster in the late 1770s, and Peter Oliver played an even more integral role in the house, working in the brothers' kitchen, craft shop, and garden. Abraham was a choir member between 1780 and 1785. Even if he did not live in the dormitory, he could have made the short walk up the street from the tannery to the brothers' house for meals, and he certainly participated in the cycle of choir meetings, prayer groups, and speakings. Thus, at the most basic levels of daily activity in the choir—eating, washing, working, worshiping, and probably sleeping in some cases—blacks and whites were united more by gender than they were divided by race.[40]

The philosophy of the choir system might even have struck a resonant chord with African Moravians. Like secret societies in West Africa, the Moravian choir as a source of order and initiation was at least roughly familiar to Africans and perhaps helped ease their entry into the Unity.

PRAYER, SONG, AND WORK provided important arenas of interracial contact and fostered a rough-and-tumble leveling in some aspects of daily life. But white and black Moravians hardly shared perfect equality: inescapably, whites were legally free, and blacks were not. Baptism gave black Brethren no instant access to power; sometimes they were treated more as wards of the church than as equal partners in the Christian drama. No black is known to have served on any of the myriad official boards and committees. Nor is there any record of black participation in congregational council meetings and elections of church officers. Enslavement posed an insoluble contradiction, for how could one be at once a brother or sister and also a slave?

This duality tinged the treatment of blacks by the church disciplinary system. Historians have called the evangelical churches the "moral courts"

40. No published material exists on the history of the Single Brothers' Choir in Salem. The most complete overview is contained in the unpublished Old Salem, Inc., Interpretive Staff Manual, sec. 9. See also Thorp, "Chattel with a Soul," *PMHB*, CXII (1988), 433–451. The choir might have originated partly in the European guild system and sustained some of its gendered social and labor functions in America. See Merry E. Wiesner, "Guilds, Male Bonding, and Women's Work in Early Modern Germany," *Gender and History,* I (1989), 125–137.

of frontier society, and in the Moravian theocracy that role was paramount. Whether stopping conversation between single men and women or reprimanding men for submitting to their "clever and quarrelsome wives," pastors forever sought to bend congregants to their vision of cooperation and morality. The Hope Brotherly Agreement of 1785, for instance, denounced as "unbecoming to our Brothers and Sisters" the "worldly Customs" of "Horse-racing, Shooting Matches, boxing and fighting, as well as all Sorts of Frolicks, such as night Spinning and Cottonpicking, and Cornhuskings at Night, intended for merriment, to which numbers of People of both sexes are invited to meeting." Those who did not "walk worthily" and indulged in such frivolities were excluded from fellowship and held in a kind of spiritual purgatory until they repented.[41]

Black Brethren received much of the same discipline as whites. But exclusion from Communion held a double meaning for black Brethren. Any time a black brother or sister spoke "insolently" to a white, shirked work, or committed a sexual offense, that act signaled a challenge not only to the church but to bondage itself. Since whites equated black acceptance of order with obedience to enslavement, excluding blacks from Communion was intended to remind them of the virtues of submission both as church members and as slaves.

Sanctions against Johann Samuel in 1782 illustrate the workings of the disciplinary machinery. There was a "wretched incident regarding the Negro Johann Samuel in Bethabara and Margaret Schor in the mill there." "Uncouth offenses easily could have arisen as a result." The elders usually left details of transgressions out of their reports, and so the nature of the incident is unclear (it is one of the few bits of evidence from the eighteenth century that even hints of the possibility of interracial sexuality). Whatever the offense, elders did not mention Margaret Schor's fate but barred Samuel

41. "Brotherly Agreement about Rules and Orders for the Brethren's Congregation in and about Hope Settlement, 1785"; Auf. Col., June 10, 1783; Thorp, *Moravian Community,* 99–100. For further context, see Elisabeth Sommer, "A Different Kind of Freedom? Order and Discipline among the Moravian Brethren in Germany and Salem, North Carolina, 1771–1801," *Church History,* LXII (1994), 221–234; William W. Sweet, "The Churches as Moral Courts of the Frontier," *Church History,* II (1933), 3–21; Henry S. Stroupe, " 'Cite Them Both to Attend the Next Church Conference': Social Control by North Carolina Baptist Churches, 1772–1908," *NCHR,* LII (1975), 156–170; and Sobel, *The World They Made Together,* 190–197. Sometimes Moravians appear to have "shunned" those they excluded but less frequently than the Amish, with whom the custom was more commonly associated.

from Communion "until he talks candidly about his past progress and we can reasonably be set at rest about the condition of his heart."[42]

Ministers viewed human nature as prone to sin and were patient with backsliders—to a point. If the elders detected a lack of self-searching in sinners, they leaned on them to intensify the quest for contrition. Their displeasure with Johann Samuel was apparent when, some three weeks after his infraction, he still had not "spoken out frankly about what ha[d] occurred in his progress nor confessed his sinfulness. We still cannot readmit him to Holy Communion." It is not known whether pressure was subsequently applied to Samuel, but a month later the elders reported that he "regrets his previous wretched behavior and asks for readmission to communion." Only final approval by the lot could confirm a miscreant's readmission, and Samuel had to wait through two drawings before rejoining select company at the Lord's Supper.[43]

A second incident involving Johann Samuel tells us a little more about Afro-Moravians' role in church discipline. In 1785, the elders learned of "a distressing story in Bethabara." "As a result, Sister Rose and the Negro Samuel remain away from communion." Again, the details of the case are vague. Anna Rosina Rose and her husband, Peter, managed the Bethabara farm and thus were Samuel's supervisors. Beyond that, it is impossible to say whether Sister Rose and Brother Samuel quarreled, conspired to break some rule, or formed a romantic attachment. After both were excluded from Communion, the Roses quit Wachovia altogether and moved to Pennsylvania.[44]

Murky as the affair remains, it suggests certain conclusions nonetheless. Insofar as both Samuel and Sister Rose were deemed co-culprits, they received the same punishment. Samuel, though enslaved, was faulted no more or less than a white person; rather, the elders treated them both as errant children. Moravian fraternalism, though never color-blind or secure, still fostered a certain limited code of justice that transcended race and racism as lenses through which congregants viewed each other.

Black Brethren might even have turned the disciplinary system to advantage. In one sense, the strict moral code might have been daunting to enslaved people seeking more control over their lives. Paradoxically, however,

42. Aelt. Conf., June 19, 1782.
43. Ibid., July 10, Aug. 7, 28, 1782.
44. Ibid., Mar. 22, 27, 1785.

the seemingly suffocating clinch of regulations actually gave slaves room to maneuver in ways they could not do outside the church. There were a great many rules to follow, but if the punishment for breaking one involved no more than suspension from Communion, blacks might have felt less inhibited about challenging them. An offense would have to be judged very serious, or would have to be repeated often, for an enslaved brother or sister to be sold.[45]

Whatever Johann Samuel did with Sister Rose, then, was done with the knowledge it was forbidden, and therefore he dared to pose an open affront to white propriety. Suppose, for example, that the two argued heatedly; if Samuel could "talk back" to a white woman and receive only a suspension from Communion instead of a whipping or worse that he likely would have received elsewhere in the South, he probably would have viewed the trade-off as acceptable. Similarly, when Abraham "behaved badly" in 1782, he received the same relatively light punishment. The price of such license was a simple admission of error and a promise to change. Like their white counterparts, blacks were forever being barred from Communion and readmitted, often as long as six months later. They could challenge slavery in small ways without permanently forfeiting stature in the Unity.[46]

Church boards resolved disputes between black and white members, as in 1787 when the Bethabara Committee mediated an argument between Johann Samuel and Bethabara farmer Johann George Aust, who complained that Samuel, searching for a horse, trespassed on his land. Samuel showed little bashfulness in counterattacking Aust during the hearing, accusing him of acting like a "reckless ruffian" who had issued a torrent of threats at Samuel. The Committee sided with the black brother, reprimanding Aust for his "disgraceful conduct."[47]

And at a time when blacks could not testify against whites in North Carolina courts, black Moravian voices were heard with relative respect in what served as the church court. In 1789, the Aufseher Collegium sought witnesses to help resolve a quarrel between two white Brethren, one of

45. Only one exception to that rule is known—Paul, of Hope, who was sold with his family to a new master in Rowan County some 20 miles away, though he continued to return to Hope for Easter services each year; see SAE, November 1802, "Nachricht von den Negern," pt. B, sec. 1, "Hope."
46. Aelt. Conf., Feb. 23, 1782.
47. Protokolle der Committee in Bethabara, Aug. 21, 1787.

whom was tavernkeeper Jacob Meyer. "The testimony of the Negro Christian, who served at that time in the tavern, can be looked upon as valid,
because his way of life is so that it shall be legitimate." Thus, in exchange for
forced acquiescence to slavery, the church's quasi-judicial system gave black
Brethren a claim in the court of divine law.[48]

FAMILY METAPHORS dominated the Brethren's concept of their place in the
world, and the church played a central role in black Moravian family life.
Historians have noted that African-American efforts to build coherent family lives during the last quarter of the eighteenth century evolved "in the
midst of a larger struggle for political independence and self-definition" during the age of the American Revolution. Though slave families were subject
to multiple disruptions, they imparted strength to thousands and conveyed
another form of African-American cultural adaptation. But little understood
is how the quest for family stability overlapped with Afro-Christianity, one
of the other emerging forms of black expression within that broader struggle. In Moravian communities, those two forces fused inseparably. Ministers
tried to shape black family life to fit their standards of propriety. But black
Brethren used their own ideals of kinship to express something far more
important—a distinct identity within the church family.[49]

Only a few isolated black families lived in the Moravian settlement during its early years. Some people were able to perpetuate long-distance relationships. On Christmas Eve 1779, Johann Samuel went "to visit his brother
on Dan River." Still, because of the relatively late development of the settle-

48. Aelt. Conf., Feb. 23, 1782; Auf. Col., Jan. 20, 1789. On the barring of black testimony in
North Carolina courts, see Ernest James Clark, Jr., "Aspects of the North Carolina Slave Code,
1715–1860," *NCHR*, XXXIX (1962), 153.

49. Mary Beth Norton, Herbert G. Gutman, and Ira Berlin, "The Afro-American Family in
the Age of Revolution," in Ira Berlin and Ronald Hoffman, eds., *Slavery and Freedom in the
Age of the American Revolution* (Charlottesville, Va., 1983), 175. On the development of
African-American family life, see also Herbert G. Gutman, *The Black Family in Slavery and
Freedom, 1750–1925* (New York, 1976); Allan Kulikoff, "The Origins of Afro-American Society in Tidewater Maryland and Virginia, 1700 to 1790," *WMQ*, 3d Ser., XXXV (1978), 226–
259; Ann Patton Malone, *Sweet Chariot: Slave Family and Household Structure in Nineteenth-
Century Louisiana* (Chapel Hill, N.C., 1992); and Brenda E. Stevenson, *Life in Black and White:
Family and Community in the Slave South* (New York, 1996). Surprisingly, few of the major
works on black family life in the early Republic and antebellum periods discuss the topic in
connection with black Christianity. The reverse critique might be directed at scholars of black
religion as well.

ment and the small size of the black population, some fifteen to twenty years passed before any kind of coherent black family life emerged.[50]

Slave marriages, moreover, faced other roadblocks, since not only were they legally invalid but they had no Christian standing in the eyes of white Brethren if the partners were not converted. Whites wanted to promote slave marriages, but only on their own terms, namely, within the church. Like many other slaveholders, white Brethren hoped that stable families would root bondpersons at home and prevent them from escaping. The idea of marriage as a calming influence occurred to the ministers during the tense 1770s when slave restlessness was at a peak. After a slave was flogged in 1776, the elders found it "desirable if our other Negroes could be married." They tried several times to arrange a match to settle Johann Samuel. On one occasion, after he was "led astray" by a "wretched" white brother (in some unspecified way), the elders concluded that Samuel "should rightly marry, and indeed soon." Marriage and the power to sanction or deny it were crucial elements in their use of religion as social control. If slaves could marry only within the church, they had an obvious incentive to convert.[51]

The church took an active part in arranging marriages for white and black members alike. "Brokering" matches might better describe the ministers' role, for the elders negotiated a complex process involving the wishes of prospective partners, the church, and the Lord's will as revealed by the lot. A single man who wished to marry had to go through the elders. He proposed a match to them, and, if they deemed it suitable, they put it to the sister in question. If she agreed, the elders sought approval from the lot, and an affirmative answer allowed the couple to marry. The elders could also decide that certain people ought to be married, again negotiating with both. But if the elders found a proposed match unsuitable or if the woman declined the offer or the Lord refused assent, the procedure would have to start all over with a different woman. The intricate procedure guaranteed individuals a say in their matrimony, although women were not allowed to initiate a marriage proposal. In theory, no one married unwillingly. In practice, the

50. Bethabara Diary, Dec. 24, 1779, in Fries et al., eds., *Records*, III, 1338.

51. Aelt. Conf., May 21, 1776, Sept. 27, Oct. 4, 1780. On Moravian views of the sanctity of marriage, see F. Ernest Stoeffler, *German Pietism during the Eighteenth Century* (Leiden, 1973), 153; Oldendorp, *Caribbean Mission*, ed. and trans. Highfield and Barac, 333. On the practice of encouraging stable slave family life as a means of social control, see Norton, Gutman, and Berlin, "Afro-American Family," in Berlin and Hoffman, eds., *Slavery and Freedom*, 184; and Genovese, *Roll, Jordan, Roll*, 452.

elders could pressure a reluctant prospective partner to acquiesce if they deemed a match advantageous for the community.[52]

Black brothers and sisters who wished to marry, or who the elders thought should marry, followed these same elaborate steps. After deciding in 1780 that Johann Samuel needed a wife, the elders went to work to find him one. "The only Negro woman here is Maria, who works in the Tavern. Thus there is no need to ask the lot about it, but rather to proceed." They decided that the couple should move into the old Single Brothers' House in Betha-bara, where Maria would take over the communal cooking. A minister, Brother Graff, "will talk with Johann Samuel himself and ask if he wants to marry Maria. After this the proposal is made to Maria." Graff's interview with Samuel was a success: Samuel agreed to marry Maria, and she accepted the match as well. Though the elders decided not to publish the banns for the couple, their betrothal would be "commended to the remembrance of the communicants" in Salem and Bethabara. "The marriage will take place Sat-urday in Bethabara in a general meeting, but one in which no strangers will be allowed. On this day a wagon will be sent out from here to carry Maria and her things to Bethabara." Nine days later, "Johann Samuel's wedding took place . . . amid a blessed sense of grace." Johann and Maria became the first Afro-Moravian couple in the South.[53]

The number of black families increased as more African Americans con-verted in the 1780s. Several black brothers tried to seek out their own part-ners, only to be stopped, not because they were black, but because they were Moravian. When Peter Oliver tried to court the sister of another slave in Salem, he was told that, "as a Brother, he cannot engage in such matters, but should wait" until the elders could "provide opportunity for him to marry." On another occasion, Abraham (who had been stolen from his wife and fam-ily in Africa years earlier) took an interest in Patty (later Anna). The elders preferred to match her to Christian, then in Bethabara, and put the couple up to live and serve in the Salem tavern. In 1783, the board arranged for Christian to come to Salem to discuss matrimony with Patty. Both partners agreed to the match, and in early December the marriage of Christian and Patty/Anna referred to above took place. "Brother Fritz, who came from Hope, married our Negro Brother Christian, of Bethabara, to the Negress

52. On Moravian marriage practices, see Gollin, *Moravians in Two Worlds*, 52–62, 110–127.
53. Aelt. Conf., Oct. 4, 11, 18, 25, Dec. 2, 6, 13, 1780.

Patty, who is a candidate for baptism. The marriage took place at the tavern."[54] They became the second black Moravian couple in North Carolina.

As for Abraham, the elders made an exception to the general rule that brothers and sisters could marry only within the church community. They proposed that his master, tanner Heinrich Herbst, buy a woman named Sarah who was serving in Bethania. The intent was to expose Sarah to more intensive Christian teaching and to wed her to Abraham. Though she was not converted, Sarah's wishes were consulted nonetheless. In July 1785, Sarah's owner agreed to sell her to Herbst, "but the event cannot take place before Sarah is willing. Therefore, when the purchase is settled, an opportunity should be provided for her to get to know Abraham." She soon agreed to the match, but, though they were married, Sarah was never baptized; Abraham was described as "very troubled" about her soul, "and he often mentioned his concern about her unhappy state of heart."[55]

As such examples show, the system of seeking or being matched to a spouse was both restrictive and empowering for black Moravians. Their choice of prospective partners was limited to mates approved by the church. Since single people had no chance to court openly, marriages based on romantic love must have been rare. Black Brethren also were forced to contend with the church's interference in their family lives. Like all slave masters, church officials wielded a heavy hand in slave family matters simply by deciding who could live where and how. On the other hand, blacks retained a measure of control in determining their partners. Men could actively seek a wife, whereas women could veto a match, though none is known to have done so.

Enslaved brothers and sisters also knew that the church wanted to legitimate their marriages. Missionary C.G.A. Oldendorp wrote disapprovingly that non-Moravian masters in the West Indies did not respect slave marriages and "continued their practice of separating married couples to suit their own convenience." In Wachovia, the church sought to preserve the integrity of black Moravian families. Married couples generally lived together (though some couples lived on separate farms in rural areas), and the church exerted strong pressure on masters to prevent the sale of Moravian or even

54. Ibid., Nov. 6, 1782, Sept. 9, Nov. 19, December 1783, June 20, 1787; Salem Diary, Dec. 2, 1783, in Fries et al., eds., *Records,* IV, 1844.
55. Aelt. Conf., June 22, July 20, 27, 1785; Memoir of Abraham.

baptized slaves. On that point the *Landarbeiter Conferenz*, a panel of ministers from the rural congregations, made an explicit directive in 1781: "When
Society members request to have children of their still-heathen Negroes
baptized—for example Jupiter's child at Douthid's—it can occur on condition
that masters be bound on their conscience to raise them for the Lord, and
not to sell them for *Profits* to outside people." At a time when the possibility
of separation from family posed a daily threat for slaves throughout America, such a pledge was no small consideration. It was also a clear incentive for
black parents to get their children baptized, and by doing so they used the
policy to form sturdy family enclaves within the larger church clan. At the
same time, of course, the preservation of family unity as an expression of a
pact between black Moravians and Christ bore all the signs of control. The
threat of sale, whether spoken or not, ominously undergirded an outwardly
benign policy.[56]

There were no interracial marriages, though the church had not always
opposed such unions. On Saint Thomas in 1738, missionary Matthaeus
Freundlich married his assistant, a free, literate mulatto named Rebekka.
She had become a devoted follower of the Brethren in the 1730s and helped
to spread the gospel among slaves on the island. Missionaries believed her
"work among the Negro women, the majority of whom were married, would
be even more effective if she were married herself" and that marriage would
erase "any misgivings concerning the propriety of her close association with
the Brethren." In North Carolina, however, the slave codes of 1715 and 1741
outlawed interracial marriages, and the Brethren certainly followed the law.
Church policy joined with legal statute to enforce strict racial lines.[57]

In fact, church records contain barely any suggestion of even clandestine
interracial relationships in Wachovia. Quite probably church moral codes
provided an important defense for black sisters against the sexual abuse

56. Oldendorp, *Caribbean Mission*, ed. and trans. Highfield and Barac, 334; LAC, June 5,
1781. Some other Protestant churches tried to enforce similar injunctions against the separation of families. Significantly, such ostensible reforms often arose after most debates in evangelical churches regarding the morality of slavery had ended and slaveholding was deemed a
matter of individual conscience. See Guion Griffis Johnson, *Ante-Bellum North Carolina: A
Social History* (Chapel Hill, N.C., 1937), 537–538; W. Harrison Daniel, "Virginia Baptists and
the Negro in the Early Republic," *VMHB*, LXXX (1972), 60–69.

57. Oldendorp, *Caribbean Mission*, ed. and trans. Highfield and Barac, 314, 318, 338–339;
Jeffrey J. Crow, *The Black Experience in Revolutionary North Carolina* (Raleigh, N.C., 1977),
30–31.

regularly visited on enslaved women by white masters throughout American slave societies. The Moravian religious culture that rigorously clamped down on unsanctioned sexuality of any kind would have punished any white brother who forced himself on a black woman, provided the offense became known. Victims could have reported such crimes to the elders and appealed for justice, as sometimes happened in other southern Protestant churches. Thus it seems likely that most black Moravian women lived in relative security against sexual exploitation by whites—no mean advantage in a time and a region when most enslaved women were highly vulnerable. Whether black *non*-Moravian women would have felt bold enough to charge white Moravian men with rape is another matter. No such cases were reported, though it is of course possible that fear silenced women victims. Had male offenders been reported, they probably would have been severely punished. The church therefore played a central role in mediating interracial gender relations.[58]

Some Afro-Moravian families began producing children quickly and steadily. Between 1779 and 1795, nine children were born to Paul and Emma in Hope, though five died in childhood. Of the seven children born to Johann and Maria Samuel between 1781 and 1801, three died young. Abraham and Sarah had no children, nor did Christian and Anna. Surviving black children, however, were members of the church community as fully as their parents or white children. Some studied with white children in what might have been among the South's first integrated schools. Johann Samuel paid annual school fees to the Bethabara Oeconomy for his children, John, Christian, Jacob, and Anna, to study the standard Moravian curriculum of reading and writing in German and English, music, mathematics, and Bible studies. Some black non-Moravian children also attended the schools. Frederic Marshall bought ten-year-old Benjamin in 1783 and gave him to Andrew Bresing in Bethabara "on condition that Bresing not rent Benjamin out to anyone. Bresing will send him to school to read the Bible and learn the religion. Benjamin is baptized." Likewise, the elders gave permission to Adam Schumacher of Salem "to send his Negro girl, who is about ten years old, to the

58. On sexual exploitation of enslaved women, see Jacqueline Jones, "Race, Sex, and Self-Evident Truths: The Status of Slave Women during the Era of the American Revolution," in Ronald Hoffman and Peter J. Albert, eds., *Women in the Age of the American Revolution* (Charlottesville, Va., 1989), 293–337; Deborah Gray White, *Ar'n't I a Woman? Female Slaves in the Plantation South* (New York, 1985).

school." At a time when many slaveholders feared that literacy would give slaves too dangerous a learning tool, the Moravians hoped for just the reverse: that literacy would help instill obedience.[59]

Black children entered the choir system as well. The most prominent example was Anna Maria Samuel, the oldest daughter of Johann and Maria Samuel. Born and baptized on Christmas Eve, 1781, Anna Maria was the first second-generation black Moravian to be raised in the bosom of the church, and as such she grew up bilingually, speaking English, the language of her parents, and German, the language of congregational discourse. "She enjoyed as a child the care and instruction of her parents, as well as school lessons in our congregation," her biography noted. "During her growing years one noticed a special inclination by her to sing; she diligently applied herself to learning congregational verses, and gladly attended the children's services and congregation meetings." She flourished in this atmosphere of worship, school, and rich Moravian music. "She expressed so frequently her desire to be taken in the congregation . . . to live in the world only for Him alone, and to partake of the forgiveness and purification of her sins through Him, whereby she could grow and prosper in His love." In June 1793, at the age of eleven, Anna Maria entered the Older Girls' Choir in Salem with much ceremony. "At ten o'clock was the reception of two children into their choir: Elis. Stockburger and black Anna Maria, both from Bethabara. At two o'clock was their Lovefeast. After that they were seen in classes, then followed the festival homily."[60]

Anna Maria now moved into the sisters' house on Salem square, where her days were filled with a full routine of choir meetings, lovefeasts, festivals, morning devotions, homilies, house conferences, and chores. She quite likely wore the distinctive clothing of Moravian women—a long dress and a *Haube*, or bonnet, fastened under the chin with a ribbon of a different color for each choir, which in Anna Maria's case meant pink for Older Girls. Moravian Bishop Spangenberg claimed that black converts "wear what we

59. Hope Church Register A; Bethabara Church Book, 1753–1792; Bethabara Ledger, 1790–1802, 44; Bill of Sale for Benjamin, Dec. 2, 1783; Aelt. Conf., Jan. 5, 1785. On Moravian education, see Madeline May Allen, "An Historical Study of Moravian Education in North Carolina: The Evolution and Practice of the Moravian Concept of Education as It Applied to Women" (Ph.D. diss., Florida State University, 1971); and Mabel Haller, *Early Moravian Education in Pennsylvania* (Nazareth, Pa., 1953).

60. Death notice of Anna Maria Samuel, 1798, in Bethabara Church Book; Single Sisters' Diary, June 4, 1793 (trans. EM).

wear," and indeed black sisters are so garbed in several eighteenth-century paintings by Moravian painter Valentin Haidt.[61]

Only one further glimpse of Anna Maria's life in the choir house was recorded. In 1795, the house diarist noted, "Our old Sister Krause was overtaken by a very painful illness. Anna Maria, who had nursed her with help for two days, also became very ill, but in her case improvement started in a week." Beyond this brief mention, the records do not disclose her precise status in the house. It is therefore difficult to pinpoint where temporal subordination ended and spiritual equality began for the only African American known to have lived in the sisters' house. Because she was enslaved and because white Moravians were not immune to the racialized exercise of power, she remained in a fundamental sense a second-class sister even while sharing her life with the adolescent girls and single women. Yet, in all likelihood, she partook of meals, slept in the dormitory, and worshiped in the prayer hall on something like an equal footing with her white companions, who, as the choir system was designed to do, became her surrogate family. The legal and social boundaries between slavery and freedom might well have blurred in the self-contained daily commotion of the sisters' world.[62]

As they married, bore children, and participated in choir life, black Brethren developed yet another layer of family: godparents, or baptismal sponsors. These fictive kin were an important part of Moravian spiritualism. In the high church tradition of medieval and early modern Europe, godparents often bore part of the responsibility for a child's religious education or assumed care of orphans. Godparenthood also reflected attempts to win social and material advantages through a link to one of higher status. In the Moravian Church, five sponsors witnessed the baptism of a child, "who as well as the Teacher lay their hands upon the Child and bless it," wrote Bishop August Spangenberg. The social assistance and educational functions of the choirs might have diminished the role of godparents among white Brethren, but they remained important figures in a child's development. "In the Congregation no one can be accepted as a sponsor who at the

61. Memorandum of August Spangenberg, Jan. 8, 1760, quoted in Lenius, "Slavery and the Moravian Church," 108.
62. Single Sisters' Diary, Feb. 10, 1795.

time is in bad standing, and shut out from the Communion," the elders emphasized in 1774.[63]

Although some form of spiritual coparenthood was embedded in most European cultures, the concept was just as familiar to Africans in the Americas. In West Africa, "spiritual parents" helped guide initiates through the lonely stages of "seeking" and communing with the spirits that culminated with a young person's formal reception into adult village society. Africans used similar spiritual mentorship practices to build extended kinship networks in New World slave societies, especially in Latin America and the Caribbean. These practices often consisted of some amalgamation of African traditions adapted to Christian godparenthood. Sponsors helped newly arrived Africans adjust to the harshness of slave society or improve children's social standing. In Saint Domingue, an observer noted how profound these fictive connections could be among African Catholics: "The respect of the Negroes for their godfather and godmother is pushed so far that it exceeds that which they hold for their father and mother. The Negroes call each other 'brother' and 'sister' when they have a godfather or godmother in common."[64]

Among Moravians, baptismal sponsorship was closely tied to African-American efforts to extend family and social links and to anchor a place in

63. From Aelt. Conf., Mar. 28, 1774, and "A Short Historical Account . . . ," 1778, in Fries et al., eds., *Records*, II, 826, III, 1013. On comparative forms of godparenthood, see Sidney W. Mintz and Eric R. Wolf, "An Analysis of Ritual Co-Parenthood *(Compadrazgo)*," *Southwestern Journal of Anthropology*, VI (1950), 341–368; John Bossy, "Blood and Baptism: Kinship, Community, and Christianity in Western Europe from the Fourteenth to the Seventeenth Centuries," in Derek Baker, ed., *Sanctity and Secularity: The Church and the World*, Studies in Church History, X (Oxford, 1973), 129–143; and Stephen Gudeman, "Spiritual Relationships and Selecting a Godparent," *Man*, X (1975), 221–237.

64. Mederic-Louis-Élie Moreau de Saint-Mery, *Description topographique, physique, civile, politique, et historique de la Partie Française de l'Isle Saint Domingue* (1797; reprint, Paris, 1958), 55. An important examination of godparenthood in slave society is Stephen Gudeman and Stuart B. Schwartz, "Cleansing Original Sin: Godparenthood and the Baptism of Slaves in Eighteenth-Century Bahia," in Raymond T. Smith, ed., *Kinship Ideology and Practice in Latin America* (Chapel Hill, N.C., 1984), 35–56. For other examples, which usually derive from Afro-Catholic societies, see Jane Landers, "Gracia Real de Santa Teresa de Mose: A Free Black Town in Spanish Colonial Florida," *AHR*, XCV (1990), 23–25; Mary C. Karasch, *Slave Life in Rio de Janeiro, 1808–1850* (Princeton, N.J., 1987), 257; and Oldendorp, *Caribbean Mission*, ed. and trans. Highfield and Barac, 263. Fundamental to an understanding of African-American godparenthood and extended kin relationships is Gutman, *Black Family*, chap. 5, esp. 220–229. See also Thornton, *Africa and Africans in the Making of the Atlantic World*, 218–219.

the sacramental fellowship. It was also, in the early years, another mechanism used by white Brethren to absorb slaves into congregations. The elders designated sponsors, usually whites in positions of authority, for the first black converts. Only adults of the same sex could sponsor adult candidates, whereas both men and women could sponsor children. When Ida was christened Maria in 1780, Catharina Meyer of the Salem tavern, two Single Sisters, and the female members of the Aeltesten Conferenz sponsored her. Christian was sponsored by male elders from Bethabara and the village supervisor.[65]

Records do not indicate whether white mentors continued to cultivate the religious progress of black inductees or whether slaves gained formal social advantages through baptismal patronage. But the meaning behind the practice is clear, at least from a white Moravian perspective. Godparents created one more link of identity between the slave and his or her companions in Christ, symbolizing and personalizing the church family as the convert's new spiritual kin. A church council expressed the relationship thus: "The entire congregation stands for the child, and the sponsors should be considered only as witnesses in the name of the congregation."[66]

Whether black Brethren indeed viewed godparents, and the congregation as a whole, in these terms is hard to know. It would be an unwarranted leap of judgment to assume that white congregants who, despite professions of spiritual equality, harbored their share of racial bias could meet black needs for an extended family. But it is certainly possible that the multiple layers of Christian kin could help blacks connect on some spiritual or social level with whites.

Godparenthood, however, soon became a way to broaden the black family through spiritual kinship with other blacks. Church authorities promoted such ties. When they designated Johann Samuel, Christian, and Abraham to sponsor Paul in 1782, they probably believed that the supervision of new converts could be more effectively handled by trusted black godparents than by whites. A similar premise had underscored their use of "national helpers," or black assistants, to help evangelize and nurture other slaves in the Danish West Indies in the 1730s. Whether whites attached significance to the shared Africanness of Paul to Christian and Abraham is not known, yet

65. Aelt. Conf., Aug. 12, 23, 1780.
66. Salem Congregational Council, Mar. 26, 1789, in Fries et al., eds., *Records*, V, 2276.

that identity probably deepened the bonds of kinship more than the elders realized. It had been eleven years since that summer day in 1771 when Abraham and Paul, then known as Sambo and Jupiter, arrived in Bethabara together, only to be separated and sold to different masters. The shared trauma of a forced march from Virginia could have created a bond of affinity between the two, much as captive shipmates during the middle passage forged ties of quasi-kinship that often endured in America. That relationship might have been formally reaffirmed by Christian baptism, with Abraham as mentor and Paul as ward.[67]

The two strengthened their spiritual link still further eight years later when Abraham served as godfather to a son of Paul and his wife Emma. The boy was christened Abraham. Slave men throughout the South frequently named sons after their own fathers, largely reflecting an African-American perpetuation of West African belief in the importance of male lineage. By encoding in his son's name his fellowship with his own spiritual father, Abraham, Paul found in baptismal sponsorship a way to adapt African practice to his American family.[68]

Such connections quickly spread throughout the black Moravian community. Adults were linked to at least two or three others through godparenthood, and the adults then sponsored each other's children. Virtually all black church members thus enmeshed themselves in a web of fictive kin relationships. Increasingly, black non-Moravians also entered the orbit by seeking baptism for their children with black Moravian sponsors. They might have believed that sponsorship would provide allies as insurance their children would not be sold. Perhaps they also sought spiritual linkages with black Brethren, though they themselves could not or did not want to join the church. But the broader implication is that godparenthood brought black Moravians and non-Moravians together through a widening vision of spiritual family.

This network was particularly strong in the rural southern tier of the settlement, where the largest number of black Moravians lived by the early 1800s. The epicenter was dominated by one person, Priscilla, who was godmother to many in the black community for more than fifty years until her death in 1834. As the only black communicant in the country congregations

67. Aelt. Conf., May 15, 1782, in Fries et al., eds., *Records,* IV, 1804. On shipmate bonds, see Mintz and Price, *The Birth of African American Culture,* 43–44.

68. Hope Church Register A, Baptisms, Aug. 22, 1790; Gutman, *Black Family,* 193–198.

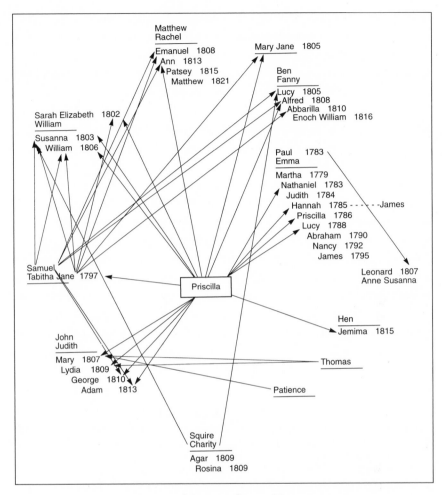

Figure 12. Baptismal Sponsorships in Hope, 1781–1815.
Arrows point from godparent to godchild. Drawn by Richard Stinely

of Hope, Friedberg, and Friedland between 1784 and 1800, she held the highest status among blacks in those areas and was a logical choice to sponsor initiates, both children and adult. "Through her loyalty and diligence she was loved and respected by white and black alike," a minister noted. Between 1783 and 1815, Priscilla sponsored three adults and sixteen children in Hope. Four of the children belonged to Paul and Emma, including one christened Priscilla. The adults included Tabitha Jane in 1797, Sarah Elizabeth in 1802, and Mary Jane in 1805. She sponsored two generations of the same family by witnessing, with her husband William, for Sarah Elizabeth's children. She was godmother for children in Friedberg and children of non-Moravian couples. Priscilla stood at the vortex of an expansive family.[69]

Other black Moravian women shared that role as elder and as a kind of spiritual coagulant. One was Anna, who, widowed after her husband Christian's death in 1789, lived for forty more years in Bethabara, Hope, and Salem. Her epitaph in 1829 described her as "careful and loving with little children, even though she did not have any of her own." African-born Anna, of course, would have been raised in a culture that revered grandparents and other elders, who took an active part in childrearing. She apparently continued that tradition in America. In slave quarters everywhere, respected "aunts" and "uncles" passed on knowledge to the young, thus playing a vital role in binding the sinews of community. But within the context of Afro-Moravian society, the importance of such elders was specifically adapted through ritual sponsorship to an extended family that secured the church's formal recognition of those spiritual links. Priscilla and Anna, in effect, were Moravian "church mothers," traditionally the most respected and powerful women in African-American churches whose authority "derived from the kinship network found within black churches and black communities."[70]

Nor were women such as Priscilla and Anna the only godparents in

69. SAE, November 1802, "Nachricht von den Negern," pt. B, sec. 1, "Hope." Baptismal data drawn from Hope and Friedberg baptismal registers and LAC diaries. In Bahia, Brazil, runaway slaves often sought the protection of godparents "who would then return the slave and ask that no punishment be given or that the situation causing the flight might be ameliorated"; see Gudeman and Schwartz, "Cleansing Original Sin," in Smith, ed., *Kinship Ideology and Practice in Latin America*, 45. It is not clear, however, who selected black Moravian godparents. If blacks did so, their choices might indicate an attempt to attach themselves to allies of higher social standing whose prestige might reflect well on them or who might buffer them or their children against possible mistreatment. If whites designated a sponsor like Priscilla, on the other hand, that choice would suggest a desire to anoint spiritual and social overseers for blacks.

70. C. Eric Lincoln and Lawrence H. Mamiya, *The Black Church in the African-American Experience* (Durham, N.C., 1990), 275. An excellent study of black Baptist women in the late 19th century that examines this theme is Evelyn Brooks Higginbotham, *Righteous Discontent: The Women's Movement in the Black Baptist Church, 1880–1920* (Cambridge, Mass., 1993). Godparents have continued to play an important role in some black Moravian communities. Rev. Cedric Rodney, the present pastor of St. Philip's Moravian Church in Winston-Salem, recalls that in the tightly knit, largely Moravian community of his youth in his native Guyana, a relative, Glen Cora Rodney, was perhaps a 20th-century equivalent of Priscilla. "Aunt Glen," as she was known, never married but was godmother to dozens of children over the course of many years (interview with author, Apr. 4, 1990). Rodney, incidentally, is the uncle of the late Guyanese historian Walter Rodney.

demand. Most people chose or were assigned between two and four sponsors, and kinship networks widened as more adults served in that capacity. Often they did so after they became communicants and their social status increased. Samuel, for example, was accepted into Hope Communion in 1800, and his wife Tabitha Jane in 1803. They joined Priscilla in sponsoring most African Americans in the Hope congregation as well as many non-Moravian children. Similar connections also developed in Bethania and Friedberg. Godparenthood bridged generational and geographic space, almost like an imaginary net of spiritual filaments spanning the dispersed farms and villages. Black Brethren appear to have employed baptism to express African notions of extended lineage in Christian form. Thus, it was through the family—broadly defined and extended—that a distinctly black Moravian community jelled within the broader Unity family, like a church within a church.[71]

Can such links tell us anything about African-American culture in the early Republic? They suggest that Christianity and family life—two sustaining pillars of black identity that are not usually discussed together—might often have interlocked and reinforced each other. For black Brethren, conversion and family formation were connected in at least four ways—through the church family of Christ, the choir family, marriage and the nuclear family, and extended spiritual kinship. Of course, the Moravians were an unusual case among Afro-Protestants in several ways, not least of which was their use of godparents, unlike Baptists, for example. Even so, Africans throughout the Americas welded familial and communal ties through what has been called the "idiom of kinship." More than we have realized, that idiom expressed an awareness of the relationship between the family of the spirit and the family of the enslaved community—a vital spark in the genesis of the black church.[72]

BLACK MORAVIANS occupied a limbo between their physical and spiritual selves as defined by whites. White Brethren thought of their world as a meshing of the secular and the sacred, the social and the spiritual. They

71. Many examples of these fictive links may be found in the Bethania, Hope, and Friedberg church baptismal registers.

72. On "idiom of kinship," see Ira Berlin, Steven F. Miller, and Leslie S. Rowland, "Afro-American Families in the Transition from Slavery to Freedom," *Radical History Review,* XLII (1988), 89. One suggestive study has described the importance of spiritual elders in guiding a

expected blacks to abide by three covenants of obligation within this cosmos: slave to dominant culture, self to community, and redeemed sinner to God. Whites presumed these three to be one and the same for blacks. As whites wiped out slaves' former selves through baptism and assimilated them into fellowship, they made them less alien, more like themselves. In so doing, they flouted a long-standing principle of New World slavery: it was easier to enslave people much less like oneself. White Brethren saw no paradox: in their world, all were servants of the Redeemer. Although proclaiming the unimportance of race in matters of the spirit, white Brethren elevated physical difference to high importance as a secular category to justify African captivity. They thereby ratified a chasm of difference between themselves and black Brethren that even the common faith could not bridge.

At the same time, the fraternalism of the Moravian Brethren contained all the era's fluid possibilities for a more egalitarian society. It marked probably the closest, most sustained contact between Germans and African Americans in early America. The concept of rebirth and inclusion in the body of Christ reordered emotional and social relations between black and white. The premise that spiritual salvation entitled African Americans to rights as integral members of a unity of the elect was not intended to topple slavery, signify social equality, or democratize the worldly order. The Moravian community of the spirit did, however, represent a laboratory in which the meanings of freedom, slavery, and race were continually tested, probed, and found pliable. On a grander scale, the same kind of experiments were conducted throughout the new Republic as people of all kinds debated who should be included in the nation's corporate identity. Whether that discussion held the potential for more dramatic racial and social leveling, no one could predict. But it inspired both hope and fear in Americans.

Living with these contradictions daily, black Moravians used the fulcrum of fellowship to try to secure themselves in an uncertain world. They sought to reconcile the sacrifices demanded by assimilation into a culture that demanded them to conform, reject "heathen" ways, and meld themselves into the collective. W.E.B. Du Bois's famous insight into the "duality" of African-American life helps us diagnose the dilemma of black Moravians. With a

---

sense of Christian unity and kinship in evangelical antebellum Gullah communities in South Carolina. But historians still know little about similar or equivalent religious constructions of family identity that African Americans might have employed elsewhere in post-Revolutionary America. See Margaret Washington Creel, *"A Peculiar People": Slave Religion and Community-Culture among the Gullahs* (New York, 1988), 288–292.

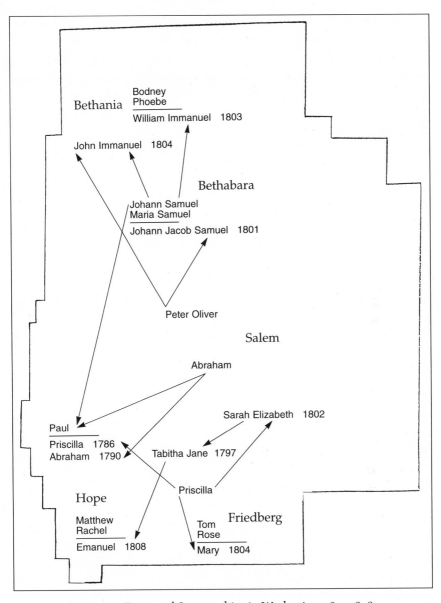

Figure 13. Baptismal Sponsorships in Wachovia, 1783–1808.
Arrows point from godparent to godchild. Drawn by Richard Stinely

foot in two worlds, they balanced different identities as Brethren and as enslaved African Americans. They sought access to the rituals and symbols of power from the masters' culture. Black Brethren spent many hours each week in close communion with whites, worshiping, working, and sometimes even living with them. Filtered though they were through the lens of racialized power, some of the intimacies and friendships among them might still have been genuine.

But when Abraham preached the gospel to other blacks, when slaves asked to celebrate a brother's spiritual "birthday," when they witnessed each other's baptisms, black Brethren affirmed an alternative fellowship of identity. Flexible, capacious, it encompassed Moravians, non-Moravians, German-speakers, English-speakers, adults, and children. Together they drank of a different spirit.

CHAPTER FIVE

. . . .

Workshops of the Lord

 A FELLOWSHIP IN CHRIST: equal parts family, congregation, and government, the Moravian Church nurtured and controlled its European and African disciples. But black Brethren were more than members of the sacramental community. They were forced to work. Indeed, white Brethren came to view slave labor as indispensable, and eventually hundreds of African Americans carried out an ever-multiplying variety of tasks.

Just as social and racial distinctions reflected the ambiguity of the Moravian religious experiment, so they blurred in the more secular daily commotion of work. White and black Moravians who prayed side by side in church also toiled together in the tannery, the pottery, and the stockyard. In the topsy-turvy Moravian hierarchy of labor division, spiritual status often mattered more than race. Here was a world where enslaved black Brethren sometimes gave the orders and free white Brethren obeyed them. Afro-Moravians gained privileges and protection in the workplace that were unavailable to most enslaved workers in late-eighteenth-century America. Black *Fremden*, or strangers, on the other hand, had little social standing, few rights on the job, and less recourse against the whims of masters. In the workshops of the Lord, divine law ordered the realms of labor and of the spirit.

Africans were brought to the Americas to work, and work dominated slave life from New England to Argentina. The theft of their labor was the reason for slaves' subjugation; clash and negotiation over working conditions and control of time formed the bedrock of antagonism between slaves and masters. In ways that are just beginning to be explored, work—for their masters and for themselves—shaped slaves' culture, their life away from the fields, their sense of personal and collective identity and even of autonomy.

147

But we little understand how the slave work experience intersected with the rise of evangelical Protestantism and Afro-Christianity in the late eighteenth century. If the South's interracial worship halls tested orthodox spiritual and social boundaries between slave and free, black and white, how did they affect work relations among them? The Moravian community of faith offers a glimpse inside an experimental laboratory where work and worship went hand in hand.[1]

To think of slave labor in early America is to think largely of production, and to consider production is to envision sprawling plantations where slaves cultivated tobacco, sugar, rice, and ultimately cotton. The picture is vastly more complicated. Enslaved African Americans worked as sailors, fishermen, and miners, as domestics and factory hands, as artisans and loggers. Though staple crop agriculture commanded the largest share of slave labor during most of the period before emancipation, slaves worked and produced in a huge array of settings. Between, around, and within the large-scale production units of the colonial lowcountry and Chesapeake and the antebellum Black Belt were important pockets of African-American life and labor that have been hidden by the historical shadow of the plantation.

We know comparatively little about the role of African-American workers in the building of southern upcountry farms and settlements. Historians regularly note the low number of blacks in the Piedmont and western reaches of the Carolinas during the late colonial period.[2] But after the Amer-

1. For three compendiums of scholarship on the importance of labor in the evolution of African-American slave culture, see Ira Berlin and Philip D. Morgan, eds., *Cultivation and Culture: Labor and the Shaping of Slave Life in the Americas* (Charlottesville, Va., 1993); Berlin and Morgan, eds., *The Slaves' Economy: Independent Production by Slaves in the Americas* (London, 1991); and Mary Turner, ed., *From Chattel Slaves to Wage Slaves: The Dynamics of Labour Bargaining in the Americas* (Bloomington, Ind., 1995). For another important overview, see John Thornton, *Africa and Africans in the Making of the Atlantic World, 1400–1680* (New York, 1992), esp. chap. 6.

2. See, for example, A[rthur] Roger Ekirch, *"Poor Carolina": Politics and Society in Colonial North Carolina, 1729–1776* (Chapel Hill, N.C., 1981), 11–12, 260 n. 59; and H. Roy Merrens, *Colonial North Carolina in the Eighteenth Century: A Study in Historical Geography* (Chapel Hill, N.C., 1964), 74–81. The few studies of slavery in Piedmont and Western North Carolina focus on the antebellum period. See, for example, Edward W. Phifer, "Slavery in Microcosm: Burke County, North Carolina," *JSH*, XXVIII (1962), 137–165; and John C. Inscoe, *Mountain Masters: Slavery and Sectional Crisis in Western North Carolina* (Knoxville, Tenn., 1989). Two of the few studies of Afro-American life anywhere west of the fall line during the 18th century are Philip D. Morgan, "Slave Life in Piedmont Virginia, 1720–1800," in Lois Green

ican Revolution, the black population increased steadily in the region as white settlers pushed west and south in search of new land, taking slaves with them. By the time of the 1790 census, blacks constituted 10–20 percent of the population of many Piedmont counties in North Carolina—still far less than along the Atlantic seaboard, but a hefty proportion nonetheless. On the small farms chiseled into the forested hill country, a different world was evolving, one of diverse ethnic complexion and social relations.[3]

Fully part of this emerging order, the Moravian settlement illustrates the extent to which African Americans shaped the changing economy of the southern backcountry in the new Republic. Wachovia's six congregations resembled a small solar system centered around the urban religious core, Salem, whose regulated commerce and industry complemented the free-wheeling farming and light crafts of the outlying villages. This ambitious mixed economy fueled a relentless demand for labor in what was still essentially a frontier settlement. Though souls were nice, it was African Americans' labor that white Moravians mostly wanted.[4]

IN SALEM, the ministers decided not only how many slaves would work but how they would work. Throughout the plantation and urban South, African Americans' position in the economic order was tied directly to their work. In

---

Carr, Philip D. Morgan, and Jean B. Russo, eds., *Colonial Chesapeake Society* (Chapel Hill, N.C., 1988), 433–484; and Philip D. Morgan and Michael L. Nicholls, "Slaves in Piedmont Virginia, 1720–1790," *WMQ*, 3d Ser., XLVI (1989), 211–251.

3. Following various county divisions, Wachovia was situated in Stokes County by 1790, when the first federal census recorded a slave population of about 9% of the total 8,535. See Walter Clark, ed., *The State Records of North Carolina*, 22 vols. (Winston and Goldsboro, N.C., 1895–1907), XXVI, 1123. An overview of post-Revolutionary western migrations is Allan Kulikoff, "Uprooted Peoples: Black Migrants in the Age of the American Revolution, 1790–1820," in Ira Berlin and Ronald Hoffman, eds., *Slavery and Freedom in the Age of the American Revolution* (Charlottesville, Va., 1983), 143–171. On the growth of backcountry slavery, though more from the masters' perspective, see Rachel N. Klein, *Unification of a Slave State: The Rise of the Planter Class in the South Carolina Backcountry, 1760–1808* (Chapel Hill, N.C., 1990); Joyce E. Chaplin, *An Anxious Pursuit: Agricultural Innovation and Modernity in the Lower South, 1731–1815* (Chapel Hill, N.C., 1993), chap. 8.

4. See Daniel Thorp, *The Moravian Community in Colonial North Carolina: Pluralism on the Southern Frontier* (Knoxville, Tenn., 1989), 107–147; Charles Christopher Crittenden, *The Commerce of North Carolina, 1763–1789* (New Haven, Conn., 1936), 91–95, 137–141; Merrens, *Colonial North Carolina*, 164–166.

the classic labor hierarchy that historians have long emphasized for the plantation economy, house slaves held the highest status, followed by artisans and, last, field hands. That basis of stratifying the slave labor force did not apply in the Moravian social order so dependent on scriptural definitions of inclusion and exclusion. In the family of the sanctified, religious fellowship rather than work determined the rise of an Afro-Moravian elite.[5]

The African sister Anna demonstrated the power of this principle during several decades of work in the Salem tavern and the Bethabara store. Fellowship gave Anna respect and bargaining power in the workplace, for in times of trouble black Moravians could turn to the church for help. There is no evidence they brought charges of cruel treatment against their masters to church boards, as black evangelicals in other churches sometimes did, but they occasionally sought protection, possibly from mistreatment. Anna, who was working in the Bethabara tavern in 1796, walked out one day, evidently in some distress, and made her way to Salem to appeal to the elders for help. They reassured her she could "go back to her workplace without fear of further consequences." In 1811, while working for a different set of tavern managers, the Strehles, Anna again fled and sought refuge in Salem. "So far all efforts have failed to persuade her to return, or to induce Brother and Sister Strehle to take her back," the elders reported. An agreement was apparently reached, for a week later she returned to Bethabara.[6]

The adjudication of the dispute revealed that Anna had a claim to protection as a sister. By leaving her workplace for Salem, she was committing a form of "petit marronnage," or short-term escape, that slaves throughout the Americas often staged to bargain for better working or living conditions. The difference in Anna's case was that she sought intervention from the ultimate master, the church, playing the card of her own status as a communicant. The elders were forced to respect the legitimacy of her appeal. Rather than punishing her or forcing her to return, they tried to "persuade" Anna as well as her supervisors, though how heavy-handed their methods were is not known. The church thus tried to negotiate harmony in the workplace and protection for slave congregants while the latter maneuvered within the zone of permissibility to make sure their rights were observed. For African-

---

5. For a discussion of plantation labor and status hierarchies, see Eugene D. Genovese, *Roll, Jordan, Roll: The World the Slaves Made* (New York, 1974), 327–331.

6. Aelt. Conf., July 20, 1796, Nov. 27, Dec. 4, 1811.

American women, who were acutely vulnerable to abuses under slavery, such defenses could be valuable indeed.[7]

Moravian brother Abraham probed many connections between work and worship during his years in the Salem tannery. His long tenure there, from 1771 until his death in 1797, made him an important figure, second perhaps only to master Heinrich Herbst. The tannery, one of the town's earliest buildings, constructed in the late 1760s, was located by the creek in the industrial district just west of town near the Single Brothers' brewery and slaughterhouse. Under the direction of Herbst, a formidable businessman and sometime member of the Aufseher Collegium, the tannery grew into one of Salem's largest and most important businesses. From the procuring of supplies in dozens of trading points throughout the region to the lengthy process of converting raw skins into leather, the tanning operations reflected the thoroughness with which Moravians integrated themselves into the backcountry economy by the early 1770s. Herbst and his agents combed the countryside buying hides, tanbark, and lime necessary for the tanning process. From Cross Creek Moravian wagons carried salt for soaking hides. Tanned products supplied one of the largest sources of revenue for the town treasury.[8]

Tanning was scarcely the most popular profession among white apprentices, which helps explain why Herbst had trouble keeping white workers and bought Abraham in the first place. The labor-intensive hide-curing process demanded the attention and skill of many men laboring long hours in the tannery's fetid stench. After washing and trimming the skins, workers soaked them in a lime solution for several weeks to loosen hair and any remaining flesh to be scraped away. Hides then soaked for twelve to eighteen months in a vat filled with ground tanbark and water. The tannic acid pro-

7. Likewise, slave members of other evangelical churches in the late-18th-century South sometimes gained protection from abusive masters. See Albert Raboteau, *Slave Religion: The "Invisible Institution" in the Antebellum South* (New York, 1978), 180–183. And in Brazil, the Catholic Church decreed in 1707 that if a slave "runs away from his master because the latter intends to treat him with relentless severity, the slave will not be taken back to him unless he first makes a sworn promise . . . that he will not mistreat him"; see Robert E. Conrad, ed., *Children of God's Fire: A Documentary History of Black Slavery in Brazil* (Princeton, N.J., 1983), 162. Many scholars have written on petit marronnage. For a synthetic discussion, see Thornton, *Africa and Africans in the Making of the Atlantic World*, 273–279.

8. Auf. Col., Dec. 21, 1772, June 2, 1773, in Adelaide L. Fries et al. eds., *Records of the Moravians in North Carolina*, 11 vols. (Raleigh, N.C., 1922-1969), II, 710.

duced by the bark reacted chemically with the skins to produce leather. After their long immersion in the tanning liquid, the hides were beaten to make them more pliable and then dried. Further finishing gave the leather a soft, polished feel. Salem boasted both a red tannery, which turned out a thick, coarse grade of leather for saddles and shoes, and a white tannery, which produced a finer grade for shoes and pants.[9]

Abraham's duties in the red tannery were not explicitly recorded, for he was neither apprentice, nor journeyman, nor master. Twenty-six years of service probably made him skilled in all aspects of the craft, and within the sphere of the workplace's unequal power relations Abraham and Herbst seem to have formed some bond of fellowship during those years together. The Mandingo Moravian might have been Herbst's right-hand man. His *Lebenslauf* carefully pointed out Abraham's niche in the church as a kind of prize convert. "He had some weaknesses in his character, which required the patience of his master and all those who were around him. On the whole he was loved by the congregation and recognized as a special example of the mercy of Jesus Christ." Perhaps realizing the perception of himself as a "special example," Abraham apparently worked his way to a sort of tenure or seniority in the tannery.[10]

A white apprentice in the tannery, Jacob Spach, learned as much when he quarreled with Abraham in 1789 and then vowed to quit. If he hoped his superiors would take his side, he was wrong. "He does not care to learn this trade and does not want to work with the Negro," the board observed. "Brother Herbst wants to get rid of him. He will hardly ever learn the trade in the right fashion. Several Brethren told him that he would repent later on, that there are so many Brethren right now who can hardly find any work." Spach's dispute with Abraham might have stemmed from racial dislike and resentment at a slave's authority. But at no point did officials reproach or punish Abraham. Instead, they blamed the altercation squarely on young Spach, whose place in the tannery hierarchy proved less secure than the African's. Both in trade experience and in religious stature, Abraham was superior to freeborn Spach. To Moravian ministers, those factors outweighed either racial or legal identity in the workplace.[11]

9. This description of tanning is drawn from Carter Litchfield et al., *The Bethlehem Oil Mill, 1745–1934: Oilseed Mill, Hemp Mill, Tanbark Mill, Groat Mill, Saaff Mill, Waterworks: German Technology in Early Pennsylvania* (Kemblesville, Pa., 1984), 55–56.

10. Memoir of Abraham (trans. EH).

11. Auf. Col., Apr. 21, 1789.

Abraham's brotherly status might also have entitled him to a bit of extra personal space that might otherwise have been denied. In 1783, the elders directed Herbst to clear "a small piece of land for the Negro Abraham in order to guard against any kind of unpleasant matters." How Abraham would use the land and the nature of the "unpleasant matters" are unspecified. Perhaps it was a garden, since slaves throughout the Americas were often allotted garden space to produce their own provisions. It was an easy concession by the masters, and one parlayed by slaves into the chance to work for themselves and sell surplus crops for cash. How common such arrangements were in the Moravian settlement is unclear, but the elders appear to have made Abraham a similar compromise, perhaps to encourage the feeling that his rights as a brother were respected.[12]

Abraham's death in 1797 revealed further close links between labor and devotions. Officials learned that he had "left a sort of testament concerning his own estate, in which he makes his widow Sarah heir of his cash money, with the condition that one Brother should keep it and give it to her from time to time as she needs it. The rest of his belongings he has given to Brothers and boys in the Tannery." A white brother, Johann Leinbach, volunteered to administer the will and pay Sarah her allowance. "Since Abraham also left some belongings about which he did not say anything in the testament, we thought that Brother Leinbach could take them and sell them as best he can for Sarah." Revealing at a number of levels, Abraham's "testament" suggests that he had some source of income from which to accumulate savings and property. Perhaps like some black Moravians, he earned an allowance or even wages. If so, such an arrangement, though not unique to the Brethren, was nonetheless unusual, given that slavery was grounded on the extraction of unpaid labor from unwilling subjects. Furthermore, besides showing an obvious commitment to his wife, Sarah, Abraham trusted the church to uphold his testament. He understood the duties of worshiper and congregation, each to the other. It was a measure of their fraternalism toward an enslaved communicant that white Brethren carried out his wishes.[13]

---

12. Aelt. Conf., Nov. 5, 1783. For an overview of the rapidly expanding literature on slaves' gardening and marketing activities, see Ira Berlin and Philip D. Morgan, "Introduction: Labor and the Shaping of Slave Life in the Americas," in Berlin and Morgan, eds., *Cultivation and Culture*, 22–45.

13. Auf. Col., Apr. 18, 25, 1797. The record of cash payments to black Moravians for labor is more explicit in Bethlehem, Pennsylvania; see Litchfield et al., *Bethlehem Oil Mill*, 89–92; Auf.

In leaving some items to fellow workers in the tannery, Abraham might also have been acting out of a sense of camaraderie. In contrast to his first ten years in Salem when he was treated with suspicion, baptism created a spiritual bridge between him and whites, clouding the boundaries between freedom and bondage and masking the violence that underpinned slavery. True, some white Brethren, such as Jacob Spach, did not like Abraham, and no one—least of all himself—forgot he was enslaved. But as a brother and coworker, the African with clipped ears formed bonds of patronage, companionship, or both with other whites—a world parallel to, and separate from, his network of spiritual kinship with blacks.

Another brother, Peter Oliver, adroitly maneuvered fellowship into a rare opportunity in another of the Moravians' key trades, the pottery, becoming one of the few enslaved Moravian artisans. The Moravians were acutely aware that skilled slaves had gradually replaced white craftsmen throughout much of the plantation South during the eighteenth century. Taking no chance that they would be marginalized in their own economy, the Brethren reserved the choice skilled trades for white Brethren. Peter was one of the exceptions.[14]

The reputation of master potters such as Gottfried Aust and Rudolph Christ carried considerable esteem throughout the region, and Piedmont folk traveled miles to buy Moravian ceramics. Oliver's chance to learn the

---

Col., Mar. 15, 1775. Evidence is more ambiguous from North Carolina. Abraham's will may also reflect an absorption of Euro-Protestant values, since Africans did not traditionally believe in the concept of savings. See Forrest G. Wood, *The Arrogance of Faith: Christianity and Race in America from the Colonial Era to the Twentieth Century* (New York, 1990), 259.

14. On black craftsmen and their displacement of white artisans, see Richard B. Morris, *Government and Labor in Early America* (New York, 1946), 182–188; John Michael Vlach, *The Afro-American Tradition in Decorative Arts* (1978; reprint, Athens, Ga., 1990); and, for a somewhat different perspective, see Jean B. Russo, "Self-sufficiency and Local Exchange: Free Craftsmen in the Rural Chesapeake Economy," in Carr, Morgan, and Russo, eds., *Colonial Chesapeake Society*, 389–432. For overviews of the Salem economy and artisans, see Fries et al., eds., *Records*, II, 830; Paula W. Locklair, "The Moravian Craftsman in Eighteenth-Century North Carolina," in Ian M. G. Quimby, ed., *The Craftsman in Early America* (New York, 1984), 273–298; Thomas J. Haupert, "Apprenticeship in the Moravian Settlement of Salem, North Carolina, 1766–1786," *Communal Societies*, IX (1989), 1–9; Catherine W. Bishir, "A Proper, Good, Nice, and Workmanlike Manner: A Century of Traditional Building Practice, 1730–1830," in Catherine W. Bishir et al., *Architects and Builders in North Carolina: A History of the Practice of Building* (Chapel Hill, N.C., 1990), 112–120; and John Bivins, Jr., and Paula Welshimer, *Moravian Decorative Arts in North Carolina: An Introduction to the Old Salem Collection* (Winston-Salem, N.C., 1981).

trade came when Christ, a former apprentice and journeyman under Aust in Salem, moved to Bethabara in 1786 to set up his own shop. Two years later, Oliver, who had been working for the Single Brothers' economy, moved to Bethabara to learn pottery under Christ. Neither an apprentice nor a journeyman in the traditional sense, he gained enough training to become a sort of assistant to Christ. The arrangement was unusual, but it did not really depart from the Moravian policy of reserving trade apprenticeships for white Brethren, since Oliver was not a formal apprentice. Church membership evidently also entitled him to consideration for artisanal training.

Religion framed Oliver's and Christ's working relationship. The church unambiguously outlined the formula for workplace harmony between the two. The Bethabara minister "talked with Peter, telling him in detail what is expected of him regarding his future course. He will also tell Christ privately that, just as Peter must be obedient, so he, Christ, must treat this Negro humanely." Christ was both master and brother to Peter Oliver, and the church could not have given more explicit counsel to both parties about what that relationship meant.[15]

Such was the slaveholder's understanding, but Oliver's grasp of the code penetrated deeper. Evidently reasoning that his "obedience" warranted further protection from the church, he pushed hard to secure it. Oliver became frightened in 1789 when Christ moved from Bethabara back to Salem to take over the master potter's duties. Another potter, Gottlob Krause, replaced Christ as the Bethabara potter, thus becoming Oliver's new master. Oliver, reported the elders, "fears that Gottlob Krause might wish to sell him at some time if a favorable opportunity arose." Even though the church owned Oliver, and Krause technically could not have sold him, the ministers were sympathetic to the enslaved brother and devised a measure to ensure his continued work in the pottery. "The problem can be remedied by Krause's issuing a bond to the effect that he cannot get rid of Peter Oliver so long as the latter conducts himself according to our *Gemein*-principles. In the event of bad behavior, however, he cannot keep him to the detriment of the town." Oliver thus savvily used the church's master-slave covenant to win protection for himself that was unusual by the standards of any eighteenth-century slave society. The right to workplace security—a right codified by an explicit written contract guaranteed by the Savior himself—

15. Aelt. Conf., Jan. 16, 1788.

amounted to a kind of freedom within slavery, a guarantee of the individual's own domain under bondage.[16]

But Oliver also experienced the limits of church membership. When Rudolf Christ moved back to Salem, he wanted to take Peter with him but was forced to leave him behind in Bethabara. Oliver wanted to marry, which Salem officials refused to permit. Since they wanted to limit the slave population in Salem, they prevented him from bringing a black non-Moravian wife to town. Church fellowship served Oliver no use in this case; white fear of black non-Moravians pushed that consideration aside. This time, Oliver's difference as an African American and as a slave overrode spiritual partnership.[17]

Peter nonetheless capitalized on his self-made opportunities. His talent as a potter flourished. Ministers noted that his "value has grown since he has learned so much from Brother Christ in the pottery"; so much, apparently, that they decided Krause, the new Bethabara potter, needed no other assistants. Oliver worked in Bethabara until 1795, when, invoking his right to church intervention in sour work relations, he complained that he had "not gotten along with his master." He asked to be allowed to work again with Christ, with whom he evidently felt lingering bonds of patronage or friendship. "The Negro Peter Oliver is still asking and praying to be taken into the Pottery. Brother Christ therefore suggested taking him into daily work." Oliver accordingly returned to the Salem pottery in 1796, where he worked for several more years, possibly even for wages, perhaps making and selling ceramic goods on the side as well. He worked toward a clear goal. "He was true in his calling and work and he brought it about through diligence in his work to the point that he could buy himself free from his status of slavery," his Lebenslauf eulogized. Thus, through a combination of luck and pluck one black brother parlayed his good standing in the church into the ultimate prize: freedom.[18]

16. Ibid., Jan. 21, 1789.

17. Auf. Col., Jan. 6, 1789.

18. Ibid., Jan. 6, 1789, Nov. 3, 1795; Aelt. Conf., Jan. 7, 1789; Bethabara Diary, Sept. 14, 1795, in Fries et al., eds., *Records*, VI, 2547; Memoir of Peter Oliver. On Moravian pottery in general and on Peter Oliver in particular, see John Bivins, Jr., *The Moravian Potters in North Carolina* (Chapel Hill, N.C., 1972), 68–69, 174; and Jon F. Sensbach, "Peter Oliver: Life of a Black Moravian Craftsman," in Sensbach, *African-Americans in Salem* (Winston-Salem, N.C., 1992), 25–40. African Americans have a distinguished history as potters since their earliest days in America. See Leland Ferguson, *Uncommon Ground: Archaeology and Early African America, 1650–1800* (Washington, D.C., 1992).

Oliver later married a free black woman named Christina Bass, who joined the church in 1802. The couple settled on a farm near Salem, raised a Moravian family, which Peter supported by selling ceramic wares until his death in 1810. Oliver's deathbed scene, recorded in his Lebenslauf, suggests that even in freedom this "esteemed Negro Brother" retained strong ties to white Brethren. "Later in his pain . . . he gave himself over considerably to the faithful care of his wife and of his [former] master Brother Christ and the other Brothers." But, like Abraham, he also partook of a separate African-American universe; at his funeral, all his pallbearers were black.[19]

Peter and Abraham found the threshold between fellowship and skilled tradework, despite the church's insistence on preserving crafts for whites. Oliver, like many slaves in the antebellum South who worked long hours saving to buy themselves or family members free, demonstrated how black Brethren could use congregational status to control their use of time to personal advantage. Time, in fact, was a crucial focus of the intersection of church life and work routines for African Americans. To white Moravians, time was a tool to be used in the service of God, whether in work or worship, and sufficient time was allotted for each. The elaborate array of services and choir meetings commanded great chunks of time each week. For black worshipers, each hour spent in prayer was another not spent in work, and the refuge of the prayer hall from the tannery's stench or the tavern's clamor might have seemed attractive. Most slaves generally did not work on Sunday, but there was no guarantee of a free day. Brethren were reminded in 1789 "not to employ Negroes on Sunday without special necessity and not without express permission of their masters." If a slave could convince the ministers of his interest in the gospel, they would decrease his workload and concentrate on his salvation. In 1787, the elders told Brother and Sister Schulz, two of the town's few private slaveholders, to "give the Negro boy time that he might use to enjoy the increasing grasping of his heart that belongs to all who are under the care of the congregation." Hence, the chance to gain more control over time—or at least to channel the use of time away from labor to spiritual pursuits—might have proven a strong incen-

19. Memoir of Peter Oliver. A diarist left the following description of Oliver's funeral: "In the afternoon at one o'clock there was the funeral of the Negro Br. Peter Oliver, who fell asleep on the 28th. In addition to our members and visitors, a large number of Negroes attended and then were given the front benches. Br. Reichel spoke on the text for the day, and led the liturgy on God's Acre. The coffin was carried by Negroes." See Salem Diary, Sept. 30, 1810, in Fries et al., eds., *Records*, VII, 3112.

tive to join the church. Time became as much a commodity for black as for white Moravians, only one to be manipulated in self-defense. As always, that prospect came with a price. A slave who pursued a closer connection with whites through the church also surrendered some control over time. Long days in the workplace and evenings, Sundays, and special festival days spent in church with whites left black Moravians less time for themselves or each other.[20]

Black Brethren sometimes tried to use church fellowship to negotiate better work assignments. One brother, tanner John Immanuel, pushed this principle as far as he could, refusing outright a request (or an order?) to sweep the chimneys of Salem. Town regulations required that kitchen chimneys in the Single Brothers' and Single Sisters' Houses and the tavern be swept every two months and all other chimneys swept quarterly. White residents delegated this grimy and thankless job to slaves when possible, and in 1812 they assigned it to John Immanuel, who must have been of slight build, and, in the Collegium's view, a suitable candidate for sweeping. He disagreed and turned them down.[21]

This boldness dismayed the members of the board, who were not used to being told no. They never forced white church members to work at any job against their will but arbitrated what they thought was a proper match of person to job. They might have conferred with some slaves about tasks as well, and Immanuel's rebuff suggests that they initially asked, rather than told, him to sweep, expecting him to agree. He must have thought he could try to play off his church standing to avoid the unpleasant task. But the church could also flex its muscles to bend a stubborn brother or sister, which it now did. "Since he has refused up to now to take over the work," declared the board, "we shall have to talk to his master, who shall make him understand the necessity and the great use the Community would have from his willingness to sweep the chimneys." What combination of threat and reward was used to "make him understand" is not clear, but it was enough to

20. Gemein Rath, Mar. 26, 1789; Aelt. Conf., Aug. 13, 1787. For another case of a slave's attraction to the contemplative life of Christianity, see Henry Melchior Muhlenberg, *The Journals of Henry Melchior Muhlenberg*, 3 vols., trans. Theodore G. Tappert and John W. Doberstein (Philadelphia, 1942–1958), II, 638. On the contrast and convergence of African and European perceptions of time, see Mechal Sobel, *The World They Made Together: Black and White Values in Eighteenth-Century Virginia* (Princeton, N.J., 1987), 21–29; and Genovese, *Roll, Jordan, Roll*, 285–294.

21. Memorandum concerning Chimney Sweeps, 1777; Auf. Col., Oct. 13, 27, 1812.

convince him of the "great use" of yielding. The limits on the value of church membership could be starkly evident.[22]

The church covenant offered no easy solutions to the burden of forced labor. Black Brethren were still classified as property, and any advantages of brotherhood or sisterhood often involved real sacrifices. But, in a religious and social system built on conformity, white Moravians also realized that their interests were served by cultivating a limited expression of black individuality, creativity, and rights. When they could, black Brethren pressed the advantage, pushing whites to abide by the Scriptures, seizing opportunities to consolidate gains—to save and bequeath money, to attain positions of skill and responsibility, and to push for protection in the workplace. Black Brethren did not necessarily absorb uncritically a Protestant work ethic to strive hard for their masters or accept and identify with enslavement; Peter Oliver's quest to gain freedom attests to a deep desire to be his own master. Rather, the church's ornate scaffold of awards, incentives, and punishments effectively gave black Brethren a voice in their own working lives—and an investment in the system itself.

BLACK NON-MORAVIANS outnumbered black church members, and as craftsmen, domestics, and laborers they sustained a larger share of the Salem economy. But whites who demanded their skills and labor also sought to limit their access to Moravian society. Shunted to the social fringe of Salem, black non-Moravians were far more vulnerable to disruption and uncertainty.

A look at the work of these men and women quickly amends the traditional picture of the Moravian economy as a closed shop operated only by sturdy German craftsmen and laborers. Ever shorthanded, the Brethren could not afford to bar outsiders entirely from the crafts they hoped to safeguard for themselves. In fact, African Americans formed a prominent bulwark of Wachovia's workforce. Slaves hired from masters in the nearby Piedmont environs often provided skilled work when the Moravians could

---

22. Auf. Col., Oct. 13, 27, 1812. In a similar case, Bethabara officials assigned the undesirable task of pumping the church organ bellows to Johann Samuel, "who however sometimes refuse[d]" and did not "see it as [his] post." After trying to spread the job around, the church fathers must have leaned on Samuel to do it again. He did it grudgingly, for they directed the minister to tell Samuel "to do his job better, as before"; see Protocoll der Hausvater-Conferenz, Bethabara, Dec. 5, 1790; Protocoll der Committee in Bethabara, Mar. 20, 1790.

find no other source. Brethren profited from the abilities of these craftsmen while preserving their goal of owning as few slaves as possible. In 1785, for example, Bethabara officials hired a "Negro who knows the craft of pottery," and Salem cabinetmaker Martin Lueck "hired a Negro who understands something about carpentry" in 1791. One advantage of such arrangements in the view of church leaders was that hired hands could be sent away if they proved disruptive. Craftsmen were typically told that any hired worker who "molests the community should be dismissed at once."[23]

African Americans helped sustain the Moravian brick and tile industry. Unlike leather and earthenware, which found their way largely into regional and Atlantic markets, bricks and tiles were intended for construction of homes and industries in Salem. The Brethren operated their own brickyard in town but found it cheaper to hire outside brickmakers than to designate one of their own in that capacity. In 1776, a church board reported that outsider "Cornelius Sale's Negro has been hired by Brother Blum at 30 shillings per month" to make bricks. Dependent on such ad hoc arrangements as their needs expanded, the Moravians searched for whatever outside labor they could find, continuing to rely on black manpower and expertise in a pinch. "Brown refuses to make roof tiles. We will see whether Ruben Fletcher will send his Negro George to make some; it is the only help we see."[24]

"The only help we see"—with plaintive but revealing words like these, white Moravians turned again and again to African-American workers. In the blacksmithing trade, lack of manpower once again overcame initial Moravian resolve to keep craftwork out of black hands. Like Peter Oliver in the pottery, one slave, Benjamin, acquired formal training in smithing from a Moravian master. When Bethabara blacksmith Matthew Oesterlein "asked for this Negro," because he saw "no hope of obtaining an apprentice any time soon," the elders agreed. Hired slaves also plied the blacksmith trade in Salem, though they gained their skills elsewhere. Master smith Samuel Schulz "cannot be without help and has therefore hired a Negro for a month." And in 1811, blacksmith Johan Sensemann hired a "Negro who has

23. Aelt. Conf., Oct. 12, 1785; Auf. Col., Dec. 27, 1791. The practice of slave hiring grew more widespread in eastern Virginia in the early Republic, and, though no comparative study has been done for the Carolina Piedmont, Moravian reliance on the practice suggests it was common there as well. See Sarah S. Hughes, "Slaves for Hire: The Allocation of Black Labor in Elizabeth City County, Virginia, 1782 to 1810," *WMQ*, 3d Ser., XXXV (1978), 260–286.

24. Helf. Conf., Sept. 4, 1775; Auf. Col., Feb. 27, 1779.

learned the blacksmith trade" when no other help was available. As such cases show, not only did white Brethren try to balance need with principle in securing skilled black labor, but black artisans had also become a prominent feature in the Piedmont workforce by the late eighteenth century.[25]

These craftsmen belonged to a transient auxiliary workforce that supplied the Moravian economy with talent and muscle. "It is still rather difficult to board and house strange workers in Salem," the Congregational Council noted in 1780. "Nevertheless, the necessity for their working here has often arisen. We need them for cutting wood, to make bricks and roof tiles or for general construction work in the community." In 1777, the "great lack of day laborers" caused forester Christian Gottlieb Reuter to "look about for a good Negro man, perhaps Abraham Martin's, for chopping wood." Hired black workers helped often with the Single Brothers' many enterprises, such as the farm and the distillery.[26]

A permanent African-American enclave developed at the Salem paper mill built in 1790 by Gottlieb Schober. One of the most enterprising of the younger generation of American-born Brethren who chafed under Salem's commercial restrictions, Schober had spent his youth working in various trades but longed to operate his own business. Though officials disallowed some of his schemes, they endorsed his bid to build a paper mill, agreeing that the Piedmont would provide an ample market for paper. With a loan from the state legislature he built the mill about two miles west of town on Peters Creek.[27]

In the mill, cotton and linen rags were broken down into a substance that made paper. Workers mixed piles of rags with water, then used a water-driven machine to beat and chop them into pulp. They poured the slush into

25. Bill of Sale for Benjamin, Aelt. Conf., Feb. 6, 1788; Auf. Col., Aug. 16, 1791, Jan. 3, 1793, Jan. 8, 1811; Bethabara Diary, Jan. 16, 1793, in Fries et al., eds., *Records*, VI, 2485. Black Americans engaged widely in smithing throughout the antebellum South. See John Michael Vlach, *The Afro-American Tradition in Decorative Arts* (1978; reprint, Athens, Ga., 1990), 108–121.

26. Gemein Rath, Feb. 10, 1780; Helf. Conf., Apr. 14, 1777. Examples of blacks hired by the Single Brothers may be found in Aelt. Conf., Mar. 2, Dec. 12, 1785, Sept. 6, 1786; Auf. Col., Mar. 21, 1786, Nov. 16, 1802, Oct. 9, Nov. 20, 1804.

27. Jerry L. Surratt, *Gottlieb Schober of Salem: Discipleship and Ecumenical Vision in an Early Moravian Town* (Macon, Ga., 1983), 33–60; Ellin Lee Rogers, "History of the Paper Mill at Salem, North Carolina, 1789–1873" (master's thesis, Wake Forest University, 1982), 2–23. Schober's was not the first paper mill in the North Carolina Piedmont; one had been established in Hillsboro in 1777. See Francis Nash, *Hillsboro Colonial and Revolutionary* (Chapel Hill, N.C., 1903), 52.

a mold that formed sheets of paper. Stacks of sheets were fitted into a press, turned by eight men, which squeezed out the water. The paper was then hung to dry on ropes. Schober's was not a large mill, but its operations still required perhaps a dozen workers, who, in the earliest days, were both black and white. Since the mill was located outside town, Salem officials cautiously allowed Schober to buy slaves. "Brother Schober is buying Negroes, whom he intends to use in his paper mill and some also on his plantation. We thought this can bring bad consequences to the community." Although the "rules for Negroes" were "not meant to extend to outlying plantations," the board still wanted Schober to consult them before buying slaves. As the mill grew more prosperous, he continued sinking capital into slaves, and by the 1820s they constituted most, if not all, of the mill's laborers, including the foreman. The paper mill held Wachovia's first industrial, privately capitalized slave workforce.[28]

Free blacks found work in Salem as early as the 1770s. Two free black families of four and six members lived just outside the town limits for many years, headed by men identified only as Sam and Scott in census and Moravian records. The Brethren often hired the two for construction and roadwork and seem not to have regarded them with the same jaundiced eye that most whites fixed on free blacks. Mainly they sought to prevent Sam and Scott, like all outsiders, from spreading impurity to the family of Christ. They threatened to cancel Sam's lease if he did not get rid of "several rather bad people" around him and "two or three women" he employed. They stopped him from selling wood he cut on their land and from letting his pigs run loose in town. When he fell into debt and "owe[d] money everywhere," the Collegium garnished his wages.[29]

Despite these incidents, Sam and Scott maintained generally good relations with the Moravians. Yet, as free people of color, their niche in the social order remained precarious. Free blacks survived with difficulty in the post-

28. Discussions of slave mill workers are in Auf. Col., Dec. 6, 1790, Jan. 10, 1792, Dec. 17, 1795, Dec. 20, 1803; and Gottlieb Schober Journal, 1789–1795, in "Salem Papermill" file, Schober Papers, Old Salem, Inc. A visitor to the mill in 1827 was given a tour by "the foreman a very intelligent black"; see Diary of Juliana Margaret Conner, June 10–Oct. 17, 1827, SHC. For a description of the papermaking process, see Rogers, "Paper Mill," 25–31.

29. Federal Census of 1790, Stokes County, N.C., in Clark, ed., *State Records of North Carolina*, XXVI, 1116; Auf. Col., Dec. 13, 1785, Apr. 29, 1788, Aug. 4, 1789, June 22, Aug. 24, 1790. Sam was granted about eight acres of land in 1777 for three years rent-free. In return, all improvements belonged to the Unity. Thereafter, he rented the land for a barrel of corn per acre annually; see Frederick Marshall Papers, no. 5, item 1, Oct. 24, 1780.

Revolutionary South, where harsh, discriminatory laws curtailed their movement, social lives, and economic activity. Many scratched out a living on the margins of slave society. Even the Moravians might have targeted free blacks for economic discrimination. Discussing wages for day laborers, the Salem Congregational Council in 1791 agreed to "distinguish between white and black daily workers," which could have meant paying blacks less, though the directive might also have referred to lower rates for hired slaves. Most of Sam's actions that so annoyed the Brethren—selling wood, hiring women, sliding into debt—in fact bespoke attempts to expand a zone of economic security around his family and the difficulty of doing so. The struggle eventually caught up with him. In 1803, the Moravians hired Sam to make a large quantity of bricks for which "he will be paid 22 shillings for 1,000 bricks and will receive the necessary kindling, boards and tools." Within two months, however, Sam "found it necessary for himself and his family to leave this region." Perhaps fleeing creditors, the law, or angry non-Moravian whites, Sam abandoned his relatively secure haven near the Brethren. Like so many hounded free blacks who took to the roads on short notice, he vanished.[30]

Confined to legal and social purgatory, other free blacks found Wachovia no safer a refuge in times of trouble than any other southern region. The Brethren had known Sam and Scott for many years, but they were wary of hiring unfamiliar free blacks. Churchmen cautioned: "We have to be careful in taking Negroes into our houses since those who have run away can easily identify themselves as being freed, so that we get into difficulties." They required free blacks to get their legal status verified by the court, and they would not risk helping free blacks in need. In the tannery, for example, Heinrich Herbst had trouble finding reliable help after Abraham's death in 1797, so he hired free blacks. The first, Aaron Moses, worked for a year before asking Herbst for a loan of 150 shillings "to satisfy the demands of a relative of his deceased master towards himself." The Collegium advised Herbst not to lend the money. A month later, Moses fled "because there are some people trying to seize him since they appear to have demands concerning his person, and they threatened to lead him away by force." A second

---

30. Gemein Rath, May 19, 1791; Auf. Col., Feb. 1, Apr. 19, 1803. Scott had also left the region for unknown reasons in 1796. On the dramatic rise of the free black population after the American Revolution and the difficulties they confronted, see John Hope Franklin, *The Free Negro in North Carolina, 1790–1860* (Chapel Hill, N.C., 1943); and Ira Berlin, *Slaves without Masters: The Free Negro in the Antebellum South* (New York, 1974).

free black hired to replace Moses was later "suspected of committing a burglary" and fled. After the failed experiment in free black labor, Herbst sought a permanent solution: he again bought slaves.[31]

As African-American skills and hands altered the shape of the Moravian economic landscape, Salem authorities regularly confronted tradesmen over their use of slave and free black labor. In one sense, the conflict manifested the hostility of southern white artisans toward black workers, particularly the skilled, during and well after the slavery era. But the peculiar Moravian twist to the familiar theme was that, unlike their counterparts in other southern towns, white craftsmen in Salem supported the hiring of black assistants, whereas the church tried to curtail it.[32]

Like so many debates in the Moravian settlement, this one was generated by changes in the aftermath of the Revolution. The tightly ordered theocratic economy had endured tremendous strains throughout the war. To cope with inflation, stagnant wages, and worthless paper money, many Brethren survived by bartering and black marketeering, despite ministers' scolding that such "usurious trades are not fit for Brethren."[33] Pressure from apprentices and journeymen for higher wages reminded authorities unpleasantly of the short-lived wage strike of 1778. They detected the insidious influence of Revolutionary rhetoric on younger, American-born generations. "Our young people want to leave their trades in order to earn higher wages on the outside without being bound," lamented the elders in 1782, correctly discerning a challenge to their interpretation of freedom and a clear threat to the community covenant. "Several people refer to their American liberty in contradiction to human order and discipline. This proves they do

31. Auf. Col., Jan. 12, Feb. 14, 1804. Some free blacks nonetheless found a seam in which to operate. In 1812, the Single Brothers, who had given up their farm and leased it to private individuals, awarded the farm contract to a free "mulatto who has been living for quite a while in our neighborhood and who enjoys a good reputation"; see Auf. Col., Dec. 31, 1811, Jan. 21, 1812.

32. See Morris, *Government and Labor in Early America*, 182–188; Bishir, "A Proper, Good, Nice, and Workmanlike Manner," in Bishir et al., *Architects and Builders in North Carolina*, 100–102; and Ira Berlin and Herbert G. Gutman, "Native and Immigrants, Free Men and Slave: Urban Workingmen in the Antebellum American South," *AHR*, LXXXVIII (1983), 1175–1200.

33. Auf. Col., June 17, 1778, Dec. 27, 1785. For an overview of the period, see Donald E. Frey, "High Prices and Bad Money: How Salem Coped during the Revolution," *Three Forks of Muddy Creek*, XIII (Winston-Salem, N.C., 1988), 13–17.

not understand the term at all, because in other free countries the individual must subordinate himself to the laws of his society, which cannot exist without this subordination." The Congregational Council decried a "spirit of variance" by which "almost no rule or arrangement can be made without arousing opposition or rebellion."[34]

Complaining of a shortage of work, Salem's youth criticized master artisans for hiring strangers, especially blacks, for lower wages, though artisans responded that blacks worked better. Town fathers partly attributed the perceived lack of work to the pickiness of young people, who wanted to do "only those things which are profitable and easy at the same time." Such attitudes thwarted attempts to regulate the economy and ensure full employment. Agreeing with them—"We should give all the work we have first to our own Brethren"—officials nonetheless chastised the young not to "make things harder and spoil their credit by asking constantly for higher wages and working badly." At a special conference in 1793, craftsmen vented their frustration at what they considered the continual questioning of their authority, the breakdown of respect among the young, and carping demands for more wages and rights.[35]

Authorities tried to solve the labor dispute by stopping the undercutting of white employment. They denied hatter Philip Transou permission to hire a black (whether slave or free is unclear) in 1788, saying, "It is no use for the community to take more Negroes in." Old fears resurfaced that blacks would bring disorder into town. When a friend of a black hired by cooper Daniel Christmann was implicated in a horse theft, the elders, "concerned lest even Christmann's Negro might become dangerous," sought to remove him from town. They also objected that slaves hired from non-Moravian masters might not be a good bargain "because Brethren cannot make much use of those who have been treated roughly and who are used to bad meals and bad clothing." But businessmen continued trying to secure them. In 1789, miller Abraham Loesch sought help for his fulling mill, and, "since he needs somebody who can really work, he thinks of taking a Negro." The

---

34. Auf. Col., Dec. 27, 1785; Aelt. Conf., Dec. 28, 1782; Gemein Rath, Aug. 4, 1785; Gemein Rath, June 19, 1783, in Fries et al., eds., *Records*, IV, 1852. On German interpretations of freedom in Revolutionary America, see A. G. Roeber, *Palatines, Liberty, and Property: German Lutherans in Colonial British America* (Baltimore, 1993), 283–310.

35. Auf. Col., Oct. 23, 1787, June 3, 1788; Conference of House-fathers and Masters, Nov. 7, 1793, in Fries et al., eds., *Records*, VI, 2482–2483.

Collegium leaned on him to hire a white brother, but two years later a white apprentice again complained that the miller "would like to release him and obtain a Negro in his place."[36]

In their efforts to secure cheap, dependable labor, some Salem masters even tried to buy slaves in outright defiance of community statutes. "It is rumored that certain Brethren have an understanding among themselves to buy Negroes for their trades instead of taking apprentices," the elders reported. "It must be stressed again what was once declared: that this is not fitting to our congregational life." When Abraham Loesch flouted the warning and bought a slave in 1791, he was reprimanded and forced to sell him. But some Moravians were warming up to the prospect of American freedom, equating it with the freedom to buy slaves.[37]

African-American women became a prominent feature of the Salem workforce as domestics in Moravian homes. Church fathers usually condemned the use of servants as a luxury that could breed idleness: "Young married people, who are well and entirely able to work, should do their own house-work, and not keep servants purely as a matter of convenience." But a family who demonstrated a need for a servant would be permitted to hire one. Single Sisters customarily served as domestics in the homes of married people, but when no sister was available elders allowed people to hire or even, on rare occasions, buy a slave.[38]

In the 1790s, subtle changes in Salem's social structure decreased the proportion of Single Sisters in the congregation. In 1781, of a population of 152, Salem had 24 married couples and 27 single women and older girls. By 1796, those proportions had shifted somewhat. Of 239 residents, there were 39 married couples and only 36 single women and older girls. The change, although hardly dramatic, was significant enough to cause more married

36. Auf. Col., May 27, Oct. 14, 1788, Dec. 24, 1789; Aelt. Conf., Aug. 1, 1787, Mar. 23, 1791. Officials were equally ambivalent about white non-Moravians, whom they also frequently hired. As with slaves and free blacks, they did not want them to displace young white Brethren from trades. But if no other help was available in a certain craft, they generally welcomed white outsiders. "We again had the wish that a few tradesmen would settle in the neighborhood, to whom we could rent small pieces of land, and who in return would serve the Community with the work of their hands"; see Auf. Col., Nov. 28, 1797.

37. Aelt. Conf., Dec. 24, 1788 (quotation); Auf. Col., Apr. 12, 1791.

38. See Aelt. Conf., Sept. 20, Dec. 20, 1780, June 19, 1782, for an unusual example of a congregant, Samuel Schulz, who gained permission to buy a slave for domestic service, since the elders "could not furnish a Single Sister to help."

couples to rent black domestic workers. In 1788, mason Gottlob Krause, who "need[ed] help for his wife," took "the Negro girl from Spach's," and hatter Johannes Reuz rented another to spin thread. Sometimes whites took black domestics because they were presumed to pose less risk of moral mishap with Moravian men than were single white women. One man bought a ten-year-old girl for domestic service because "a Negro girl can be lodged there with less misgiving than a white person."[39]

These women and girls, who often worked beside white mistresses to tend gardens, prepare food, produce textiles, and raise white children, bore the consequences of the near-pariah status of black non-Moravians. Hired slaves came from Piedmont farms and communities in a wide radius around Wachovia, and their service separated them for months, even years, from family and social connections at home. They were trapped by two lines of Moravian logic. On one hand, they were unable to join the church because they were rented on six-month or annual contracts and remained temporary residents. On the other hand, because town officials sought to limit the black population in Salem, domestics were forbidden to have families in town or to court potential mates. Deprived of these outlets, domestic women found themselves doubly marginalized.[40]

Indeed, whether free or slave, black non-Moravians claimed none of the security of the congregational order. Regarded as unregenerate outsiders, they were several notches lower than black Moravians in the estimation of white congregants and more vulnerable to capricious treatment. In 1790, several Brethren were scolded for "beating a Negro who has destroyed one of their fish baskets . . . instead of reporting it to his master." Since record-keepers always referred to black church members by name, the beaten man was probably not Moravian. Although nominal rules against ill-treatment of outside slaves existed, the offenders drew no more than a reprimand. Yet had the man been a church member, they would have had no more right to

39. "Summary of the Brethren and Sisters in Wachovia Congregations at the Close of the Year, 1781," and Wachovia Memorabilia, 1796, in Fries et al., eds., *Records,* IV, 1664, VI, 2555; Auf. Col., May 27, July 15, Oct. 7, 1788; Aelt. Conf., Dec. 22, 1787. Similar examples of African-American domestics are reported in Auf. Col., Aug. 20, 1789, Mar. 8, 1796, Dec. 10, 1799, Mar. 4, 1800, Mar. 26, 1805, June 17, 1806.

40. Church policy regarding family life for black non-Moravians is set forth in Auf. Col., July 19, 1814; and Gemein Rath, Aug. 22, 1814. The fragmented family life of hired slaves is discussed in Hughes, "Slaves for Hire," *WMQ,* 3d Ser., XXXV (1978), 260–286.

beat him than a white brother and would have been punished severely. Unlike congregants, moreover, black non-Moravians had no right to appeal to a higher church authority in cases of abuse.[41]

Perhaps because they had no stake in the system that confined them, enslaved non-Moravians sometimes used the workplace more freely than black Brethren to stage acts of resistance. They found ways to avoid doing tasks, particularly unpleasant ones such as sweeping chimneys, by turning in maladroit work: "Krause's Negro boy tried to sweep the chimneys. However, he did not do his job as well as he should have," and the job was thrust on a white Moravian. Similarly, in 1806 "the mulatto boy of Johann Volz tried sweeping the chimneys but was not very skillful and gave it up again."[42]

A slave named Peter, who worked in the Salem tavern, displayed real talent for vexing authorities with more flagrant misdeeds. Neither Peter nor his wife, Louisa, was Moravian, nor, apparently, did they want to be, and they felt no obligation to abide by the rules. The elders warned tavernkeeper Jacob Blum in 1787 "not to let his Negro Peter have too much freedom" and complained that "Peter and his wife are becoming overly troublesome in their behavior toward Blum." The elders told Blum to "treat his Negro Peter more sternly than he had in the past so that he does not overstep his bounds." They also instructed a minister to tell Peter "that he must, as a Negro, behave in obedience to the regulations" and that they would try to sell him if he did not do so. The following year, Blum admitted to his superiors a desire to "get rid of the Negro Peter" but could find no buyer.[43]

Perhaps aware of this failure, Peter continued to taunt his masters. In 1789, officials complained: "Since Peter has acted yesterday and other days before that rather indecently, Brother Blum was asked to stop it. If he does not change his behavior he will be sent away." The threat again proved toothless. As herdsman for the tavern's cattle, Peter used his position to expand his mobility around town. He "often goes into the forest with a gun, which cannot be allowed to a Negro; he is also often with the [free] Negro Sam, and he not only chases the horses but also the cows. We thought

41. Auf. Col., May 18, 1790. One might compare the case with that of Abraham Loesch, who was expelled from Salem in 1792 for beating his white non-Moravian apprentice. Such a penalty, compared with the mere reprimand to those who beat the black man, suggests the distinction white Moravians made between white and black outsiders (Jan. 31, 1792).

42. Ibid., July 28, 1801, Aug. 20, 1806.

43. Aelt. Conf., Sept. 19, Dec. 22, 1787, Jan. 19, 1788.

it would be better if the tavern would not use a horse to get the cattle in." The following year, Peter was denied further permission to ride his horse, because he was "driving the cattle on horseback and with dogs into the community," which could "easily lead to an accident." Possibly sensing the Moravians' loss of patience, Peter and Louisa made several belated attempts to make amends. Louisa once asked for baptism but was turned down by the lot.[44]

It might have been Peter who tended George Washington's horse when the president visited Salem and stayed at the tavern for two days in 1791 during the last leg of his southern tour. Louisa might have cooked meals for Washington's party. Nonetheless, churchmen concluded in frustration: "For a long time we have wished to get rid of the Negro Peter with his whole family in the tavern. We find more and more traces that he is harmful to our youngsters." The family was sold by the church to George Hauser, a blacksmith in Bethania. For the next dozen years, the Brethren, wary of using enslaved workers at the tavern again—or at least defiant outsiders such as Peter and Louisa—employed only white church members and hired hands.[45]

Moravian policy promoted division among African-American workers. In this Christian social order where work was considered an extension of the soul, the church created a multi-tiered labor system, not simply of the free and the unfree, but one compartmentalized by a complex interpretation of race, gender, age, legal status, and spiritual status. The melding of Africans and Europeans, and of free and slave labor, framed by a tenaciously held Christian cohesion, produced an economic and social order utterly out of step with the plantation and urban economies of the South. The strength of white Moravians' religious vision depended on its flexibility, and they tried to adapt Salem's tightly controlled labor system to the needs of the frontier. They created a hybrid labor force by fusing the guild system of the Old World with a limited form of New World slavery. But the tenuous balance between congregational exclusiveness and slave labor would be

44. Ibid., June 7, 1788, Apr. 21, 1790; Auf. Col., Aug. 21, 1787, Apr. 21, 1789, June 22, 1790.
45. Auf. Col., Aug. 16, 1791. On Washington's stop in Salem, see Adelaide L. Fries, "George Washington's Visit—1791," *Winston-Salem Journal and Sentinel*, May 22, 1932, reprinted in *Three Forks of Muddy Creek*, X (Winston-Salem, N.C., 1983), 37–44; Kenneth J. Zogry, "A Research Report and Historic Furnishings Plan for the Salem Tavern," 1991, Old Salem, Inc., 59–69.

repeatedly tested in the nineteenth century as more white Brethren clamored for slaves.[46]

CRAFTS AND COMMERCE drove the Salem economy. But it was the land—nearly one hundred thousand fertile acres skewered on the three forks of Muddy Creek—that sustained the bulk of Wachovia's people. On small farms and in the scattered "villages of the Lord," the red Piedmont clay demanded a relentless struggle for its yield. Men, women, and children, black and white, congregation members and outsiders—all were called to the scythe and the plow. Two annual crops of wheat, oats, barley, and rye were sowed, harvested, and threshed. Fruit had to be picked and dried, animals tended and slaughtered, corn shucked, gardens planted, and fields manured. "This was a busy day, cutting and drying hay, and mowing the oats, which are short and thin on account of the drought," Bethabara minister John Michael Graff reported in June 1772. "The currants were picked and seventy gallons of currant wine made. . . . Our Sisters have finished the sheep-shearing." Life in the countryside turned around the cycle of the seasons and the caprices of the weather. Surveying a frostbitten orchard in the spring of 1779, a Bethabara diarist lamented: "Last night it was so cold that this morning all the fruit looks as though it had been cooked."[47]

African Americans played a central role in the agricultural cycle of the Moravian settlement. The young cattle hand Sam managed the Bethabara stockyard in the 1760s, and within a few years desperate church leaders in Bethabara absolutely depended on the husbandry of black workers. The village had always been a site of both agricultural and industrial production, but its economic identity floundered after 1772, when most crafts and trades were moved to Salem. Having given birth to Salem, Bethabara was prac-

46. The Moravians' problem was related to Carl Bridenbaugh's diagnosis of labor on the frontier: "The medieval guild system, based as it was on restriction of the labor supply, could not survive under colonial conditions where labor was always at a premium"; see Bridenbaugh, *The Colonial Craftsman* (New York, 1950), 6.

47. Bethabara Diary, June 15, July 3, 1772, Apr. 23, 1773, Apr. 19, 1779, in Fries et al., eds., *Records*, II, 735, 736, 779, III, 1333. A full study of Moravian agricultural practices has yet to be undertaken, although Daniel B. Thorp has suggested some preliminary findings and directions for research in "Assimilation in North Carolina's Moravian Community," *JSH*, LII (1986), 19–42.

tically gutted. The population fell from a high of 136 in 1768 to 54 in 1772, a third of it children. Of commercial enterprises, only a few crafts, a couple of mills, a tavern, a distillery, and a store were left. Although Bethabara remained a backcountry trade entrepôt, most remaining congregants were expected to earn their bread by farming. Church leaders considered converting the economy to plantations based on slave labor, but the plan never took shape, probably because of the high cost of slaves.[48]

Nonetheless, Bethabara's skeletal workforce could no more accomplish unassisted the task of daily survival than Salem Brethren, so they likewise leaned heavily on slave labor. Slaves worked in the Bethabara tavern and store, in industries and homes, and on the congregational farm, one of few surviving vestiges of the communal economy. Congregants pooled their efforts to raise crops, livestock, and poultry on the farm for the common benefit. But Bishop John Michael Graff explained in 1778: "Each year it becomes more difficult because of the lack of Brothers; ours are getting older and older and are passing away. The greater part of the land-work must be done by Negroes or other day-laborers, which at this time are very hard to get and cost four times as much as before."[49]

A key figure in this effort was Johann Samuel, one of the scant remaining single men and experienced workers in Bethabara's economy. Samuel represented a startling case of blurred social, racial, and religious lines of authority within the Moravian fellowship. He quickly rose to a supervisory position on the communal farm. The slave driver or overseer who directed other slaves is a familiar figure in the history of southern plantations. Yet Johann Samuel supervised both black workers *and* white Brethren. In 1777, the elders debated where to assign a young white named Christian Loesch for work. Noting that Loesch "seems to have most inclination for farmwork," they assigned him to live with the Single Brothers' Choir in Bethabara and to "work under Johann Samuel." The older, more experienced slave brother held more authority than the young, free, white one. Neither man's reaction to the inverted labor hierarchy was reported, nor were details of their

48. Wachovia Memorabilia, 1768, 1772, in Fries et al., eds., *Records*, I, 371, II, 664; Marshall to the Unity Diener Department, Nov. 3, 1771 (trans. EM). An overview of Bethabara's post-1772 development is Raymond F. Willis and R. Jackson Marshall III, "Archaeological and Archival Studies at Historic Bethabara Park: Proposed Visitor Center Site" (unpublished report, Wake Forest University Archaeology Laboratories, 1985), 84–91.

49. Graff to Unity Vorsteher Collegium, July 3, 1778 (trans. EM).

subsequent relationship. But once again, racial and legal distinctions in the workplace tumbled as expediency demanded and as the realms of work and fellowship merged.[50]

Brother Samuel also supervised a small staff of slaves at the farm. As in Salem, slaves in Bethabara were owned by the church whereas individual congregants were allowed to own slaves only outside the town limits. A youth named Moses helped Samuel work the farm and drive teams on trading forays through and beyond the Wachovia tract. Another, Stephan, tended the communal cattle that foraged through open country and forest, a job that, although solitary, gave him enviable independence from the masters' scrutiny. "Stephan shall stay with the cattle the entire day and bring them home in the evening. He can take his dinner with him. . . . We will be satisfied if Stephan fetches the cattle on time, without expecting additional work from him the same evening." The relative autonomy of cattle herding might have produced a free-spiritedness that the Bethabara Committee wanted to curb by forbidding "Negroes to search for lost horses or cattle in the forest without informing the village first."[51]

Samuel and his wife, Maria, perhaps because of their senior communicant status, formed the nucleus of Bethabara's small black population, which also included Anna and her husband, Christian. Officials encouraged black communal affinity. Black and white Brethren had once shared communal meals, but the town committee decreed in 1788 that "the Negroes will eat together at the Samuels', and [administrator] Brother Kühnast will see that their meals are cooked separately." Officials' intent in cultivating this kind of African-American social solidarity is not entirely plain. They might have wanted to promote the patronage by elder Moravians of younger slaves

50. Aelt. Conf., Jan. 21, 1777 (trans. ES). Samuel remained a central figure in the farm's management. A white brother, John Holland, was designated farm superintendent in 1785, but when the elders concluded three years later that the farm was "suffering under John Holland's bad management," they divided the duties among three supervisors, appointing Samuel to "take care of the crops as chief farmhand," while two white sisters took care of swine, fowl, and the communal cooking. The arrangement proved temporary; a white farm supervisor was appointed less than a month later. But Samuel probably retained much responsibility for farm production. See Aelt. Conf., Mar. 13, 1788.

51. Graff to Unity Vorsteher Collegium, July 3, 1778 (trans. EM); Wirtschafts-Conferenz in Bethabara, Mar. 6, Apr. 24, May 11, Sept. 22, 1786. The same board also assigned Stephan to milking duties with others in 1787, perhaps to bring him under closer supervision (May 7, 1787).

such as Moses and Stephan in hopes of steering them toward the gospel. Or perhaps they were showing signs of an incipient racial separatism.[52]

By the late 1780s, the church began to phase out slaveholding in Bethabara along with the communal farm, both of which were a drain on the congregational treasury. Ministers opened some acres to private use while reducing cultivation on the rest. The town's white population was climbing again, reaching about one hundred in 1790, and leaders felt less need to use slave labor. Stephan was sold in 1792, Moses a year later. The Samuel family and a few others were left, including Anna, widowed since the death of Christian in 1789. But by 1796, the Bethabara Committee concluded that "it would be better if there were no Negro slaves in the village." Maria Samuel was freed by the church, according to the promise the Moravians had made in 1778 to emancipate her in seventeen years. Following their mother's legal status, the Samuel children were freed by the courts in 1797; daughter Anna Maria Samuel moved out of the Single Sisters' House in Salem and back to Bethabara. Wishing that "Johann Samuel could be established to earn his own bread," the church obtained a state legislative act freeing Samuel in 1800, and the family rented a farm outside the village. The old communal economy of Bethabara ended, and the Samuels were launched into the uncertain world of freedom.[53]

In the countryside, however, a new economic order was quietly emerging that would overshadow these developments. This order contained the genesis of a larger-scale plantation system based on slave labor. In contrast to the endless wrangling over slaveholding regulations in Salem and, to a lesser extent, in Bethabara, the church had little to say about the private ownership of slaves on the sprawling farm tracts of Wachovia. Many white Brethren took advantage of more liberal policies in the countryside to buy slaves. By 1800, nearly all slaves owned by the Moravians lived in farming

52. Committee in Bethabara, Apr. 8, 1788. The congregation had eaten together since the earliest days of Bethabara and had continued to do so after 1772. Maria Samuel, in fact, assumed the communal cooking duties after her marriage to Johann in 1780.

53. Aelt. Conf., Mar. 18, 1785, May 17, 1797, Dec. 27, 1799, Feb. 11, 1801; Wirtschafts-Conferenz in Bethabara, July 10, 1786; Committee in Bethabara, Mar. 14, 1796; Bethabara Diary, Mar. 6, 1797; "An Act to Emancipate John Samuel, the property of F. W. Marshall of Stokes County," 1800, in Marshall Papers. As the administrator of Wachovia, Marshall held legal title to church-owned slaves. According to a 1796 North Carolina law, masters could manumit slaves for "meritorious service" only with the permission of county courts or by state legislative act. See Franklin, *The Free Negro in North Carolina*, 20–21.

communities, where markedly different patterns of African-American life began to emerge. By the end of the eighteenth century, the Bethania area emerged as the major African-American enclave in Wachovia. It was there that plantation agriculture took root, on a small scale at first, but expanding steadily during the antebellum era.

Slaveholdings grew in Bethania largely because of the unusual character of the place. Founded in 1759, Bethania was Wachovia's first planned community, laid out in the precise, rectilinear fashion of villages in eastern Germany with which the Moravians were familiar. Each resident was allotted about twenty-two acres of orchard and farmland in various plots throughout the two-thousand-acre town lot. An observer described Bethania in 1793 as "a few plain but well built houses, surrounded by a beautiful assemblage of little farms, cultivated in the German manner, and exclusive of the farmers and their families, it contains, Wagon-makers 4; Blacksmiths 4; Weavers 3; Silversmiths 1; Shoemakers 2; Tanners 2 and six distilleries." Near the edge of what had been the northwest Carolina frontier, Bethania tapped several key trade routes, including the Great Wagon Road from Pennsylvania, which streaked between Bethania and Bethabara toward the southwest.[54]

From the beginning, Bethanians showed a pugnacious independence that irritated church leaders. Such contrariness might have been the result of the town's volatile mixture of longtime church members and new converts who settled there during the Seven Years' War. The elders complained endlessly that Bethanians, particularly the newcomers, "seek after their own cause more than that of the Saviour, and neglect the training of their children." Common infractions ranged from socializing at cornshuckings to marrying without the church's permission.[55]

Bethanians were particularly driven by a strong economic individualism. A new, aggressive generation was eager to expand business opportunities

54. Thorp, "Assimilation in North Carolina's Moravian Community," *JSH*, LII (1986), 19–42; Michael O. Hartley and Martha Brown Boxley, "Bethania in Wachovia" (a preservation plan prepared for the Bethania Historical Society, 1989), 7–35; "Letter from the County of Surry, N.C., to a Gentleman in Halifax," Feb. 20, 1793, *The North Carolina Journal of Halifax*, reprinted in *Old Salem Gleaner*, XVI, no. 1 (Summer–Fall, 1972), 4. See also Robert W. Ramsey, *Carolina Cradle: Settlement of the Northwest Carolina Frontier, 1747–1762* (Chapel Hill, N.C., 1964).

55. Aelt. Conf., Aug. 12, 1780. For other examples, see Aelt. Conf., May 3, Oct. 25, 1786, Sept. 2, 30, Nov. 11, 1789. See also Jo Conrad Butner, "A New Town in Wachovia," *Three Forks of Muddy Creek*, V (Winston-Salem, N.C., 1978), 1–11.

and propertyholdings. To the ministers, this desire conveyed a greater interest in profits than in salvation. The misplaced priority, they feared, would "draw people from this region to land, so that they consequently lose sight of the Saviour and the *Gemeine*." They lamented: "Some selfish aim usually lies at the root of the wish to set up a farm at some distance from Salem. This inclination is gaining the upper hand more and more among our young people."[56]

Despite the elders' grumbling, Bethania's tradesmen-farmers were acting legitimately within the church's own rules. Private landownership, after all, had driven settlement in the Moravian countryside since the 1760s, when the Unity offered land at cheap prices to lure settlers. Now, as the century closed, such families as the Hausers, Conrads, and Loesches acquired tracts piece by piece outside the Bethania town limits, consolidating holdings of several hundred acres.[57]

On these rural estates, free from the regulations of town life, landowners increasingly used slave labor to raise crops and manage industries. A different kind of slaveholding emerged there and in the southern country congregations such as Hope and Friedberg, where individual Brethren, not the church, owned slaves. By the 1790 census, Bethanians owned the largest number of slaves of any Wachovia congregation, seventeen. George Hauser, Jr., owned eight, and a handful of others owned one or two slaves. The Salem congregation, by comparison, collectively held eight slaves and Bethabara ten. By 1802, Wachovia Brethren held seventy-three slaves according to the following distribution: Bethania, thirty-six, Hope, twenty, Friedberg, twelve, Bethabara, three, Friedland, one, and, surprisingly, only one in Salem.[58]

Slaves produced much of the corn, wheat, and other crops grown on Bethanian farms. Liquor production, a major part of the local economy, de-

56. Aelt. Conf., Apr. 26, 1786, Sept. 22, 1790.

57. The land transactions of one family, the Conrads, may be followed in the Conrad Family Papers, Duke University Manuscript Collection, Perkins Library, Durham, N.C. How families such as the Conrads were able to assert economic dominance in Bethania during the late 18th and early 19th centuries has not been fully studied. Further investigation in court and church records may reveal consolidation of holdings through intermarriage and kinship.

58. Federal Census of 1790, Stokes County, N.C., in William L. Saunders, ed., *The Colonial Records of North Carolina*, 10 vols. (Raleigh, N.C., 1886–1890), XXVI, 1115–1123; SAE, November 1802, "Nachricht von den Negern in der Wachau," pt. A. Another eight free blacks were members of Moravian congregations in 1802, and hired laborers increased Wachovia's black population further.

pended partly on slave labor.[59] African Americans probably helped cut the huge amount of wood needed to fire distillery kettles (so much wood, in fact, that the forested countryside was denuded), and they worked in the distilling process. In 1800, the Bethania Committee warned George Hauser, Sr., "not to use the Negro in his distillery because he is almost constantly drunk, and it is to be feared that harm would come to the town through his negligence with fire." Like all slaves who staged subtle workplace protests by feigning incompetence or illness, George might in fact have drunk to escape work.[60]

Black workers, some of them free, made many of the bricks for a new church built in Bethania between 1806 and 1808. Searching for construction workers, the town committee gave a chilling glimpse into the economics of labor in the early Republic. "Because we need so many construction day-workers, it would be best to rent several Negroes. Not only can we get them for lower wages than white people, but they stay at their work much better than whites."[61]

CARPENTERS AND COOKS, tanners and teamsters, blacksmiths and brick-makers—African Americans were often the only help the Moravians could see. Their immersion in this one corner of North Carolina shows that, despite their small numbers compared to the plantation societies of the Americas, black Americans played a more important role in the backcountry economy during the late eighteenth and early nineteenth centuries than generally recognized.

At the same time, the Moravian example reveals the transformative po-tential of evangelical Protestantism to shape work and social relations in

59. "The manufacture of grain liquors is pushed forward here with great spirit, and fur-nishes a market for the wheat, rye, barley, buckwheat, etc. of that part of the country," wrote a neighbor. "By that means the farmer econimises [sic] on the part of transportation, and his produce becomes a *cash article* in any county in the state"; see "Letter from the County of Surry," in *Old Salem Gleaner*, XVI, no. 1 (Summer–Fall, 1972), 4.

60. Committee in Bethania, Nov. 30, 1800. Christian Loesch, the same person who received his early agricultural training from Johann Samuel (see above, note 50), owned a distillery and tannery in town in which his five slaves worked. When the Bethania congregation took over these businesses and Loesch's store in 1804, he continued to own the slaves but received an annual rent for their use. See Committee in Bethania, Oct. 16, 1803; HCfG, Nov. 7, 1803. The deforestation of the Bethania countryside because of the liquor trade is discussed in Aelt. Conf., Dec. 13, 1797.

61. Bethania Committee, May 29, June 10, July 20, Aug. 19, 1806, Jan. 17, 1807 (quotation).

post-Revolutionary slave society. White Brethren viewed slave labor as a means of production, but they also defined enslaved (and free black) producers by their place in the Christian order. Black Brethren used Christianity to anchor their own place in that order and as an economic bargaining device to improve their working lives, whereas black strangers were mostly shut out from that sanctum. In crucial ways, of course, the Moravian settlement was unique. But its story suggests that, in parts of the evangelical South, workplace and worship hall were intimately joined for many slaves and masters. The implicit social radicalism of that connection stood as a possible check to the expansion of plantation slavery. White Moravians' growing eagerness to buy slaves was forcing a conflict between Christian ideology and slaveholding that they had long tried to avoid.[62]

62. Though several scholars have probed the emergence of evangelical Christianity in the Revolutionary and post-Revolutionary era as a vehicle of both white paternalism and a means of negotiation between masters and slaves, none has specifically investigated the connection between Christianity, slavery, and labor relations. My suggestion that these social and economic factors were closely linked not only in the Moravian communities but in the broader southern society must therefore remain only a hypothesis and a suggestion for further research. See Sobel, *The World They Made Together*, 178–213; Sylvia R. Frey, *Water from the Rock: Black Resistance in a Revolutionary Age* (Princeton, N.J., 1991); and Alan Gallay, "The Origins of Slaveholders' Paternalism: George Whitefield, the Bryan Family, and the Great Awakening in the South," *JSH*, LIII (1987), 369–394.

· · · · · · · · · · · · · · · · · ·

CHAPTER SIX

The Unseemly Kiss

 GOTTESACKER—God's Acre—the Moravians called their graveyards, where the faithful were laid when they "went home" to Jesus. In Moravian towns, God's Acre usually occupied the crest of a hill above the village, the most sacred of spaces, where the intersection of cedar-lined alleys in the form of a cross restored the dead to the wellspring of Christian time. After sixteen years as a Moravian, Abraham took his place there in 1797. In his final illness, his memoir reported: "It was edifying to see him with his pains, which he felt mainly in his abdomen, so quiet, patient, and free from all fright of death, yea, the calmness and the well-being of his soul sparkled in his countenance. When he was asked what would be mainly comforting to him, he prayed like a child the verse: The blood and righteousness of Christ are my adornment and dress of honor." And so the African brother was buried in the Salem God's Acre beside fellow members of the Married Men's Choir, eternally together in the democracy of death.[1]

But how long could black and white Brethren continue to share this figurative and literal common ground? And did they really share it? Black and white Moravians might have interpreted death, as they did life, in different ways. Like Moravians, black Christians of many faiths also spoke of "going home" in death, and so seemingly the two traditions overlapped in Moravianism. But blacks did not always have the same home in mind as whites. For many, particularly African-born Christians like Abraham, the

---

1. Memoir of Abraham (trans. EH). The symbolic recreation of Calvary is the obvious connection between Moravian graveyards and hills, but on the mystical association of mountains and elevated places in world religions generally, see Mircea Eliade, *Cosmos and History: The Myth of the Eternal Return*, trans. Willard R. Trask (New York, 1959), 14–15.

phrase "going home" often represented the soul's final flight back to Africa after a long night of captivity in America. For others, it meant freedom in Jesus through spiritual release to a haven where there were no white people. In either case, going home to share his eternal rest with white Brethren might have been exactly what Abraham wanted to avoid.[2]

The distinction bespoke the unresolved tension in the congregational world of the Moravians. Marshaled by the church in defense of slavery and by the enslaved in defense of their lives, the Bible demarcated the line between inclusion and exclusion. Frail and limited even at its best, the fellowship of the awakened still shrank the worldly gap between white and black, slave and free. Barely twenty years after Johann Samuel, the South's first black Moravian, joined the church, the egalitarian spirit that once drove Moravian missionaries across the ocean to the West Indies showed signs of fraying. The alluring charms of their adoptive land called to white Brethren ever more insistently. Casting their eyes beyond Wachovia, they saw white Americans throughout the young country feverishly buying land and slaves and tightening racial boundaries in social and political life. The temptations of freedom, property, and profits begged the fundamental question— did being a Moravian mean the same thing in 1800 as it did in 1770? While their fellow Brethren's ideals dangled in the balance, the question was just as pertinent for black brothers and sisters.

WHITE AMERICANS clinched their independence in 1783, but black Americans did not give up the quest for theirs. Although the disappointment of crushed hopes that had risen so high during the war might have plunged some into despondency, others had quite the opposite reaction. The political settlement between Britain and the United States denied half a million enslaved Americans their share of basic human dignity. But the example of thousands who had made their way to liberty during the war furnished inspiration for those still in bondage. During the 1780s, slaves continued to run away and to rise in scattered acts of rebellion. In the wake of the slave revolt on Saint Domingue in 1791, fresh waves of armed rebellions, arson,

---

2. Lawrence W. Levine, *Black Culture and Black Consciousness: Afro-American Folk Thought from Slavery to Freedom* (New York, 1977), 34–35; David R. Roediger, "And Die in Dixie: Funerals, Death, and Heaven in the Slave Community, 1700–1865," *Massachusetts Review,* XXII (1981), 163–183.

and escapes rippled up and down the eastern seaboard, culminating in Gabriel's thwarted uprising near Richmond in 1800. Whites brutally punished
offenders and passed oppressive new laws to keep both bondpersons and free
blacks in check. The spiral of slave resistance, white fears, and repression
kept tensions high as the nineteenth century dawned.[3]

Though whites heavily outnumbered blacks in the Moravian settlement,
the conflicts at work throughout the South were keenly felt there as well.
No overt slave uprisings were reported. But many slaves pressed hard to
expand or overcome limits on their mobility and actions. Black non-Moravians were especially apt to defy authorities, avoiding work, traveling without permission, and speaking rudely to whites often enough that by 1785
churchmen insisted: "The Negroes will be reminded of their duty toward
their masters." They scolded a white couple for displaying "no gift for
training their Negro boy and keeping him within proper bounds. It is to be
feared that he might run away." Black social life was expanding, and the
board sought to control it, ruling that "nightly visits of the Negroes in the
village as well as by strange Negroes on Sundays must be restricted or
prohibited as far as possible." In case the message was lost on either blacks or
whites, Salem's board stated it more forcefully the following year: "The
masters of the Negroes shall be told that they must not let them have too
much freedom."[4]

Too much freedom, or too little? Here was the nub of African-American
resentment and the ministers' anxiety. What did terms like "duty" and
"proper bounds" mean? A key question continued to involve clandestine
interracial contact. Leaders in the Single Brothers' Choir complained that a
black youth in Salem "continues to go walking sometimes with the boys.
We would gladly grant him that company . . . but as long as he has no

3. Herbert Aptheker, *American Negro Slave Revolts*, 2d ed. (New York, 1987), 206–243;
Eugene D. Genovese, *From Rebellion to Revolution: Afro-American Slave Revolts in the Making
of the Modern World* (Baton Rouge, La., 1979); Winthrop D. Jordan, *White over Black: American Attitudes toward the Negro, 1550–1812* (Chapel Hill, N.C., 1968), chaps. 10, 11; Sylvia R.
Frey, *Water from the Rock: Black Resistance in a Revolutionary Age* (Princeton, N.J., 1991);
Julius Scott, "The Common Wind: Currents of Afro-American Communication in the Era of
the Haitian Revolution" (Ph.D. diss., Duke University, 1986); Jeffrey J. Crow, "Slave Rebelliousness and Social Conflict in North Carolina, 1775 to 1802," *WMQ*, 3d Ser., XXXVII
(1980), 79–102; Douglas R. Egerton, *Gabriel's Rebellion: The Virginia Slave Conspiracies of 1800
and 1802* (Chapel Hill, N.C., 1993).

4. Aelt. Conf., Apr. 27, 1785, May 17, Sept. 4, 1786; Committee in Bethabara, Oct. 15, 1787;
Auf. Col., Aug. 21, 1787, Apr. 29, 1788.

connection with us, we believe it best to act very carefully, especially toward our boys." The Bethabara Committee warned in 1787 that "no one should buy anything from strange Negroes without knowing how they came by it, because complaints have already arisen." North Carolina law forbade unauthorized interracial trading, and Moravian officials wanted white Brethren—the majority of whom still did not speak English—to understand the dangers of ignoring or defying the statute. Brethren in Salem were reminded in 1789 that "according to the laws of this country they are subject to punishment if they purchase anything from a Negro slave without the master's written agreement, especially if it is something which possibly does not belong to the slave at all."[5]

Both white and black continued to ignore the warnings. Bethabara distiller Johann Muecke was instructed in 1790 to "neither sell nor give our Negroes any liquor without orders." The Bethabara Committee learned that "various white Brothers and Sisters in the village have engaged the Negroes in an indecent manner, from time to time secretly using them to work at night in return for promises of drink." Here was the real problem: using "other people's property" in such a way made blacks "boisterous and insolent to their masters."[6]

At least one slave might have equated the liberty to pursue white companionship with a rejection of Moravian teachings. In Bethabara, Moses showed no interest in Christianity until late 1789, when the elders reported hopefully: "An alteration has been apparent in the Negro Moses ever since he attended the baptism of Susanna Ritter in Bethania. He is perplexed about himself and is pondering a desire to belong to the Saviour. Brother Ernst would do well to admit him to the doctrinal instruction in religious truths." Moses' attraction to the gospel proved fleeting. Barely three weeks later, in 1790, he rode out late one night with a white youth, Ludwig Micke. When pastor Ernst reprimanded both boys, Moses responded "insolently." "This time he shall be given only a warning," committeemen decided, "but if it happens again we shall be more severe." Moses' disregard for Moravian rules affirmed an unwillingness to be domesticated, perhaps even a disdain for them and their religion with which he had so recently flirted. He resisted

5. Protocoll der Haus-Conferenz der ledigen Brüder, March 1789; Committee in Bethabara, Dec. 13, 1787; Salem Gemein Rath, July 30, 1789. See Ernest James Clark, Jr., "Aspects of the North Carolina Slave Code, 1715–1860," *NCHR*, XXXIX (1962), 154–156.

6. Committee in Bethabara, Jan. 11, May 30, 1790; James A. Padgett, "The Status of Slaves in Colonial North Carolina," *JNH*, XVI (1929), 300–327, esp. 306–309.

further overtures, and in 1793 the elders confessed there was "no hope for the conversion of the Negro Moses, and now, at his own request, he has been placed elsewhere."[7]

All of this activity suggests a many-sided dispute about liberty and cross-racial encounters. Ministers sought to restrict black and white fraternizing to the approved arenas of church and workplace. Black Moravians perceived a threshold of security in interracial fellowship. Many black non-Moravians rejected that approach but cultivated illicit relations with whites as a gateway to greater day-to-day freedom.

At the same time, perhaps in response to such contact and to black restiveness, some white Brethren began defining new boundaries between themselves and blacks. They had always assumed that black people were physically different but that the gospel would submerge worldly disparities in a spiritual fellowship of the awakened. But by the 1790s, many whites had come to believe that black Brethren *were* different, that racial identity mattered even in affairs of the spirit.

Whites started to question the presence of blacks within the worship hall itself. In 1789, seating arrangements for black non-Moravians in the Salem *Gemein Haus* came under scrutiny by the Congregational Council. "As on Easter morning a good many Negroes come and sit among the white people, which does not accord with the customary thought of people in this country, the Saaldiener [sexton] shall hold them at the door and then show them to a back bench if there is room." The directive betrayed a new concern about what outsiders might think of them. Removed as they sought to remain from the outside world, the Moravians still depended on good relations with others for trade and for their continuing military exemption. By trying to avoid giving offense, church leaders encouraged white Brethren to apply social stigmas against black non-Moravians in a spiritual setting.[8]

7. Aelt. Conf., Dec. 24, 1789; Committee in Bethabara, Jan. 18, 1790; Aelt. Conf., Jan. 30, 1793, in Adelaide L. Fries et al., eds., *Records of the Moravians in North Carolina*, 11 vols. (Raleigh, N.C., 1922–1969), VI, 2476.

8. Salem Gemein Rath, Mar. 26, 1789, in Fries et al., eds., *Records*, V, 2276. Indicative of the sensitivity toward outsiders' opinions was this advice to Brethren in 1786: "It has been observed that some people, born either here in America, or hailing from England, Scotland or Ireland, consider it a personal insult if called Irishmen. This appellation should therefore be avoided." Or again, in 1795: "Although we do not object to people doing little odd jobs on Sundays, they should avoid doing them in front of their houses, because strangers are prone to take offense at that, and the laws of the country are against work on Sunday"; see Gemein Rath, Oct. 8, 1795, Feb. 2, 1786. This theme is treated extensively for a somewhat earlier

The racial divisions in church seating did not apply to black Brethren. It was one thing to separate people who were outside the fold, quite another to take such steps against brothers and sisters in Christ. Ministers continued to believe strongly that black and white Brethren should worship together. Other whites, however, were beginning to desire separation from *all* blacks. In 1792, white congregants in Salem boldly tried to sit apart from black Brethren in church. Surprised, ministers spoke up to suppress the rising tide of race consciousness they had indirectly helped to foster. "We must not be ashamed of those Negroes who belong to our community and, as has happened before, let them sit all by themselves in congregation worship and even during Holy Communion," admonished the Congregational Council. "They are our Brothers and Sisters and different treatment of them will degrade ourselves to the rank of ordinary people and will be a disgrace for the Community."[9]

The elders were worried. Gone was the concern for the opinions of outsiders, who were now spoken of contemptuously as "ordinary people" with whom the Brethren would be "degraded" and "disgraced" to suffer comparison. Churchmen now believed it more important to stop the ebbing of a value that made the Unity distinctive. Discrimination against blacks, they feared, would mark a surrender to base motives of which the chosen people could have no part.

Yet the signs of shift were unmistakable. The elders were stunned just five years later, in 1797, by astonishing news from one of the country congregations, Friedberg. An African-American girl had been studying the Scriptures under minister Martin Schneider with the intention of being baptized. She had asked permission to attend a meeting of the Older Girls' Choir, and Schneider agreed. But word of the plan got out to the congregation, and a protest was organized by a coalition of girls and parents who, according to the elders, had "persuaded these people not to tolerate any Negro in these meetings. And so when he [Schneider] wished to hold the last meeting, they all walked out. It is now known for certain that the situation is to be blamed not only on the girls, but especially on some of the mothers." The elders moved at once to remind congregants that "not the slightest distinction between whites and blacks can be made in matters of the spirit."

period in Daniel B. Thorp, *The Moravian Community in Colonial North Carolina: Pluralism on the Southern Frontier* (Knoxville, Tenn., 1989).

9. Gemein Rath, Dec. 6, 1792.

The hasty response showed their sense of urgency in shoring up the imperiled Unity ideals. A minister spoke to the errant single women individually about their "bad behavior," and the parents who instigated the walkout received a stern lecture as well.[10]

"Not the slightest distinction in matters of the spirit." The scene is worth reimagining for its stark evocative power. A young black girl wanted to follow Christ and worship with a white congregation whose ideals of fellowship she had heard much about. Under a minister's tutelage she studied the gospel diligently in anticipation of the time she would join. On the appointed day she was to attend the meeting, she entered the church, no doubt with some mix of eagerness, pride, and shy self-consciousness. But angry discussions had taken place behind the scenes. The girls, primed for the moment by their parents, rose and stalked out of the church. After an investigation, reprimands were issued all around, and the girl entered the choir—but to what coldness and muted hostility?

The implications of the incident can hardly be spelled out too strongly. In the 1720s, the early Moravian missionaries to the West Indies had burned with a sense of divine purpose to spread the gospel to Africans. They had been beaten and imprisoned, tropical fevers had plundered their ranks; yet they embraced what they regarded as the privilege of serving as God's messengers. Thousands of blacks had been baptized. But in North Carolina, as the eighteenth century drew to a close, a new generation of white Moravians walked out in protest rather than suffer a black in their midst. The militancy of the young women's manner shocked the elders as much as the spirit of their rebellion. Had the fiery sense of mission been so diluted in just sixty years, wondered the elders, that the Unity's collective purpose was in jeopardy? What, indeed, had happened?

THE YOUNG RACE REBELS of 1797 staged their walkout in a remote meetinghouse amid the fields and forests of the Piedmont countryside. Far from being culturally isolated, however, they joined a rising din of antiblack voices heard with depressing familiarity throughout the young American Republic. As they had done since the struggle for their own independence, a generation of white Revolutionaries and their children struggled to square

10. Aelt. Conf., May 3, 1797; LAC, June 1, 1797.

their rhetoric of liberty and equality against their lack of enthusiasm to apply those words to African Americans.

Unwilling to share power with blacks, white Americans developed a new brand of racial ideology during the last two decades of the eighteenth century that denied blacks a place in the emerging post-Revolutionary political and social order. African enslavement had always been defended by whites on the grounds that Africa itself was a dark continent of barbarous idol worshipers and that Africans in America remained an inferior people who needed exposure to the benefits of European civilization. That reasoning was susceptible to the argument that, if blacks in America were degraded, it was only because slavery kept them so, and because slaveholders purposely locked them in ignorance. Blacks were naturally as intelligent as anyone else, environmental theorists insisted, and with proper education they could function in society as well as any white person.

To trump this logic, intellectuals such as Thomas Jefferson developed a new racial doctrine that blacks were inherently and biologically inferior, had not advanced mentally after several generations of life in America, were incapable of doing so, and hence did not deserve to share political or social equality with whites. Such reasoning enabled whites to contend that the republican ideology of liberty did not apply to blacks. Racial identity replaced the legal status of slavery or freedom as the determinant of social distinction. In the eyes of many whites, blackness itself, whether of a slave or a free person, now signified an immutable badge of social inferiority. In essence, white Americans were defining what an American was and who was allowed to participate in setting the agenda of the young nation. Cultural anthropologists now suggest that ethnic identities evolve through contact with other ethnic groups and the creation or maintenance of boundaries of social difference between them. Thus, to solidify their emerging identity as Americans, whites excluded, or tried to remake, those different from them, particularly African Americans and native Americans in the early nineteenth century. The evolving ideology of racial categories ultimately signified the wielding of massive cultural, social, and economic power.[11]

11. Jordan, *White over Black*, pt. V; Ronald Takaki, *Iron Cages: Race and Culture in Nineteenth-Century America* (Berkeley, Calif., 1986); David Brion Davis, *The Problem of Slavery in the Age of Revolution, 1770–1823* (Ithaca, N.Y., 1975); David R. Roediger, "Whiteness and Ethnicity in the History of 'White Ethnics' in the United States," in Roediger, *Towards the Abolition of Whiteness: Essays on Race, Politics, and Working Class History* (London, 1994),

Evangelical Christianity played a contradictory role in this new order. With its emphasis on spiritual likeness rather than difference, on acceptance rather than rejection, the religion of the awakenings served as a potential check on emerging definitions of racial domination and subordination. But that very emphasis on Christianity as the only legitimate faith also enabled whites to view conversion as a crucial tool in the cultural crusade to domesticate blacks and Indians and induce them to accept the social superiority of the white race. If evangelical Protestantism had heralded one possibility for black and white Americans to surmount racial differences to build a more egalitarian society, that prospect began to ebb in the early nineteenth century. Camp revivals continued to draw black and white worshipers together, and some white evangelicals persisted in denouncing slavery. But their voices grew fainter. The economic survival of slavery was at stake. White evangelicals, including many slaveholders, who once might have used their religion to attack slavery and the social order, increasingly muted the social critique implicit in their emphasis on spiritual equality. Now, as the Moravians had always done, they stressed that the spiritual regeneration of black and white Christians in no way implied social equality. In congregation after congregation during the 1790s and early 1800s, Methodists, Baptists, and others sidestepped or killed proposals to outlaw slaveholding by members or to devise a plan for the gradual emancipation of slaves. In time, they would harden their defense of slavery based on the Scriptures.[12]

The embrace of the revivals dissipated early in the nineteenth century as whites separated themselves, or other whites, from blacks during worship. Congregations segregated blacks at the back of the church or in balconies. African-born Omar ibn Said was thrown in jail for praying in a white church in Fayetteville, North Carolina. One group of white Baptists in Virginia installed a wooden partition down the middle of the church dividing black and white worshipers on either side.[13]

181–198. On the definition and maintenance of ethnicity, see Fredrik Barth, ed., *Ethnic Groups and Boundaries: The Social Organization of Culture Difference* (Boston, 1969); George De Vos and Lola Romanucci-Ross, eds., *Ethnic Identity: Cultural Continuities and Change* (Palo Alto, Calif., 1975); Richard D. Alba, *Ethnic Identity: The Transformation of White America* (New Haven, Conn., 1990).

12. Davis, *Problem of Slavery in the Age of Revolution*, chap. 4; H. Shelton Smith, *In His Image, but . . . : Racism in Southern Religion, 1780– 1910* (Durham, N.C., 1972); Frey, *Water from the Rock*, chap. 9; Forrest G. Wood, *The Arrogance of Faith: Christianity and Race in America from the Colonial Era to the Twentieth Century* (New York, 1990).

13. W. Harrison Daniel, "Virginia Baptists and the Negro in the Early Republic," *VMHB,*

Such physical barriers perfectly captured the spirit of the greater psychological barriers the slaveholders wanted to erect. The implied racial leveling of integrated worship evoked an atavistic fear in them—fear that slaves would think too highly of themselves and that the logic of slavery itself would unravel. Driving a new wedge between slaves and nonslaveholding whites would further prevent the possibility of a cross-racial challenge to slavery of the sort that Gabriel's uprising threatened.[14]

Regarded as dangerous examples, free blacks also felt racial harassment in previously integrated worship halls. In the face of rising discrimination, the efforts of African Americans to secure religious self-determination fostered the rise of independent black churches in Philadelphia, New York, Boston, Charleston, and many other towns.[15]

These cataclysmic changes in post-Revolutionary social relations helped shape the course of racial realignment among the Moravians. Fault lines in their own social structure made them more vulnerable to such pressures. Both from the inside and the outside, the communitarian ideals enunciated by the Unity as far back as 1727 came under duress by the end of the eighteenth century. Many Brethren chafed under economic and social constraints. Ministers decried what they saw as the absorption of worldly notions of liberty by impressionable Brethren. In increasingly strident tones,

LXXX (1972), 60; "Autobiography of Omar ibn Said, Slave in North Carolina, 1831," *AHR*, XXX (1925), 793. The aftermath of segregation within southern churches later in the antebellum period is explored by various authors in John Boles, ed., *Masters and Slaves in the House of the Lord: Race and Religion in the American South, 1740–1870* (Lexington, Ky., 1988), esp. Larry M. James, "Biracial Fellowship in Antebellum Baptist Churches," 37–57, and Robert L. Hall, "Black and White Christians in Florida, 1822–1861," 81–98.

14. A Virginian blamed the rebellion on "liberty and equality," spread in part by the "Methodists, Baptists and others, from the pulpit, without any sort of reserve. What else then could we expect than what has happened?" (*Virginia Herald* [Fredericksburg], Sept. 23, 1800, quoted in Jordan, *White over Black*, 396). For more evidence of white participation in slave conspiracies, see Aptheker, *American Negro Slave Revolts*, 233–234.

15. The literature on the birth of independent black churches is voluminous. For a reassessment, see Will B. Gravely, "The Rise of African Churches in America (1786–1822): Re-examining the Contexts," in Gayraud S. Wilmore, ed., *African American Religious Studies, an Interdisciplinary Anthology* (Durham, N.C., 1989), 301–317. See also Edward D. Smith, *Climbing Jacob's Ladder: The Rise of Black Churches in Eastern American Cities, 1740–1877* (Washington, D.C., 1988); Gary B. Nash, *Forging Freedom: The Formation of Philadelphia's Black Community, 1720–1840* (Cambridge, Mass., 1988), chaps. 4, 6. On the rise of black churches in North Carolina, see C. Eric Lincoln, "Black Religion in North Carolina: From Colonial Times to 1900," in Jeffrey J. Crow and Robert E. Winters, Jr., eds., *The Black Presence in North Carolina* (Raleigh, N.C., 1978), 9–24.

the elders castigated their flock for greater attention to affairs of the pocket-book and the courthouse at the expense of the heart.

The elders were wrestling with the symptoms of changing demographics and the resulting pressure on community principles. By the 1790s, an ever-greater number of Brethren had been born in America. The old guard, born in the 1720s and 1730s in places as diverse as Württemberg, Denmark, and Saxony, were dying off; their places were taken by second and third genera-tions whose experiences differed considerably. For those born in Europe, the conviction to join the Unity arose out of spiritual yearning, awakening, conversion, and sometimes persecution. But as all evangelicals discover, neither a conversion experience nor an automatic desire to live by the same codes can be deeded to the next generation. The sons and daughters of early converts often felt fettered by the church's elaborate machinery to preserve and transmit its values.[16]

Challenges came from artisans and apprentices, enterprising young busi-nessmen frustrated by economic regulations, ambitious farmers bent on increasing their land and slaveholdings, and young people eager to marry as they chose. Such defiance calls to mind the more familiar struggles of Pu-ritan elders to recharge a perceived waning commitment to the founders' ideals in rising generations. To Moravian churchmen, likewise, each infrac-tion expressed a surge of rising individualism against the constraints of the corporate body.[17]

16. Insofar as it is possible to quantify changing attitudes, or declension, one study finds that by the 1790s regularly one-fifth to one-quarter of the Salem congregation was excluded or abstained from Communion, as opposed to one-tenth in the 1760s. In addition, between 1771 and 1801, "a total of 78 people (out of a population which averaged between 150 and 200) were either excluded from the *Gemeine*, expelled, or left Salem before they were formally expelled as a result of disciplinary measures"; see Elisabeth W. Sommer, "Serving Two Mas-ters: Authority, Faith, and Community among the Moravian Brethren in Germany and North Carolina in the Eighteenth Century" (Ph.D. diss., University of Virginia, 1991), chaps. 3, 4.

17. Some of these themes are explored in Michael Shirley, *From Congregation Town to Industrial City: Culture and Social Change in a Southern Community* (New York, 1994), chaps. 1, 2; Jerry L. Surratt, "The Role of Dissent in Community Evolution among Moravians in Salem, 1772–1860," *NCHR*, LII (1975), 235–255; Surratt, *Gottlieb Schober of Salem: Disciple-ship and Ecumenical Vision in an Early Moravian Town* (Macon, Ga., 1983); Norma Taylor Mitchell, "Freedom and Authority in the Moravian Community of North Carolina, 1753–1837" (master's thesis, Duke University, 1962). A parallel pattern of change and secularization in other Moravian communities, particularly Herrnhut and Bethlehem, is described in Gillian Lindt Gollin, *Moravians in Two Worlds: A Study of Changing Communities* (New York, 1967); and Alice M. Caldwell, "Liturgical and Social Change in Moravian Communities, 1750–1823," *Communal Societies*, IX (1989), 23–38.

The leadership's armor for shielding the flock from profane influences was formidable indeed, but hardly impenetrable. The soldiers, refugees, and travelers who flooded Wachovia during the Revolution brought worldly ideas that lasted long after the messengers had left. Try as they might, ministers could not keep the Brethren isolated from the swirl of political events around them as a new nation developed. The lure of political involvement proved attractive. Several Brethren won election to the state assembly in the early 1800s, whereas others were reproved by the elders for publishing an open letter to Congress in the *Raleigh Register* in 1808.[18]

Toward the end of the century, yet another serious challenge threatened Moravian solidarity. The wave of religious revivals that came to be known as the Second Great Awakening surged across the South from Kentucky through the Carolinas and Virginia. Evangelical preachers patrolled central North Carolina vying for souls, often at the Moravians' doorstep. The Brethren generally supported evangelical labors by other faiths, except when their own people were the targets. A Bethania diarist reported in 1799: "A certain young man, who used to belong to us but has turned to the Methodists and serves them as a preacher, had announced a meeting for this place today. As no house was emptied for him he preached on the public street. . . . We would be glad to forget this meeting, which was intended to annoy us, if he had not announced a similar meeting for two weeks hence." The threat seemed even more serious in 1804, when Methodists brashly asked to use the Moravians' own pulpit in Salem to proclaim the word. "We are glad that they proclaim the Gospel," conceded the Brethren unconvincingly, "but we believe that we dare not give over our church to other denominations, and prefer that they should hold their meetings outside our town."[19]

18. Mitchell, "Freedom and Authority," 131–132. Despite their desire to bar church members from politics, leaders took a keen interest in political debates of the 1780s. Because of their heavy dependence on trade, they supported policies favoring creditors. In 1788, the Brethren cast their support for pro-Constitution delegates to the State Convention. North Carolina rejected the Constitution on the first ballot, but a second convention later adopted it, to the Brethren's satisfaction; see Salem Diary, Mar. 13, 1788, "To the Unity's Vorsteher Collegium," November 1789, and Wachovia Memorabilia, 1792, all in Fries et al., eds., *Records*, V, 2217, 2283, 2352.

19. Bethania Diary, Feb. 24, 1799, Auf. Col., Oct. 16, 1804, in Fries et al., eds., *Records*, VI, 2635, 2783. The threat, as the Moravians saw it, had begun long before the revivals of the early 1800s. See, for example, LAC, May 3, 1782, ibid., IV, 1804. A good account of the Methodist penetration into Moravian territory is Larry E. Tise, *The Yadkin Melting Pot: Methodism and Moravians in the Yadkin Valley, 1750–1950, and Mt. Tabor Church, 1845–1966* (Winston-Salem, N.C., 1967). See also John B. Boles, *The Great Revival, 1787–1805* (Lex-

The Methodist challenge was quite direct in the more vulnerable country congregations, and the elders' fears proved well founded when Brethren began defecting. "Generally, each Sunday the Methodists hold a service less than a mile from the Hope *Gemein Haus,* and just at the time of our service," reported a diarist in 1806. The results were plain: "At Hope only a few came to the service, as a Methodist preacher, James Douthit, was preaching a mile away at the home of our neighbor Thomas Douthit." Perhaps some second- and third-generation Brethren turned to Methodism to rekindle emotional faith and a connection with God they felt was lacking in Moravian worship.[20]

Though buffered from the press of worldliness by congregational cohesion, many younger American-born Brethren thus identified more with the land of their birth than with an increasingly distant European heritage. Questioning the faith of their parents was one index of change; so was a shift in racial attitudes. The adolescent girls who walked out in protest in 1797 were born in the early to mid-1780s, and the parents who encouraged them were probably born in the 1760s—most of them in America. Whatever notions of cross-racial tolerance their elders had tried to impart, the young had come of age in America. By rejecting blacks, white Moravians now declared themselves to be Germans no longer, but good Americans. Even more specifically, perhaps white Moravian women, whose own status in the church was slipping, were proclaiming a newfound sense of racialized gender identity by rejecting black women as Christians and as women.[21]

Yet a metaphor of innocence corroded by outside forces is an incomplete explanation for the rise of antiblack sentiment. White Moravians embraced African slavery; they had endorsed servitude and worldly hierarchies for

---

ington, Ky., 1972); Guion Griffis Johnson, "Revival Movements in Ante-Bellum North Carolina," *NCHR,* X (1933), 21–43.

20. Salem Diary, Dec. 22, 1805, May 25, 1806, in Fries et al., eds., *Records,* VI, 2815, 2850.

21. The dimensions of gendered change in the Unity toward the end of the 18th century have only begun to be explored, but research indicates that, after the death of Count Zinzendorf in 1760, church leaders moved the Unity's policies toward women in more conservative directions. Women's roles in church leadership, for example, were severely limited. See Beverly Prior Smaby, "Female Piety among Eighteenth Century Moravians," and Elisabeth Sommer, "Weak Worktools? Female Authority in the Eighteenth Century Moravian Community" (papers presented at the conference "The Quiet in the Land? Women of Anabaptist Traditions in Historical Perspective," Millersville University, Millersville, Pa., June 1995). This theme is explored in Jon F. Sensbach, "Interracial Sects: Race, Gender, and the Moravian Church in Early North Carolina," in Catherine Clinton and Michele Gillespie, eds., *The Devil's Lane: Sex and Race in the Early South* (New York, 1997), 154–167.

three hundred years, and they were eager to make slavery work for them in their adopted land. For Moravian farmers, slave labor was the key to penetrating the expanding Piedmont marketplace. As their investment in slaves increased, the growth of the African-American workforce in places like Bethania, Hope, and Friedberg magnified the tensions between spiritual egalitarianism and slavery. White Brethren had found it relatively easy and magnanimous to incorporate small numbers of blacks into the sacramental fold. It was quite another story to drink from the same chalice as thirty blacks, or fifty, or a hundred.

The issue was more complicated than a simple clash between piety and profits, because Moravian racial and scriptural ideology had always sought to reconcile the two. But an emerging capitalist order was helping to refigure a people who had cast themselves in the image of the primitive Christians. Indeed, the Moravian story echoed in one form or another throughout the early Republic, as the market revolution created new imbalances of wealth and power or reinforced old ones, often along racial lines. The Moravian experience, though partly rooted in the Americanization of a distinctive Germanic people, reflected larger patterns being played out on a grand scale throughout the new nation.[22]

The effects of cultural adaptation on white Brethren in North Carolina emerge in even sharper relief beside their counterparts in Pennsylvania. African slavery among Brethren in Bethlehem, Nazareth, and other congregations was already well on the wane by the time the state legislature passed its gradual emancipation bill in 1780. By the late eighteenth century, no more slaves are known to have been held by Pennsylvania Moravians. A few free blacks, some emancipated by the church, continued to worship in biracial congregations as late as the 1850s. The two North American Moravian provinces, then, veered in sharply different directions as each identified with emergent sectional beliefs. One went toward slavery, the other freedom. As white North Carolina Brethren amended their racial views to

22. The literature on the subject is vast, but see, for example, Allan Kulikoff, *The Agrarian Origins of American Capitalism* (Charlottesville, Va., 1992); Sean Wilentz, "Society, Politics, and the Market Revolution, 1815–1848," in Eric Foner, ed., *The New American History* (Philadelphia, 1990); Charles Sellers, *The Market Revolution: Jacksonian America, 1815–1846* (New York, 1991); Christopher Clark, *The Roots of Rural Capitalism: Western Massachusetts, 1780–1860* (Ithaca, N.Y., 1990); Shirley, *From Congregational Town to Industrial City;* and Michael Merrill, "Putting 'Capitalism' in Its Place: A Review of Recent Literature," *WMQ,* 3d Ser., LII (1995), 315–326.

match those of the majority of white southerners, Pennsylvania Brethren not only shunned slavery but proved slightly more liberal racially than many white northerners.[23]

At the cusp of the nineteenth century, a tangle of forces shaped the racial beliefs of white North Carolina Brethren. These conflicts came to a head in the summer of 1802, when they faced the threat of slave rebellion. Again, religion and revolt were linked. As the Great Revival moved east from Kentucky into North Carolina in late 1801, camp meetings furnished ideal settings for slaves to gather and plan insurrections, often under the leadership of slave preachers. A general rising in eastern North Carolina was planned for June 10, 1802, but the conspiracy was discovered on June 2. The leaders were arrested and tried, many were hanged or deported, and panic spread among whites throughout the region. For the rest of the summer, patrols harassed slaves suspected of complicity, forcing confessions and executing many.[24]

Once word of the thwarted uprising spread west, Stokes County authorities tightened watch in and around Wachovia. On July 16, Moravian "Brethren Kapp and Strehle spoke with Sam [Johann Samuel] about the Negro disturbances." "White patrollers were at the tavern, and visited him, warning him that no Negro might be on the streets without a certificate and that he should secure one." The rebellion scare jolted white Moravians. Though on heightened alert, they were still exempt from bearing arms on slave patrols. Even before the alarm had passed, however, they instead sought a more lasting way to subvert slave revolt. Ministers turned to what they knew best: the Bible. They concluded that their efforts to convert blacks had

23. Although no thorough study has yet been undertaken of the African-American presence in Pennsylvania Moravian congregations, these observations are based on examination of a sampling of church records in the Moravian Archives, Northern Province, Bethlehem. For a study of the African-American emancipation experience in Pennsylvania in the late 18th century, see Gary B. Nash and Jean R. Soderlund, *Freedom by Degrees: Emancipation in Pennsylvania and Its Aftermath* (New York, 1991).

24. Crow, "Slave Rebelliousness and Social Conflict," *WMQ*, 3d Ser., XXXVII (1980), 96–102; John Scott Strickland, "The Great Revival and Insurrectionary Fears in North Carolina: An Examination of Antebellum Southern Society and Slave Revolt Panics," in Orville Vernon Burton and Robert C. McMath, Jr., *Class, Conflict, and Consensus: Antebellum Southern Community Studies* (Westport, Conn., 1982), 57–95; and Thomas C. Parramore, "Conspiracy and Revivalism in 1802: A Direful Symbiosis," *Negro History Bulletin*, II (April–June, 1980), 28–31. Two reappraisals of the rebellion are Douglas R. Egerton, " 'Fly across the River': The Easter Slave Conspiracy of 1802," *NCHR*, LXVIII (1991), 87–110; and Thomas C. Parramore, "Aborted Takeoff: A Critique of 'Fly across the River,' " *NCHR*, LXVIII (1991), 111–121.

lagged in recent years and that a more concerted missionary appeal was needed. They told a visiting congressman from Georgia in August, "In our experience the Negroes who accepted the Gospel served their masters more faithfully than formerly."[25]

The church at once began planning a series of monthly meetings designed to teach Christianity to slaves through the Unity's missionary wing, the *Societät zu Ausbreitung des Evangelii unter den Heiden,* or Society for the Propagation of the Gospel among the Heathen. The society had been formed in Bethlehem, and a North Carolina chapter was begun in 1788, but until 1802 most of its efforts concentrated on dispatching missionaries to south-eastern Indians, most notably the Cherokees in northwest Georgia.[26] The slave revolt scare of 1802 suddenly awakened the society to the realization that hundreds of thousands of slaves urgently needed evangelizing, starting in the Moravians' own backyard. They would spread the gospel to their own slaves, seeking "from time to time to incorporate one or another of them into our fellowship through Holy Baptism." Pastors also might have seen in the mission a chance to rekindle a flickering evangelical spirit and reunite a white population gone astray. "The Society wished that the renewal of grace, love and simplicity in the Unity of Brethren might be accompanied by an outpouring of the witness spirit in our congregations here."[27]

Not surprisingly, the idea for the local mission was championed by spokesmen from Friedberg and Bethania, where some of the largest slave concentrations in Wachovia lived. They took their cue from slaveholders in Hope, who had already begun such an effort in late 1801. These English Brethren, perhaps responding to widespread African-American restless-

25. Bethabara Committee, July 16, 1802; Salem Diary, Aug. 31, 1802, in Fries et al., eds., *Records,* VI, 2701.

26. Wachovia Memorabilia, 1788, in Fries et al., eds., *Records,* V, 2212. On Moravian missions to the Cherokees, see William G. McLoughlin, *Cherokees and Missionaries, 1789–1839* (New Haven, Conn., 1984), esp. chap. 2. Moravian missionaries operated their farm at the mission station in Springplace, Ga., with slaves hired from nearby Cherokee slaveholders.

27. Wachovia Memorabilia, 1802, in Fries et al., eds., *Records,* VI, 2690. The society called for a report on efforts to evangelize to blacks in Wachovia. The result was an annual summary between 1802 and 1805 of local missions. Totaling some 40 handwritten pages in German, these reports provide a key source for analyzing the African-American population of Wachovia in the early 19th century; see SAE, November 1802, "Nachricht von den Negern in der Wachau," preamble. On plantation missions, see Albert J. Raboteau, *Slave Religion: The "Invisible Institution" in the Antebellum South* (New York, 1978), chap. 4; and Milton C. Sernett, *Black Religion and American Evangelicalism: White Protestants, Plantation Missions, and the Flowering of Negro Christianity, 1787–1865* (Metuchen, N.J., 1975).

ness, "expressed a wish that now and then appointed meetings for the Negroes in the Settlement might be kept, as many grow up very ignorant." In
Hope's early years, the church had taken an interest "only in those few
Negroes in whom one could notice the workings of holy grace," such as
Paul, Priscilla, Samuel, Tabitha Jane, and a few others. But the Hope Committee concluded that separate meetings would give a better forum to "present the truths of our beliefs to them in a clear and more comprehensible
manner." Twenty blacks attended the first meeting in December 1801. They
"appeared to be pleased, and their remarks thereafter showed that this arrangement especially satisfied them." Meetings continued on a quarterly
basis, then increased to once every two months and by June 1802 to once a
month. They proved popular, drawing about fifty worshipers each time,
including members of the Hope congregation and non-Moravians alike.[28]

These meetings pointed the way. By the third week in July 1802, barely a
month after the slave uprising in eastern North Carolina, the Friedberg
Committee proposed separate meetings for blacks every eight weeks on the
Hope model. Ministers favored the idea but cautioned that "because one
hears that disturbances have arisen among the Negroes in our region as
well, and that the military patrols are searching for runaway Negroes, of
whom several have been taken as prisoners to Germanton [county seat of
Stokes], we should be very careful with these Negro meetings, and consider
it wise to request the masters of the Negroes to give them a pass to the
meetings." Reluctant Bethania slaveholders similarly feared that "the passage of many Negroes through our neighborhood will bring only opportunities for disorder and complaints."[29]

Ministers, however, lobbied slaveholders hard to accept the plan and by
August had persuaded them it was their "duty" to support the mission.
Tapping into African-American information networks, ministers told slaves
to spread the word to others outside Wachovia, but with the warning that
after meetings "they should not swarm around the village but return home
at once, failing which those who disobey will be turned away in the future."
Noting that most slaves spoke German—including, perhaps, those owned by
German Lutherans to the north of Wachovia—churchmen had high hopes

28. Hope Committee Minutes, Oct. 11, 1801; SAE, November 1802, "Nachricht von den
Negern," pt. B, sec. 1, "Hope." Significantly, the decision to increase the meetings occurred in
late June, presumably soon after the fear of slave insurrection reached Wachovia, although the
connection was not explicitly made by the Hope Committee; see LAC, June 25, 1802.

29. LAC, July 23, 1802; Committee in Bethania, Aug. 1, 1802.

for the mission in Bethania. Some blacks had attended meetings with whites and were already singing Moravian hymns at home. Indeed, some sixty to seventy attended the first meeting on September 12. Minister Carl Gotthold Reichel sang a few verses "in which the Negroes joined as well as they could," and spoke on Titus 2:11–13: "Denying ungodliness and worldly lusts, we should live soberly and righteously and godly in this present world." Reichel then came right to the point, explaining that, since the passage "was about servants and about their duties toward their masters, they should take the words of the text to heart and believe in them." The listeners' only reported reaction was a diplomatic remark "that the meeting was blessed with the noticeable presence of the Saviour." Perhaps more heartfelt was the enthusiasm of white non-Moravian observers, who told Reichel that "surely in this way the Negroes would best be kept in their bonded subordination."[30]

This emphasis on obedience notwithstanding, African Americans seem to have responded to these overtures with cautious interest. In 1802, there were fifteen black Moravians in Wachovia: Peter Oliver in Salem, the six-member Samuel family and Anna in Bethabara, and Samuel, Tabitha Jane, Paul, Priscilla, Sarah Elizabeth, Matthew, and Charity in Hope. But most of the predominantly agrarian black population was non-Moravian. Their large numbers at the first meetings might have reflected a genuine desire by many to hear preaching of some kind and a wish by others simply to attend a communal meeting, though a dose of coercion by whites is possible as well.

Ministers tried to cultivate slaves' enthusiasm by resorting to proven evangelizing techniques used seventy years earlier in the West Indies. In Hope, the two black communicants, Priscilla and Samuel, were appointed sextons and "were requested to be attentive to the declarations of the Negroes and to communicate them to the pastors." In much the same way as the national helpers had done on Saint Thomas, the two black Moravians with the highest status served as surrogates for the preacher, mediating between him and the audience. By designating certain brothers and sisters as envoys to their companions, the ministers hoped to cultivate and control scriptural discussion among the enslaved.[31]

Some responded to the outreach by joining one congregation or another.

30. Committee in Bethania, Aug. 23, 1802; SAE, November 1802, "Nachricht von den Negern," pt. B, no. 3, "Bethania."
31. SAE, November 1802, "Nachricht von den Negern," pt. B, sec. 1, "Hope."

Jack, a slave of Christian Conrad's in Bethania, attended meetings regularly and pressed minister Reichel for baptism. The Bethania Committee hoped in 1803 that Jack's conversion "might have a blessed influence on our Negroes here, with whom Jack has no association, but who more often mock him." It is not clear whether other blacks shunned Jack because he had shown an interest in conversion, or whether he sought religion because he was an outcast among his fellow slaves. In any case, his baptism with the name John Immanuel in early 1804, under the sponsorship of Johann Samuel and Peter Oliver, was hailed as "the first fruits of our work among the Negroes" in Bethania. In Hope, Jenny, a slave of Robert Markland, asked for baptism in 1804. Observing that "she still appeared to be somewhat ignorant and from her conversations it was clear she believed simply that through baptism she would obtain all she yearned for," the ministers urged her "to give her whole heart to the Saviour, and he would not deny her baptism." Baptized and christened Mary Jane in 1805, she joined the Hope congregation.[32]

The linguistic abilities of many of the new converts again show the closeness with which black and white shared their lives. When Jack was christened John Immanuel, the minister "made a short talk to the candidate, speaking in German which the man understood better than English." According to his biography, Immanuel was born in Amelia County, Virginia, in 1775 and must have come to Wachovia at a young age. In his early years, he "lived with Bro. and Sister Christian Conrad in the vicinity of Bethania." Evidently assimilated into the Conrad household, he must have lived and worked almost exclusively with German-speaking people, virtually sequestered from English-speakers.[33]

Likewise, present at the baptism of a black infant in Bethania in 1803 were "most of the Negroes of the village, all of whom understand German." But the languages used by blacks varied even within Wachovia itself. A minister reported: "As most Negroes in Friedberg understand German better than English, the meetings are held in German there, but in Hope and Bethania they are held in English." Such enclaves of German-speaking blacks, wherever they existed in early-nineteenth-century America, were relatively

---

32. Committee in Bethania, May 23, 1803, Nov. 18, 1805; Bethania Diary, Jan. 8, 1804, in Fries et al., eds., *Records*, VI, 2789–2790; SAE, November 1804, "Bericht von der Arbeit der Bruder unter den Negern hiesiger Gegend," pt. 1, "Hope"; LAC, June 21, 1805.
33. Bethania Diary, Jan. 8, 1804, in Fries et al., eds., *Records*, VI, 2789.

small by the standards of the majority, who spoke English or Afro-English creoles. They nonetheless reaffirmed the cultural and linguistic diversity of blacks in North America, who in various places spoke French, Spanish, Dutch, and a host of African and Indian languages.[34]

Their immersion in the culture of white Brethren, combined with the message of Christian redemption, disposed some African Americans to seek fellowship. But the mass conversion the ministers hoped for never happened. "With regret we must recognize that most of them still have no desire to come from the shadows into the light and to convert from the power of Satan to God, and that when a ray of hope shines on one or another of them it quickly disappears," confessed a pastor in 1803. That year, the number of black Moravians had increased only to eighteen, by 1805 to twenty-one, and twenty-eight by 1807.[35]

Something more subtle than mere indifference was happening. Blacks who refused the bait offered by the Brethren had their reasons. One was that the mission spawned a struggle over control of slave family life. Ministers had noticed that many slaves were not married by church standards. "In Bethania it is repeatedly the case that unwed Negresses have children," which pastors found "distressing" because they had "taken an interest in giving them the Gospel." Slaveowners were reminded "that it is their duty to do their utmost to have their Negresses lawfully married." Apparently, the pastors sought to impose arranged marriages upon slaves, who would have none of it. "Negroes and Negresses here in town would not marry each other, because for their part they wish to make their own choices," admitted the Bethania council. "One Brother remarked that if he had an adult Negro

34. Bethania Diary, Feb. 13, 1803, in Fries et al., eds., *Records*, VI, 2752; SAE, November 1802, "Nachricht von den Negern," pt. B, sec. 2, "Friedberg." See Gwendolyn Midlo Hall, *Africans in Colonial Louisiana: The Development of Afro-Creole Culture in the Eighteenth Century* (Baton Rouge, La., 1992); Jane Landers, "Gracia Real de Santa Teresa de Mose: A Free Black Town in Spanish Colonial Florida," *AHR*, XCV (1990), 9–30; William Gehrke, "Negro Slavery among the Germans in North Carolina," *NCHR*, XIV (1937), 307–324. For a summary of literature on black-white linguistic interchange in Anglo-America, see Philip D. Morgan, "British Encounters with Africans and African-Americans," in Bernard Bailyn and Philip D. Morgan, eds., *Strangers within the Realm: Cultural Margins of the First British Empire* (Chapel Hill, N.C., 1991), 203–207.

35. SAE, November 1803, "Nachricht von den Negern in der Wachau," pt. 3, "Bethania"; SAE, reports from 1803–1805; Wachovia Memorabilia, 1807, in Fries et al., eds., *Records*, VI, 2884.

and an adult Negress they would not want to marry each other because one would not be right for the other."[36]

This sudden interest in slaves' nuptial affairs after years of white indifference must have puzzled and annoyed black non-Moravians who wanted the independence to conduct their family lives as they chose. The church even considered threatening to sell slaves who persisted in "unlawful Connexions." Day to day, the enslaved bowed to the masters' will in so many ways. This time, their defiance wore down the ministers. Responsive neither to threats nor cajoling, they proved as resistant as church leaders had feared. By simply refusing to marry partners selected for them, African Americans managed to preserve a margin of cultural autonomy. In November 1803, the society admitted that "so many difficulties have arisen in opposition to this matter—especially on the part of the Negroes themselves—that nothing has yet happened." Ministers held out hope that continued preaching would evoke the desired change. But the reverse might have happened— resentment over the marriage issue perhaps hardened blacks against the Brethren.[37]

Something else deterred blacks from joining the church. "The reason that not as many come to the meetings as in the beginning," ventured a minister in 1803, "is that the affair is no longer new to them, and moreover, that they attend the meetings of other religious faiths more often." Still, he conceded without much enthusiasm, "if they at least hear the word somewhere, and are thereby stirred to run to the arms of the shepherd, then we are satisfied in our hearts."[38]

African Americans were indeed seeking other sources of spiritual nourishment. In camp meetings, log churches, barns, and fields, evangelical preachers drew hundreds of black and white seekers eager for the participatory drama of spiritual awakening. A Baptist meeting near Hope in 1803 drew "most of the Negroes." Inspired by such meetings, black audiences eagerly sought more exhortation. One day in 1804, Brother Reichel, the Bethania minister, noted: "Two Methodist preachers, who live in the neighborhood, preached in the orchard behind the tavern, and a crowd gathered from the neighborhood. It was more quiet and orderly than we expected.

36. HCfG, Apr. 4, 1803, in Fries et al., eds., *Records*, VI, 2740; Committee in Bethania, May 30, 1803.

37. Committee in Bethania, June 13, 1803; SAE, November 1803, "Nachricht von den Negern," pt. 3, "Bethania."

38. SAE, November 1803, "Nachricht von den Negern," pt. 3, "Bethania," pt. 4, "Hope."

One woman went into a kind of ecstasy, and began to shout." But the meeting drew an unexpected result. After the preaching ended at one o'clock, the hour that monthly meetings for blacks were held, most black listeners went quickly from the orchard to the Bethania prayer hall to hear more preaching. "This was a blessed sign that the meetings are important and dear to them," Reichel concluded.[39]

Perhaps; but worshipers might have invested a deeper meaning in the chance to hear back-to-back sermons. Going from one meeting to another, measuring one preacher against the other, they must have carefully weighed the value of what they heard. The pressure on them to convert was strong. But they could compare messages and styles, take what they liked from each, discard the rest, and shape the assorted fragments into a vision of Christianity that addressed their needs. Some joined Moravian congregations, whereas others chose the Methodists. Thus, when Moravian ministers complained that African-American audiences remained unmoved and aloof, a closer version to the truth was that they were very interested in Christianity. In fact, they were conducting a lively experiment in finding and adapting a faith to their own desires, not to those of the masters.

Whatever inspiration they drew from white ministers, moreover, many blacks found a clearer, alternative voice in a slave preacher named Lewis who lived near Bethania. Black preachers played an important role in spreading Christianity through southern slave quarters and free black communities. Exhorters such as Lewis commanded great respect among African-American listeners. A glimpse of him in action was recorded by the Bethania diarist in March 1804. "This morning, in the God's Acre for Negroes, there was the burial of a Negro boy named Bob, belonging to our Br. George Hauser. The Negro Lewis, who belongs to Mr. Jean, living some miles from here, held the service, which went in a quiet and reverent manner. They call Lewis their preacher, because he sometimes goes out and preaches to his race; he belongs to the Methodists." Lewis, reported the diarist with approval, "spoke to the gathered Negroes on the sinfulness of men, whereby death is forced on all men, but how they have been redeemed by the bitter suffering and death of Jesus Christ, how his spilled blood cries of mercy for all men."[40]

---

39. Salem Diary, July 31, 1803, in Fries et al., eds., *Records*, VI, 2730; Bethania Diary, Sept. 16, 1804.

40. Bethania Diary, Mar. 27, 1804. Part of this episode is translated in Fries et al., eds., *Records*, VI, 2791.

Nothing in this brief portrait suggests any overt subversiveness in Lewis's style or rhetoric. Having encouraged and trained slave preachers to assist their own missionary work, the Moravians viewed him, not as a threat, but as an ally—as long as his exhortation remained to their liking. Yet his message addressed the lives of black auditors as no white person could and in shades of meaning well hidden from slaveholders and ministers. Lewis's popularity reflected the growing appeal of Christianity among the region's black population. As their expanding baptismal sponsorship network showed, black Americans wove themselves in a web of spiritual kinship that overlapped with, but expanded far beyond, the Moravian church family.

They really had no choice. At the same time white Brethren tried to get them to join the church, the drumbeat for racial separatism grew louder. Ministers could not understand how those contradictory forces worked against the mission. Once, church leaders had quelled antiblack sentiments. But by the early nineteenth century, they joined the chorus of voices questioning the black presence in fellowship. If one moment signaled a watershed in their shifting consciousness, it was the summer of 1802 and the start of meetings for black non-Moravians. Only five years earlier, in 1797, the elders had reacted with indignation when the Older Girls in Friedberg protested a black girl in their midst. Events of 1802, however, made the ministers view African Americans in another light, as objects of intense—and separate—evangelical attention. That new perspective spawned a critical look at interracial worship.

Whites continued to make an issue of seating in church. In 1803, several congregations confined black listeners to the back of the church. In Friedberg, "the Brethren believe it would be well if Negroes who come to the meetings would sit in the most rear benches." Not surprisingly, blacks reacted to such disdain by avoiding whites. "Our Negroes always explain their absence from our general meetings with the excuse that white people do not want to sit with them," noted the Bethania Committee, whose solution, like their counterparts' in Friedberg, was to reserve several back benches for blacks. In Salem, likewise, "certain benches in the Saal will be designated for Negroes so that they also can attend other public meetings."[41]

41. Committee in Friedberg, Oct. 30, 1803; Committee in Bethania, Dec. 29, 1803; Aelt. Conf., Jan. 12, 1804. On special occasions, blacks actually sat at the front of churches. In 1804, the induction of Jack into the Bethania congregation as John Immanuel was "attended by a considerable number of Negroes who were seated on the front benches" as well as by many whites. The important point, however, is that whites were consciously separating themselves

Since neither Friedberg nor Bethania had black members in 1803, the zeal for separate seating was aimed at black non-Moravians. It is unclear whether black Brethren such as Priscilla, Johann Samuel, or Peter Oliver were also forced to the back of the church. But at some profound level even they no longer held the same respect with whites. The rituals that had always celebrated the universalism of Moravian fellowship steadily gained stark new racial overtones.

Black Brethren, for example, had always taken part in the *Pedilavium,* or foot washing ceremony. In 1809, the Bethania minister, Simon Peter, asked the elders for clarification of the church's foot washing policy. "Brother Peter wanted to know how to proceed with Negro Brothers and Sisters in the Pedilavium," the board reported. They gave him a clear answer: "The Conference regarded it for the best that they should be present but should not be washed." Once intimate participants in this ceremonial cleansing of sin and pride, black Brethren were now expected to stand aside and observe whites wash each other's feet. What lesson they were to derive as spectators is unclear. "If I then, the Lord and the Teacher, have washed your feet," Christ admonished the disciples, "ye also ought to wash one another's feet" (John 13:14). Once these words were an unconditional code for the Brethren to live by. Now, either they no longer took the command literally, or their interpretation of scriptural literalness had changed. If Christ was still re- garded as the Chief Elder of the Unity of Brethren in 1809, his opinion had lost clout.[42]

Nothing symbolized the profound changes at hand more vividly than the fate of the kiss of peace. Of all the Moravian rituals, the kiss signified the pinnacle of Christian love and union, the final mystical celebration with which Brethren were inducted into the Unity. But by the early nine- teenth century, even the kiss was drowning in the rising tide of white race- consciousness. In March 1808, the elders reported that "the Negro couple William and Chrissy will be received into the congregation of Bethania at a private meeting, as it would not be seemly to give Negroes the kiss of peace in a public service." Discussing the same subject in 1814, the Hope Commit-

from blacks, not simply from non-Moravian strangers; see Bethania Diary, Jan. 8, 1804, in Fries et al., eds., *Records,* VI, 2789.

42. Aelt. Conf., Sept. 6, 1809 (trans. author). Bishop August Gottlieb Spangenberg set forth the importance of foot washing in the early Unity in *An Exposition of Christian Doctrine as Taught in the Protestant Church of the United Brethren or Unitas Fratrum,* ed. and trans. J. Ken- neth Pfohl and Edmund Schwarze (1778; reprint, Winston-Salem, N.C., 1959), 450–452.

tee set forth in even more bare and painful terms just how dramatic the shift in thinking had been. Reverend Samuel Kramsch, reported the Committee diarist in English, "wished to know the opinion of the Committee whether the reception of Negroes in the congregation by a Kiss as it is customary was anyway disagreeable to be performed in a meeting of the Society. It has been allways done so here as in other congregations, but as times and circumstances change, scruples have been started lately." The solution? "The Committee thought it would be best if our young people were not present and the transaction performed in a meeting of grown persons."[43]

Once a transcendent exchange of the holy spirit, the kiss of peace had become a thing of poison, tainted with impurity like the kiss of Judas. The sight of a white person's lips touching black skin was now deemed repugnant by whites, who feared that such gestures would pollute the minds of their children, might perhaps even suggest interracial sexuality. Times and circumstances had changed, and "scruples [had] been started"; no trace of regret colored the minister's words. The lesson was as clear as its implications were startling: there *were* differences between black and white—irrevocable, unbridgeable, absolute differences, in the world of the spirit and of the flesh. God himself had ordained two separate spheres, and it was no longer the work of men and women to merge them.

That lesson—insistently repeated, rigidly enforced—leached into the minds of the young. John Henry Leinbach, born in Salem in 1796, lived his formative years as the walls were being erected between black and white. In 1832, on a journey north, he encountered a black passenger on a coach ride to Newark, New Jersey. "When I came to the stage," he wrote (in English), "the seats were all occupied but one, which I had to take, on the middle seat, and fronting me sat an African in full glory, staring me right in the face, and entangling his black legs in mine; rather disagreeable to a Southern man."[44]

At the time Leinbach wrote, the Brethren had been implanted in North

<hr>

43. Aelt. Conf., Mar. 16, 1808, in Fries et al., eds., *Records,* VI, 2927; Committee in Hope, Aug. 7, 1814.

44. Journal of John Henry Leinbach, May 19, 1832, Old Salem Library, Winston-Salem, N.C. Leinbach's life is the subject of Isabel Veazie, "Master and Apprentice," *Three Forks of Muddy Creek,* III (Winston-Salem, N.C., 1976), 49–57. Leinbach was already a fourth-generation American. His great-grandfather Johann was born near Frankfurt, Germany, in 1712 and later emigrated to Pennsylvania and in 1765 to Bethania. All his children were born in America. John Henry Leinbach's father Johannes was born in Bethania in 1766 (personnel files at Old Salem, Inc.).

America for nearly a century, and though plenty of German-born Brethren still lived in the Salem of his youth, Leinbach considered himself thoroughly American. Even more to the point, he thought of himself as a Southerner, with the sectional and racial loyalties and prejudices of other proslavery whites. In firm repudiation of his people's own past, he and other whites of his generation now found physical contact with a black person "rather disagreeable for a Southern man." Like so many other European immigrants and their descendants in America, white Moravians had found, in the negation of blacks, a perfect foil for their emergent national identity as Americans.

One by one the divisions were codified. It was predictable, then, that black and white would come to be separated in death as in life. In the earliest sections of God's Acre in Salem, Bethabara, and Hope, black Moravians had always found a final resting place alongside white brothers and sisters. The flat headstones stretching over the hills in long, orderly rows bore the simplest of inscriptions—name, birthplace, date of death, age—but revealed much about the multilingual nature of these early settlers united by their belief in Christ. Brothers and sisters from Saxony, Württemberg, Denmark, Holland, England, and Pennsylvania lay side by side in their separate choir groups. Among them may still be found today fading headstones that read "Abraham—Neger [Negro]—Guinea," "Christian der Mohr [the Moor]," "Katharina Negerin [the Negress]," and others that inscribe a necrology of spiritual leveling on the landscape. Here indeed was a loyal fellowship of death.

But in 1816, Salem officials determined that *all* blacks, Moravian and non-Moravian alike, would be buried separately from whites, and they set aside space for that purpose outside the town limits in a former parish graveyard previously reserved for non-Brethren. In such official directives, we miss the discussion, around town or in the boardroom, behind the decision, so it is impossible to say whether any white Brethren raised voices of disagreement. If so, their dissent was buried. The spirit and the effect of the ruling were unmistakable. The last black Moravian buried among white Brethren in the Salem God's Acre was Peter Oliver, who died in 1810.[45]

45. Auf. Col., Oct. 21, 1816. No similar directives have been found for segregation in the other graveyards. But only one black burial after 1810 has been found in those locations, 85-year-old Priscilla, who as late as 1834 was buried in the graveyard at Hope, perhaps as a last gesture of respect for a woman who had lived most of her life with white Moravians.

Anyone seeking a road map of the changing social order of the young Republic could find it plainly scrawled in this mortuary geography of racism atop the gentle Carolina hills.

WITH OFFICIAL BLESSING, white Moravians now found they could get away with the most petulant expressions of disdain for the previous norms of interracial worship. Even though black congregants continued to be buried in the Hope graveyard after they were banned from the Salem burial ground, for example, they no longer automatically received respect from whites. The Hope Committee ruled in 1817 that gravestones should be provided for plots lacking them. Congregant John Peddycoard, disregarding previous expectations that masters would provide stones for slaves, was "not willing" to do so for his former slave, the baptized sister Tabitha Jane, believing that her husband, Sam, had "enough money to get one." The Hope minister asked Sam, who was "willing to procure a stone for his deceased wife Tabby." How Sam had the money for a stone is not known, but his willingness to spend what must have been precious savings reflected an evident realization that African Americans had to strive that much further to honor each other's spirituality in the absence of white decency.[46]

It was little wonder that black interest in Moravian preaching came to what the ministers described as "a complete standstill." The separate meetings continued for a while and then fizzled out altogether by 1808. Some years later, in 1814, the Hope minister Kramsch asked his Committee "what the reason had been that the former Negro meetings were dropt." In his view, "there was no particular cause known, except the indifferency in attending them." Here and there a black supplicant still applied to join the church. But they were scattered figures. African Americans could hardly be blamed for shunning those who counseled patience, subservience, and worship from the back bench.[47]

Some clung to the congregational order they knew, perhaps hoping in

46. Hope Committee, May 2, 11, June 15, 1817.

47. SAE, November 1804, "Bericht von der Arbeit," pt. 1, "Hope"; Committee in Hope, Apr. 3, 1814. Racial discrimination against blacks also cropped up in the Moravian mission outposts to the Cherokees. Missionaries at the station in Springplace, Ga., said in 1819 that any blacks admitted to the mission would be "assigned special seats" at Communion and "the cup is given them last of all." Not surprisingly, the Brethren made only one black convert there, in 1827; see McLoughlin, *Cherokees and Missionaries*, 48–49 n. 23.

time to return to favor with whites. Yet a number of black congregants, possibly believing they had little left to lose, challenged Moravian moral codes with growing defiance. The Hope Committee in 1811 confronted the "painful necessity of excluding from the Congregation the Negro woman Mary Jane, commonly called Jenny, who belongs to Captain Markland, on account of a very criminal connexion with a strange Negro-man." Another sister of long standing, Anna (now known more commonly as Nancy), repeatedly vexed whites with a confrontational attitude. Long a servant in the Salem tavern and then in the Bethabara store and tavern, she had a testy relationship with her masters and had sought the protection and intervention of the elders at least twice in previous years. Finally in 1815, when tavernkeepers Johann and Maria Kummer "could not agree with her any more," they gave Anna / Nancy to Kramsch in Hope. There she "lost her congregational privileges through her bad behavior" and was allowed to regain them only by "showing an improvement in her course." She showed no inclination to do so. By 1818, she had "become a burden" to the Kramsches, was moved to Salem, and once again was barred from worship, though officials seem to have made no effort to sell and be rid of the aging but insubordinate former sister for good.[48]

Two other Moravians launched an especially bold assault on the church's authority. John Immanuel, whose master sold him away from Bethania to Salem in 1808, worked at the tannery and worshiped with the town congregation. In 1811, he got into trouble by carrying on an apparent affair with free mulatto Christine Oliver just three months after the death of her husband, Peter. Immanuel, town leaders noted, "seems to have taken a liking for Christine Oliver. Because of his crude and careless behavior he has several times caused a scandal in the community." Officials considered whether the two could marry, taking into account his status as a slave and hers as a free person. They agreed to give him two days a week for five years "to let him establish his own livelihood." Two weeks later, Immanuel "admitted that he ha[d] worked in the evenings in the house of the widowed Sister Oliver, and also that he ha[d] found his night's lodgings there if it grew too late. He promised to be more careful about his behavior and good morals." But later Immanuel was "trapped several times during the night" at Christine's, causing "great scandal and upheaval." The board scrapped

---

48. Hope Committee, Feb. 3, 1811, Jan. 22, 1815; LAC, Jan. 20, 1815, July 3, 1818; Aelt. Conf., June 22, 1818, in Fries et al., eds., *Records*, VII, 3375.

plans to marry the pair and banished them from the congregation. After threatening to sell Immanuel, the Collegium relented, but he remained an outcast. Christine's lease on a piece of land near Salem was canceled, and she was forced to move, leaving her children to the authority of the courts. Christine's downfall reaffirmed the precariousness of free black life in the new Republic. Peter Oliver's long struggle to gain freedom and establish his family's independent livelihood had ended in the tragic dispersal of his survivors just a few months after his death.[49]

Such episodes might have reflected black Brethren's disgust with white separatism and a reciprocal desire to abandon the church. They might also have reflected a general pattern of continued African-American unrest in the early nineteenth century. Slave plots and small-scale uprisings continued to ripple across the South in the aftermath of Gabriel's Rebellion and the conspiracy of 1802. Slave resistance intensified between 1809 and 1815 in response to economic depression brought on by soil exhaustion, the embargo and nonintercourse acts, and the War of 1812. As the United States moved toward open hostility with Great Britain in 1812, both black and white southerners drew lessons from the American Revolution. As in that war, many slaves tried to exploit the political and military turmoil by running away to the British, who again dangled the carrot of liberation. Slaveowners, often expressing more fear of rebellious slaves than of the British, clamped down with predictably repressive measures.[50]

All of these conditions came home once more to Moravian territory. Whites moved quickly to head off an increase in black insubordination. The number of church-owned slaves in Salem had increased slightly since the

49. The relationship between John Immanuel and Christine Oliver is chronicled in Auf. Col., Jan. 8, 23, Feb. 19, 26, Mar. 5, 1811. In 1811, the Collegium warned: "The mulatto woman Oliver, who is trying to find a place on the Unity land in our neighborhood, should not be given permission because of the ill conduct of her life. We wish she would leave the neighborhood for good." Christine had also been stripped of her two children even before then. Israel and Nancy Oliver were both quite young when, soon after the death of their father, a county court ruled that Christine was unable to care for them, removed them from her custody, and bound them to white familes as indentured servants. A free black woman had little chance against the legal apparatus of the state. Her affair with Immanuel, if indeed it was such, might have been an effort to compensate for the loss of husband and children within a span of two months; see Auf. Col., Nov. 6, Dec. 27, 1810, Mar. 3, June 25, 1811.

50. Aptheker, *American Negro Slave Revolts*, 23–27, 241–244; Frank A. Cassell, "Slaves of the Chesapeake Bay Area and the War of 1812," *JNH*, LII (1972), 144–155; Sarah McCulloh Lemmon, *Frustrated Patriots: North Carolina and the War of 1812* (Chapel Hill, N.C., 1973), 122, 196–198.

beginning of the century, and, though they remained but a small handful of people, together with hired slave and free black workers they were a source of suspicion to whites. "The Negro lodged in the vacant house is going to be moved to some other quarters, because he is keeping company," the Salem board reported in June 1809. In September, whites voiced fears that "meetings of the Negroes in the Tavern will be of evil consequences." Blacks perceived as troublemakers were purged. "Brother Stotz will dismiss the Negro Humphrey because of his impudent behavior. We also wished to get rid of Dick and his wife bought for the Tavern, because their behavior is very bad also." In January 1812, a free Negro who won a contract to operate the Single Brothers' farm was warned not to "hold meetings there with other Negroes or accommodate any of them or any other persons."[51]

Reports of slave rebellions—real or imagined—confirmed their fears. In April 1812, a Virginia slave testified about a planned revolt in Rockingham County, North Carolina, adjacent to Stokes County, in which slaves "said they were not made to work for white people, but they (the white people), were made to work for themselves; and that they (the negroes) would have it so." In July 1812, Salem leaders were alarmed by reports of a plot in Huntsville, a small town ten miles west of Salem. "There was also the rumor that they would put their hostile intentions into action next Thursday, when some authorities are to be elected here in Salem and the neighborhood." Four armed Brethren patrolled the town on election day, and no disturbance was reported. In 1813, touchy authorities reported "a gathering of many Negroes of the neighborhood at the place of the Negro Dick, who is property of the Community Diaconate and lives a mile from here. Brother Stotz will tell him this cannot happen again." In Bethabara: "A Negro who had worked for Brother Kummer for a year and a day had been under suspicion for a considerable time. Yesterday morning a theft in the store was discovered, and the Negro this morning was taken in chains to Germanton."[52]

White Brethren's need to control a potentially rebellious servile class forced them into a seeming paradox regarding their desire not to bear arms.

51. Auf. Col., June 27, Sept. 12, 1809, Jan. 23, 1810, Jan. 7, 1812.

52. Aptheker, *American Negro Slave Revolts*, 252–253; Auf. Col., July 12, 1812, Feb. 3, Oct. 26, 1813; Salem Diary, Aug. 13, 1812, in Fries et al., eds., *Records*, VII, 3169. Whites remained intensely interested in regional cases of black rebellion throughout the decade. In 1819, many Moravians traveled to Germanton, some 15 miles north in Stokes County, to witness the trial and hanging of a slave who had murdered his master; see Salem Diary, Oct. 21, Nov. 12, 1819, in Fries et al., eds., *Records*, VII, 3405.

During the Revolution, they stockpiled arms and ammunition in case of a slave uprising while pleading exemption from military service for either side. Likewise, in the War of 1812 white Brethren clung to their exemption, yet by participating in the Stokes County system of slave patrols they shouldered arms to support slavery. Both they and the state distinguished between bearing arms against an external foe (the British) and an internal one (enslaved African Americans). Even many Brethren could agree on the necessity of upholding the system in which they were by now so thoroughly enmeshed, although elders complained that service in court-appointed slave patrols was not wholesome for their youth.

In fact, elders expressed concern that some men seemed to delight in searching black homes, interrogating slaves, perhaps even roughing them up in the fashion of other slave patrols. "Some time ago the court appointed three young single Brethren to the patrol over the Negroes in this neighborhood," they noted in 1814. "It appears that in filling this office they are going further than is well or necessary. They shall be admonished to show more of the Brotherly character." Salem officials, observing that "the control over the Negroes of this neighborhood is disadvantageous to the young men," asked the court "not to have a new patrol appointed next year. If this is not possible, we wish the task would not fall on young, inexperienced Brethren." The request was denied; the court again appointed two young single men as patrollers. The episode again demonstrated the constant tension within white society generated by the church's efforts to make slavery compatible with brotherliness. As the boards saw it, slave control was needed but distasteful and a bit ethically awkward; at the very least, Brethren should be a little gentler about it.[53]

In this tense era, black friendship continued to hold an exotic and daring appeal for some white Brethren. Although most whites now wished to exclude blacks from their company, others secretly sought them out. White offenders who were caught meeting furtively with blacks were punished severely. The Bethania Committee reported in 1816, for example, that "the single Anton Hauser here in the village, on the second Christmas day of the

53. Aelt. Conf., June 1, 1814, in Fries et al., eds., *Records,* VII, 3236; Auf. Col., Aug. 2, Dec. 20, 1814. During the latter stages of the war, the North Carolina General Assembly did, in fact, rescind the Brethren's exemption from military service, along with that of the Quakers and Mennonites. Moravians, however, continued to forbid their members to bear arms and instead set up a fund to pay substitutes. The war ended before they had to draw on it; see Auf. Col., Nov. 22, 1814, Feb. 21, 1815.

past year, took part in a *Negro-Frolick* in this neighborhood." Hauser was excluded.[54]

Such episodes only reinforced the church's desire to enforce racial boundaries in all walks of life. Concern over the effects of slaveholding on whites, combined with mounting racism and fear of slaves, erupted in a major controversy over the presence of slaves in Salem. The debate arose in 1814, when church officials tried to entice Frederick Schumann, a physician in Bethania, to move to Salem to serve as town doctor. Schumann showed interest but wanted to bring his slaves with him, including a woman and her four children. The town board, willing to let him bring the woman but not her children, protested that the increasing number of slaves would harm the town. Schumann offered to leave behind or sell two of the children, but the board remained firm. In demanding that Schumann sell all the children, town leaders showed the limits of their concern for preserving the slave family. In August 1814, the Salem house fathers, masters, and members of the Congregational Council gathered to consider the Schumann case and to reevaluate the entire subject of slaveholding in town.[55]

Out of the conference arose the clearest articulation yet of the church's position. Participants contrasted the "seeming advantage and some profit and convenience in keeping Negro slaves" with "the greater disadvantage to the outer and inner welfare of the congregation." Young white women, it was said, might "become work-shy and ashamed of work; and there would be increasing difficulty in holding growing boys to the learning of a profession, in restraining them from dangerous tendencies, and in leading them into outward morality and inward growth in good." Congregants agreed that, although "the ownership of Negro slaves is often a consequence of the lack of white labor in our neighborhood, . . . the disadvantages outweigh the advantages." The group reaffirmed the old rule that individuals could not own slaves and that residents should seek permission to rent them.[56]

The church made one crucial departure from its long-standing principles.

---

54. Committee in Bethania, Feb. 14, 1816. On black Christmas celebrations, see Genovese, *Roll, Jordan, Roll*, 573–579; Charles Joyner, *Down by the Riverside: A South Carolina Slave Community* (Urbana, Ill., 1984), 134–137; Robert Dirks, "Slaves' Holiday," *Natural History*, LXXXIV (December 1975), 82–90. On the connection between Christmas and slave rebellion, see Elizabeth A. Fenn, " 'A Perfect Equality Seemed to Reign': Slave Society and Jonkonnu," *NCHR*, LXV (1988), 127–153.

55. Auf. Col., July 19, 1814.

56. Gemein Rath, Aug. 22, 1814.

A clause stressed that "in the question of the holding of Negroes no differ-ence shall be made" between black Moravians and non-Moravians. Thus it was more important to keep down the number of bondpersons than to allow an increase even in Moravian slaves. Fear and dislike of blacks—in part because they were black and in part because they were enslaved—now su-perseded their religious status.[57]

Such measures kept the permanent enslaved population in Salem fairly low. Frederick Schumann agreed to settle on a plantation outside the town limits where he was permitted to keep his slaves. Church-run businesses and a few congregants owned a handful of slaves in town. Several served on the Salem tavern staff, others worked for the tannery. A slave named Sam worked as a maintenance man and laborer for the Single Sisters' Choir, in which capacity he was termed "almost indispensable." His wife, Elizabeth, served as a domestic in the Salem Boarding School for Girls, which had been opened in 1803 as a school for non-Moravian girls and would become one of the South's best-known boarding schools in the antebellum period.[58]

In addition, ten church-owned slaves lived on the Salem plantation just southeast of town, which by the early nineteenth century had come to be known as the "Negro Quarter." This group of workers raised crops and tended animals for the benefit of the Salem congregation, of which some, ironically, were still members. Exactly when and how the Quarter came into being is unclear, but its development suggests whites' desire to affirm a wider social distance between themselves and blacks corresponding to their growing wish to exclude blacks from worship. For the first time, an identi-fiably African-American social enclave or neighborhood was part of the Salem landscape, situated apart from whites, outside the town limits. The spatial realignment locked in place the new psychological order.[59]

Salem tradesmen still used hired slave and free black labor, but town leaders continued trying to stop the displacement of white artisans by slave

57. Ibid. A somewhat different translation of these minutes is provided in Fries et al., eds., *Records,* VII, 3544–3548. A more extensively cited discussion of the issue may be found in Philip Africa, "Slaveholding in the Salem Community, 1771–1851," *NCHR,* LIV (1977), 286–290. See also Shirley, *From Congregation Town to Industrial City,* 47–50.

58. Auf. Col., Aug. 6, 1811, Apr. 21, 1817. See also S. Scott Rohrer, "Friederich Schumann and His Slaves: Portrait of a Plantation," Old Salem, Inc., 1990.

59. Auf. Col., Feb. 3, 1808, in Fries et al., eds., *Records,* VI, 2926; Bill of Sale, George Hauser to Christian Benzien, Oct. 4, 1810; Inventory of Salem Plantation, May 31, 1817, in Fries et al., eds., *Records,* VII, 3557; Bills of Sale folder; Auf. Col., Aug. 30, 1814.

apprenticeships. When joiner Johann Belo asked permission to train a slave in 1816, the Collegium sharply answered that to do so "would lead to the ruin of our economic constitution" and threatened to banish anyone who disobeyed. Clarifying their stand in 1820, officials insisted: "While slaves might contribute initially to skilled trades and professions," ultimately "these Negroes are the ruin of the whole community, since the industriousness and ingenuity of the whites, mainly that of the youngsters, on which finally all the wealth of such a place depends, will come to an end. The immediate consequences of having such Negroes work in our trades would be the sad custom of laziness and all evils deriving from this great vice." Conceding that "the help of Negroes in many cases is indispensable" and that "it is practically impossible to ban everyone with a black skin from our Community," the board nonetheless reaffirmed its prohibition on teaching trades to any blacks, slave or free.[60]

The web of rules confirmed a complex set of racial divisions that whites had been widening for more than thirty years. White Brethren had made clear their desire to be free of black company in worship, in housing, and in burial. They had set aside a Negro Quarter outside Salem. Like all slaveowners, they feared the slave class they had become dependent on and stepped up surveillance in times of unrest. Their exhaustive efforts to curtail slavery in town were entirely consonant with all of these efforts. The antislavery regulations could be seen as a rearguard effort to protect free white labor and preserve the old ways against modernization. But it was just as true that the Brethren wanted the benefits of slave labor without admitting blacks into their congregations—as scores of hired slaves might have attested.

The new racial masonry steadily collapsed the difference in white thought between black Moravians and non-Moravians: all were to be swept aside. One final step remained.

BLACK PRAYER MEETINGS begun early in the century marked a preliminary attempt by whites as well as many blacks to distinguish the African-American religious experience from white worship. That idea, tentative at first, took years to evolve; several dozen blacks remained members of Moravian churches even as they worshiped with all-black groups. By 1822, Moravian leaders decided the time had come for a final, radical break. They devised

60. Auf. Col., Jan. 22, 1816, Jan. 24, 1820.

a plan to revive a mission that would for the first time include a separate black congregation.

The impetus for the scheme arose from the Female Mission Society, which was formed in January 1822 to support Unity missions throughout the world but especially at home for blacks who had not heard the Moravian message. The society called on the Provincial Helpers' Conference to "take under consideration what could be done for the Negroes, in and around Salem, in regard to Religion among them so that they are served not only with the preaching of the Gospel, but that in consequence they might also come to Holy Baptism and the Holy Communion and might get a church for them alone."[61]

In delicate language, officials tried to sum up the preceding thirty years to explain why an all-black church was now needed. "From time to time, some Negroes had indeed become members of the Brethren's Congregation in Salem, Bethabara, Bethania and Hope, who were also communicants. But in the subsequent period it became more and more evident that the relationship of whites and blacks to belong together to one and the same congregation was subject to many a difficulty and unpleasantness." More precisely: "Experience had shown that the Negroes shrank from mixing in a Christian Congregation of white people and it was just as unpleasant for the whites to be served with the Sacraments of the church in fellowship with blacks." Such an analysis seemed more indicative of the recent past than of the earliest years of biracial fellowship. It furthermore glossed over the obvious premise that if blacks "shrank" from mixing with whites it was because whites had done their utmost to make them feel unwelcome. Nonetheless, the logic of their confection drove ministers to conclude that "it might not only be more pleasant for both sides to be separated from each other, but also that many a black sheep might find its way which might otherwise stay back because of shyness." As a result, "there was the wish that the Negroes and colored people might be served in such a way that they would form their own church organization and a congregation exclusively for them." Hinting of embarrassment, the statement suggests that an all-black church would erase whites' ambiguity over their relations with black Brethren while soothing their guilt over excluding them.[62]

White Brethren, moreover, never abandoned their belief that religion was

---

61. Report of the Directors of the Female Mission Society in Salem, Feb. 14, 1822 (trans. EM).
62. Ibid.; Negro Congregation Diary, Introduction.

the best source of slave control. As reports of slave insurrections continued making news in the early 1820s, the Brethren tirelessly preached on behalf of slavery. In 1822, a master near Lexington, twenty miles south of Salem, allowed a Moravian missionary "to preach to the slaves on his plantation, as he knew well that the Brethren would not speak to them of freedom but of the Gospel and of obedience." Such reasoning no doubt bolstered support for the new congregation.[63]

A final reason for the founding of the church is that African Americans themselves might have lobbied for it. All over the country whites were pushing blacks into the back bench, the upper gallery, or out of church altogether. In many cases black Christians quit churches before they could be evicted. Responding to mounting discrimination, African Americans might have pressed Moravian ministers for their own church or at least for a resumption of separate meetings. Black Bethanians in 1819 sent a delegation to minister Peter Wolle asking for occasional preaching, which he provided. While further evidence is scanty, the possibility exists that white and black Moravians alike agreed on the need for separate black worship.

For whatever reasons, African Americans were at last formally removed from Moravian churches. They held their first meeting on March 24, 1822, at the Negro Quarter outside Salem. More than fifty slaves and free blacks attended. The pastor was Abraham Steiner, formerly a missionary to the Cherokees in Springplace, Georgia, and more recently inspector of the Salem Boarding School for Girls. After prayer, singing, and the baptism of two infants, Steiner asked the group whether they wanted to continue attending separate meetings. "All manifested their pleasure over that," the minister reported in the new church diary he began to keep, "and some of them said they would gladly have gone to the services more frequently but that they had not done it only because they felt ashamed to go into a meeting of the white people. Some said, 'We black people love each other and are happy to see each other and therefore will gladly come to the meetings which will be held for us.'" The worshipers' response might have told the pastor what he wanted to hear, but it also indicates a certain guarded candor about

63. PAC, Aug. 13, 1822, in Fries et al., eds., *Records,* VII, 3514. On slave unrest in the early 1820s, see Aptheker, *American Negro Slave Revolts,* 266–267. Although the link between religion and social control remained a staple of white Moravian thought, the new mission work cannot be linked directly to fears caused by Denmark Vesey's insurrection scare of 1822. That plot was uncovered in May, some five months after Moravian Church leaders began planning their new mission.

their treatment and about their preference to have nothing more to do with whites.[64]

Steiner then told them of plans to form a separate congregation under his pastorship; whites meant to keep firm control and would scarcely permit a black minister to lead them. Any members "who would be guilty of a disorderly walk or who would be the cause of offence and scandal would have to be excluded." The minister also forbade "diversions" before or during services and urged them to return home "quickly and quietly" afterwards.[65]

There was one further condition. When blacks were received into the congregation, "instead of the kiss, a handshake will be deemed more suitable and proper." The stipulation seemed anticlimactic after all that had happened earlier, yet it conveyed a powerful symbolism.[66]

White Moravians found themselves unable to live with the implications of their own ideology. Their need as slaveholders to subdue a captive population by defining it as even more different and inferior gradually surpassed their earlier commitment to spiritual fellowship. Their exclusion of blacks mirrored the rise of new barriers in a nation that had won political independence but was not ready to acknowledge the full humanity of African Americans. The changes sweeping the country helped white Brethren abandon crucial parts of their cultural legacy and embrace the new Republic's emerging racial polarities. Like all immigrants to America, white Brethren faced, resisted, and in the end often accepted compromise and the purge of their memories in the name of adaptation. Along the way, any prospects for a more open society that might have been heralded by a time of relative fluidity simply drained away.[67]

African Americans had always had tenuous access at best to Moravian

64. Negro Congregation Diary, Introduction.

65. Ibid. On Steiner's earlier careers, see Frances Griffin, *Less Time for Meddling: A History of Salem Academy and College, 1772–1866* (Winston-Salem, N.C., 1979).

66. LAC, Apr. 19, 1822. Although racially motivated reasons had spurred the church to restrict the kiss as a ritual of induction for blacks earlier in the century, the ceremony had fallen into general disfavor by the 1820s. The Herrnhut Synod of 1824 authorized congregations to use the hand of fellowship instead; see Kenneth G. Hamilton and J. Taylor Hamilton, *History of the Moravian Church: The Renewed Unitas Fratrum, 1722–1957* (Bethlehem, Pa., 1967), 183. See also Jacob John Sessler, *Communal Pietism among Early American Moravians* (New York, 1933), 204.

67. For discussion of the issue of assimilation by immigrants to America, see John Higham, *Send These to Me: Immigrants in Urban America*, rev. ed. (Baltimore, 1984), esp. 9–13, 175–197; Russell A. Kazal, "Revisiting Assimilation: The Rise, Fall, and Reappraisal of a Concept in American Ethnic History," *AHR*, C (1995), 437–471.

society, which by definition was church society; now they were squeezed to its outer rim. By 1822, blacks might have viewed their final exclusion from the church with embittered relief. The enthusiasm with which they embraced their own church reflected a desire to escape the humiliation being heaped on them. Like scores of African Americans throughout the nation who founded churches during these years, black Moravians welcomed the chance for a greater hand in shaping their own religious lives. Yet, unlike many worship halls, particularly those of free black Christians, theirs was not independent of white control. From the earliest days, black congregants and white leaders struggled for the soul of the church.

HE HAD COME TO WORK in the young settlement of Bethabara in 1766, a sixteen-year-old youth hired to tend the stockyard. Within a few years, Johann Samuel had become the first black Moravian in North Carolina and had risen to overseer of the Bethabara farm. Though a slave, Samuel was possibly one of the most prominent of Brethren, white or black. But his foothold in the church, ever precarious, slipped. Emancipated at the age of fifty in 1800, Johann Samuel lived his last twenty-one years in troubled freedom.

He and Maria still worshiped in Bethabara, but freedom brought them less rather than more social acceptance by whites. In 1801, soon after Johann's emancipation, the elders explicitly told them to set up their new household outside the town limits. A year later, they denied them permission to move into town. The barriers were going up, and the Samuels found themselves on the wrong side.[68]

The family struggled to make their new farm work. Their best years had been spent in slavery; now Johann was hard-pressed to support them. They had trouble meeting rent payments to the church, and committeemen complained constantly about the poor repair of the house and barn. "The Negro Br. Johann Samuel complains of poverty, says that it is impossible for him to pay his rent, and asks consideration because he has grown old in the service of the Diaconie," they noted in 1804. "To make things easier for him it was agreed to remit his rent for last year and the current year, on condition that he put a new roof on his house, that is one side of the roof for each year."[69]

68. Aelt. Conf., Feb. 11, 1801, and Bethabara Memorabilia, 1801, in Fries et al., eds., Records, VI, 2679, 2683; Bethabara Committee, June 30, 1802.
69. HCfG, Dec. 3, 1804, in Fries et al., eds., Records, VI, 2783. Two committee members

The family clung to their home and what meager living they could wrest from the land. Aside from the Widows' and Widowers' Choirs, the church had no formal system of elder care. Many older Moravians relied on their children for support. But, of the seven Samuel children, three were dead, and the survivors were only sixteen, twelve, seven, and three in 1804. Manumitting the Samuels had been an act of limited magnanimity. Having drained the parents' productivity, church leaders removed the burden of supporting the family from their budget and were content to remit the rent on occasion and chip in other kinds of charity.

Within the family there must have been a sense of abandonment and solitary struggle. Poverty eventually drove them to desperate acts. "This afternoon there was a most unpleasant incident," the Bethabara Diary reported in February 1813. "The Negro family Samuel, to the dishonor of the congregation to which they belonged, have been stealing from Br. and Sr. Strohle, and were arrested, tried, and sent as prisoners to Germanton." The family was evidently released soon thereafter, for in March another warrant was sworn out for Samuel's arrest for failure to pay sixty dollars in rent.[70]

The two episodes evidently stirred some whites into a belated realization of the Samuels' plight. "Their lease has been cancelled, and they have been told they must vacate the property by April 2," a church board noted. "They are far behind in their rent, and if execution is levied the old people will hardly be able to live. This must be borne in mind, and while the execution must be allowed to proceed their household goods must then be lent to them for their use." When their property was put on public sale, church officials bought most of the farm equipment and livestock and lent them back to the Samuels: five sickles, a plow, a mattock, Dutch oven, iron pot, shovel, pewter basins and plates, bowls and saucers, a coffee mill, four cows, and three horses.[71]

---

reported in 1802, for example, that "the house and barn were in extremely bad condition" and that "they did not see how the harvest could be protected from rain and weather, because the barn had no planks." Samuel "did not know or understand" that his rent-free contract for the first five years after emancipation was about to expire and had no idea how he would pay rent; see Committee in Bethabara, July 14, 1802.

70. Bethabara Diary, Feb. 23, 1813, in Fries et al., eds., *Records,* VII, 3211; Frederick Marshall Papers, no. 5, "The Negro Sam Affair," item 4. On the economic difficulties of free blacks in North Carolina, see John Hope Franklin, *The Free Negro in North Carolina, 1790–1860* (Chapel Hill, N.C., 1943), 121–162.

71. HCfG, Mar. 8, 1813, in Fries et al., eds., *Records,* VII, 3204; Marshall Papers, no. 5, "The Negro Sam Affair," item 3.

Banished from the congregation and forced to move, the Samuels settled on a farm near Bethania, where they lived for the next eight years. The records tell nothing of this twilight season, but perhaps their children, having grown to adulthood by then, were better able to support their parents. In June 1821, a Salem minister "went to a neighboring plantation and held the funeral of the married Negress Maria Samuel, who passed out of time yesterday; she had dropsy. Formerly she and her widowed husband, Johann Samuel—who is suffering from consumption—belonged to the congregation in Bethabara, and helped with the farm work there." Just three weeks later, a diarist tersely recorded: "The Negro Johann Samuel died in our neighborhood."[72]

Two short mentions in a church diary; that was all. The most the diarist could recall about their lives was that they had "helped with the farm work." It seemed to matter little, in 1821, that Johann Samuel had lived among the Moravians for fifty-five years and Maria for forty-three, that they had been the first African-American man and woman to embrace the faith in North Carolina and had taken Communion as Brother Johann and Sister Maria. By the end of their lives, they witnessed the evisceration of blacks from the church they helped sustain.

In 1822, as black congregants worshiped in their new church, they sang Moravian hymns to the seraphic accompaniment of classical violins. The musicians were three brothers—Christian, John, and Jacob Samuel, the sons of Johann and Maria.

72. Bethania Diary, June 2, 27, 1821, in Fries et al., eds., *Records*, VII, 3488.

· · · · · · · · · · · · · · · · · ·

CHAPTER SEVEN

A Separate Canaan

THE EXILES GATHERED at the Negro Quarter outside Salem in March 1822. Reminiscent of so many earlier Christian groups, the fifty slaves and free blacks who crowded into a slave cabin that day hungered for a chance to worship without harassment. Perhaps they compared themselves to the small band of persecuted Moravian Brethren who had taken refuge on Count Zinzendorf's estate in Saxony exactly a century earlier. If white Moravians recognized this irony, they did not acknowledge it. Whatever the Unity had once stood for, times had changed, as the Hope minister so bluntly admitted in 1814; "scruples [had] been started," and racial consciousness had overpowered the inclusive embrace of gospel.[1]

As these refugees banded together in prayer, they were acting out their own version of a long-running drama begun even before the first enslaved Africans arrived in America. That was the struggle to find and hold onto a faith to bolster them in a perilous world—a struggle that was perhaps the most important cultural adaptation Africans made in their new environment. Religion has been the ark of the African diaspora in America. The black church, both in its institutional embodiment and in its more personal form, individual faith, has nurtured, taught, and protected worshipers for nearly five hundred years.[2]

1. Committee in Hope, Aug. 7, 1814.

2. The literature on the black church and the role of religion in African-American life is vast. Standard works include Carter G. Woodson, *The History of the Negro Church*, 2d ed. (Washington, D.C., 1921); E. Franklin Frazier, *The Negro Church in America* / C. Eric Lincoln, *The Black Church since Frazier*, Sourcebooks in Negro History (New York, 1974); Benjamin

By the 1820s, as the new congregation took shape in Salem, black Americans sought to express their religious selves in many ways and many places: in open-air camp meetings where, clothed in white robes, they waded into the sin-cleansing rivers; in plantation mission meetings and white-approved "praise houses"; in the balconies of segregated evangelical churches; in the privacy of cane thickets and "hush harbors" where slave preachers had exhorted them out of the masters' sight; and in urban free black churches where, as nowhere else, they had the power to control the destiny of their own worship.[3]

Born during a Revolutionary era that brought enslaved and free African Americans abundant—and frequently disappointed—hopes of release from racial oppression, the church became a vessel of black identity. Both a product and an agent of emergent Afro-Christian sensibilities, the church served many roles as refuge from racism, seedbed of black cultural nationalism, vehicle of spirituality and self-expression, and locus of social and political organization.[4]

Elijah Mays and Joseph William Nicholson, *The Negro's Church* (New York, 1969); Gayraud Wilmore, *Black Religion and Black Radicalism* (New York, 1983); Lawrence W. Levine, *Black Culture and Black Consciousness: Afro-American Folk Thought from Slavery to Freedom* (New York, 1977); C. Eric Lincoln and Lawrence H. Mamiya, *The Black Church in the African-American Experience* (Durham, N.C., 1990); Theophus H. Smith, *Conjuring Culture: Biblical Formations of Black America* (New York, 1994); Albert J. Raboteau, *A Fire in the Bones: Reflections on African-American Religious History* (Boston, 1995); Timothy E. Fulop and Albert J. Raboteau, eds., *African American Religion: Interpretive Essays in History and Culture* (New York, 1997).

3. On "praise houses," see Margaret Washington Creel, *"A Peculiar People": Religion and Community-Culture among the Gullahs* (New York, 1988), 233, 277–281. Segregated worship in early southern Christianity is discussed in John B. Boles, ed., *Masters and Slaves in the House of the Lord: Race and Religion in the American South, 1740–1870* (Lexington, Ky., 1988). On camp meetings, river baptisms, cane thickets, and "hush harbors," see Albert J. Raboteau, *Slave Religion: The "Invisible Institution" in the Antebellum South* (New York, 1978), 219, 226–227. On the flowering of free black churches, see Will B. Gravely, "The Rise of African Churches in America (1786–1822): Re-examining the Contexts," in Gayraud S. Wilmore, ed., *African American Religious Studies: An Interdisciplinary Anthology* (Durham, N.C., 1989), 301–317.

4. For a tidy summary of how this process might have worked, see Charles Joyner, *Down by the Riverside: A South Carolina Slave Community* (Urbana, Ill., 1984), 141–143. A sampling of the vast outpouring of works treating the fusion of African and Christian beliefs among enslaved peoples in the Americas (in addition to those cited above) includes Mechal Sobel, *Trabelin' On: The Slave Journey to an Afro-Baptist Faith,* 2d ed. (Princeton, N.J., 1988); Eugene D. Genovese, *Roll, Jordan, Roll: The World the Slaves Made* (New York, 1974); Donald G.

Yet black congregations and churches were spheres not only of collective African-American expression and unified action but of intense debate, even struggle, as well. Subject to strong pressures from within and without, black churches reflected both the cooperative and competing agendas of their members as well as the reality of life in a white-dominated society. For members of the new congregation in Salem, the chance to worship apart from whites was an experiment in self-definition. In one sense, they remained a missioned people under the control of a white pastor, without complete freedom to choose or direct preaching and worship as they wanted. White Brethren, like slaveowners and ministers throughout the South, drew strong connections between slave Christianity and social control. For their part, congregants gathered in their new forum to create an alternative moral space where they might mold the Christian message to fit their own spiritual and social needs.

Such spaces had always existed, wherever black Americans prayed—perhaps clandestinely—or discussed religious beliefs and their application to the demands of a harsh life. To create a church under the constraints of slave society required an act of equal parts faith and will. It is certain that black seekers committed such acts regularly in antebellum America. But rarely was any written record left of their efforts, performed as they so often were in stealth by people either unable to document their actions or who found it prudent not to do so. Only slightly more frequently did white observers note the workings of the black church emerging around them, and usually then as a source of fear, disdain, or curious exoticism. And so the multiple origins of one of America's great institutions of cultural assertion and resistance remain elusive.[5]

Mathews, *Religion in the Old South* (Chicago, 1977); Sterling Stuckey, *Slave Culture: Nationalist Theory and the Foundations of Black America* (New York, 1987); Roger Bastide, *The African Religions of Brazil: Toward a Sociology of the Interpenetration of Civilizations,* trans. Helen Sebba (Baltimore, 1978); Mary C. Karasch, *Slave Life in Rio de Janeiro, 1808–1850* (Princeton, N.J., 1987); and Richard Price, *Alabi's World* (Baltimore, 1990).

5. Scholars have, of course, tapped a huge amount of source material about slave religious life—spirituals, conversion accounts, ex-slave narratives, travel journals, church minutes, and other documents that have brought much about the "invisible institution" to light. My point here is that, despite the enormous amount of writing on the role of religion in African-American life, we still know comparatively little about what was required to create and sustain the black *church,* particularly the slave church, as an institutional form in early national or antebellum America.

In 1822, Abraham Steiner, the white pastor of Salem's new black congregation, began to keep a journal to apprise the Female Mission Society and other church councils of its activities. Writing in German, Steiner made weekly reports on worship services and special ceremonies, about what congregants said and did, and about their lives and deaths. He accentuated the pages with biographies of black Christians, some of them several pages long, which were read aloud at their funerals. This diary, continued by Steiner's successors well into the 1880s, is a rare and little-known source for nineteenth-century African-American religious history. From its pages we can watch a congregation germinate, grow, and survive, week by week, month by month, year after year in a society that militantly sought to control black self-expression and collective action. Combined with baptismal and marriage records and other sources, it provides one of the most detailed eyewitness accounts we have of African-American congregational life in the antebellum South. It is, in effect, a kind of Genesis story of one black church.[6]

Of course, the diary is not written by black eyewitnesses or participants, and the text reflects its authors' pronounced biases of race and class and their zeal to bend the congregation to their own moral vision. Like any account, its maddening gaps and silences invite speculation rather than certainty. But if read carefully from the inside out, the diary reveals much about the motives and thoughts of black worshipers in the act of cultural creation. Far from being invisible or inarticulate, they emerge from the pages as thoughtful and savvy people skilled at sustaining a community of faith within the limits allowed them. Church records help us peer through a small gap in the screen of secrecy behind which slavery forced its captives to act. Through the screen, we glimpse at least part of what the church meant to its practitioners and how they made it work. "We black people love each other . . . and will gladly come to the meetings which will be held for us," the supplicants

6. The Negro Congregation Diary fills many hundreds of handwritten pages. Between 1822 and 1856, ministers jotted entries in German script. Those pages have been translated by Elizabeth Marx. After 1856, when Moravian officials switched to English as the church's language of record, diary entries were likewise kept in English. Other sources pertinent to the black congregation include annual reports by ministers of the congregation, contained in the files of the Landarbeiter Conferenz; the "Church Book for the People of Colour in and about Salem," a register of baptisms and deaths; and the minutes of official governing boards of the Moravian Church.

told Steiner at the start of the mission. What that declaration signified would soon become clear in the spring of 1822.[7]

THE THRONG at the first meeting in the quarter was a mosaic of familiar and new faces. Many of the old guard of black Brethren had long since died: Christian in 1789, Abraham in 1796, Peter Oliver in 1810, Tabitha Jane and Sarah Elizabeth in 1816, and, more recently, the Samuels in 1821. Others had been expelled, such as Christine Oliver and Mary Jane in 1811, the married couple William and Chrissy in 1814 after a drunken fight, and the couple Matthew and Rachel in 1819 for lack of attendance at meetings. Moravian territory was now home to a younger generation of African Americans, most of them farm laborers, paper-mill workers, and domestics who probably had little contact with the church, given the climate of racial antipathy.

But a few important figures from an earlier time survived to help create the congregation. This small nucleus represented vital cables of continuity spanning the previous forty years. They carried vivid memories of earlier generations' search for a usable faith. One was Anna (now known more commonly as Nancy), one of the first black sisters, who had lost her fellowship privileges through "bad behavior" and was now living in the Negro Quarter outside Salem by 1818. Another familiar face at the early meetings in 1822 belonged to John Immanuel, the German-speaking native of Virginia who, after being banished from the Salem congregation in 1811, was also without a church. In subsequent years, he yearned for a restoration to fellowship, and in March 1822 he walked to Friedland to ask the Moravian minister's permission to join the congregation there. Pastor Christian Buchholz was reluctant, telling Immanuel that, "as he had belonged earlier to the congregation in Salem, had been baptized by the Brethren, and had gone to Holy Communion," he should "tie the thread that had been broken" and

7. Negro Congregation Diary, 4. For a general theoretical overview of the efforts of subordinate people to resist oppression in both public spaces controlled by the powerful and spaces concealed from them, see James C. Scott, *Domination and the Arts of Resistance: Hidden Transcripts* (New Haven, Conn., 1990). Scholars have been aware for some time of the invisible or secretive dimensions of slave Christianity, which were often expressed out of sight and earshot of whites. In Salem, and perhaps in other mission churches as well, some of these invisible aspects of black Christian worship and thought found expression in a highly visible public forum nominally controlled by whites.

offered to speak on Immanuel's behalf to Salem officials. Thus, the first black meeting just two weeks later came at an opportune time to meet Immanuel's spiritual longing.[8]

Others were no strangers to Moravian practice as well. The slave couple Bodney and Phoebe, who lived on the church farm near town, had joined the Salem congregation in 1810; it was in their cabin that the worship group first assembled in March 1822. John, born in 1799, had been baptized as a child by the Friedberg pastor and later joined the Hope congregation. The Samuel children, free blacks John, Christian, Jacob, and Anna, had been raised and educated in the Bethabara congregation, though they had been banned after their parents' downfall in 1813.[9]

And Henny, or Hannah, who lived near Hope, had never been a member of a Moravian church but had attended various meetings through the years, asking unsuccessfully for baptism. She again asked pastor Abraham Steiner in 1823, who replied: "She had already presented this concern for more than 20 years from time to time, but one had never noticed in her a true purpose to dedicate herself entirely to Jesus. [Asked] why she came to church so seldom, she said that during the week she is hired out by her mistress and so does not have time to do anything for herself, which she has to do on Sundays and also has to do her own washing." Henny's testimony gives valuable insight into the obstacles facing some slaves who sought fellowship. Unremitting labor for their masters and in their own households left many exhausted and with little time for worship. Henny nonetheless persevered and was at last baptized in March 1824.[10]

All of these people had either been members of, or once had close association with, the Moravian Church. Yet white officials designated the new mission church, not a Moravian congregation, but rather a generic "Christian Congregation" that might evoke a broad regional appeal. At an administrative level, the new congregation would be considered part of the Moravian Church's missionary outreach rather than a component of its congregational structure. At the far more important symbolic level, the decision reasserted white Brethren's radical claim of the spiritual apartness of blacks.

---

8. LAC, Mar. 8, 1822.

9. Probably the son of Tom and Rose, John appears in the Friedberg Register as having been baptized on June 18, 1809, sponsored by Priscilla, Tabitha Jane, and Samuel—further links to a previous generation of black Moravians; see Negro Congregation Diary, Nov. 28, 1838.

10. Negro Congregation Diary, June 11, 1823.

Whites emphasized the forced distancing of former black Brethren from the Moravian Church and their formal separation into a different religious sphere. Christians they might be, but Moravians they were no longer.[11]

That distinction did not mean a complete end to all white Moravians' spiritual engagement with black congregants. In fact, dozens of white women helped support the new congregation to varying degrees through their involvement in the Female Mission Society. Evangelical work to local blacks had been a prominent reason for the society's founding, and the cause remained central to its mission. Members collected funds for pastor Steiner's salary and other expenses, and many women, such as Steiner's own sister, Sarah, took an active part in congregational life by attending services, helping instruct congregants, and sponsoring baptisms of black children. However motivated by sincere Christian conviction and willingness to worship with black congregants the sisters might have been, their participation in no way represented a subversive challenge to the racial boundaries of the 1820s. Rather, their work helped strengthen these boundaries by reaffirming and taking place entirely in the separate realm of the black congregation. Whites could worship in African-American space if they chose, but blacks could no longer worship in white space.[12]

Early meetings of the black fellowship in the spring of 1822 took place every two weeks at the Negro Quarter or in a barn at Conrad Kreuser's plantation outside Salem. Steiner would speak soberly to the group, in English, "imparting instruction in the fundamental truths of Christianity and Christian doctrine. . . . When they were asked whether they had grasped and understood everything well, some said, 'Not entirely, but with frequent repetition, it will probably become clear.'" On one occasion, "an old Negro gave a very Christian counsel to the Negroes and told them how happy he was that they now have the opportunity in their own services appointed for colored people to hear the Gospel, but that the principal thing is that Jesus

11. Negro Congregation Diary, 4–5; Bericht der Provinzial-Conferenz in der Wachau zur Vorbereitung für den Synoden der Brüder-Unität (Report of the Provincial Conference in Wachovia in preparation for the Synod of the Unity of Brethren), Salem, July 1824, in Beilagen zum Synodus (Supplements to the Synod), 2a, 60, 1825, Archiv der Brüder-Unität, Herrnhut, Germany.

12. Plentiful minutes and other records would permit a detailed examination of the Female Mission Society, which lies beyond the scope of this study. See the translated but unpublished Report of the Directors of the Female Mission Society in Salem.

live in their hearts, of which they must be assured through his Spirit." After that exhortation, "the Negroes sang two more hymns together."[13]

Three communicants—Bodney, Phoebe, and John Immanuel—held their first Communion in the conference room of the Salem Gemeinhaus on May 19. Steiner noted of this first session that "even in this small group there was the blessed feeling and comforting awareness of the nearness of the unseen Friend of the poor." A fourth communicant, Christian David, joined this group in July 1811. (Perhaps of symbolic significance, his christened name matched that of the leader of the Moravian refugees who had settled on Zinzendorf's estate in 1722.) "After a preceding personal address," Steiner jotted in the diary, "the Negro David received the blessing of Confirmation for his first-time participation of this great blessing." A "blessed Holy Communion with four communicants followed."[14]

On weekdays, between preaching, Steiner visited outlying plantations and the paper mill to talk to blacks about spiritual matters. During these trips, and on their own visits to the pastor, African Americans with little prior experience in Moravian worship eagerly embraced the congregation. Enoch, a slave in Gottlieb Schober's paper mill, wanted his desire to join the church registered publicly and recorded formally as a measure of permanence. In July, Steiner told worshipers that "the Negro Enoch, according to his desire, was the first one whose name was written down" as an applicant to the fellowship. The minister later "visited in the paper mill and had a conversation with Enoch, who expressed his longing for grace and his desire to belong to the Saviour." Enoch's wife, Nancy, also spoke with the pastor, and, though she hitherto had been "devoted to the world and its pleasures," her "unrest had become great and she could no longer refuse to think earnestly about how she could obtain grace and forgiveness and be saved." Other applicants included John Immanuel's wife Sarah—whom he had married in September 1822—as well as Lewis, a slave working for the Single Sisters.[15]

Steiner encouraged these supplicants but told them sternly that "no one should join such a fellowship just to please me or anyone else, that I would rather have a few upright souls than a large number of hypocrites." Regarding baptism, he believed there was "only a vague understanding on the part

13. Negro Congregation Diary, Apr. 14, May 5, 1822.
14. Ibid., May 19, 1822, July 11, 1824.
15. Ibid., July 7, 17, 1822.

of some and none at all among others, of how such a transaction is carried out among us." He explained to the group "what is expected of a candidate for baptism and what he must believe and want with all his heart before Holy Baptism may be administered to him."[16]

After instruction and the drawing of a positive lot, worshipers who demonstrated knowledge of Christian precepts and a sober temperament received baptism. Following further instruction, candidates were admitted to Communion with a handshake. Slaves and free blacks who had previously been communicants in Hope, Friedberg, or Friedland could hold that status without further qualification. Candidates who had been baptized elsewhere could join the congregation but needed the approval of the lot to receive confirmation.[17]

Under these conditions, the congregation grew at a modest but steady pace. By 1824, it claimed eight communicants and six regular or noncommunicant members, five awaiting baptism, and one temporarily barred from worship. In 1826, the congregation numbered sixteen: communicants Bodney, Phoebe, John Immanuel, Nancy (Anna), Lucy Ann Sarah, Christian David, Hannah Louisa, Elizabeth, Elisabeth Jane, and Rosa Lucy Ann and noncommunicants John, William, Fanny, Susanna, Sabina, and Nancy. Most lived on farms within a one- or two-mile radius around Salem, but some came every other Sunday from as far away as Hope, five miles south of Salem, and Bethania, six miles northeast. Besides these formal members, another sixty to seventy slaves (and some free blacks as well) regularly attended services but declined to commit themselves to full association. Wistfully, Steiner wished that these people "would become not only listeners but followers of the Word." Nonetheless, the congregation had become a magnet for black seekers eager for fellowship.[18]

From the beginning, black Brethren understood that this was to be *their* congregation. Whatever agenda the white authorities had in mind for them, whatever oversight the ministers exercised, blacks knew that for the first time they would have a say in shaping their world of worship. Indeed,

---

16. Ibid., July 7, Nov. 5, 1822. Competing denominational beliefs about baptism could sometimes cause confusion. James, a congregant who had been baptized as a child, worried when told by Baptists in 1830 that infant baptism was worthless. Steiner reassured him the Moravians thought differently; see LAC, Feb. 4, 1830.

17. LAC, Nov. 12, 1823.

18. LAC Bericht, Aug. 21, 1824; church roster in Negro Congregation Diary, Sept. 20, 1826 (inserted on page 45 of transcript).

congregants had their own church council to help them do so. The functions of the board and the limits on its power are not clear. Certainly members would not have been able to set policy independent of white approval. Nonetheless, the council must have given church members the rare sense of exercising some organizational authority in their own spiritual lives.[19]

Every chance to act on this conviction held special significance, but probably no occasion was more important than the construction of a new church in the fall of 1823. Abraham Steiner proposed the building of the church in February 1823 in response to the increasing popularity of the prayer meetings. "The Negroes continue to attend the service held at fourteen-day intervals," reported the Provincial Elders' Conference. "It is hard for Brother Steiner to hold these services at distant points, and not many suitable places are available." Members agreed "that it would be advantageous and useful, and that it would further the plan, if a separate church should be built for use of the poor Negroes." Salem was chosen as the most central location in the Moravian territory. The Conference selected a site at the south end of town, beside the former parish graveyard that in 1816 had been designated the blacks-only graveyard. Significantly, as if to formalize in structural and spatial terms the removal of blacks from white congregational society, the site was well away from the heart of town, symbolically on Salem's spiritual and social fringes. The church and graveyard together became a center of sacralized African-American space immensely important to the region's black population.[20]

The church building would be "32 by 28 feet in size, and 12 feet high," ruled the board. "On the south gable there shall be an 8 foot addition for the use of the minister. In the wall between this room and the church there shall be a chimney, with a fire-place in the church and another in the room. Along the west wall there shall be a porch where the Negroes may gather before a service." Congregants themselves would build the church with logs cut on

19. Whether the council was elected by the congregation or appointed by the pastor is unknown. The only known reference to the council suggests it had the authority to make recommendations regarding worship. "At the request of the church council of the Negro church, Br. Bechler preached a sermon in their church"; see Salem Diary, Jan. 31, 1830, in Fries et al., eds., *Records*, VIII, 3913.

20. PAC, Feb. 4, 1823, in Fries et al., eds., *Records*, VIII, 3637. On the social significance of the location of the church to a new racial categorization of space in the Salem landscape, see Niels R. Taylor, "The Landscape of Alienation in Nineteenth Century Salem, North Carolina" (master's thesis, University of South Carolina, 1992).

Figure 14. *Salem from the North West.* The black church is shown on the far right. Unknown artist, 1832. Watercolor. Courtesy Moravian Archives, Southern Province, Winston-Salem, North Carolina

Unity land. Ministers evidently convinced local slaveowners that the church would strengthen social control of the slave population, for they agreed to share the cost of the building with the Female Mission Society.[21]

Work was under way by July, crammed into spare hours during the long days of the growing season. "Shingles, boards and logs have been brought but because of the great amount of field work, the Negroes have not been able to do anything on it." Finally, on September 27, a Saturday, "thirty Negroes gathered to lay up the logs for the church for Negroes. The Female Mission Society has with pleasure undertaken to bear the expense. All went off well."[22] A sense of communal cooperation and energy must have been

21. Aelt. Conf., Feb. 26, 1823, Auf. Col., Mar. 3, 1823, in Fries et al., eds., *Records,* VIII, 3637, 3638.

22. Report of the Directors of the Female Mission Society in Salem, July 7, 1823; Salem Diary, Sept. 27, 1823, in Fries et al., eds., *Records,* VIII, 3632.

high among the congregants at their task, fueled by the knowledge that they were building their own worship house.

Predictably, not all whites saluted their labors. Perhaps memories of Denmark Vesey's thwarted uprising in Charleston in 1822 lingered in the minds of Salem residents. At a meeting of the Congregational Council, someone asked "whether the gathering of the Negroes might become a nuisance for the citizens? Recently they have been seen more often in the yards, and in that way have become better acquainted with the location and condition of the individual houses in the town. When their church is ready for use precautionary measures must be taken, and arrangements must be made that they go home directly after the close of services. Whether the Negroes shall be taught reading and writing has not yet been decided."[23]

Preparations continued nonetheless. On two Saturdays in late November and early December, the Congregational Council reported: "Several Negroes were here to plaster the inside of the church." The building was at last pronounced ready, and on December 28, 1823, some ninety blacks and a large number of whites gathered for a day of services consecrating the church, highlighted by the baptism of a woman, Sarah, and the induction of a couple, Lewis and Sabina.[24]

Within this temple of logs, boards, and plaster, congregants could now focus their efforts to create a moral universe. A formidable array of obstacles faced them. Steiner remained firmly in control of worship, and, though the congregation was not officially Moravian, he sought to shape its tone, style, and practice to Moravian standards. Indeed, through his evangelizing years among the Cherokees, the minister had much experience in attempting to repress signs of "heathen" culture. In contrast to many slave churches in the South, he allowed no spirituals or other African-American songs; there was no ring shout, hand clapping, or emotional exhortation inside this church.[25]

23. Salem Congregational Council, Oct. 16, 1823, in Fries et al., eds., *Records,* VIII, 3647–3648.

24. Negro Congregation Diary, Dec. 6, 21, 28, 1823. Weatherboarding was added to the building's exterior in 1827; see Female Mission Society Minutes, July 8, 1827.

25. On Steiner's earlier missionary career, see William G. McLoughlin, *Cherokees and Missionaries, 1789–1839* (New Haven, Conn., 1984), 35–53, 60–68. A fair representation of what Steiner had in mind for the congregation may be seen in a list of rules adopted by Moravian missionaries in 1793 for their congregation of Delawares in Ohio: "None shall live with us who will go to other places to feasts and dances. . . . None who will bring whiskey into our town. . . . None who keeps a whore. . . . No man who forsakes his wife nor woman who

Congregants might well have carried out such practices covertly beyond the walls of the church, but, inside, their services followed the pattern familiar to all Moravian churches: sermons and sober discussions based on daily texts, lovefeasts, Moravian hymns, Communions, and a cycle of special festivals. An 1825 inventory of a few simple items belonging to the church reflects the kinds of activities that drove congregational life: Communion dishes and a little basket, shrouds for adults and children, hymnals, baptismal dishes and two baptismal cloths, grave-digging tools: spade, pickax, shovel, and rope for lowering. One departure from traditional Moravian practice was the apparent absence of a formal seating arrangement according to choir division.[26]

Blacks did not subscribe easily to Steiner's version of spiritual expression in worship. From the days of the earliest meetings in 1822, a struggle developed between pastor and congregation over the boundaries of emotional release during prayer services. The conflict reflected not only a dispute over the appropriation and expropriation of power but the continuing adaptation of African-American cultural idioms as well. On one occasion, the Methodist slave preacher Lewis, who had distinguished himself in the early-nineteenth-century revivals that swept through the Piedmont, attended a service where he "began to sing a hymn and thereafter delivered an exhortation and offered a prayer." As Steiner described the scene:

After that the Negro Hercules sang two hymns and offered prayer. Already during the first one—Lewis's—several Negroes went out, but

---

leaves her husband. . . . No son or daughter who abuses their parents. . . . None that uses witchcraft or such like things. . . . None that will doctor or be doctored after the wild Indian manner. . . . None that paint, shave, shear, or dress themselves as the heathen do"; see McLoughlin, *Cherokees and Missionaries*, 44.

26. Negro Congregation Diary, June 26, 1825. The absence of a choir system is suggested by a black Methodist's refusal to attend Moravian services in the 1840s because converted and unconverted listeners sat together, in contrast to his own church; see Report of the Negro Congregation in and around Salem, Feb. 8, 1843, in Fries et al., eds., *Records*, IX, 4733. Archaeological investigation, furthermore, has shown that burials in the graveyard by the church followed no choir system as in traditional graveyards. They were, however, apparently separated by sex, a later departure from a 1773 directive that burials not be divided by age or sex in the Strangers' Graveyard from which the black graveyard developed. See two reports prepared by Leland Ferguson for the Winston-Salem, Forsyth County, Kernersville Preservation Council: "A Report on Archaeological Testing of the St. Philips Moravian Church and Parish Graveyard," 1992, and "Hidden Testimony: A Perspective from Historical Archaeology on African Americans and Cemeteries in Old Salem," 1994, 21.

when the latter, who does not have the best character, had begun, the exiting was general. Those who remained behind began to sigh aloud and to repeat and finally during the prayer of Hercules, Lewis began to aggravate those who were leaving and shortly there was some commotion and disorder. I calmed them down again and went out to those who left to invite them to come back in, when they explained unanimously that they did not want any disorder in their services and no one should talk except the preacher. They came back with me to the meeting when I explained to them how they were to behave in the future and forbade them all loud shouting and uproar. Thereafter everything was extraordinarily quiet and I could give them some more instruction in Christian Doctrine.

Although some of Hercules' listeners reacted with the call-and-response pattern familiar to worship and preaching in African and African-American traditions, others preferred silence, perhaps indicating greater absorption of Euro-American styles. Their disagreement, in any case, indicates a robust engagement with the definition of their own modes of worship even as whites tried to steer the congregation in prescribed directions.[27]

Congregants also reacted to Steiner's preaching, restrained as it undoubtedly was, in ways that surprised and displeased him. He spent a good deal of time trying to stamp out what he considered heathenish outbursts associated with spirit possession. This practice, widely followed by African Americans throughout the South, represented a melding of both African and Christian concepts of spiritual rebirth. Worshipers "under conviction" were commonly seized by a trance or an overwhelming flood of the holy spirit that led to conversion through emotional and physical release. While preaching a sermon at the paper mill in December 1822, Steiner held the attention of most listeners "in spite of some disturbance due to the convulsive attacks of a Negress, who had to be taken out." Later, at the end of the same service, "another Negress had severe attacks," which prompted another reprimand from the minister. "As several believed that both cases were not natural but supernatural—as they said: They are 'under conviction'—and that this can

27. Negro Congregation Diary, June 2, 1822. Similar tensions, less well documented, undoubtedly occurred in hundreds of black churches. On call-and-response patterns in African-American worship, see Dena J. Epstein, *Sinful Tunes and Spirituals: Black Folk Music to the Civil War* (Urbana, Ill., 1977); Stuckey, *Slave Culture*, chap. 1; Roger D. Abrahams, *Singing the Master: The Emergence of African American Culture in the Plantation South* (New York, 1992).

easily lead to fanaticism, I explained to them how this can have its natural causes and also that we do not consider such occurrences as any indication of an awakening or conviction."[28]

Moravian officials grew more alarmed as a new wave of Methodist and Baptist camp meetings rolled across North Carolina in the 1820s. Even some white Brethren now "shouted" and testified noisily in church, and, though Steiner blamed the rising cacophony on Methodist influences, whites might just as easily have adopted the practice from blacks through the vehicle of the camp meetings they both attended. At the end of a service at the log church in June 1824, a slave woman, Sarah, "had an ecstasy or religious convulsion and twitching, as is usual in some Methodist services." Sarah, wrote Steiner, "fell down and screamed with strong twitching and thrashing on every side. Two strong Negroes held her down until she finally clapped her hands and cried aloud, 'Glory, glory.' It lasted a long time and the disturbance caused by this gave me the occasion to express my displeasure at such outbursts. She continued clapping her hands for a long time and turned her head and eyes, but as things had become more quiet, I began the service with the article of Christian doctrine about God."[29]

The conflict between minister and congregation over such forms of worship did not embody a simple dispute between "emotional" versus "rational" religion. Moravians had always emphasized that faith derived more from an emotional, heartfelt relationship with God than from the study of theology or a reasoned calculation of divine intent. The inner spirit, they

28. Negro Congregation Diary, Dec. 1, 1822. On spirit possession, see Sobel, *Trabelin' On*, esp. chap. 5; Raboteau, *Slave Religion*, 10–11, 35–37, 63–73; Erika Bourguignon, "Ritual Dissociation and Possession Belief in Caribbean Negro Religion," in Norman E. Whitten, Jr., and John F. Szwed, eds., *Afro-American Anthropology: Contemporary Perspectives* (New York, 1970), 87–101.

29. Negro Congregation Diary, June 13, 1824. "Almost everywhere people talk about the usual questions: 'What *is* true religion? *How* am I to acquire it?' " wrote a Friedberg minister in 1833, noting also that three Moravians in the Friedberg and Hope congregations were said to have shouted in meetings; see LAC Bericht, August 1833. Excerpts from this report are found in the Friedberg Diary, Aug. 6, 28, 1833, in Fries et al., eds., *Records*, VIII, 4117–4118. A similar example is contained in a report from Friedland in the LAC Bericht, May 3, 1836. See also Guion Griffis Johnson, "Revival Movements in Ante-Bellum North Carolina," *NCHR*, X (1933), 21–43; Johnson, "The Camp Meeting in Ante-Bellum North Carolina," *NCHR*, X (1933), 95–110; and see, esp., Larry E. Tise, *The Yadkin Melting Pot: Methodism and Moravians in the Yadkin Valley, 1750–1850, and Mt. Tabor Church, 1845–1966* (Winston-Salem, N.C., 1967), chaps. 4, 5, on the Methodist-Moravian rivalry and the influence of Methodism on the Moravian Church.

believed, though grounded in a private exchange between worshiper and God, promoted a shared experience of faith among congregants. In Salem's black church, rather, it was the expression of emotion that was at stake. Whereas the pastor sought to cultivate an inwardly directed experience of Christ among worshipers, the congregants considered the Holy Spirit an irrepressible force to be projected outward in ecstatic release that engulfed the faithful in communal celebration.

During the middle and late 1820s, however, the congregation gradually conceded to Steiner the contest over visceral displays of emotion during services. It was an issue on which the pastor clearly refused to give ground, and African Americans evidently concluded that continuing to express openly the ecstasy of the inner spirit might jeopardize the fate of the church. Not that they suppressed spirit possession altogether. In 1833, when a minister visited an ill slave, Lucas, at the paper mill, he "found him in a very gratifying state of heart, but it is to be regretted that he bases his conversion so much on dreams, visions and other fantasies." Another consideration might have persuaded congregants to acquiesce to Steiner on worship styles: they were free to attend religious meetings elsewhere that provided attractive outlets for spiritual expression.[30]

When possible, worshipers often preferred to attend meetings led by black preachers. Moravian officials permitted these exhorters to hold forth as long as they seemed to serve white purposes. A preacher named David (it is unclear whether he was slave or free) and three other black preachers, for example, held a meeting for slaves on Jacob Conrad's plantation in Bethania in 1823. Slaveholder Abraham Loesch also permitted David to lead his slaves in singing and instruction in the evenings to "perhaps keep them from mischief."[31] In June 1824, attendance at the log church "was not as large . . . as usual, for a black preacher was preaching . . . near Germanton and some of them went to hear him out of curiosity." Likewise, in 1825:

30. Negro Congregation Diary, Nov. 8, 1833. When the pastor, Renatus Schmidt, visited Lucas again two weeks later, however, he "found him in a more gratifying state of mind. His pretended visions had disappeared. He blamed himself for being a great sinner, whose only hope when he has to depart from the world is that he would be accepted through Jesus' merits because, he said, he had nothing good to present"; see Negro Congregation Diary, Nov. 25, 1833.

31. LAC Bericht, Sept. 7, 1823. David also received permission to hold a meeting for slaves in Bethania in 1827 on the condition that "his behavior is not offensive"; see LAC, June 28, 1827.

"The service today was not well attended as many blacks had gone to the funeral at Lawrence Hauser's near Bethabara, which was conducted by a black, Lewis, who preaches frequently." White Brethren were obliged to respect Lewis's acclaim. "Well-known among the African people as a good preacher, the famous Negro Lewis today held a burial service, first in the village and then at Jacob Conrad's for two recently deceased Negro children." By 1830, Lewis and four other black preachers were granted licenses to preach.[32]

As late as 1836, at the height of another Methodist revival in the Piedmont, Lewis still captivated black audiences from miles around. By then a veteran of more than thirty years of exhortation and revival meetings, he retained his touch as perhaps the key religious spokesperson for African Americans in the area. In June 1836, Pastor Renatus Schmidt reported: "The services here were omitted entirely because the Negro Lewis was preaching in this neighborhood and all the local church Negroes were there." Lewis and other black preachers provided a unifying voice for a wide network of black Christians.[33]

Because of most black preachers' affiliation with the Methodists, congregants in Salem absorbed and used the vocabulary of Methodists and Moravians almost interchangeably. A meeting for slaves held by a Moravian minister in Bethania in 1827 illustrated how denominational distinctions could blur. "In the afternoon there was a well attended meeting for Negroes. With the help of several leaders from among them verses from our Hymn Book were sung to their own tunes."[34]

On many Sundays, congregants went to Methodist meetings or to a camp revival if one was in progress. In June 1832, there were "only a few present" at Steiner's sermon, "as most of them had gone to a Methodist service," whereas in July 1835 services "had to be omitted entirely because of the Camp Meeting in Clemenstown." Similar examples could be repeated at length. Moravian ministers realized they could not compete with the appeal of such gatherings to worshipers eager for intense "seeking" and emotional release. Methodist churches such as Jerusalem Church in Forsyth County competed with the Brethren for members among the local black popula-

32. Negro Congregation Diary, June 26, Nov. 13, 1825; LAC, Sept. 10, 1826; Tise, *Yadkin Melting Pot*, 56.

33. Negro Congregation Diary, June 5, 1836.

34. Bethania Diary, Mar. 25, 1827, in Fries et al., eds., *Records*, VIII, 3820. A latter-day editor has added the words "presumably Methodist" after the words "their own tunes."

tion. By 1850, Jerusalem's membership roles contained the names of slaves owned by Moravians, such as Blum, Boner, Fries, and Zevely.[35]

Moravian pastors evidently tolerated congregants' preference for Methodist meetings on the reasoning that at least they were hearing some kind of preaching. For African Americans, however, the camp meetings provided an alternative if temporary forum for worship. When the meetings were over, they returned refreshed to their own church. Where white evangelicals saw denominational competition for souls, blacks saw a chance to enrich their spiritual lives in as many settings as possible. Thus, Methodist camp meetings and black-led services formed the basis of compromise between the congregation and Steiner. Both sides understood that such outlets made it easier for black worshipers to accept the reserved tone of Moravian services.

At the same time, black Christians did not confine their spirituality to the four walls of a church. They regarded spirituality less as a matter of formal church affiliation and theological distinctions than quality and variety of worship and social exchange. Energized by an expansive view of their religious world, they experimented with different forms and beliefs, adapting to both opportunities and realities. Black congregational life assumed a fluid, permeable character. Although membership in the church remained small—between fifteen and twenty communicant and noncommunicant members through the 1840s—the extended church family was much larger. Many meetings drew sixty or seventy people, occasionally as many as one hundred; other times only a handful showed up. Sporadic attendance did not reflect an inconstant commitment to the church but rather a broader view of fellowship in a climate of severe constraints on movement, sociability, and self-expression.

DIFFERENCES OVER WORSHIP styles telescoped a larger conflict between Steiner and the congregation over behavior, both inside and outside the church. The minister, as a faithful servant of Moravian slaveholders, viewed the church as a tool of slave control. Like his fellow Protestant missionaries throughout the plantation South, he peppered his sermons with frequent

35. Negro Congregation Diary, June 7, 1832, July 13, 1834, July 24, 1835; Larry E. Tise, "The Churches," in *Winston-Salem in History,* X (Winston-Salem, N.C., 1976), 19. Forsyth County, the location of the modern city of Winston-Salem, was created out of Stokes County in 1849.

reminders to slaves, bolstered by New Testament texts, to obey their masters. Inevitably, punishment and discipline meted out by Steiner were designed to mold the behavior of congregation members not only as Christians but also as slaves.[36]

For their part, parishioners saw church life as a forum for energetic engagement in their own spiritual affairs, which sometimes meant vigorous disagreement with the minister and with each other. Sharp contention often arose over the church moral code. In March 1823, for example, Steiner reproved the congregation for what he took as misconduct: "At the close there was another serious discourse to all about the offensive disturbances which had occurred a week ago. The unseemly behavior of various ones was held up to them and the consequences of that were presented to them. They were reminded to open their hearts to the Spirit of God, and if they follow his voice, it would guide them to a Christian life. They all promised that they would let that occurrence serve as a warning."[37]

Such unnamed "offensive disturbances" might have been related to worship, but because services provided a rare moment of social fellowship, black congregants inevitably angered each other at times, perhaps over disagreements both sacred and secular. In October 1824, after a "really blessed service, the Evil One was active in some women and led them astray into a quarrel with each other and it would have come to blows between them if others had not intervened." These fellow worshipers "held up to them the outrage to carry on in such a refractory way after a worship service, and particularly after the one we had just had, and I also took the opportunity to rebuke them seriously for their behavior."[38]

36. On antebellum Protestant evangelical efforts to inculcate submissiveness among slaves through the mission, see Raboteau, *Slave Religion*, chap. 4, esp. 168–171; Creel, *"A Peculiar People,"* chap. 7; Anne C. Loveland, *Southern Evangelicals and the Social Order, 1800–1860* (Baton Rouge, La., 1980), chap. 8; Milton C. Sernett, *Black Religion and American Evangelicalism: White Protestants, Plantation Missions, and the Flowering of Negro Christianity, 1787–1865* (Metuchen, N.J., 1975); and Donald G. Mathews, "Charles Colcock Jones and the Southern Evangelical Crusade to Form a Biracial Community," *JSH*, XLI (1975), 299–320. For an indication of the Moravians' philosophy of the relationship between social and spiritual control of slaves in the Danish West Indies, see C.G.A. Oldendorp, *History of the Mission of the Evangelical Brethren on the Caribbean Islands of St. Thomas, St. Croix, and St. John*, ed. and trans. Arnold R. Highfield and Vladimir Barac (1770; reprint, Ann Arbor, Mich., 1987), 334.

37. Negro Congregation Diary, Mar. 16, 1823.

38. Ibid., Oct. 31, 1824.

The incident prompted Steiner to impose sterner measures to preserve his concept of orderly worship. He used a standard Moravian missionary device of appointing two slaves as *Saaldiener*, or sextons, to oversee decorum. The Brethren first employed the technique of designating an elite cadre of converted slaves to help control others in the Saint Thomas congregation in the 1730s. Priscilla and Samuel served as sextons for blacks-only meetings in Hope in 1802.

In similar fashion, Abraham Steiner named free black Jacob Samuel and slave John Immanuel to the post in 1824, noting that his own teachings seemed to have "made a good impression on both Negroes." Indeed, John Immanuel apparently had already taken on a leadership role himself early in the life of the young congregation. There was precedent for his action, for in 1804 on behalf of slaves in Bethania he asked a minister for a special lovefeast. Likewise, in July 1822, he went to Steiner as a sort of spiritual go-between: "In the evening John Immanuel came and after he had first of all taken care of his own concern, he presented the concern of others, especially that of Enoch and his wife Nancy. . . . He also mentioned that the Negro Shepherd seeks for the good with tears and that he had conversed with him about it. He was told that the next time he should bring Shepherd to me." This willingness to serve as a liaison between pastor and congregation seems to have made him an attractive candidate to help enforce Steiner's vision of order.[39]

Immanuel's appointment as sexton in 1824 also completed his resurrection from spiritual exile, marking him now as a key figure in the church. As one slaveholder described the sextons' role, "Old John and Jacob Samuel . . . always see that everything is in good order." After one sermon, Steiner reported: "The sextons brought to me three young men who had permitted themselves frivolity during the service, in order for me to give them a reprimand for their unbecoming behavior; this happened, and they were instructed by others how they had to behave in gatherings for divine worship. We hope that this will be instructive for the young people." The sextons also helped the pastor comfort the sick and dying. "I went with the Negro Brother John Immanuel to the paper mill to visit the Negro Richard, who is ill, just as I had already visited him frequently during the previous week." Communicant Christian David, appointed sexton in the early 1830s,

---

39. LAC Bericht, Dec. 2, 1824; Negro Congregation Diary, July 17, 1822.

visited an ailing slave, Lucas, and "at his request he had offered a prayer at his bedside and commended him to the grace and mercy of the Saviour."[40]

In these capacities, sextons served the pastor's interests. But they also viewed themselves as spiritual custodians responsible for improving the lives of worshipers in substantive ways. In 1833, when the fence posts around the graveyard were decayed, John Immanuel offered to cut and set new posts himself. And in late December 1834, without notifying authorities, he undertook a drive to collect money for a new iron stove in the church. During the previous winter, part of the church had burned when sparks escaped from the stove, igniting a beam. White authorities had considered doing without fire in the church as a precaution but concluded that, because "the poor Negroes are often thinly clothed in cold weather and have no place to warm themselves, we must seek to help them."[41]

It is possible they still had done nothing a year later, whereupon worshipers took it upon themselves to buy a new stove before the advance of winter. Clearly they meant their church to be as much a physical sanctuary as a psychological one. Yet this display of black assertion displeased the pastor who, in a "thorough interview with John Immanuel," made sure the latter understood the limits of his post. "We tried to make clear to him that the office of Church Administrator, as some are accustomed to say, is only nominal and that in the Negro Church his only responsibility is that of church sexton, that in the future, he should undertake nothing which is not involved in this office without our knowledge or order, least of all to collect money to get for the church one or another item which occurs to him. If there is money to be collected, for a lovefeast for example, Sister Steiner will take care of that in the future." The minister praised congregants for "devotion to their church" but warned them not to try to collect money for such projects in the future "because it could be misunderstood or thought wrong." "Perhaps some other means could be found in time to get such a

40. Francis Fries Letters, Nov. 13, 1829, in Fries et al., eds., *Records,* VIII, 3876; Negro Congregation Diary, Aug. 6, 1826, Apr. 29, 1827, Nov. 17, 1833. Similarly, pastor Renatus Schmidt, who replaced Steiner in 1833, reported in August 1834: "Some of the charges against James were unfounded but since he has given offense and caused annoyance through carelessness, on the 9th, in the presence of Bro. David and John Immanuel we talked with him earnestly and advised him that *for the time being* we could not consider him as a communicant. We talked very lovingly and seriously with him."

41. LAC Bericht, Sept. 7, 1833, Dec. 29, 1834. On the inadequacy of slave clothing, see Paul D. Escott, *Slavery Remembered: A Record of Twentieth-Century Slave Narratives* (Chapel Hill, N.C., 1979), 39–40.

stove for them, something which they really need. This was very well accepted by the Negroes."

Of course they had no reason at all to "accept" the censure, and the pastor himself might have wondered about the effectiveness of his scolding. To drive the point home, he lectured them two weeks later to be "grateful" for their church building and for the opportunity, "which they have more than many others of their color in this state, to be instructed in the Word of God." Finally, in early January, the Female Mission Society bought an iron stove for the church. Once again, parishioners and pastor had effected a compromise, albeit an unequal one. By secretly organizing on behalf of their church, congregants spurred white officials to action and ultimately got what they wanted. But the issue represented a contest for control of the church in which blacks were forced to maneuver subtly behind the curtains of power drawn open or shut at will by whites. To authorities, the stove meant little next to the issue of who obtained it, and how. They granted black desires only on terms that would leave no doubt who was in charge.[42]

The episode also illustrated the tension inherent in the role of sexton. John Immanuel's actions reveal a sense of commitment to the congregation that made him far more than a mouthpiece for white authority. Like many African-American leaders at other times and in other places, he faced the delicate problem of maintaining the trust of both whites and blacks. He had been anointed by whites who believed his experience and respect within the black community could help preserve their sense of Christian order and discipline. As elites often do, they used the device of designating surrogate authorities drawn from those they control, in effect, encouraging the dominated to police themselves.

But Immanuel and other sextons also defended the interests of worshipers when they could. They were a vital force in shaping the spiritual and moral direction of the church. Though they did not necessarily speak for all congregants, they represented a view that seemingly counseled patience and conformity to white expectations as a measure of Christian virtue and prudence. In helping to discipline wayward members, however, Immanuel might have seen himself as a watchman of the congregation whose survival depended on unity, mutual support, and recognition of the seriousness of their purpose. Such a stance perhaps lay behind an appeal by an elderly slave

42. Negro Congregation Diary, Dec. 7, 1834. These admonitions were delivered by Steiner's successor, Pastor Schmidt.

named Tom, who, though not a sexton, one day in 1825 took upon himself the task of admonishing the congregation. "The old Negro Tom made an exhortation to the church group to the effect that they do not come here to carry on foolishness or to do something unseemly, and that therefore everything indecent should be avoided. He did this because it had already happened several times and it was beginning again that some of the males were instigating others to laughter."[43]

In the many-layered struggle for control of the church, when whites forbade one form of behavior, they generally had to offer some form of compensation in return, which blacks made their own. A prime example is music. Slaves elsewhere sang spirituals about their longing for freedom, about crossing the river Jordan, and about their self-identification as the children of God. In ring shouts, they clapped, danced, stamped their feet, and sang in African-inflected rhythms. Spiritual as this music was, it was condemned by Moravian church officials as heathenish. Only Moravian music was sanctioned in the log church. Yet, by taking what they were given and adapting to this European tradition, congregants nonetheless built a rich vocal and instrumental vocabulary.[44]

As in any Moravian church, a basic musical form was the *Singstunde*, or singing service, in which the pastor interwove a spoken sermon with hymn stanzas sung by the congregation. On a typical Sunday in 1824, for example, "the sermon was on Matt. 11:28–30 and after that there was Bible study and a Singstunde." In 1824, the free black brothers Jacob and Christian Samuel added their considerable instrumental talents to the assembly's musical range. "During the second service there was the baptism of a child and after that Singstunde, during which those who were there were practiced in singing some melodies, for which the Negroes Jacob and Christian played the violin, which they had already done for all the singing today and which will happen frequently from now on."[45]

43. Negro Congregation Diary, Aug. 7, 1825 (quotation). Creel, *"A Peculiar People,"* 283–284, contains a brief but lucid discussion of elders in slave Baptist congregations among antebellum South Carolina Gullahs.

44. On sacred African-American music, see Epstein, *Sinful Tunes and Spirituals;* Stuckey, *Slave Culture,* Introduction; John White, "Veiled Testimony: Negro Spirituals and the Slave Experience," *Journal of American Studies,* XVII (1983), 251–263; Eileen Southern, *The Music of Black Americans: A History* (New York, 1971); and Robert Simpson, "The Shout and Shouting in Slave Religion of the United States," *Southern Quarterly,* XXIII, no. 3 (Spring 1985), 34–47.

45. Negro Congregation Diary, Aug. 8, Sept. 19, 1824, Mar. 4, 1827.

The Samuel brothers had spent a great deal of time in musical training and self-education. They had attended the Moravian school in Bethabara during the late eighteenth and early nineteenth centuries, where music was a standard part of the curriculum. Christian Samuel had "stored up in his memory a treasure of hymn stanzas and tunes. . . . He had a particular gift for music and frequently accompanied the hymn singing in the church on the violin." Jacob Samuel had evidently done the same, and a third Samuel brother, John, "had learned to read German fluently and write and had also learned a number of hymn verses and their tunes. In music he had gone so far without instruction that he could play the violin quite well and could also play the flute which he used mostly for choral singing."[46]

Musicians held high status in southern slave communities, and the Samuels' musical ability, combined with their free status, undoubtedly earned them much esteem among fellow congregants. Moravian documents do not report whether their sister, Anna Samuel, also had musical training or played for the congregation. But largely because of the three brothers' playing, the musical canvas of Salem's black church must have differed greatly in form, texture, and emotional appeal from most southern congregations, black or white.[47]

Music consoled John Samuel as he lay on his deathbed in 1825. "In spite of the fact that he was so weak and that he talked so indistinctly, he did testify that he did not think of his departing from here below as being fearful for him but rather comforting. Several Negroes had come together during this and as his sister said that the singing of hymns cheered him up particularly, various stanzas were sung and after that he was commended to the Good Shepherd in a prayer for guidance and waiting." Singing accompanied such African-American death vigils elsewhere, as family and friends helped

46. Ibid., Mar. 22, 1825, Mar. 20, 1826.

47. Ibid., Dec. 26, 1824. See Paul A. Cimbala, "Fortunate Bondsmen: Black 'Musicianers' and Their Role as an Antebellum Southern Plantation Slave Elite," *Southern Studies,* XVIII (1979), 291–303. The status that accomplished violinists like the Samuels might have commanded is suggested further by the observation of a British traveler in the South in 1833: "The supreme ambition of every negro is to procure a real violin. By saving the few pence which are given them, selling chickens, and robbing a little, if necessary, they generally contrive to make up the sum. An instrument of music seems necessary to their existence"; see John Finch, *Travels in the United States of America and Canada* . . . (London, 1833), 237–238, quoted in Roger D. Abrahams and John F. Szwed, eds., *After Africa: Extracts from British Travel Accounts and Journals of the Seventeenth, Eighteenth, and Nineteenth Centuries concerning the Slaves, Their Manners, and Customs in the British West Indies* (New Haven, Conn., 1983), 388.

the spirit of the dying pass into the afterlife safely. The deathwatch was common to many traditional African cultures and might have infused Afro-Christian practice in America. Even Samuel's dying declaration that death did not trouble him might have reflected a fusion of compatible elements of Moravian doctrine and received African sensibility. Likewise, as John's brother Christian Samuel "went home," he apparently regarding music as necessary to hasten his spiritual transport to the unseen spirit world, so much so that he left explicit instructions for his burial. "Once he expressed the wish that at his funeral No. 406 out of our English hymnal, 'Jesus, will I never leave,' be sung," his biography noted, and his wishes were followed.[48]

Music and liturgy in the black congregation reflected Euro-Christian forms in many cases, but African Americans used them effectively nonetheless. Scholars have focused much attention on the adaptation and continuity of African influences in Afro-Christian worship, such as music, the ring shout, and burial practices. But form is only important in the service of an idea. The ways people worship can obscure understanding of the beliefs they express, though the two issues are often inseparable. The religious expression of black congregants in Salem, therefore, cannot be understood solely by the forms of worship to which they were confined. Like other black Americans, they adapted what was available to their purposes.

Barred from singing spirituals or other African-American songs in church, they sang Moravian hymns to the accompaniment of their own violins. In the absence of a ring shout, they held a lovefeast. Black Brethren planned and arranged events themselves in traditional Moravian fashion. On the Sunday after Christmas in 1824, "there was a general lovefeast, organized by the Negroes themselves, for which also many white Brothers and Sisters from Salem were present." During the lovefeast, "a hymn was sung by some of the Negroes and one of them accompanied it on the violin." Ritual in whatever form nourished a common purpose.[49]

Worshipers embraced the congregation; they took a proprietary interest

---

48. Negro Congregation Diary, Mar. 20, 1825, Mar. 19, 1826, and, for other examples, Nov. 10, 1826, Jan. 18, 1829. On these themes, see John S. Mbiti, *African Religions and Philosophy* (New York, 1969), chap. 14; Sobel, *Trabelin' On*, 200; Raboteau, *Slave Religion*, 261. Death vigils were a communal event among the Gullahs in South Carolina; family and friends gathered to comfort and help the dying "cross de ribber" safely; see Creel, *"A Peculiar People,"* 308–312, esp. 311; and David R. Roediger, "And Die in Dixie: Funerals, Death, and Heaven in the Slave Community, 1700–1865," *Massachusetts Review,* XII (1981), 169–170.

49. Negro Congregation Diary, Dec. 26, 1824.

and pride in it. They wanted it to be more than a place to be ministered to, one rather that served them in ways they themselves defined. As early as October 1822, a delegation of congregants visited Steiner at his home and "presented the desire that they and others had for more frequent services." Again, in 1834, they applied for more preaching and were told that, "in accordance with their desire, in the future there would be services every Sunday." Many felt a sense of personal identification with the church. They wanted to testify, to let others know about their joy. John's joining of the congregation in 1824 was announced to the assembly "in compliance with his expressed desire." Tom, a noncommunicant, wanted more participation in church ritual, professing his "chagrin that although he was an admirer of Jesus, he was not allowed to be at the last Communion on Good Friday but was refused admittance by the official." The postponement of one Communion, because several members "were not in the right frame of mind," disappointed others: "Those who had been baptized and had been received were to have been there as observers, which had been announced to them and for which they had been very happy, and now all of a sudden, their joy and ours was dampened."[50]

The church became an important place to celebrate or solemnize life passages. Congregants took keen interest in each other's weddings, baptisms, and confirmations. They did not confine their activities to Sundays. They came out especially for funerals at the graveyard beside the log church, even taking precious free time after work during the week to review the life of the dead and bid farewell. At the burial of the aged sister Anna (now usually known as Nancy) on a Friday afternoon in September 1829, congregants listened as Steiner, reading from the short biography he had written, recalled her life: "She had been born in Africa and had been brought to this land as a slave when she was young. Here she lived in different places until she came to Salem more than fifty years ago, where she was baptized and admitted to the Holy Communion." After the death of her husband, Christian, Anna / Nancy remained a widow for forty-one years. "She was faithful and punctual in the work assigned to her and was treated more like a maid than as a slave," Steiner read, glossing over her earlier predilection for challenging authority. "She had her peculiarities, but when one learned to know her better, one found that she knew whom she believed in, and in whom she placed her trust, and she was patient with all kinds of rudeness.

50. Ibid., Oct. 3, 1822, Apr. 18, 1824, Apr. 13, 1825, Nov. 2, 1834.

For the last several years she was not able to go out much any more, but a few years ago she was still here for the Holy Communion and explained that she had again strengthened herself with the Savior's look of love. . . . Her age cannot be given, but it must have been more than eighty years." Listeners' reaction to the funeral reading went unreported. However compact the narrative was, it nonetheless must have helped congregants remember and honor the long life of one of the first black sisters in North Carolina. Examples of such memorial services and other kinds of ceremonies could be compounded at length, but the evidence suggests that congregants derived meaning from them and that the vibrancy of their fellowship flowed, not from feigned enthusiasm or white-enforced attendance, but from their own emotional investment in the sacramental community.[51]

Although attendance fluctuated for much of the year according to agricultural work cycles, the weather, and the proximity of Methodist camp meetings, special days in the Moravian worship calendar invariably brought crowds. Christmas, Pentecost, Lent, and a series of Moravian memorial days were certainly important and always drew big numbers. But without question the high point of the year was Easter. The Moravian Church that so derived its identity from the redemptive agony of Jesus replenished its spiritual core during Passion Week. In white Moravian churches, daily services commemorated each step of Christ's passage to martyrdom and resurrection, building to a high emotional pitch on Good Friday, when in an early afternoon service a solemn prayer was uttered at the hour of his death. Though the black congregation technically was not Moravian, Easter was also the pivotal week of its annual worship cycle. Congregants generally were not allowed to worship from Monday through Thursday, but Palm Sunday, Good Friday, and Easter Sunday services remained elemental parts of their Passion Week.

It is scarcely surprising that black worshipers should have taken such an interest in Easter, since they knew a great deal about suffering and could identify with Christ's Passion. Many Moravian-owned slaves received time off to attend Good Friday services, so it is also possible that church attendance was swelled by some who sought to evade an afternoon's work. In one typical year, 1825, "between one and two o'clock in the afternoon a nice group came together for whom the story of the day about Jesus' suffering was read," followed by prayer and Communion with seven communicants.

51. Negro Congregation Diary, Sept. 4, 1829.

Easter Sunday services drew even larger audiences. As early as 1823, when Steiner still occasionally conducted services at the paper mill, he reported that on Easter Sunday "there were only a few present at the beginning, but little by little, so many came that there was no room at the end, so the sermon was prolonged in order that something might be said even to those who came last." At 9:30 on the morning of Easter Sunday in 1838, the congregation prayed the Easter Litany on the graveyard beside the church, then moved inside to hear Pastor Schmidt's preaching. "The church could not hold the large number of listeners. Several had to find places on the gallery." Worshipers sometimes prolonged the emotional intensity built up during Passion Week. On Easter Monday in April 1827, "there was a love-feast for the black church fellowship, which they had organized, at which many white Sisters were present." Thus, though not complete masters of their own worship, congregants exploited a rich variety of outlets provided by such occasions to express their spirituality.[52]

What kind of faith did black Christians in the Salem church espouse? Since they were so heavily exposed to Moravian teachings, did their beliefs differ from those of black Protestants elsewhere in the antebellum South? Enslaved African Americans saw clear parallels between their own tribulations and the struggle of the Israelites to escape Egyptian bondage and regain freedom in Canaan. Reflecting an African concept of time that compressed past and present into one, spirituals spoke of striving Old Testament heroes such as Moses, Abraham, and Jacob as though they were alive and helping slaves in their daily struggle. The spirituals spoke in both veiled and explicit language of spiritual and physical liberation. Captives identified with the suffering Jesus and saw his martyrdom as a ransom for their oppression. Their faith expressed both sorrow over bondage and joy that God believed in them and took their side. The slaves' sacred world was also alive to the presence of spirits who could be manipulated or supplicated for good or malign purposes. Conjury provided for slaves access to an alternative source of spiritual control beyond the power of the master.[53]

52. Ibid., Mar. 30, 1823, Apr. 11, 1825, Apr. 27, 1827, Apr. 15, 1838.
53. Overviews of slave theology are many, especially those based to one extent or another on analysis of spirituals. See, among others, Raboteau, *Slave Religion*, chap. 5; Stuckey, *Slave Culture*, Introduction; Sobel, *Trabelin' On*; Genovese, *Roll, Jordan, Roll*, bk. 2; Levine, *Black Culture and Black Consciousness*, 3–80; and Olli Alho, *The Religion of the Slaves: A Study of the Religious Tradition and Behavior of Plantation Slaves in the United States, 1830–1864* (Helsinki, 1976).

Congregants in Salem left a less-extensive personal testament of their faith than that encoded in the slave spirituals and narratives. They sang no spirituals—in church, at least—nor did they leave a body of oral testimony regarding their belief. It is difficult to determine what they took from Moravian doctrine, added from other sources such as the Methodists (including black preachers such as Lewis), and refashioned into a theology to suit their own needs. Nevertheless, it is possible to glimpse through the filtered lens of descriptions recorded by white ministers what these black Christians might have thought about their relationship to God.

Like the early black Moravians, a new generation of seekers in the 1820s embarked on spirit "travels" involving recognition of sin, restless seeking for spiritual release, and a personal vision of redemption. In an important narrative—in fact, the first female slave narrative—Mary Prince, a West Indian slave who attended Moravian meetings in Antigua in the 1820s, portrayed the process thus: "I dearly loved to go to the church, it was so solemn. I never knew rightly that I had much sin till I went there. When I found out that I was a great sinner, I was very sorely grieved, and very much frightened. I used to pray God to pardon my sins for Christ's sake, and forgive me for every thing I had done amiss; and when I went home to my work, I always thought about what I had heard from the missionaries, and wished to be good that I might go to heaven."[54]

Likewise, Jesse, a slave living near Salem, described bouts of searching as intense as Mary Prince's. Steiner reported: "For a long time he has been feeling his sinful need deeply and anxiously, and has been crying constantly to the Lord for mercy, until Jesus finally appeared to him and comforted him with his forgiveness. This had happened twice and now he prays to him whenever he feels moved to do it and that this is often."[55]

54. Mary Prince, *History of Mary Prince, a West Indian Slave* (London, 1831), in Henry Louis Gates, Jr., ed., *The Classic Slave Narratives* (New York, 1987), 207.

55. Negro Congregation Diary, Sept. 23, 1827. Though the congregation was composed predominantly of slaves, similar testimony from a free black, Joseph Davis, may be found in the Negro Congregation Diary, Nov. 10, 1826. Although he owned land and a house and had more power, wealth, and freedom of movement than enslaved parishioners, Davis still groped for spiritual direction. "He testified that he did not have anything good to present, but that he did believe that Jesus Christ had come into the world to redeem and save sinners, and that gives him confidence." On the "seeker's" soul journey to conversion, see also Sobel, *Trabelin' On*, 108–128; Alho, *Religion of the Slaves*, 182–186; and Clifton H. Johnson, ed., *God Struck Me Dead: Religious Conversion Experiences and Autobiographies of Negro Ex-Slaves* (Philadelphia, 1969).

Since the Moravian Church was so Christocentric, Steiner and other ministers preached heavily—though not exclusively—from the New Testament. That does not mean that congregants necessarily adopted wholesale Pauline Christianity with its stress on obedience that was emphasized by whites. We may assume they knew about and identified with Old Testament heroes like Moses, Daniel, and Joshua, as did other black Christians. Some were literate and could read the Old Testament for themselves, discerning strong parallels for their own liberation struggle. Even more important, blacks in Salem were part of a larger web of Afro-Christians in Piedmont North Carolina and beyond who worshiped, learned from each other, and exchanged ideas in many different settings, some sanctioned by whites, others not. In other words, the services, music, and prayer within the log church constituted only part of these converts' religious lives.

It seems safe to say that from this shared pool of knowledge congregants developed a theology similar to that of other black Christians around them. Such a theology served two different purposes. On one hand, it emphasized God's immediate presence in their lives as a deliverer or savior, an active and omnipresent ally against degradation. At the same time, their faith no doubt counseled patience and a belief in a better afterlife as well. Both tendencies, for example, might be read into the testimony of Budney: "In many difficult occurrences in his family, about which he was accustomed to pour out his troubled heart, he never lost trust in his Savior, that he would help him through and some day take him to his heavenly kingdom; and that in his family, the Lord would in the end turn everything to the best." And in a "Speaking," or conversation with the minister, a candidate for Communion said: "I have experienced that the Savior can make the rough places smooth and what is uneven, he can make level." In the end, theology among black worshipers in Salem, as among enslaved African Americans elsewhere, grew out of their experience of oppression. They translated the private relationship between God and the believer into a collective affirmation of spiritual and physical salvation.[56]

56. Negro Congregation Diary, Nov. 27, 1824, Jan. 29, 1829. Raboteau, *Slave Religion,* Genovese, *Roll, Jordan, Roll,* and Levine, *Black Culture and Black Consciousness,* emphasize the liberating Old Testament–inspired strains in slave religion. Orlando Patterson, however, contends that slave Christianity was Pauline in its "overwhelming preoccupation with Christ and the crucifixion and in its ethical and symbolic dualism, its paradoxical tension between the ethic of judgment and the ethic of the redeemed sinner." "Jesus and his crucifixion dominate the theology of the slaves and not, as recent scholars have claimed, the Israelites and Exodus

Worshipers might also have expressed those beliefs through the subtle use of cultural practices adapted from African traditions. At least some of the burials in the graveyard by the church were apparently marked or decorated by small objects such as shards of broken mirror, marine shells, pebbles, and scissors; several graves were enclosed by small rocks. Though the full meaning behind such fragments cannot be known, it is quite possible they belonged to the deceased and were intended to convey spiritual power on the journey to the afterlife. The use of such objects for ritual purpose was common in Africa and in much of African America. It is unclear whether such practices persisted in Salem with the knowledge of white Moravians, who might have viewed object-strewn graves as heathenish superstition. With or without white approval, the objects provide potentially strong material testimony of the lingering—though usually secretly expressed—power of African-inspired beliefs in the Moravian settlement, perhaps providing a form of cultural resistance to Euro-Christian values.[57]

What drew many into the Salem church's orbit was its transregional and cross-denominational attraction. Yet such a kaleidoscopic complexion defied universal appeal. Some blacks held strong opinions about religion that differed from practices in the Salem church. In 1840, the minister was visited by "a black who lives about 9 miles from here" who had attended the service earlier that day. He had been baptized by the Baptists sixteen years earlier but was later expelled because he worked on Sundays. When he asked the Moravian minister's opinion about working on Sunday, the latter replied: "In Holy Scripture we are commanded to sanctify the day of rest and therefore that transgressing of this commandment could not be seen as good. Thereupon he went into an endless judging that I also was considering him unworthy." For ministers both Moravian and Baptist, the Bible was unequivocal and could not be contravened. But this literal interpretation posed a problem for enslaved Christians seeking to earn money by working for themselves, since Sundays were generally their only free days. The connec-

story." This "Pauline dualism," in Patterson's view, reconciled the seemingly opposing theological poles in slave religion of liberation and obedience; see Patterson, *Slaves and Social Death: A Comparative Study* (Cambridge, Mass., 1982), 74–76.

57. Ferguson, "Hidden Testimony," 42–48. See also Robert Farris Thompson, *Flash of the Spirit: African and Afro-American Art and Philosophy* (New York, 1983), 132–142; John M. Vlach, "Graveyards and Afro-American Art," *Southern Exposure,* V (1977), 161–165; Elizabeth A. Fenn, "Honoring the Ancestors: Kongo-American Graves in the American South," *Southern Exposure,* XII (1984), 42–47.

tion between slave religion and economic advancement is little understood. But if this case of one worshiper's frankness and willingness to return a minister's criticism is revealing, then some slaves, interpreting the Scriptures more liberally, believed spiritual "worthiness" compatible with Sunday labors.[58]

A second exchange showed that some blacks shunned the Salem church because of doctrinal differences. A black man named David, described by the Moravian minister as "a cripple who can get around only with much effort on two crutches . . . and is a zealous defender" of the Methodists, refused to attend services in the black church because "he would not know where to sit. Our way of holding meetings is not right, for the sheep and the goats were all mixed together, which should not be for the converted and those who are beginning to take thought and those who are still unconverted should all, each one in a class for themselves, sit alone and this was the reason he would never come to the negro church, for he could not decide to sit among the mixed groups." This Christian's precisely ordered view of worship clashed with the Salem church's improvised looseness. Though the ethos of collective celebration remains among the most striking outward features of slave Christianity, in fact that dimension rested on intensely private experience. Despite its broad regional appeal, Salem's black congregation could no more satisfy everyone's idea of worship than any other church.[59]

YET THE MORAVIAN CHURCH claimed allegiance from a devoted core. A crucial reason was that by the 1820s slaves in the Moravian communities found themselves more embattled than earlier generations. Most glaringly, families were more vulnerable to separation by sale. In the eighteenth century, though black Moravian marriages carried no legal standing, the church

58. Negro Congregation Diary, Jan. 19, 1840. The minister reporting the incident was Thomas Pfohl. Abraham Steiner had died in 1833, and his successor, Renatus Schmidt, was called to the Cherokee Mission in 1838. See the account of Mary Prince, a slave on Antigua in the 1830s, who recalled that slaves were forced to work on Sunday mornings, after which "those that have yams or potatoes, or fire-wood to sell, hasten to market to buy a dog's worth of salt fish, or pork, which is a great treat for them. It is very wrong, I know, to work on Sunday or go to market; but will not God call the Buckra [white] men to answer for this on the great day of judgment—since they will give the slaves no other day?" See Prince, *History of Mary Prince,* in Gates, ed., *Classic Slave Narratives,* 206.

59. Report of the Negro Congregation in and around Salem, Feb. 8, 1843, in Fries et al., eds., *Records,* IX, 4733.

frowned on the division of families. By the 1820s, however, that measure of security had eroded. Apart from a few slaves owned by the church, slaveholding was concentrated in the hands of individuals outside Salem who operated beyond the bounds of church control and felt freer to sell slaves with impunity. A crucial change in marriage procedure reflected this shift. In 1822, Steiner told the congregation that "those who wanted to be married in the future must present written permission from their masters and mistresses."[60]

With that decree, ministers recognized that control of enslaved Brethren's family lives had passed to slaveowners. In earlier years, ministers monitored the selection of mates; now they surrendered that prerogative to masters. In late 1823, the elders took no interest in the marriage of a slave named Patsey, owned by Wilhelm Fries. "Br. Fries asked concerning the marriage of his Negress to the free Negro Jacob on his plantation. Conferenz replied that it had nothing to do with that."[61]

With control over slave marriages transferred from the church's hands to their own, many Moravian masters, following other Protestant slaveholders throughout the South, gradually came to disregard the entire concept of the integrity of the slave family. A church board described the issue in 1824:

Hitherto Br. Steiner has married Negro slaves by the Book of Common Prayer, like white persons. It is not within the power of the Negroes to promise that they will live together as married people, for it often happens that one or the other is sold by the owner, or by his executor, and they are completely separated. Some of them also break the marriage bond lightly. We were therefore of the opinion that this custom should cease; and if those who belong to the congregation wish to marry, their purpose shall simply be announced, they shall be admonished to live as Christian husband and wife, and the blessing of God shall be wished for them.

60. Negro Congregation Diary, Sept. 1, 1822. The decision was reiterated in LAC, Jan. 2, 1824.

61. Aelt. Conf., Dec. 30, 1823, in Fries et al., eds., *Records*, VIII, 3650. Patsey was not a member of the congregation but was closely affiliated with it, and undoubtedly Abraham Steiner hoped to bring her into the fold. The elders' lack of interest in the marital status of a potential convert thus seems strongly indicative of a desire to cede control of decisions regarding marriage to slaveowners. By comparison, in 1803 the Bethania church board applied strong pressure to both masters and slaves—with limited success—to arrange Christian marriages for slaves.

In the 1760s, a Moravian missionary excoriated non-Moravian slaveholders in the West Indies for separating married slave couples. Sixty years later, the church bowed to the desires of white Brethren now heavily enmeshed in the slaveholding system by allowing them to do the same thing.[62]

Moravian and non-Moravian slaveholders alike in the Piedmont region were responding in part to external economic factors. The closing of the legal African slave trade in 1808 made the domestic slave trade more profitable. The rise of the cotton kingdoms to the southwest early in the nineteenth century created a powerful demand for slaves. Although white Brethren were contemptuous of slave trading as a profession, some were quite willing to supply the trader with human merchandise. One discovers, for example, two appalling scenes in 1836 involving the sale and separation of Christian slave families that would have been less likely to occur thirty-five or even twenty-five years earlier. "There was much comforting to be done today because the wife of our Communicant Brother James, who belongs to Miss Rose, was sold and taken to Alabama; likewise the brother and sister of Safe," reported Renatus Schmidt. And two months later, the minister noted that "a member of our little congregation and the property of the deceased Joshua Boner, had the sad fate of being sold to a slave trader, namely the married Maria, a received member." Besides the obvious shock and sorrow of seeing their friends, family, and fellow worshipers sold, such incidents drove home to congregation members how vulnerable they had become.[63]

Two major reasons related specifically to Moravian culture explain this new willingness of some white Brethren to separate families and to sell even

---

62. PAC, Jan. 6, 1824, in Fries et al., eds., *Records*, VIII, 3694; Oldendorp, *Caribbean Mission*, ed. and trans. Highfield and Barac, 334. It should also be pointed out that some enslaved parishioners who were sold were owned by non-Moravian masters over whom the church governance had no control. Comparison with another slaveholding society, Brazil, reveals a similar schism between religious authority and the masters with regard to slave marriage. See Robert E. Conrad, ed., *Children of God's Fire: A Documentary History of Black Slavery in Brazil* (Princeton, N.J., 1983), 151–152, 159, 175–176, 189. In the American South, Protestant churches sometimes suggested strongly to slaveholding members to do everything in their power to maintain slave unions, but enforcement was weak; see Raboteau, *Slave Religion*, 183–184. The more the Moravian Church withdrew from such supervision in the marriages of slaves, therefore, the more it resembled other mainline Protestant denominations.

63. Negro Congregation Diary, Aug. 7, Oct. 5, 1836; Michael Tadman, *Speculators and Slaves: Masters, Traders, and Slaves in the Old South* (Madison, Wis., 1989); Allan Kulikoff, "Uprooted Peoples: Black Migrants in the Age of the American Revolution, 1790–1820," in Ira Berlin and Ronald Hoffman, eds., *Slavery and Freedom in the Age of the American Revolution* (Charlottesville, Va., 1983).

communicant Christians. Both stem from the changing nature of their settlement itself. The first is that slave conversion to Christianity no longer carried the same social or spiritual prestige with white Brethren as in former years. The idea of living, working, and worshiping alongside African Americans in the Salem choir houses would have been strange to white Moravians of the 1820s. As enslaved Moravians came to be regarded as Christians apart, some whites found it easier to discount whatever moral imperative they had felt earlier to respect slave families.[64]

A second and related reason is that by the 1820s the church itself wielded less influence over its members than in earlier years. One might characterize this change in part as a growing secularization of Moravian society. Half a century of protest against church regulations by rising generations had resulted in a gradual weakening of the elders' control and a rise in individual freedom, at least for white Brethren. The Unity Synod of 1818 in Herrnhut, for example, had voted to discontinue the use of the lot in determining marriages. The elders thus exercised less and less control over all marriages, white as well as black. Even more important was a rise in economic independence, particularly in Salem, where the church sought to restrict competition and individual enterprise in favor of a carefully regulated guild system. Brethren kept trying to wriggle free of what they saw as the stifling control over business and trade, and they slowly gained headway.[65]

As Moravian society gradually separated into distinct spiritual and secular spheres, blacks felt the impact. The burgeoning of slavery in the countryside,

64. This harsh view was by no means universal among white Brethren. George Logenauer's will of 1834, for example, stipulated: "My negro woman Betty and her child I leave to my heirs on condition that they not be sold out of their families; it is my will not to misuse them while they behave well." But that at least some white Brethren now were quite willing to split families indicates a great change in social relations. It is also worth pointing out that the rise of racial segregation begun in the 1790s did not end in 1822 with the formation of the black church. Officials kept finding new ways to separate people. In 1828, for example, "bodies of Negroes will no longer be taken to the corpse-house at the church but will be brought directly to the Negro church." See Stokes County Wills, III, 270, Stokes County Courthouse; Auf. Col., Jan. 22, 1828, in Fries et al., eds., *Records*, VIII, 3845.

65. For overviews of social and economic developments in Salem, see Jerry L. Surratt, "From Theocracy to Voluntary Church and Secularized Community: A Study of the Moravians in Salem, North Carolina, 1772–1860" (Ph.D. diss., Emory University, 1968); Surratt, "The Role of Dissent in Community Evolution among Moravians in Salem, 1772–1860," *NCHR*, LII (1975), 235–255; Philip Africa, "Slaveholding in the Salem Community, 1771–1851," *NCHR*, LIV (1977), 271–307; Michael Shirley, *From Congregation Town to Industrial City: Culture and Social Change in a Southern Community* (New York, 1994).

where it was largely unregulated by a weakened church, left the enslaved more at the mercy of the masters. The church exercised little oversight of slaveholders' use and treatment of bondpersons. Ministers could occasionally intercede with masters to ameliorate the lot of a slave, but in general even the church acceded to masters' wishes. Sometimes enslaved Christians were forced to sacrifice worship for duty, as in 1831 when several missed Communion "because they had to carry out orders of their owners."[66]

Such barriers to religious fulfillment could dominate a slave's life, and there was apparently little a minister like Steiner could do—or chose to do—about it. He wrote of Penelope, for example, a widow who died in 1827: "The deceased had lived a difficult and oppressed life in material things and for that reason she rarely came to church, but she did testify when one talked with her that her only hope was in the merciful grace of God." There is no evidence Steiner ever tried to intercede with Penelope's owner (though it is unknown whether he was Moravian or non-Moravian) to ameliorate what even he perceived as a "difficult and oppressed life." Indeed, he proved unsympathetic to another woman's complaint that work interfered with worship. "A Negress said that she had not been present at the service because she had been detained at the Paper Mill," he reported in 1823. "She was told that this was only an excuse with which she would not get by on that [judgment] day, and if she had been at the service, she would have heard of such excuses for not accepting God's grace."[67]

Church officials occasionally flexed their muscles on slaves' behalf against the authority of the masters, at least in spiritual matters. In 1833, Christian Friedrich Denke resigned as pastor of the Friedberg congregation and moved to Salem, where he and his wife bought two slaves, Samuel and Elizabeth, who were members of the black congregation. "Samuel and Betzi expressed their great joy that they had now received new masters in Bro. and Sister Denke; even though they still have to continue to work for their former owner Hauser until August, Bro. Denke issued the order yesterday that they must enjoy the attendance of the services here without any hindrance." But on other occasions, attempts at ministerial intervention met resistance. "I spoke with the owners and asked them to allow their Negroes to have the

66. Similarly, all communicants took Communion in December 1829 "except one who was hindered from coming" because she had to serve her owners; see Negro Congregation Diary, Dec. 6, 1829, Dec. 4, 1831.
67. Ibid., Oct. 12, 1823, Feb. 4, 1827.

day (off) on the coming Saturday in order to fence the God's Acre," noted Pastor Schmidt in 1836. "Various ones had many difficulties, so that on Saturday only seven Negroes came for that, and only half of the fencing was accomplished." The will of the church was at times arbitrarily subverted by masters.[68]

Facing these pressures, black Christians made their church even more of a spiritual fortress. For those who had nothing except their church and each other, solidarity became life's organizing principle. Indeed, the seemingly stern discipline meted out to wayward members by sextons like John Immanuel and Jacob Samuel becomes more understandable in this light. Given the fragility of slave family life, any deviance detected by these community guardians threatened the group.

Church and family overlapped. Entire families three generations deep belonged to the church. Many couples were married in the worship hall; others joined the congregation and were received into Communion together. Thus some defined their marital relationship to each other at least partly through a shared commitment to the church. Family members took a strong interest in whether parents, children, or mates embraced the gospel. John Immanuel was troubled by his daughter Mary's lack of interest in religion despite her upbringing among Moravian church members who had given her much instruction. His efforts to "make her aware of her need for real salvation" bore no fruit until she fell sick and repented on her deathbed.[69]

Baptism or church affiliation earned applause from kin, even in distant communities. In 1822, Steiner was "visited by Enoch's mother, who belongs to the Baptist Church" in Yadkin County. "She told me something of her experiences, which were quite evangelical," noted the pastor. "It seemed particularly comforting to her to notice a changed frame of mind in her children at the Paper Mill from what she had previously seen as they seem to seek now earnestly after the Kingdom of God." When another woman, Rose, was baptized in 1825, "her children, some of them grown and living far away, were all present, and the church was also packed full; among those present were many white Sisters and children." Rose considered the ceremony a milestone important enough to send word to her children, who in turn traveled miles across the Piedmont to witness it. Thus, just as strong

68. Ibid., June 30, 1833, Apr. 1836.
69. Ibid., Sept. 20, 1830.

family ties could influence people to convert, religion conversely strengthened family bonds among the enslaved, even across great distances.[70]

Moravian ministers baptized hundreds of black children. Rules permitted baptism for children of unbaptized parents as long as slaveowners agreed to give them a Christian upbringing. From the start of his ministry, Steiner exhorted parents to "bring up their children as much as they can in the fear and admonition of the Lord."[71] Baptism was the crucial first step to incorporating slave children into the church community, and black parents quickly took advantage of its possibilities. What did it mean for them to seek baptism for their children? Although the rite's full significance to them can never be known, a partial answer may lie in the elaborate black Moravian baptismal sponsorship networks that first flourished a generation earlier. Building on surviving fragments of these connections, black congregants in the 1820s expanded godparenthood far beyond anything yet seen.

At a time when slavery afforded most Afro-Christians few formal sources of personal security and social cohesion that whites would honor, baptism might have provided both. Most godparents were congregants with relatively high status whose patronage might shelter slave children. Not surprisingly, John Immanuel, the most prominent communicant, and his wife, Sarah, sponsored thirteen children between 1824 and 1829. Among them were several free children, which may further confirm this enslaved couple's stature. One child, in fact, was the daughter of Anna Samuel, whose father, Johann, had himself sponsored John Immanuel in 1804. The symmetry of this relationship projects a sense of spiritual continuity through the generations.[72]

Congregants amplified further links to earlier black Moravians. Free blacks Nancy and Israel Oliver, the children of Peter and Christine Oliver, had grown to adulthood by the 1830s, joined the church, and sponsored several children. And another of Johann and Maria Samuel's children, the sexton Jacob Samuel and his slave wife Patsy, sponsored seven children. If the number of sponsorships indicated a person's status, then other elite members of the church community included Betsey (eight), Samuel and

70. Ibid., Sept. 9, 1822, Oct. 16, 1825.

71. LAC, Apr. 19, 1822; Negro Congregation Diary, Nov. 5, 1822.

72. Register of Infant Baptisms, in "Church Book for the People of Colour in and about Salem" (hereafter cited as "Church Book").

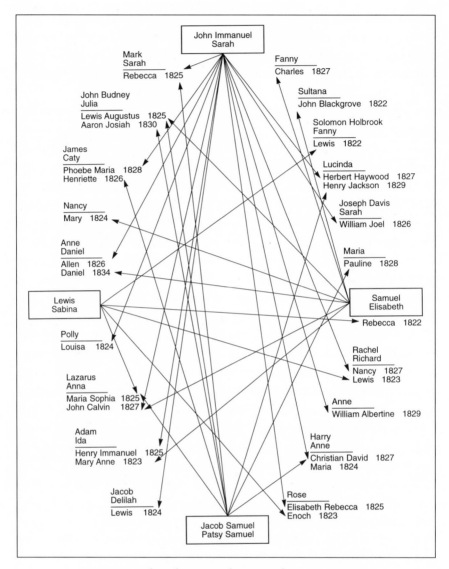

Figure 15. Selected Baptismal Sponsorships, 1822–1834.
Arrows point from godparent to godchild. Drawn by Richard Stinely

Elizabeth (seven), and Susanna (four). But dozens of other adults also sponsored children, resulting in an even more extensive web of fictive-kin relationships that encompassed nearly everyone connected to the congregation.
In fact, this kinship network suggests a church community reaching far
beyond the twenty or so communicant and noncommunicant members to

enfold hundreds of African Americans in the region (see Figure 15). Some black parents also chose (or perhaps were appointed) white godparents for their children, possibly to secure protection from well-placed whites. These sponsors were usually teachers or other helpers such as Abraham Steiner's sister Sarah.[73]

In the absence of precise information about how baptismal relationships worked, we again must rely on indirect evidence to suggest that they served both symbolically and practically as important extensions of the nuclear family. John Immanuel, for example, like grandparents, "aunts," "uncles," and other relatives or quasi-kin in slave societies, helped socialize children, specifically into the church. "Since his baptism in the year 1803, on January 6," his short biography observed, "each year on this day, formerly in Bethania and later in Salem, he took pleasure in inviting a number of children of our members to an afternoon vesper, which they enjoyed together." Immanuel "was a great friend of the children, who loved him, and often on Sundays a number of them would go to talk with him." Since slave parents often lived apart with different masters, godparents might have stepped in to assist in childrearing, a role that took on even greater importance by the 1820s. Indeed, perhaps for that reason parents often chose people from the same farm or plantation to sponsor their children. Thus, baptism and sponsorship were the vital cords tying a dispersed black community to the Salem church.[74]

Both adults and children gained another benefit from the church—the chance to gain literacy. Though many African Americans had learned to read in Moravian schools or through association with the church, ministers never undertook a systematic effort to give blacks formal instruction until 1827, when several women in the Female Mission Society began a Sunday school at the black church. The project defied conventional Southern slaveholding thought, since several states forbade slave education by law.[75]

73. Register of Infant Baptisms, in "Church Book." Examples of John and Sarah Immanuel's sponsorship of free children are nos. 27, 28. White sponsors are listed in nos. 39, 41.

74. Death notice of John Immanuel, in Negro Church Diary, Aug. 25, 1835, in Fries et al., eds., *Records*, VIII, 4196. That Immanuel invited "a number of children of our members" to vesper may indicate that he was an influential uncle to white children as well. On the slave community as an extended family, see Herbert G. Gutman, *The Black Family in Slavery and Freedom* (New York, 1976), chap. 8; and John W. Blassingame, *The Slave Community: Plantation Life in the Antebellum South* (New York, 1972), chap. 3.

75. There were nonetheless several illegal schools for slaves in the antebellum South, including three others later in North Carolina (in Raleigh, Fayetteville, and New Bern). In

Yet white Moravians continued to regard literacy, if properly taught, as a tool for social control. Rather than fearing that bondpersons might put reading to subversive use, whites were confident that the enslaved would read firsthand and absorb a message of submissiveness in the Bible. Schools were essential components in the Unity's missionary efforts worldwide, including Caribbean slave societies. Danish West Indian authorities thought so highly of the social benefits of the Moravians' educational efforts that the governor required *all* slaves in Saint Croix and Saint John to attend Moravian schools in 1838. Some three thousand children thereby gained access to a rudimentary formal education. In Salem, a diarist reported in March 1827: "Today several Sisters began to teach the Negro young people, in their church, giving them instruction in English spelling, and reading." About twenty pupils attended. Whites and blacks quickly came to regard the school as a success. By May, some forty pupils attended the weekly lessons. In June, Steiner reported that "school was lively and was supported by blacks and whites." The following month, the Female Mission Society bought primers for the students.[76]

Both adults and children took advantage of the school. Historians have noted the great desire of enslaved African Americans to read and write, and many found clandestine ways to learn what was generally prohibited them. There is much evidence from Salem to confirm this thirst for formal learning. For many, literacy was the key to uncovering the secrets of the Bible. It was said of John, one of the original congregants, that "chiefly through his own efforts he had acquired a significant mastery of reading and through that had made for himself a not meager knowledge of the Holy Scriptures, something not usual for one in his situation." The death notice of Phyllis,

---

addition, some masters personally taught slaves to read and write, whereas other slaves attended school with whites. W.E.B. Du Bois estimated that about 5% of the slave population was literate. See John Hope Franklin, *From Slavery to Freedom: A History of African Americans*, 7th ed. (New York, 1994), 137; Genovese, *Roll, Jordan, Roll*, 563; Guion Griffis Johnson, *Ante-Bellum North Carolina: A Social History* (Chapel Hill, N.C., 1937), 541–543; and Janet Duitsman Cornelius, *"When I Can Read My Title Clear": Literacy, Slavery, and Religion in the Antebellum South* (Columbia, S.C., 1991). Though some evangelicals criticized laws against teaching slaves to read, most obeyed and instructed slaves orally instead; see Loveland, *Southern Evangelicals and the Social Order*, 233.

76. Salem Diary, Mar. 4, 1827 (quotation); Negro Congregation Diary, Mar. 4, May 27, June 10, 1827; Female Mission Society, July 8, 1827.

who died in 1828, observed: "She attended church and school faithfully; in the latter she was an apt pupil."[77]

Likewise, a moving description of the departure of Ellen from Salem in 1829 gives valuable insight into the kind of two-way interracial education that might have been more common in the South than recognized. "The Negress Ellen took leave of us with a moved heart as she is going away from our area with her owners. . . . She was an intelligent pupil and in a short time had gone far in reading, singing and memorizing, of which she made good use with the children of her owners. She had already said farewell in Sunday school earlier and as they were singing a farewell hymn for her, everything broke down into such weeping that one could hardly continue singing."[78]

By May 1829, out of a class of about forty students, twelve "now can read fluently in the Testament, the rest are more or less advancing in spelling." As an encouragement, readers received "a Bible, or Testament, accompanied with some tracts." Congregants saw the school as a vehicle not only for learning but for teaching each other as well, since some "coloured persons are now employed to assist in teaching." Examinations confirmed many students' eagerness. "After the sermon there was an examination in the school," reported Steiner in November 1829. "The greater number of those [whites] present manifested their satisfaction with the progress of the Negroes in reading and memorizing." That month, sixty pupils attended class.[79]

The school thus furnished another testing ground for black and white expectations in which both sides ceded terrain for perceived gain. Driven by a combination of piety and pragmatism, whites saw education as an instrument of control, despite the risk that slaves might put their schooling to potentially subversive uses. Blacks viewed the school as a vehicle for knowledge, vital practical skills, and mutual instruction. Their price was a curricu-

77. Negro Congregation Diary, Dec. 7, 1828, Nov. 28, 1838. Carter G. Woodson observed that slaves "almost worshipped the Bible, and their anxiety to read it was their greatest incentive to learn" (quoted in Raboteau, *Slave Religion*, 240).

78. Similarly, the obituary of Peter Rose in 1833 notes: "He had been a faithful scholar in the Sunday school which had formerly been conducted for the Negroes and had learned to read well"; see Negro Congregation Diary, Apr. 27, 1829, Nov. 28, 1833.

79. *Weekly Gleaner* (Salem), May 26, 1829 (in archives at Old Salem, Inc.); Negro Congregation Diary, Jan. 4, Nov. 8, 29, 1829.

lum steeped in Pauline doctrine. Both sides could probably judge the project a success by these lights. From the school emerged a core of literate congregants who might continue to keep reading and writing alive in the slave community, secretly if necessary. Whether literacy actually bred a deeper sense of humility in these Christians is unclear. To the extent that no complaints linking insubordination to literacy surfaced, whites might have concluded that their efforts were worthwhile.

In any case, a more naked exercise of power halted the experiment after only four years. In January 1831, North Carolina lawmakers followed other southern states and prohibited the teaching of reading and writing to slaves on the grounds that it "has a tendency to excite dissatisfaction in their minds, and to produce insurrection and rebellion, to the manifest injury of the citizens of this State." Like all slaveholders, the legislators were alarmed by the publication in 1830 of *An Appeal to the Colored Citizens of the World,* an abolitionist tract by free black David Walker, and sought to prevent slaves from reading its incendiary message. Violators of the ban on slave education would receive thirty-nine lashes.[80]

In Salem, Steiner gave a sermon to the congregation on "the resigned devotion to the will of God," then announced the bad news, though arithmetic lessons were excepted and would continue. He admonished the slaves "to submit to the specification of the law and their superiors without murmuring and willingly; this would not only lighten their station but also indicate that they believe in Jesus Christ." The minister continued: "Since the school had gone on for about three years every Sunday with them, that those who had taken good advantage of it had advanced so far that they could read well and that they can edify themselves from the Word of God. . . . On the other hand, that those who were negligent or indifferent, have to blame themselves that . . . they have missed that which they can now no longer reach." Sunday school continued but now with an emphasis on arithmetic and

---

80. "A Bill to Prevent All Persons from Teaching Slaves to Read or Write, the Use of Figures Excepted," Legislative Papers, 1830–1831 session of the General Assembly, excerpted in Lindley S. Butler and Alan D. Watson, eds., *The North Carolina Experience: An Interpretive and Documentary History* (Chapel Hill, N.C., 1984), 209–210. On David Walker's *Appeal,* see Vincent Harding, *There Is a River: The Black Struggle for Freedom in America* (New York, 1981), 86–94; Peter P. Hinks, *To Awaken My Afflicted Brethren: David Walker and the Problem of Antebellum Slave Resistance* (University Park, Pa., 1996). For white reaction to Walker's *Appeal* in North Carolina, see Johnson, *Ante-Bellum North Carolina,* 515–516.

memorization of verses. Students' reaction to the ban was not reported, though it can be imagined.[81]

THOUGH WHITES VIEWED the black church largely as a means of tightening cultural domination over slaves, they held no illusion that it would do so. The best indication that black congregants did not fully internalize an ethic of obedience is that whites never assumed they had done so. White Brethren who professed the doctrine of Christian love and forbearance had no reluctance reinforcing the message with periodic displays of force. Officials closely monitored church services to prevent plots from germinating. In August 1825, the elders warned that after Sunday services "the Negroes are gathering at various places in town, which might easily cause trouble." Slaves were reminded "to go home quietly after a religious meeting."[82]

Whites continued on guard throughout the fall and winter of 1825, especially after a slave revolt was discovered in eastern North Carolina in December. Slave preachers were again blamed for inciting the uprising, said to be planned for Christmas Eve. The alarm spread to Salem. "All sorts of rumors regarding the Negroes are in circulation. The congregation *Vorsteher* [supervisor] is requested to employ several able Brethren to be on guard on Christmas Eve during the lovefeast, and on New Year's Eve during the services. They shall keep a quiet but sharp watch in the town. It would also be well to have a second watchman on duty every night from Christmas to New Year. This shall be kept secret from the Negroes." The Christmas lovefeast and all evening meetings for blacks were canceled. "Many colored persons were ashamed" to attend services, wrote Steiner, because "many bad reports had been spread against them and some of their enemies wanted to take advantage of that to do them harm." Congregants probably stayed away more out of fear than shame.[83]

African Americans suspected of causing trouble were purged, even those

81. Negro Congregation Diary, Jan. 16, 1831.

82. Aelt. Conf., Aug. 31, 1825, in Fries et al., eds., *Records*, VIII, 3746. See also Herbert Aptheker, *American Negro Slave Revolts*, 2d ed. (New York, 1987), 264; R. H. Taylor, "Slave Conspiracies in North Carolina," *NCHR*, V (1928), 20–34; and Johnson, *Ante-Bellum North Carolina*, 510–521.

83. Johnson, *Ante-Bellum North Carolina*, 515; Auf. Col., Dec. 12, 1825, in Fries et al., eds., *Records*, VIII, 3748; Negro Congregation Diary, Dec. 25, 1825.

of long standing in the church. Prominent sexton Jacob Samuel lost his church post after Salem officials accused him in 1827 of passing liquor to slaves on the Wilhelm Fries plantation where he was working. The board vowed to "sue him legally if he causes more disorder among the slaves." Fries agreed to dismiss Samuel once harvest season was over. Samuel's association with the church seems to have ended, and Enoch, a communicant who worked at the paper mill, replaced him as sexton in 1830.[84]

When Samuel fell ill with dropsy in 1833, a minister found him "dejected." Samuel "complained that he had shortened his life through sinning and especially through the use of brandy." A week later, Samuel was still drawing sustenance from the bottle and "not really repentant—as he professed—about his bad life." Jacob Samuel might have suffered from more than the usual frightful psychic toll on free blacks in a slave society. This literate, bilingual, and cultured man was raised in the bosom of the Moravian Church and then ousted from it. Later, asked to mediate between slaves and masters, Jacob Samuel endured the pressure—and perhaps resentment from blacks—of bending to white expectations. Caught between two worlds, perhaps he fitted in neither. He died an alcoholic and an outcast from congregations both white and black in October 1833.[85]

Wachovia was engulfed in the cycle of panic and retaliation that swept the South following Nat Turner's revolt in August 1831. In late September, rumors of uprisings in nearby Montgomery and Davidson Counties galvanized whites into emergency action. A volunteer Moravian company and a Stokes County militia reinforced the night watch. Wild reports reached Bethania that "200 Negroes had assembled in the neighborhood of Lexington, were murdering the people there, and by evening would reach Salem." Slaves there were "forbidden on pain of death to leave their lots." After services at the black church, "some of the Negroes were stopped by the patrol and were alarmed." The reports proved false and the militia eased its alert.[86]

---

84. Auf. Col., July 23, Aug. 6, 1827; Negro Congregation Diary, Dec. 25, 1830. In 1833, an older communicant, Christian David, also took on some of the responsibility for visiting the sick and reprimanding rule breakers; see Negro Congregation Diary, Nov. 25, 1833.

85. Auf. Col., July 23, Aug. 6, 1827; Negro Congregation Diary, September and October 1833.

86. The incident is described in the Salem Diary and Bethania Diary, Sept. 26, 1831, in Fries et al., eds., Records, VIII, 3972, 4006; and Negro Congregation Diary, Sept. 25, 1831. See also Charles Edward Morris, "Panic and Reprisal: Reaction in North Carolina to the Nat Turner

Yet distrust gnawed at white Brethren. Pastors intensified their use of the church as a forum to reinforce discipline, issuing "serious admonitions" about "disorderly" behavior and reminding slaves "how they are to act when they come and when they go home, to and from the services" and forbidding them to play ball in the meadow by the Salem tavern.[87]

These measures were overshadowed in August 1835 by a new spasm of fear occasioned by a seemingly innocent church celebration. On August 23, some three hundred slaves and free blacks gathered at the log church for a sermon and lovefeast commemorating the 103d anniversary of the beginning of the Moravian mission to Africans in the Caribbean in 1732. Not expecting so large a crowd, authorities were caught off guard. Bethania minister George Frederic Bahnson described the event: "Today there was a largely attended meeting in Salem for Negroes. The rumor reached the Negroes that anyone could attend the lovefeast by paying 6¼ cents. They came from 20 miles around Salem. It is the opinion of our people that it is at this time inadvisable for the Negroes to use such a pretext for gathering in such a mass. They were too proud to go on foot and hired horses and wagons from all quarters." Whites must certainly have been amazed, and probably frightened, by the sight of hundreds of blacks pouring into Salem from across the region by horse and wagon dressed, no doubt, in their Sunday best.[88]

Bahnson's reaction revealed a standard blend of alarm and condescension that large gatherings of black people evoked in whites. Although attributing the slaves' hiring of transportation to excessive pride, he considered their religious meeting a "pretext" for more subversive motives. And perhaps it was. Yet whites underestimated the symbolic importance and holiness the lovefeast held for blacks, since the historic foundations of their own church were being exalted.

A closer look at the event and the chronology behind it suggests that black congregants and hundreds of others walked or rode across the Piedmont landscape out of a profound awareness of their actions and that they invested deep layers of meaning in the occasion. The date they celebrated was August 21, 1732, when the two missionaries Leonard Dober and David

---

Insurrection, 1831," *NCHR*, LXII (1985), 29–52; and Peter H. Wood, "Nat Turner: The Unknown Slave as Visionary Leader," in Leon Litwack and August Meier, eds., *Black Leaders of the Nineteenth Century* (Urbana, Ill., 1988), 21–40.

87. Negro Congregation Diary, Jan. 25, Apr. 12, 1835.

88. Bethania Diary, Aug. 23, 1835, in Fries et al., eds., *Records,* VIII, 4202.

Nitschmann arrived in Saint Thomas to begin preaching to the Africans bound to serve out their lives in the cane fields. One hundred years later, that event was marked quietly in the black church in Salem when, on August 26, 1832, Pastor Steiner gave a sermon on the second letter of the Ephesians followed by "a short narrative of the Brethren's mission among the heathen." He did not report how the assembled congregants responded, and the 101st anniversary the next year went unobserved in the church.[89]

But, at some point, congregants ascribed a strong intellectual and emotional appeal to the idea of locating in time and commemorating the beginnings of both the mission and their own church. In 1834, congregants must have spread the word in advance that the anniversary was again to be celebrated, for many African Americans attended the service. Minister Renatus Schmidt described the occasion:

> On August 24th, we celebrated solemnly the beginning of our mission on August 21, 1732, 102 years ago, and very many Negroes had come for this. First there was the sermon on Acts 2:38–39. After that the two baptismal candidates: Jeremias (a Negro belonging to Adam Fishel from the neighborhood of Friedberg) and Sam (a Negro belonging to Jacob Shor, also from there), answered clearly and distinctly the questions prescribed in the baptismal liturgy; after a prayer and with a thrice repeated pouring [of water] they were baptized into the death of Jesus with a mighty feeling of the near presence of God's grace. . . . Finally the baby daughter of the Negress Lucy was baptized with the name Sarah Elisabeth. In the second service the entire Negro congregation had a lovefeast. It was a day of blessing which the Lord provided for us.

Whatever significance black Christians attached to the celebration, by the time of the 103d anniversary the following year, in 1835, they had already solidified a tradition of commemorating it. The event was advertised two months in advance by Pastor Schmidt who, on June 14, 1835, announced: "On August 23 of this year we would again celebrate in a solemn way the beginning of the mission work among the Negroes on August 21, 1732." The impressive turnout two months later of three hundred black worshipers "large and small" as well as the Female Mission Society testified to the

89. Negro Congregation Diary, Aug. 26, 1832, August 1833.

ceremony's prominence as a cultural emblem in the minds of the Piedmont's African-American population.[90]

The large attendance also demonstrated that, though the event was nominally sponsored by whites, blacks thought otherwise. Neglecting to discard the idea that they might shape the direction of their own church, black planners took furtive control over arrangements for the lovefeast. Who did so is unknown; perhaps it was the church council or sextons. Behind the scenes, they had carefully organized and publicized the ceremony during the previous two months in their own communities, employing black communication networks to spread news of the event to slave quarters far into the central Piedmont. Congregants thus turned the traditional Moravian lovefeast into an act of cultural appropriation.

Part of these organizers' incentive might have stemmed from a lingering desire to assert their own economic will and earn money for the congregation. Pastor Schmidt had rebuked them earlier in the year for their attempt to buy a stove, but evidently they still had not given up trying to raise funds independently for church projects. At "6¼ cents," admission to the lovefeast for three hundred attendees, church members might have raised as much as twenty-five dollars. The more important point is that planners saw the event as an entrepreneurial opportunity by recognizing that many African Americans valued the ceremony highly enough to travel miles and pay a few precious cents to attend. The lovefeast was a special event indeed. But what exactly were the celebrants commemorating?

The deep symbolic resonances of the festival are hard to verify in the absence of direct black testimony. One explanation might be that these Christians saw themselves as paying homage to the first generation of African converts who originated a tradition of black Moravianism that spawned their own church. In so honoring their spiritual progenitors, supplicants might have been pursuing a truncated African-American adaptation of traditional African ancestor veneration, hearkening back to a kind of creation myth embedded in recorded time.

But perhaps the three hundred celebrated something more on August 23; suppose they were testifying to their membership in a wider Afro-Christian family without borders. Theirs was a congregation, after all, that traced its sources to Africa, Saxony, and the Caribbean. In the 1780s, Abraham fol-

90. Ibid., Aug. 24, 1834, June 14, 1835.

lowed with interest news from Moravian missions in the West Indies and in turn preached to fellow slaves in Carolina. From the earliest days of the Salem congregation in 1822, black seekers had been aware that they were part of a historical international Afro-Moravian network. In October 1822, Steiner read them a passage from the *Periodical Accounts*, a Unity publication, "about the mission to the Negroes in the West Indies Islands and Surinam, for which the Negroes were very glad, expressed their astonishment and made some appropriate comments." Periodic updates remained a regular feature of church services, invariably drawing enthusiastic response from worshipers. Indeed, some drew inspiration from the overseas Brethren with whom they explicitly compared themselves. In 1825, Steiner read aloud a report "from Saint John's in Antigua for the year 1821, and then some of them commented that even though we are smaller in number than those, it really depends on us whether we have a similar experience of grace as those on that island."[91]

The phrase "depends on us" is particularly revealing, for it reflects congregants' awareness of their own power to create a community of faith. In celebrating the West Indian genesis of the Moravian mission, perhaps black congregants in Salem 103 years later were invoking cultural memory to affirm their identification with a broad Atlantic family of black Christians that remained vibrant in their own time. Much as black parishioners used godparenthood to cast a spiritual—and ecumenical—net across the region, they might have viewed themselves as part of a giant web of Christian fictive kin that transcended local and regional boundaries.

For whatever reasons, blacks streamed into Salem as never before to bear witness. But though the meeting went off without incident, whites were deeply shaken in the aftermath of what was probably the largest gathering of slaves ever in the area. Their alarm was traceable not only to memories of Nat Turner but more immediately to a slave plot uncovered in Madison County, Mississippi, just two months earlier. Word of the foiled revolt reached Salem at about the same time as the huge lovefeast, although whether earlier or slightly later is unclear. Upon reading a newspaper account of the Mississippi incident a few days after the Salem celebration,

91. Ibid., Oct. 6, 1822, Feb. 6, 1825. Less-detailed references to reports from the mission field are described in diary entries for November and December 1824, August and November 1832, October and December 1833.

Bahnson noted that "excitement in the South seems to be great, even here our people begin to be afraid of black insurrection."[92]

Whites at once associated the Mississippi report with the potential for local danger. A hastily convened conference of ministers ruled that in the future only blacks who "in some measure" belonged to or were associated with the congregation would be permitted to attend lovefeasts. Strangers would not be allowed to attend simply by paying admission. Large gatherings of slaves would have to end because they spawned "unsettling rumours of Negro insurrections" that could jeopardize the church itself, since "everywhere there are people who look dimly on all such efforts among the blacks."[93]

The controversy thus laid bare a fissure in white thought about the black church. White Brethren had organized it in part as an exercise in control. They got more than they bargained for. Blacks embraced the church so tightly that the experiment threatened to backfire. When so many worshipers jammed the church that they became objects, not of evangelism, but of terror, their religion was illuminated as truly subversive. Ministers insisted the church could remain an agent, not an enemy, of social order. Both sides agreed that black celebration of the gospel should not endanger white security, and, ultimately, that security rested on armed might. For black Christians, the result was unequivocal: further surveillance and more controls on their religious and social expression.

JUST TWO DAYS after the lovefeast, the death of the venerable church elder John Immanuel marked the passage of one of the last of the old guard of black Brethren (though he was survived by Budney's widow Phoebe, who died in 1860 at the age of ninety). Immanuel's funeral reflected the esteem accorded him by black and white alike as well as a sense of generational turnover. "Thirty Negroes and so many brothers and sisters from the town came so that the church was quite full," reported Pastor Schmidt, whose

92. Diary of George Frederic Bahnson, Aug. 27–28, 1835, Old Salem, Inc. Accounts of the Mississippi plot include Christopher Morris, "An Event in Community Organization: The Mississippi Slave Insurrection Scare of 1835," *Journal of Social History*, XXII, no. 1 (Fall–Winter 1988), 93–111; and Laurence Shore, "Making Mississippi Safe for Slavery: The Insurrectionary Panic of 1835," in Orville Burton and Robert C. McMath, Jr., eds., *Class, Conflict, and Consensus: Antebellum Southern Community Studies* (Westport, Conn., 1982), 96–127.

93. LAC, Sept. 3, 1835.

eulogy recalled Immanuel's baptism in 1804, his subsequent wandering "astray," and continued: "For many years he had been serving faithfully in the Tavern here. He was one of the 14 Negro Brothers and Sisters with whom this little Negro Congregation was organized 12 years ago on December 28, 1823. Since then he has been serving as sexton of this Negro Congregation very faithfully and conscientiously." Inducted into a white congregation and ending his life as a leader of a black one, this brother had tried, with his limited authority, to moderate the growing duress felt by African Americans around him.[94]

But perhaps another dynamic was at work as well. The church had a seating capacity of several hundred; although three hundred blacks had crowded inside for the lovefeast just two days earlier, only thirty attended Immanuel's funeral. The two events were entirely different, and attendance at the funeral could not possibly match that of the lovefeast, the product of months of organizing. Since the funeral was held on a Tuesday afternoon, many blacks might also have found it impossible to leave work to attend. Perhaps ambivalence toward John Immanuel kept others away. Whites filled the church to pay respects, whites who viewed him as some combination of esteemed fellow Christian, example for other slaves, and community leader who could be counted on to enforce discipline among blacks. Could his popularity with whites have been an index of his relative unpopularity among blacks? The awkwardness of mediating between white authority and black constituents might at last have robbed Immanuel of some black parishioners' respect.

The church lost more followers in 1836 for a different reason. A group of twenty-four Moravian-owned slaves, including a communicant member of the congregation, James, were freed and sent to Liberia. Seventeen of them were emancipated by Frederick Schumann, the physician whose proposed move to Salem in 1814 had ignited a controversial debate over the town's slavery regulations. In subsequent years, his slave workforce on his plantation outside Salem gradually increased before he liberated all in 1836, an occasion that brought a mixture of joy and sorrow to the black congregation. "On October 23, the whole congregation had a lovefeast for those Negroes who in two days will embark for Africa in order to get their freedom there," recorded the church diary. "At the end, the Communicants had the Holy Communion. The Negro Brother Jim, who belongs to the above

94. Negro Congregation Diary, Aug. 25, 1831.

mentioned company was present for the last time and was commended to the Savior in particular for blessing and safe keeping." A fortnight later, two couples married at Schumann's plantation before leaving for Liberia. The minister found it "encouraging that their separation from the church in which they have been hearing God's Word for such a long time was painful to them."[95]

Although he attributed their distress to the impending loss of opportunity to hear about the gospel, they also mourned the loss of the church family to which they had long been connected. They testified (reported Schmidt) that "nothing about their departure would grieve them so much as that they must miss the meetings and see themselves separated from us." These faithful, some of whom had worshiped with Anna, now turned toward the land of her birth. Joyous as they were over a beckoning new life, they knew they probably would never see their companions again.[96]

The pilgrims' anguish reflected an emotional commitment to the church that did not come easily or without cost but evolved through tense and persistent engagement with authority. Congregational life reflected a contest over the use and meaning of ritual, prayer, and physical space. In this rare sanctioned forum for black social and religious gathering, the stakes were high. Congregants labored to define the church in their own terms,

95. Ibid., Oct. 23, Nov. 5, 1836.

96. LAC Bericht, Nov. 5, 1836. Frederick Schumann's decision to free his slaves evidently stemmed less from humanitarian reasons than from the contentious doctor's long-running feud with Salem officials. After years of squabbling over his plantation lease with the church, Schumann tired of the struggle and agreed to free his slaves and send them to Liberia; see S. Scott Rohrer, "Friedrich Schuman and His Slaves: Portrait of a Plantation," research report, Old Salem, Inc., 1990, 13. The emigrants sailed from Wilmington on Dec. 30, 1836, arriving in Monrovia on Feb. 3, 1837. Most settled in the town of Millsburg, where several died soon thereafter in the unfamiliar tropical climate. Nothing is known of the survivors' fate. In 1839, two more freed black congregants, the sexton Enoch Morgan Alexander Schober and his wife, Nancy (both recently freed by the will of Gottlieb Schober), also migrated to Liberia, departing from Norfolk on the American Colonization Society's ship *Saluda* and arriving in late 1839. They identified themselves as members of the Moravian Church, and Enoch described himself as a preacher. In Liberia, they rejoined members of the earlier group, but later one emigrant wrote to Gottlieb Schober's son, Emanuel, in Salem that Enoch and Nancy had died shortly after their arrival in Liberia; see Negro Congregation Diary, July 21, 1839, Feb. 2, 1840; "Report of the Managers to the American Colonization Society, at Its Twenty-first Annual Meeting," *The African Repository and Colonial Journal*, XIV, no. 1 (January 1838), 1–2, "Twenty-third Annual Meeting of the American Colonization Society," XVI, no. 5 (March 1840), 67–69. See also James Wesley Smith, *Sojourners in Search of Freedom: The Settlement of Liberia by Black Americans* (Lanham, Md., 1987), 161–162, 181.

both openly and covertly, taking what whites offered—or allowed them—and more. Often they prudently acceded to white-imposed limits. But the church diary suggests how enslaved Christians, in Salem and perhaps in similar fashion in hundreds of other black churches, could maneuver underneath the veil of power to make their church a community of the spirit with an inner life not entirely visible to whites.

The theological dimensions of Afro-Christianity are often invoked to explain the value of faith as a tool of psychological resistance for the enslaved. Christianity might well have fostered in some slaves an otherworldly focus on a better life in the hereafter, thus serving as a vehicle of white control; others used religion as a prophetic ideology of cultural autonomy and liberation. Undoubtedly, both elements informed the thinking of black Christians in Salem and elsewhere. We might move beyond these two poles to focus on the way enslaved Christians used their church to build a collective identity.

Slave religion, though grounded in personal revelation, was more than a theological statement of faith; it operated as an entire cultural system. Historians have spoken—if at times too glowingly—of the slave community as an extended family. The genius of the emerging black church is that it expressed that kinship connection in religious terms. The black church conflated worship, family, and community. Congregants prayed together, taught each other, feuded, planned events, reprimanded the wayward, and comforted the dying. Afro-Christianity shaped an ethos for daily life, a code for political organization. The logs and boards enclosing Salem's black church had been erected by worshipers' own hands. Lovefeasts and festivals held inside honored their God. At the same time, the camp meetings, black-led prayer groups, and behind-the-scenes organizing testified to a thriving religious consciousness of which the mission church was but one expression. To these supplicants, the church remained an ark of hope.[97]

97. For a critique of the historiographic treatment of the slave community, see Peter Kolchin, "Reevaluating the Antebellum Slave Community: A Comparative Perspective," *JAH*, LXX (1983–1984), 579–601.

· · · · · · · · · · · · · · · · ·

CHAPTER EIGHT

Transfiguration

ELECTION DAY, August 1835. In Bethania, crowds milled in front of the store as they did in towns and hamlets across antebellum America. Voting day in the age of the "common man" was a public and communal event, centered on the courthouse or the general store and conducted amid an air of festivity and politicking. In the crowd at Bethania, wrote minister George Frederic Bahnson, were both "whites and blacks, it being a kind of frolic and holiday for all—some were pretty far gone in consequence of frequent treats, that disgrace of our elections." Grumble he might, but the scene was typical of antebellum southern society in at least one respect. Black and white people intermingled continually in daily affairs, even on occasions like elections that crystallized the limits of American democracy. By their presence in the crowd that day, African Americans asserted a symbolic claim to the voting rites denied them.[1]

Despite its great disparities in wealth and power, the South was hardly a racially compartmentalized society. The lives of whites and blacks—slave as well as free—intersected in many milieus: sacred and profane, urban and rural, in labor and recreation, in enmity and friendship. They worked side

1. Diary of George Frederic Bahnson, Aug. 13, 1835, Old Salem, Inc. On the theatricality of elections and the use of alcoholic "treats" to sway voters in colonial Virginia, see Rhys Isaac, *The Transformation of Virginia, 1740–1790* (Chapel Hill, N.C., 1982), 110–113. On election day in the 18th century, Moravian church elders attempted to enforce bloc voting among congregants. "It is better for all the Brethren to vote alike, for if they vote for others, even though they are worthy, there is danger that some unworthy man may be elected because of a divided vote"; see Gemein Rath, Feb. 26, 1784, in Adelaide L. Fries et al., eds., *Records of the Moravians in North Carolina*, 11 vols. (Raleigh, N.C., 1922–1969), V, 2029. As a measure of the cultural assimilation of North Carolina Moravians, the practice had ceased by the 1830s.

by side, drank and gambled together in defiance of the law, and sang hallelujah at camp meetings. They swapped stories and folk beliefs; they mingled on city streets and at backcountry cockfights. Planters blustered without irony of their obligation to their extended black and white families, while forcing their sexual demands on enslaved women. Cultural exchanges and influences flowed back and forth among black and white people, though tempered and shaped in countless complex and skewed ways by racial slavery. Historians have only begun to analyze how black and white entered and altered each other's conscious and unconscious minds.[2]

But if daily, face-to-face contact characterized relations between white and black, the emotional quality of that interaction is another matter. In many ways, the record points to profound psychological divisions in the plantation world. One historian, for example, has identified the late eighteenth century as a period of growing social separation between masters and slaves in Virginia, as wealthier planters adopted an "increasingly individualized way of life" that diverged from the growing communal ethos among African Americans. Other work has refocused attention on the abuse inherent in a system that depended on force to keep captive workers in check. Physical punishments and the separation of families by sale produced among bondpersons deep-seated distrust and hatred of masters and, according to one historian, a "wide chasm between the mental world of master and slave." The rich dimensions of African-American slave culture suggest alternatively an incipient Pan-African nationalism that stood outside, and in explicit rejection of, the culture of the masters.[3]

2. A volume assessing interracial exchanges before the Civil War is Ted Ownby, ed., *Black and White Cultural Interaction in the Antebellum South* (Jackson, Miss., 1993). A sampling of other important works that address the theme include John B. Boles, ed., *Masters and Slaves in the House of the Lord: Race and Religion in the American South, 1740–1870* (Lexington, Ky., 1988); Elizabeth Fox-Genovese, *Inside the Plantation Household: Black and White Women of the Old South* (Chapel Hill, N.C., 1988); Charles C. Bolton, *Poor Whites of the Antebellum South: Tenants and Laborers in Central North Carolina and Northeast Mississippi* (Durham, N.C., 1994), chap. 2; and, especially, for an earlier period, Mechal Sobel, *The World They Made Together: Black and White Values in Eighteenth-Century Virginia* (Princeton, N.J., 1987).

3. Isaac, *Transformation of Virginia*, 306; Paul D. Escott, *Slavery Remembered: A Record of Twentieth-Century Slave Narratives* (Chapel Hill, N.C., 1979), 28. Works reemphasizing the harshness of plantation regimes and white control include Michael Tadman, *Speculators and Slaves: Masters, Traders, and Slaves in the Old South* (Madison, Wis., 1989); Norrece T. Jones, Jr., *Born a Child of Freedom, Yet a Slave: Mechanisms of Control and Strategies of Resistance in Antebellum South Carolina* (New London, 1990); and Peter Kolchin, *Unfree Labor: American*

To consider the terms on which white Moravians and African Americans lived is to view their relationship over the span of half a century. Their social world in the 1830s little resembled that of the 1780s. Yet there they were, still together, their lives still entwined, facing each other now with new rules, changed perceptions. How stark were the divisions between them, and how much could they admit of the other in their worldview?

THE DEFINING REALITY of the new Moravian racial code was that by the 1830s far more African Americans were doing a far larger share of the work. By 1830, the approximately 1,500 white Moravians owned about 350 slaves, about five times the number they owned in 1800. In Stokes County as a whole, the total white population was 13,122 against 2,841 slaves and 233 free blacks. Enslaved people thus constituted about 20 percent of the population in Wachovia, a figure slightly higher than their proportion of the total county population, about 17 percent.[4]

This steady rise occurred because during the early nineteenth century a handful of Brethren consolidated large holdings in land and slaves outside Salem, particularly in Bethania. The eagerness with which white Bethanians sought to expand their human property was one of the first things noticed by minister Bahnson, a native of Denmark who received a call to serve the Bethania congregation in 1835 after teaching at the Moravian school in Nazareth, Pennsylvania. "You do not see any silver anywhere in town," he remarked in his diary. "Land and slaves are the principal things, wherein they invest money." Bahnson might have exaggerated; his comment was no doubt colored by his outsider's initial astonishment at a slave society. But his observation contained more than a kernel of truth, for by the 1830s a new breed of Moravian slaveholders dominated the landscape. Christian Loesch (sometimes anglicized to Lash) owned 3,098 acres and

Slavery and Russian Serfdom (Cambridge, Mass., 1987). The best representative of a black nationalist perspective is Sterling Stuckey, *Slave Culture: Nationalist Theory and the Foundations of Black America* (New York, 1987).

4. Figures tabulated from the Federal Census of 1830, Stokes County, N.C. Far and away the largest slaveholder in the county was Peter Hairston, a non-Moravian, with 293 slaves living on his plantation in northern Stokes County near the Virginia border. By 1835, Salem was the largest congregation with 482 members, followed by 382 in Friedberg, 225 in Friedland, 218 in Bethania, 128 in Hope, and 102 in Bethabara; see Bahnson Diary, Nov. 26, 1835.

thirty slaves, Jacob Conrad, 2,127 acres and twenty-six slaves, Abraham Conrad, 1,125 acres and fifteen slaves, and John Conrad, twenty-one slaves. All lived in Bethania. In 1830, Frederick Schumann owned thirteen slaves on his farm outside Salem; his holdings increased before he freed all seventeen slaves in 1836. These five men held more than a quarter of all slaves owned by Brethren in 1830. The Moravian Church owned another nineteen slaves, most of whom lived on the Unity farm south of Salem. Such holdings were small potatoes next to the slaveowning heavyweights of the South, and, in fact, most Moravian slaveholders owned from one to five slaves. But individually and collectively, white Brethren put much faith in slaveholding as a key to prosperity.[5]

By the early nineteenth century, moreover, Moravian slaveholding had become overwhelmingly rural and connected to the agricultural economy. This development had far-reaching implications, because it meant that the experience of most enslaved workers in Wachovia had changed between 1800 and 1830. In the eighteenth century, the slave workforce was divided between urban crafts and services and rural agriculture. The rough workplace parity fostered by church membership allowed some enslaved Brethren to rise to key positions of authority. But by the 1820s, work relations between whites and blacks had grown far more stratified. The predominantly rural, plantation-based slavery that characterized Wachovia in the nineteenth century was less egalitarian than the largely urban, church-regulated slavery of the eighteenth. Blacks and whites appeared less as coworkers than as slaves and masters. What happened in Wachovia was thus akin to a transition during the colonial period in the Chesapeake, South Carolina, the West Indies, and elsewhere from frontier society, with elastic race relations, to plantation economy, with more rigid and divisive racial boundaries.[6]

5. Bahnson Diary, July 16, 1834; population figures from Federal Census of 1830, Stokes County, N.C.; acreage from 1830 List of Taxables, Salem District, Stokes County, NCDAH. Bahnson (1805–1869) was born in the Danish Moravian congregation town of Christiansfeld, received his education in Herrnhut, and migrated in 1828 to Pennsylvania. He served as pastor in Bethania between 1834 and 1838 before being called to Bethlehem. He returned to North Carolina as minister at Salem in 1849 and in 1860 was consecrated as bishop. See Alice Henderson North, "New Minister at Bethania," *Three Forks of Muddy Creek*, I (Winston-Salem, N.C., 1974), 23–24.

6. See Philip D. Morgan, "British Encounters with Africans and African-Americans, circa 1600–1780," in Bernard Bailyn and Philip D. Morgan, eds., *Strangers within the Realm: Cultural Margins of the First British Empire* (Chapel Hill, N.C., 1991), 190; and Peter H. Wood,

One example illustrates these changes. In 1779, a white brother, Johann Christian Loesch, had worked under the supervision of the enslaved Brother Johann Samuel at the Bethabara communal farm. Later, after moving to Bethania, Loesch became a slaveholder himself, in fact the largest in Wachovia, and several of his sons owned slaves as well. In 1835, a witness described a startling scene. Loesch's son, Louis, "kicked one of the black women, and when his father spoke about it, he picked up a stone to throw it at his old grayheaded parents." A revolution in social relations had taken place in one generation. Although Christian Loesch had trained under a slave supervisor, that idea would have seemed preposterous to his son, who delighted in abusing slaves. No minister raised his voice in admonishment, either for Louis's mistreatment of the slave or for his stone-wielding impudence to his own parents, which by itself was astonishing by the standards of an earlier era. The fear expressed by some eighteenth-century Moravians and a host of antislavery theorists had come to pass. Slavery and its attendant culture of violence corrupted and depraved those who proclaimed themselves God's messengers.[7]

Whites erected further mental barriers to divide themselves from black workers. Over the years, white Brethren gradually embraced a more rigorous racial categorization of labor. By the 1820s, they believed that at least some kinds of labor should not be done by blacks, either slave or free, and that other kinds of work should be done *only* by blacks. Domestic and custodial work, for example, was now deemed too demeaning for whites. The evolution of this attitude must be traced again to the gradual acculturation of second- and third-generation Brethren. Count Zinzendorf believed that *all* work done in the Lord's name was sacred and chose a domestic example to illustrate his point: "When a maid cleans a room, she does a service to God." Indeed, during the eighteenth century, many Single Sisters served as domestics in homes and occasionally even in the Salem tavern. But after about 1803, tavern proprietors, catering to the wishes of non-Moravian patrons who "like to be waited on by Negro servants rather than white," had begun to use slave domestic labor almost exclusively in the tavern. Thus, the Brethren's own reasons for using black tavern servants had evolved since the 1760s, when they sought to protect white women

---

Black Majority: Negroes in Colonial South Carolina from 1670 through the Stono Rebellion (New York, 1974), chap. 4.

7. Bahnson Diary, June 26, 1835.

from rowdy male behavior. Now they wanted to cater to their patrons' racialized preferences for service.[8]

This accommodation to tavern customers' expectations in time became part of white Moravians' own racial view of the world as they, too, associated domestic and service work with blacks. "Single Sisters and other white service people are often not to be had for either good words or money," noted Salem's Congregational Council in 1820. "No white man will be found to take over the job of hostler in the tavern and it cannot even be expected of any white person to attend to such a job." Indeed, the Single Sisters indicated the low esteem with which they now regarded service labor when, in 1828, they wanted to hire a custodian for their house. The sisters declared themselves "embarrassed to command white people, and so need a Negro." George Bahnson similarly linked domestic work with African Americans, noting his intent to "get Simon Stolz's black girl for waiting at table and doing other 'black' work in the [Bethania] school."[9]

Salem's town statutes of 1814 and 1820 likewise codified the belief that blacks should be restricted to unskilled work—indeed, that they were best suited for such work. These rules not only limited slavery in town but expressed a vision of the perceived inferior role of black people as well. Thus, in 1822 Christian Briez was allowed to rent a slave to do only unskilled "rough work" in the tannery. Blacksmith Christian Vogler was forced to dismiss a free black he had hired to assist him and to train Vogler's own son. In the 1770s and 1780s, church leaders had sought to limit black access to town trades, but the church allowed whites to hire skilled slave and free black artisans when necessary and even relaxed the rules on occasion by permitting a few slaves to be trained under master craftsmen. By the 1820s,

8. Zinzendorf paraphrases Martin Luther; see Otto Uttendörfer, *Zinzindorfs Weltbetrachtung: Eine systematische Darstellung der Gedankenwelt des Begrunders der Brüdergemeine* (Berlin, 1929), 37; Aelt. Conf., Nov. 21, 1804; Auf. Col., Dec. 4, 1803. Some Single Sisters did serve briefly in the tavern in the 1820s.

9. Gemein Rath, Feb. 3, 1820; Auf. Col., June 7, 1828; Bahnson Diary, Oct. 13, 1836. Dozens of examples of domestic service by African Americans may be found in the Aufseher Collegium minutes of the 1820s. Changing attitudes toward work by whites, Moravian and otherwise, foreshadowed later racialized notions of domestic service. For a study of the comparable contempt of middle-class white women for household work and their employment of African-American women as domestics in the 20th century, see Phyllis Palmer, *Domesticity and Dirt: Housewives and Domestic Servants in the United States, 1920–1945* (Philadelphia, 1989). See also Jacqueline Jones, *Labor of Love, Labor of Sorrow: Black Women, Work, and the Family from Slavery to the Present* (New York, 1985), 127–134.

there were no loopholes: henceforth, all skilled craft work in Salem would be reserved for whites.[10]

Thus, the racialization of work roles complemented the rise of a plantation economy at the same time blacks were being weeded from Moravian congregations. These interlocking changes reinforced each other, widening the social and spiritual distance between white and black, erasing any ambivalence about their relationship that might have nagged at whites. These emergent cultural, economic, and demographic realities, fifty years in the making, contained profound implications for African-American culture and for the ways blacks and whites regarded each other. Though black and white inhabitants of the Moravian communities crossed paths daily, they now lived in distant worlds.

As the debate festered among white Moravians over the use of slave labor in Salem, it was in the Moravian countryside that the real centers of black life flowered in response to the plantation economy and to social separation. By the 1820s, most enslaved workers in Wachovia probably lived and worked much like those elsewhere in the region—that is, in an agricultural setting. Moravian farms differed little from typical farms and small plantations throughout the southern Piedmont, where farmers owned less land and fewer slaves than along the Atlantic seaboard, and instead of cultivating cash crops such as cotton and tobacco they produced food crops for self-sufficiency or for sale to eastern markets. Slaves raised grain and tended livestock, although by the 1840s cotton cultivation had spread west as well. Moravian farms, like many in the Piedmont, concentrated heavily on corn production. Slaves could be put to work more regularly throughout the year raising corn rather than wheat, which was less labor-intensive.[11]

Oral testimony from Betty Cofer, a former slave, regarding the end of the antebellum period, indicates the diversity of occupations on one Moravian plantation. Cofer was born in 1856 on the plantation of Beverly Jones, a physician in Bethania who had married into the Moravian Conrad family. The plantation, with about forty slaves, was relatively large by Moravian standards. The men, Cofer recalled, were "Mac, Curley, William, Sanford, Lewis, Henry, Ed, Sylvester, Hamp, and Luke. [They] worked in the fields and yard. One was stable boss and looked after all the horses and mules. . . .

10. Auf. Col., Jan. 7, 14, 1822, Jan. 10, Feb. 7, 1825.

11. Rosser Howard Taylor, *Slaveholding in North Carolina: An Economic View,* The James Sprunt Historical Publications, XVIII (Chapel Hill, N.C., 1926), 35–38.

We had our own mill to grind the wheat and corn and we raised all our meat." The women were "Nellie, two Lucys, Martha, Nervie, Jane, Laura, Fannie, Lizzie, Cassie, Tensie, Lindy, and MaryJane. The women mostly worked in the house. There was always two washerwomen, a cook, some hands to help her, two sewin' women, a house girl, and some who did all the weavin' and spinnin'." The plantation strove to be as self-sufficient as possible. Agricultural and domestic production were closely connected:

> We raised our own flax and cotton and wool, spun the thread, wove the cloth, made all the clothes. We made the mens' shirts and pants and coats. One woman knitted all the stockin's for the white folks and colored folks too. I mind she had one finger all twisted and stiff from holdin' her knittin' needles. We wove the cotton and linen for sheets and pillowslips and table covers. We wove the wool blankets too. Leather was tanned and shoes was made on the place. 'Course the hands mostly went barefoot in warm weather, white chillen too. We made our own candles from tallow and beeswax. We wove our own candle wicks too.[12]

None of these observations marks the experiences of Cofer or her family and friends as very different from those of thousands of slaves on medium-sized plantations in the South. In fact, the similarity of her recollections to those of other ex-slave narratives is in itself remarkable, for it confirms how dramatically the life and work experiences of African Americans in the Moravian lands had changed in a generation.

The growth of slave quarters marked a key feature of the rise of plantation agriculture. Though we know little about African-American housing in the eighteenth century, the relatively low number of slaves scattered throughout the Moravian tract probably meant there were few concentrations of them living in separate quarters. Many might have lived with their masters, and in a few cases black brothers and sisters lived in the Salem choir houses. But by the early decades of the nineteenth century, as some planters' holdings multiplied, more and more slave cabins dotted the landscape, including larger clusters of cabins containing more people. The rise in the number of slave quarters such as the Negro Quarter outside Salem signaled

---

12. George P. Rawick, ed., *The American Slave: A Composite Autobiography*, XIV, North Carolina Narratives, pt. 1, Contributions in Afro-American and African Studies, no. 11 (Westport, Conn., 1972), 168–169.

an effort by whites to put more physical distance between themselves and the black population they considered increasingly alien. Such compounds arose on the various estates of the Lashes, Conrads, and others. Lingering memory of ancient practice might even have informed such housing arrangements, as, for example, on the Jones plantation, where boys and single men lived in the "boys' cabin," a sort of latter-day Single Brothers' House.[13]

It was the quarters that provided the social spaces where African-American culture thrived. That culture emerged clearly at times such as the autumn cornshucking frolics that revealed the social fault line between white and black. Cornshuckings were customary throughout America wherever rural folk gathered to strip the husks from mounds of corn piled high after the harvest. Communal harvest rituals of this kind were common to both the European and West African traditions. Collective work efforts were both sacred and festive, since they involved both prayer and thanks to a god or spirit for a bountiful crop as well as celebration of the earth's fruits through postharvest feasting and dancing.[14]

The early Moravians in Germany, although attempting to suppress what they regarded as profane outbursts of popular exuberance, nonetheless incorporated a much-muted version of the harvest ritual into their sacred cosmos. Harvesters sang special hymns as they worked, and a formal harvest festival and thanksgiving sermon were part of the annual worship cycle. These festivities carried over into America, although not always in a form the church considered morally healthful. Farming communities like Bethania and Hope expressly forbade Brethren to participate in cornhusking frolics, but ministers were forever scolding violators. The harvest lost some of its sacred aura (although thanksgiving ceremonies continued), and by the

13. Rawick, *The American Slave*, XIV, 173. Three log cabins, perhaps including Betty Cofer's, may still be seen today at the Conrad site.

14. For an overview of cornshucking in early America, see Nicholas P. Hardeman, *Shucks, Shocks, and Hominy Blocks: Corn as a Way of Life in Pioneer America* (Baton Rouge, La., 1981). On African harvest rituals, see John S. Mbiti, *African Religions and Philosophy* (New York, 1969), 73, 77, 85, 98, 234; Sobel, *The World They Made Together*, 52–53. On European agricultural celebrations, see Denys Thompson, ed., *Change and Tradition in Rural England: An Anthology of Writings on Country Life* (Cambridge, 1980), 8, 135, 197. One has only to look at Pieter Brueghel the Elder's scenes of harvest merriment in early modern Flanders to see the centrality of such events in preindustrial European life. See Bob Claessens and Jeanne Rousseau, *Our Bruegel* (Antwerp, 1969), plates 31, 32 (after 112), etching 26 (after 230). A West African counterpart is John Biggers's 1959 painting, *Jubilee—Ghana Harvest Festival;* see Dallas Museum of Art, *Black Art—Ancestral Legacy: The African Impulse in African-American Art* (Dallas, Tex., 1989), 249.

1820s the church gave up policing agrarian activities. Through the frolics, white Moravians tailored European custom to American practice.[15]

African-inflected harvest rituals, meanwhile, continued in attenuated form throughout the South. Africans sang work songs while planting and harvesting rice, tobacco, corn, sugar, and other crops. During harvest festivals on the Georgia Sea Islands, recalled a former slave, "We hab big feas. Ebrybody bring some ub duh fus crops. We all gib tanks fuh duh crop an we dance an sing."[16]

In an annual routine of forced and often monotonous toil, cornshuckings provided welcome times of enjoyment. Planters sponsored these nighttime frolics by inviting slaves from neighboring plantations to join their own workforce. Usually divided into competing teams under the leadership of a "captain," workers sang or chanted for hours in a rhythmic call-and-response fashion as they shucked. Often their songs voiced overt or subtle criticism of slavery and satire of the master. Regarding the show as vastly entertaining, white observers described the frolics as riveting spectacles of music and merrymaking. Lavish feasts provided by the master lasted far into the night.[17]

15. On Moravian harvest festivals in America, see Salem Diary, Nov. 16, 1823, and Bethania Diary, Oct. 26, 1823, in Fries et al., eds., *Records*, VIII, 3634, 3664. See also F. Ernest Stoeffler, *German Pietism during the Eighteenth Century* (Leiden, 1973), 158. The efforts of the early church to curb similar expressions of popular culture in early Herrnhut are discussed in Elisabeth W. Sommer, "Serving Two Masters: Authority, Faith, and Community among the Moravian Brethren in Germany and North Carolina in the Eighteenth Century" (Ph.D. diss., University of Virginia, 1991), chap. 2. On the incorporation of pagan festivals such as harvest and fertility rituals into Christian worship in medieval and early modern Europe, see Keith Thomas, *Religion and the Decline of Magic* (New York, 1971), 47–50; and Peter Burke, *Popular Culture in Early Modern Europe* (New York, 1978).

16. Charles Joyner, *Down by the Riverside: A South Carolina Slave Community* (Urbana, Ill., 1984), 58–59; Wood, *Black Majority*, 61–62; Dena J. Epstein, *Sinful Tunes and Spirituals: Black Folk Music to the Civil War* (Urbana, Ill., 1977), chap. 9, esp. 172–176; Eugene D. Genovese, *Roll, Jordan, Roll: The World the Slaves Made* (New York, 1974), 315–319; Georgia Writers' Project, *Drums and Shadows: Survival Studies among the Georgia Coastal Negroes* (1940; reprint, Athens, Ga., 1986), 127–128 (for other examples, among many, see 131, 141, 159, 165). An appendix also includes a selection of descriptions of harvest festivals among various African cultures (222–223). On the broader context of WPA interviewers' attempts to transcribe the speech patterns of black Georgians in the 1930s, see Charles Joyner's introduction to the 1986 edition of *Drums and Shadows*, ix–xxiv.

17. For an excellent study of cornshucking celebrations and their broader implications, see Roger D. Abrahams, *Singing the Master: The Emergence of African American Culture in the Plantation South* (New York, 1992).

Although the workers at many shuckings were exclusively black, in some southern regions dominated by yeoman farmers cornshuckings were often all-white affairs. In still other areas, blacks and whites shucked corn together, sharing these times of hard work and festivity, as they often did in the Moravian communities. "Every evening there is husking at some house or other" in Bethania, noted George Bahnson. "All the neighbors help each other and all done, they have a grand feast, sometimes not very long before midnight." As he described one such frolic in 1834: "The whole yard was filled with corn heaps, all hands being busy with shocking which is generally a tolerably frolicsome time, with such as are fond of amusements of a rather noisy description. Neighbors black and white assist each other and have shocking frolics almost every evening."[18]

Though the festival had European and African roots in common, even these times of seeming cultural convergence convey the impression of two peoples socially and culturally distant from each other. As the shuckers went about their work, the "whites converse together but the blackees sing, that you can hear them ever so far," reported Bahnson. "One of the songs used to be: Johnny Miller up town, Johnny Miller downtown, which was constantly repeated."[19]

In this scenario, the frolic seemed less a time for interracial contact than for informal separation according to different cultural meanings blacks and whites invested in the occasion. White Moravians apparently regarded the cornshucking as a time for collaborative labor, socializing (primarily with each other), and quiet merriment. African Americans converted an occasion that could otherwise be seen as more forced drudgery into a participatory drama of communal celebration. In the propulsive chant driving the workers onward—the vocal equivalent of a drumbeat—African rhythmic forms adapted to new words and tunes to produce African-American music. There in the cornfields, the slaves' songs expressed an inventive spiritual release, the same kind of sensibility that also infused their celebrations on holidays. "We were awakened between 1 and 2 AM by noise made with an old drum, pipes and cowbells," noted Bahnson. "The negroes thus celebrated the 4th of July."[20]

18. Bahnson Diary, Oct. 10, 13, 1834. For varying accounts of cornshuckings that were either all black, all white, or racially mixed, see Abrahams, *Singing the Master,* 77–81, 225, 286, 294.

19. Bahnson Diary, Oct. 10, 1834.

20. Ibid., Oct. 20, 1836.

The postshucking feast expressed a similar psychological distance. In some parts of the South, blacks and whites ate together, whereas in other regions, including Wachovia, they ate separately. At one shucking in Bethania, "no whites had been asked on account of the additional trouble which they give as regards the eating part." Evidently, the host believed that black and white should eat separately but either recognized the difficulty of enforcing such a division at a free-for-all affair like a frolic or considered it too much bother to prepare separate tables. Since church officials had tried to enforce social segregation between black and white in the secular realm for many years, some whites followed either policy or regional custom at mealtime.[21]

In any case, on this occasion black shuckers proceeded with the celebration. "The negroes hollowed for life such songs as: Miss Eliza's fond to marry, oh! oh! oh! which must be heard in order to be appreciated," wrote Bahnson. "There were assembled more than 30 negroes, all as happy as larks. They continued husking until about 10 o'clock, whereupon they feasted on pies, meat, cabbage etc. till nearly 11 o'clock and it was midnight before dishes were cleared and put away. . . . After midnight you could hear the negroes coming back to town singing and hollowing as if they were paid for it. The fine moonlit evenings are well calculated for such sport."[22]

Though husking frolics provided enslaved workers one of their few permissible arenas for social gathering and collective affirmation, the line between joy and pathos at these occasions could be fine. Participants brought with them all the accumulated frustration and the experience of violence in captivity. Although frolics were intended to release tension in harmless ways, oppressed people sometimes used such celebrations to vent their stored rage against each other, as happened at a husking party in Bethania in 1818. A slave named Harry died after "violent pains in his lower belly, perhaps the result of a fight a short while ago with another Black during a cornhusking." Music and laughter were not always successful in quelling daily indignity. But whether cornshuckings brought fights or, more commonly, festivity, they showed the cultural divergence that had been widening for years between black and white in Moravian towns, churches, and farms.[23]

Economic trade likewise reaffirmed the divide even while cultivating a

21. Ibid.

22. Ibid., Oct. 28, 1835, Oct. 20, 1836. The minister's "happy as a lark" theme was widely echoed in many other descriptions of cornshuckings by southern apologists as evidence of the benevolence of slavery; see Epstein, *Sinful Tunes and Spirituals,* 174–175.

23. Diary of Peter Wolle, Nov. 28, 1818.

certain cross-racial interdependence. Throughout the South, slaves operated thriving subeconomies that earned them a small degree of self-sufficiency while siphoning money away from whites. By hiring their labor for cash in their spare time or selling craft work or agricultural produce, many slaves accumulated savings and even property. Masters found the practice a useful concession to relieve social tension.[24]

African Americans in Moravian territory engaged in many such activities. In Bethania, they regularly supplied whites with firewood. Observed Bahnson: "The saw is used only at Salem, here with us, everything is done with the axe. Negroes generally attend to such wood concerns, during their free time, principally in the evening. I try to pay them regularly, hence they are very willing to do anything of the kind. Grabs's negro was busy cutting our wood till quite late in the evening." Slaves could earn "25 cents for a 4-horse load—but you ought to see how large the pieces are."[25]

Slaves cultivated their own gardens in the evenings and on Sunday, their free day. On the Sabbath, wrote a Bethania doctor in 1828, "you can see the poor African feel this leisure day. And he appears quite free. He goes out in his little piece of land and prepares it for the spring." Phillis, a slave of M. Blum, was "permitted to sell cucumbers and receive pay for those she sold before." Slaves hunted and trapped game for their own as well as their masters' tables and to sell. Gottlieb Schober gave bond of 100 pounds for "his Negro man slave named Enoch to hunt upon his own land and plantation with a gun to preserve his Stock or kill game for his family." Bahnson "bought some hares at 3 cents apiece," and, he wrote, we "trust we shall be pardoned for having done it on the Sabbath, the only day the negroes have

24. North Carolina law attempted to regulate trade between whites and enslaved blacks. A 1788 statute required masters to give slaves written permission to trade with whites. In 1826, the legislature restricted trade even further by issuing a list of goods that slaves could not sell without a written permit, mostly pertaining to liquor and agricultural products and equipment; see Ernest James Clark, Jr., "Aspects of the North Carolina Slave Code, 1715–1860," *NCHR*, XXXIX (1962), 155. An overview of the acquisition of capital and property by slaves and free blacks is Loren Schweninger, *Black Property Owners in the South, 1790–1915* (Urbana, Ill., 1990). A representative sample of the prolific scholarship on African-American marketing activity and its implications for social and economic life is Ira Berlin and Philip D. Morgan, eds., *The Slaves' Economy: Independent Production by Slaves in the Americas* (London, 1991).

25. Bahnson Diary, Sept. 13, Oct. 31, 1834. The minister complained regularly of being "cheated" by slaves who, he claimed, often tried to supply less than a full load. In disgust, he finally decided to cut his own wood and "thus save a little money which I used to throw away upon blacks, who try to cheat wherever they can"; see entries for Nov. 5, 20, 1834, Dec. 23, 1837.

free." African Americans also sold handicrafts to whites, often undercutting prices charged by white craftsmen. Bahnson bought some chairs in Betha-bara made by whites, "made of a kind of coarse reed at 20 cents apiece, but I have been told, one can get them for 12½ cents with the negroes." Cases such as these must have spurred the elders' efforts to prohibit competition from skilled black craftsmen in Salem.[26]

Through diligent work and careful savings, slaves were thus able to ex-pand their range of action and buy more goods for themselves. When a traveling circus camped outside of Bethania in 1836 ("roaring lions, and a band, 40 wagons, 90 gray horses and 60 men"), "the show people did not get a cent" from Bahnson's family. "The black man Louis was the only person who had 75 cents to spare." The extent of personal acquisition of prop-erty and savings by slaves in Wachovia as compared to those elsewhere is not well documented. Nonetheless, the slaves' extensive internal economy stemmed from their determination to take advantage of a certain autonomy allowed them by masters.[27]

Most important, slave marketing, gardening, and hunting in Wachovia were rural, not urban, activities, a distinction born of the direction slave-holding and African-American life had taken. Although slaves maintained lively market activity in many southern and West Indian towns, they had been banned from doing so in Salem and Bethabara by churchmen who wanted to stamp out any kind of urban freelancing by white and black alike. They had also believed that such concessions to slaves were unnecessary. Instead, their aim had been to incorporate slaves into the church as an incentive to encourage obedience—an outlet that such activities as market-ing served elsewhere. That strategy ended with the advent of religious separation, although tight restrictions on slave marketing remained in Sa-lem. As slaveholding became an increasingly privatized, rural institution in

26. George Follett Wilson, *Journal, April 27, 1828–September 30, 1830,* ed. Evelyn H. Wilson (Greenville, S.C., 1984); Memorandum, Sept. 19, 1830, and Bond, June 13, 1829, in Stokes County Slave Records, Miscellaneous Records, NCDAH; Bahnson Diary, Aug. 4, 1834, Mar. 8, 1835. Wilson also noted that some masters hired slaves to work on Sundays, presumably keeping some or all of the wages or hiring fee (72). Enoch was sexton of the black congregation in Salem in the 1830s.

27. Bahnson Diary, Aug. 23, 1836. "A lesson for the Ultra Abolitionists, that the slave goes to see a show, to pay for which his master thinks himself unable," intoned the minister. "Far be it from me to defend slavery, but still farther to join the fanatic Abolitionists of the extreme gauch."

the nineteenth century, the slaves' economy correspondingly grew because it was encouraged in the countryside.

Though trade regularly brought blacks and whites together in Bethania by the 1820s, the exchanges indicated only impersonal economic links generated by unequal power relations. Allowing slaves to hunt and market might have provided outlets for social tension, but it did nothing to bring African Americans back into the inner Moravian family where they once had been.

Songs of satire, songs of praise. The same rural folk who chanted in the cornfields strengthened their ties through religion. African Americans drew no sharp line between Christian and non-Christian forms of expression but wedded them in an aesthetic and spiritual continuum. In stylistic terms, this often meant in much of the South that the rhythmic clapping, singing, and dancing of the cornshuckings and other celebrations were simply transposed into the ring shouts of slave religious services. Although the spirit of the ring shout certainly infused the shuckings, white Moravian watchfulness prevented ring shouts in black religious services (though they might well have taken place secretly). Afro-Christians expressed in other ways the same collectiveness they displayed in the workplace.[28]

Not only did many black worshipers form links with Salem's new congregation, but at their request all-black prayer meetings resumed in Bethania about the same time, often led by Lewis or other black preachers. No formal congregation in Bethania was organized from these meetings until 1845, but they served as a kind of satellite African-American church in the rural Moravian lands. As with Salem's congregation, through baptism and godparenthood black Bethanians constructed an elaborate intra- and inter-plantation latticework of spiritual kinship. This is not to suggest they lived in an idyllic, autonomous world far removed from white intrusion and control. Rather, it was precisely that ever-present invasiveness that made the need for such support so paramount.[29]

28. African-American cultural continuities are explored in Stuckey, *Slave Culture;* and Joyner, *Down by the Riverside.*

29. Many references to black meetings in Bethania may be found in Fries et al., eds., *Records,* VIII. See, for example, Bethabara Diary, Apr. 3, 1823, 3652; Bethania Diary, Aug. 3, 1823, Sept. 10, 1826, Mar. 25, 1827, 3661, 3786, 3820. African-American baptisms are recorded in Bethania Church Register, esp. 108–130, 201–222, 437–492.

In part because of the Methodist presence in the countryside near traditional Moravian strongholds such as Bethania, Christian worship had a freewheeling quality that brought black and white together more frequently than in Salem. "Here people 'get religion' by the wholesale at every campmeeting, and they count and calculate from that day on," complained George Bahnson, worried by frequent white Moravian defections to the Methodists. When black and white seekers "got religion" together at meetings, whites often emulated the African-American style of joyous spiritual release. "A negro belonging to Br. Hn. Butner had been at the camp meeting and coming home declared, such unbecoming things he, mind a negro, had never seen, nor did he ever intend going again," noted Bahnson approvingly. And even as African Americans in Bethania attended all-black monthly meetings, many also worshiped in the Moravian church there, though they were not members of the congregation and sat apart from whites. "Blacks of both sexes have their particular benches, under the windows, opposite the table," noted Bahnson. Within segregated contexts, religious venues still brought black and white together.[30]

Yet the death and burial of a slave named Sus in Bethania in 1835 showed how limited even that contact could be. "In the evening black Sus property of Christle Grabs died, in consequence of a late confinement," reported Bahnson. "Neglect on the part of her owners was probably the visible cause of her death. They called in no assistance until it was too late." The minister wrote this account of her funeral the next day:

The church was opened for the occasion. How it pleased our blacks. They were at liberty to occupy the middle of the church while the whites seated themselves on or below the choirs (galleries). There were a goodly number of blacks, all of whom are owned by members of our congregation.... I addressed them on Mark 1, 15 and they seemed to be very attentive. Age of deceased unknown. Of mourning not much could be noticed either, though she had 3 children and at least 3 brothers, one of whom Jacob is said to be somewhat sad, as was also the youngest child Matilda, about 2 years old. After preaching, preparations were made taking the corpse to the graveyard, more than half a

---

30. Bahnson Diary, Aug. 10, Oct. 1, 1834, Feb. 7, 1836. African-American influences on whites in evangelical worship are explored in Sobel, *The World They Made Together,* 178–213.

mile from here. A one-horse carryall was loaded with the coffin and the mother of the deceased, whites and black followed in whatever order they chose, viz. none whatever. We had to go through town, out to the mill, beyond which is the negro graveyard on a tolerably good hill; no fence, no tombstones, nothing of the kind, only a few graves. Some of my companions, viz. Christle Grabs and others beguiled the time by smoking, which I did not think was suitable but it was only a poor black! I prayed the second litany in English and then all returned. At the grave everything was conducted very decently by the blacks.[31]

The funeral suggests conflicting layers of emotional engagement with African-American death. The apparent lack of mourning by Sus's family and friends might have reflected, not an absence of sorrow, but a desire to restrain emotion in front of a white audience and release their grief in private. Sus's funeral sermon in the white church was evidently a gesture of respect from the Bethania congregation, especially since it is not certain that all deceased blacks were so honored. Whether all whites shared a genuine respect for the dead, or whether some attended from a grudging sense of obligation, is unclear. The traditional seating order in church was sym-bolically reversed, blacks now occupying the center and whites relegated to the side benches normally reserved for blacks. The arrangement suggests white deference to the sanctity of death and a tacit admission of its leveling of the social order.

Yet how different it all was from years past! When the African brother Christian died in 1789, Moravian musicians accompanied his funeral with the traditional serenade of *Posaunen*, or trombones, from the balcony of the Bethabara Gemeinhaus. He was buried in God's Acre as the congregation looked on in solemn observance of the "homegoing." Now, in 1835, Sus was buried in an isolated, unmarked African-American graveyard, as her owner, who had refused to call a doctor for her in time, watched from a distance, smoking a cigarette in profound disrespect. It was for black mourners to extract dignity from the occasion by turning the ritual farewell to the dead into an act of affirmation for the living. Though the graveyard had no fence or stones, it was their graveyard, and a consecrated one too—consecrated not

---

31. Bahnson Diary, May 6, 1835. Mark 1:15: "The time is fulfilled, and the kingdom of God is at hand: repent ye, and believe in the gospel."

by the Moravians but by the Methodists, who claimed the real allegiance of many African Americans. From this perspective, white Moravian condescension at the gravesite probably was irrelevant to blacks.[32]

Given the mixed messages broadcast by white Brethren, some blacks spurned Christianity to return the contempt they absorbed every day. A slave named Adam turned his anger in such a way on George Bahnson in 1835. Adam had suffered a stroke and lay ill in his cabin when the minister visited him. As Bahnson entered the hut to find Adam lying on the floor, "a long dark streak showed me, that he had just unburdened himself of some fluid. It was very disagreeable but I sat down near him." Adam "could not at all speak intelligibly, so that I may be mistaken, but when I asked him whether he wished to go to heaven I understood him to say No!" The minister persisted with an "admonition to apply to the Savior," but "the poor fellow looked so cross and little pleased that I fear my poor words appeared to him nothing but foolishness." Bahnson tried again two days later, finding Adam "stretched out before the chimney, containing no fire." Gagging from the stench of the cabin, the minister "sat down on a three-legged stool and spoke to the sick man in his pantaloons made of domestic carpetstuff, but he could give me no satisfaction." Giving one last try two months later, Bahnson found Adam "in a pitiful spiritual condition. He cursed and did such godless things and said drily that all Negroes curse."[33]

Perhaps sensing his impending death (which in fact occurred a few months later), Adam took a measure of delight in throwing Christianity back in the minister's face, cursing and taunting him. Adam's barb that "all Negroes curse," said with a sarcasm plain to Bahnson, could be read as a satire of white notions of black uncouthness. Alternatively, it might also have meant that behind a facade of Christian humility blacks really did curse—whites. Perhaps Adam meant to give Bahnson a rare glimpse behind the facade to show him that the white mission to breed black docility had failed. Repudiating Christianity could be as powerful an assertion of identity as embracing it.

32. Bethania Diary, Sept. 1, 1833, in Fries et al., eds., *Records,* VIII, 4106. Although the number of African Americans formally affiliated with Methodist churches in the area is not known, the Methodists did find some success in their concerted effort to win black souls. Methodist camp meetings proved a more consistently alluring source of spiritual release for black worshipers in the countryside than anything the Moravians could offer. See above, Chapter 7.

33. Bahnson Diary, Oct. 13, 15, 1835; Bethania Diary, Jan. 21, 1836, in Fries et al., eds., *Records,* VIII, 4236.

Whatever his meaning, Adam's mocking made it clear he regarded the minister and his slaveholding religion, not himself, to be in a "pitiful spiritual condition." They would get no deathbed conversion from this sinner.

IT WOULD BE WRONG to imply that blacks and whites by this time had nothing to do with each other outside the realm of work, trade, and occasionally religion. They continued to find common ground in some arenas and to leave cultural imprints on each other. Language remained one crucible of complex social exchange reflective of several broad cultural shifts. German continued as the primary language of most white Moravians and probably at least some African Americans through the first few decades of the nineteenth century, but by the 1820s the Americanization of the Moravian settlement yielded increasing linguistic fragmentation. Seventy years after the German settlement of Wachovia, English had made strong inroads among younger whites while remaining a second language to older generations.[34]

George Bahnson observed this linguistic transition with dismay, for it seemed to him a sign of cultural confusion. "The younger generation, if able to read at all, can read only english," he noted in 1834. The effect, as he saw it, was to disrupt the unity of the Bethania congregation. "It is a great pity that the young people receiving in english what little 'learning' is given them cannot understand preaching in german as well as in english, whilst the real 'Stamm' [core] of the congregation prefer the german so decidedly as hardly to admit english on any solemn occasion, funerals excepted, when both languages are used in succession."[35]

The demands of bilingualism sometimes annoyed the minister. After one sermon he complained: "Until the very commencement of divine service I have to talk upon cows and corn, pigs and wheat in the German language

34. Recognizing that in time English would supersede German as the language of the American Brethren, church officials tried to provide controlled instruction in English toward the end of the 18th century. In 1789, a Salem minister began reading classes in English for men and boys, and in 1803 the church decided to "have English preaching every fourteen days instead of monthly, especially that we may encourage more general use of the English language among us." Years of such fitful measures were needed to cultivate thorough confidence with English among white Brethren; see Salem Diary, Feb. 5, 1789, June 23, 1803, in Fries et al., eds., *Records,* V, 2264, VI, 2730.

35. Bahnson Diary, Nov. 26, 1834, May 9, 1837. On the wider context of linguistic change of which the Moravians were part, see William H. Gehrke, "The Transition from the German to the English Language in North Carolina," *NCHR,* XII (1935), 1–19.

and then all at once, preaching begins in English. The discourse ought to have been much better, but it is rather difficult to collect one's thoughts." On several occasions, strange medleys of German words spliced with English caught his ear, symptomatic to him—as they are to us—of broader cultural hybridization. He quoted one speaker as saying, "Er hatt anyhow a sortee von her notions gehat, es zu postpone" (roughly, "Anyhow, he has had notions of postponing it"). Another said simply, "Ich bin sehr gepleased" ("I am very pleased"), grafting the German *ge-* prefix to an English word. Not surprisingly, the perceived linguistic decline of the younger generation, in the minister's mind, mirrored an ominous slide away from Moravianism to Methodism or even irreligion by young Brethren. Indeed, the rising use of English among whites reflected the acculturation that had so influenced their changing attitudes toward race.[36]

In fact, however, that transition was being aided by African Americans themselves. At least some, perhaps many, younger whites gained their first exposure to English from black housekeepers and perhaps other workers. Charles Brietz, born in Salem in 1811, recalled many years later that in school, where instruction was still in German, he had an advantage during English lessons. "The boys being jealous of my abilities in this, always plagued me, saying I learned it from a Negro woman belonging to my father, which no doubt, was partly true." Brietz's experience, although evidently unusual in Salem, was probably more common in the countryside where the black population was so much greater. Just as African-American domestics gave thousands of white children across the antebellum South many of their first lessons in language and other cultural forms, they served as linguistic midwives for white Brethren.[37]

At the same time, many blacks remained conversant in German. Through

36. Bahnson Diary, Aug. 1, 15, Sept. 3, 1835. "Br. John Schor is a staunch Moravian," he wrote (Aug. 18, 1834), "but all but one of his children have either joined the Methodists or followed a practice which is but too common in our parts, to belong to no religious denomination whatever." For examples of German-English hybrids elsewhere in North Carolina, see Gehrke, "Transition from the German to the English Language," *NCHR*, XII (1935), 3.

37. Account by Charles G. Brietz, Old Salem, Inc. Brietz also allowed that his father's business dealings in English gave him early exposure to the language. For an example of a similar kind of cross-racial teaching in the Danish West Indies in the 1760s, see C.G.A. Oldendorp, *History of the Mission of the Evangelical Brethren on the Caribbean Islands of St. Thomas, St. Croix, and St. John*, ed. and trans. Arnold R. Highfield and Vladimir Barac (1770; reprint, Ann Arbor, Mich., 1987), 154.

the first years of the nineteenth century, black bilingualism achieved varying degrees of fluency in German and English. As late as 1823, a diarist describing the baptism of a black child in Bethania could write that "more than thirty Negroes attended, and as most of them understood German Br. Pfohl spoke to them about the way of eternal salvation." Few words spoken by blacks have been preserved, but some undoubtedly spoke in German-English hybrids similar to those used by whites.[38]

On the other hand, fewer blacks probably spoke German as a *primary* language than in earlier years. The more than fivefold black population increase between 1800 and 1830 owed something to natural increase but even more to the purchase of English-speaking slaves from outside the Wachovia tract. Slave children were more likely to be socialized into English-speaking slave quarters rather than German-speaking white homes. Religious segregation removed one of the key arenas of black-white contact and along with it the need for many blacks to master German. One sign that fewer blacks might have been at ease with German by the 1820s is that Abraham Steiner apparently preached in English in the Salem log church, though he might have been attempting to reach out to a broader regional constituency. In 1836, when Bahnson gave a Sunday sermon in German to a racially mixed audience in Bethania, "all [were] able to understand the german language except perhaps two or three black women."[39]

German probably remained entrenched strongly enough in the Moravian settlement that many African Americans retained at least some familiarity with it, undoubtedly until well after the Civil War in some cases. But the influence of German as a cultural stamp on African Americans weakened, partly because of the growing social distance between black and white and partly because of white Moravians' own loosening grip on the language.

Folk beliefs furnished another matrix of cultural exchange. This secret

38. Bethania Diary, May 12, 1823, in Fries et al., eds., *Records*, VIII, 3660. Blacks grew up speaking German in other parts of North Carolina as well, and we gain the briefest of glimpses of their ability from the reminiscences of a former slave who recalled fragments of the language as late as the 1930s. Laura Dry, who lived in Cabarrus County as a child and was interviewed in 1934, remembered the words *Deitsch schwaetze* (to speak German), *geh' weg* (go away), and *hall Maul* (shut your mouth); see William H. Gehrke, "Negro Slavery among the Germans in North Carolina," *NCHR*, XIV (1937), 311.

39. Although documentation is incomplete, bills of sale survive for several dozen slaves bought by Moravians from non-Moravian owners after 1800; see Bills of Sale file, Slavery box; Bahnson Diary, Feb. 7, 1836.

world of cures and charms, of spirits and divination, common to both Africans and Europeans in early America, is only tantalizingly hinted at in the Moravian records. Yet evidence suggests that whether within, parallel to, or in repudiation of the Moravian faith, black and white people together explored ways of tapping into unsanctioned sources of spiritual power out of sight of the church elders.[40]

The Brethren acknowledged a lively, unseen spirit world that they considered an arena of struggle between Christ and Satan. The elders condemned, but could not stamp out, such potent expressions of popular belief as fortune-telling and charms that courted a power other than Christ's. Lay Brethren were known to consult conjurers and magicians for illnesses, for help in tracking lost animals, or in craft work. Vexed that "superstitious belief in witchcraft and unnatural things [had] not yet ceased" among the Congregation, ministers in 1807 deplored "congregation members who believe far too much in magic and sorcery and have sought the counsel of the so-called wizard [Hexenmeister]." Folk belief in spells, incantations, and perhaps even curses flourished side by side with Christianity in the cosmology of many white Moravians as well as African Americans.[41]

These forms of popular culture persisted and intermingled among whites and blacks into the nineteenth century, though from the available fragmentary reports it is impossible to discern precisely how. George Wilson, a

40. On African folk practices and their mingling with European popular culture in America, see Sobel, *The World They Made Together;* and Albert J. Raboteau, *Slave Religion: The "Invisible Institution" in the Antebellum South* (New York, 1978), 33–35. On European roots of Euro-American popular culture, see Thomas, *Religion and the Decline of Magic;* Burke, *Popular Culture in Early Modern Europe;* and William Monter, *Ritual, Myth, and Magic in Early Modern Europe* (Athens, Ohio, 1983). On their continuance in America, see Jon Butler, *Awash in a Sea of Faith: Christianizing the American People* (Cambridge, Mass., 1990), chap. 3; and David D. Hall, *Worlds of Wonder, Days of Judgment: Popular Religious Belief in Early New England* (New York, 1989).

41. Aelt. Conf., Feb. 22, 1786; LAC, Aug. 14, 1807. Other examples are found in Gemein Rath, June 5, 1783; and Aelt. Conf., Mar. 13, 1788. On folk culture among Germans in early America, see Stevenson Whitcomb Fletcher, *Pennsylvania Agriculture and Country Life, 1640–1840* (Harrisburg, Pa., 1971), 340–343; Elizabeth W. Fisher, " 'Prophesies and Revelations': German Cabbalists in Early Pennsylvania," *PMHB,* CIX (1985), 299–333; A. G. Roeber, " 'The Origin of Whatever Is Not English among Us': The Dutch-speaking and German-speaking Peoples of Colonial British America," in Bailyn and Morgan, eds., *Strangers within the Realm,* 269–271; and Henry Melchior Muhlenberg, *The Journals of Henry Melchior Muhlenberg,* 3 vols., trans. Theodore G. Tappert and John W. Doberstein (Philadelphia, 1942–1958), I, 349.

Bethania physician, noted a powerful belief in witches among some of his patients who begged him for potions or charms to ward off evil magic. In 1828, he visited an elderly woman a few miles from Bethania who claimed to be bewitched by a black man. "All at once she said, don't you see that old Negro man peeping through the crack? It is him has brought me to this. Oh Doctor, do give me something that will kill him or keep him from my house. . . . Oh, that Negro will kill me. Every night he is here." The doctor also visited a slave woman who claimed to be bewitched but whom he diagnosed as pregnant. And minister George Bahnson wrote of a man plagued by the "attacks of witches and evil spirit, whom he defies by cutting the air with his knife and making crosses, like the Catholics."[42]

On the eve of the Civil War, such folk beliefs still flourished, providing cross-racial cultural influences. Former slave Betty Cofer remembered in the 1930s that, though she did not "know much about spells and charms," during her childhood "most of the old folks believed in 'em. One colored man used to make charms, little bags filled with queer things. He called 'em 'jacks' and sold 'em to the colored folks and some white folks too." However sketchy such anecdotal evidence, the tenacity of folk beliefs suggests that they were rooted deeply in a long exchange between Germans and African Americans since the earliest days of the Moravian settlement.[43]

Cases of suspected interracial sexual relationships indicated that black and white people were drawn to each other in more personal ways. A slave woman in Salem was accused of trying to "seduce a white boy" in 1827. "Being a dangerous person for our young people, this Negro woman therefore cannot be tolerated any longer in the Community," Salem officials warned, sending her away. In 1828, a woman living in the Single Sisters' House left Salem after she was accused of being on "too familiar terms with a free Negro serving in the Sisters' House."[44]

Black and white lives intersected at many points. They maintained a host of economic, social, and religious connections with each other, some of them quite intimate. But all of these kinds of contact were informal, often impersonal, sometimes clandestine. Some expressed sneaky defiance of official policy designed to separate black and white in isolated worlds. Yet cross-

42. Wilson, *Journal*, ed. Wilson, July 24, 1828, 79, 155; Bahnson Diary, Sept. 29, 1834.
43. Rawick, ed., *The American Slave*, XIV, 170.
44. Auf. Col., Sept. 3, 23, 1827, June 7, 1828.

racial relationships were qualitatively different from the consistent, daily closeness linking black and white Brethren in earlier generations. The fraternalism that once infused the concourse of black and white Brethren gave way to the standard paternalism of slaveholders unable to live with the implications of their earlier beliefs. Were it ever possible the Christian covenant could have promoted more social equality rather than less, that chance had long since disappeared by 1820. Across the antebellum South, black and white people encountered each other every day, but the antagonism and inequality that tainted their dealings belied the reality that another way had once beckoned. They lived in worlds they made apart.

WHETHER DAVID, a slave living on a plantation near Bethania with his master, Solomon Transou, understood his life in such terms is impossible to say. Nor is much else known about the man. His age, family life, religious beliefs—the details are blank. George Bahnson described a brief encounter he once had with David in 1834. Ever suspicious of black woodcutters, the minister accused David of trying to shortchange him on a load of wood. "Oh the negroes are so cunning!" Bahnson fumed. "They get paid by the load, the less favorably the spot is situated, the smaller must the load be, on which account the rogue had chosen" a location more than a mile outside of town. Bahnson refused to buy the load. "Honesty is the best policy as I told the negro, the most disgusting fellow in town." Who was cheating whom was, of course, a matter of perspective.[45]

Like many slaves, David tried to supplement his private economy by taking goods from whites. After having "stolen some fresh pork at Saml Schaubs" in 1836, he was "brought before the justice and punished with 20 lashes inflicted upon his bare back by a cowskin. Last Sunday he received 15 each of which was yet visible on his poor back." Evidently the whippings were only a prelude to further punishment, for two months later, in January 1837, he was sold for transport to the Deep South. As Bahnson described the scene on the main street of Bethania: "Between 20 and 30 blacks were driven through town by one Martyn on their way to Alabama. Sol. Transu's David was among them. None of them was however handcuffed and they seemed pretty jolly. It is for all a revolting sight. How can a person have anything to

45. Bahnson Diary, Nov. 5, 1834.

do with this infamous trade in human bones and sinews? They pay most enormous prices for negroes. Sol. Transu got $900 for his."[46]

David, however, did not go south. Before traveling very far, he apparently was bought by another slaveholder from whom he seems to have escaped. The next report places him, not in Alabama, but in the jail at Germanton, the Stokes County seat ten miles northeast of Bethania. On December 13, 1837, he and a fellow black prisoner named John Blair destroyed the jail in a bold but futile attempt to escape, causing a regional sensation. The timing of the breakout was more than coincidental. Court dockets at first described David's partner Blair as a runaway slave but later called him a free Negro, about thirty years old. He had been held prisoner for more than a year and had been advertised according to law, without response. On the morning of December 13, the county court ordered the sheriff to "advertise and sell the said Negro or Mulatto who calls himself John Blair." That very day, George Bahnson reported: "Dave the notorious negro, formerly belonging to Sol. Transu, had put fire to the jail at Germanton to escape it. He had been caught though, together with another runaway who had also escaped from the red house at Germanton."[47]

Who actually set the fire? It might have been Blair, who had learned he was to be sold. Yet the court seemed to presume David's guilt. Indicted for arson, the pair were held in the Guilford County jail until April 1838 when they were called to court. Blair might have agreed to testify against David to save himself, for the court ordered him to "give evidence in behalf of the State against David a Slave or . . . he shall give sufficient security in the sum of $200." In October 1838, Blair and David both entered preliminary pleas of not guilty. Blair was tried and acquitted but was sent back to Guilford jail nonetheless. David was remanded to Rockingham County to await trial, but court minutes give no further trace of him, and his fate remains a mystery.

46. David's whippings were not isolated events in Wachovia. A slave girl was whipped for stealing some shoes from Bahnson's home. With standard slaveholder reasoning, her master, Abraham Conrad, was reportedly angry about the theft, "for he provides well for them, that there is indeed no necessity for their stealing, but they cannot help it"; see Bahnson Diary, Nov. 1, 1836, Jan. 27, Feb. 4, 1837.

47. That David was bought before he could be transported to Alabama is suggested by court minutes that reported a year later: "Lyne Glen and Wm Gellarten the owners of David a Slave came into Court and admit notice"; see Stokes County Minute Dockets, Superior Court, Oct. 10, 1838, NCDAH; Stokes County Court of Pleas and Quarter Sessions, Dec. 13, 14, 1837, NCDAH; Bahnson Diary, Dec. 13, 1837.

If, as is probable, he was tried and convicted with the aid of Blair's testimony, his fate would have been clear. By North Carolina law, the punishment for arson was death.[48]

We are left, then, with the haunting image of two desperate captives fleeing a burning jail and one of them mounting the gallows after a thwarted escape. Almost seventy years had passed since the manacled and battle-scarred Africans Sambo and Jupiter arrived in Bethabara and since Johann Samuel first knelt in prayer as a Single Brother. Had David ever heard of them?

The Moravian story is a parable of America—of dreams for a regenerated world, of the battleground of race, of the pressures of assimilation, and of promises left in ash. "Go and make disciples of all the nations," the risen Christ told his apostles (Matt. 28:19), and seventeen centuries later the Moravian Brethren responded. Like others before them, they left Europe to build a new Jerusalem across the sea. They would remake America. Fired with the ideal of freedom in Christ, they vowed to make their Jerusalem a model of racial fellowship, within the limits of their understanding of that idea. In the organic totality of their world, religion shaped their notion of racial identity and every other aspect of their relations with African Americans. White Brethren never renounced slavery or even questioned its morality. But they shared with black Brethren a common language, whose vocabulary was the foot washing, the Communion cup, and the kiss, that gave some basis for mutual empathy and respect—for a breathtakingly brief moment.

Intoxicated with the spirit of individual liberty and possibility in a new nation that brashly trumpeted those ideals, white Moravians wanted more freedom—freedom to make money, to follow private impulses, to buy land and slaves. More freedom for themselves meant less for African Americans. The cultural lessons the descendants of the original Moravian immigrants learned in America provided powerful reinforcement for this equation. They learned that it was difficult and unrewarding to resist the seductive racial language of an emerging American nationalism. White America, they were assured, would not regard them unkindly for spurning black Brethren. With scarcely a nod to the past, they gave in. America had remade *them*.

Black Moravians' absorption into this church society emerged from a desire for self-determination yet also expressed sober awareness of their

---

48. The case of David and Blair is described in Stokes County Minute Dockets, Superior Court, Apr. 9, 12, Oct. 19, 1838, NCDAH. On North Carolina arson law, see Guion Griffis Johnson, *Ante-Bellum North Carolina: A Social History* (Chapel Hill, N.C., 1937), 645.

limited ability to grasp it. Their experience reflected an enduring reality of African-American history that conformity to join the inner sanctum of white society earns favors but comes with a price. Ultimately, the bargain left them with utter betrayal.

Black Brethren embraced the rituals, symbols, spiritual regeneration, and inclusive metaphors of Christianity. Through the church they expressed a sense of redemption, spiritual kinship, and opposition to racial oppression. That consciousness, already well in place during the era of biracial worship, flourished in exile after the founding of the black church. Being pushed out of an integrated church and to the margins of Moravian society was not the end of the world for African Americans. One people's social and cultural margin is another's center. For black Christians, that new center was their church, and, like the old Moravian Church, through it the black congregation absorbed and framed their outlook on virtually every aspect of life.

Yet for some African Americans, it was not enough to create an alternative cultural and social space within slavery. They were the insurgents who wanted out, like the Virginia slave who uttered the perfect epitaph to the American Revolution in 1800. On trial after a failed revolt, he cheekily claimed that, in striking a blow for freedom, he had done only what George Washington had done.[49] And like David, who, with equally deft symbolism, struck at the prison of slavery by leaving a jail in smoking embers. To these rebels, the New Jerusalem lay beyond, on a distant hilltop.

49. Douglas R. Egerton, *Gabriel's Rebellion: The Virginia Slave Conspiracies of 1800 and 1802* (Chapel Hill, N.C., 1993), 102.

AFTERWORD

. . . .

In the opening months of the Civil War, the cornerstone was laid to a new brick church for Salem's African-American congregation. When it was finished in December 1861, the building, just a few feet away from the old log church and the graveyard, combined a simple but handsome design with commodious worship space. Built in Greek Revival style, the church sported a bell tower, large windows, white trim, and paneled doors. In the sanctuary, rows of yellow pine pews lined either side of the central aisle. From those pews, several hundred African Americans watched on May 21, 1865, as a Union cavalry chaplain took the pulpit. Quoting from I Cor. 7:21, he asked: "Were you a slave when called? Never mind. . . . For he who was called in the Lord as a slave is a freedman of the Lord." Then, in words repeated many times throughout the South that spring, the chaplain said: "According to the proclamation of the President of the United States, the slave population of this State was now free." As the site of the announcement that ushered them from slavery to freedom, the brick church became the new African-American house of passage.[1]

By the time the day of jubilee arrived, the black presence in the Moravian communities was larger than ever, and white Brethren's ability to envision a cross-racial earthly kingdom was less than ever. The previous two decades had seen the intertwined expansion of slavery and the demise of Salem's holy experiment. Defiant townsmen clamored more insistently for the right to own slaves, and the church had trouble holding them at bay. Businessman Francis Fries opened a woolen mill at the north end of town with slave labor in 1840. But when he refused to give bond for the slaves as required by town statute, other white Brethren protested, igniting yet another round in the dreary debate over slavery regulations. Finally, the Congregational Council

1. S. Scott Rohrer, "Freedman of the Lord: The Black Moravian Congregation of Salem, N.C., and Its Struggle for Survival, 1856–1890," Old Salem, Inc., 1993, 11–15, 22.

Figure 16. Black Churches in Salem, circa 1862. *The 1823 log church stands
at the far right. Beside it to the left is the African-American graveyard,
and in the center is the congregation's brick church completed in 1861.*
Courtesy, Collection of Old Salem, Winston-Salem, North Carolina

voted in January 1847 to revoke all rules restricting the use and domiciling
of slaves in Salem. The wider context of the decision was clear. Many Brethren, concluded the board with resignation, "let themselves be guided merely
by their own private interests, and that therefore everybody objects stubbornly to any regulation, which would hamper his own interest."[2]

The end of Salem as a church town was not far off. In 1849, Stokes
County was divided, and Wachovia formed the core of a new county, Forsyth. Wanting to keep county governmental functions out of Salem, the
church sold a parcel of land north of town for a new county seat, Winston.
But in 1856, town officials recognized: "We already have a considerable
population living in our midst who are not members of our congregation,
whereby the original idea of a congregation town or place where the members of our community, unmixed by others, could build themselves up in

2. Congregational Council, Aug. 28, 1846, quoted in Philip Africa, "Slaveholding in the
Salem Community, 1771–1851," *NCHR*, LIV (1977), 304. The debate culminating in the final
dissolution of the rules is more amply documented in Africa's article.

their most holy faith, has for a number of years already been lost sight of."
The council abolished the lease system, and two years later the church began
to put Salem lots up for public auction. The Christian theocratic ideal had
ended without ceremony or noticeable lamentation.[3]

As restrictions on slaveholding collapsed and Salem's congregation town
status ended, slaveownership immediately increased. Moravian industrial-
ists such as Fries used slave labor heavily. By 1858, the town's population
stood at 1,155, including 100 black males and 61 black females, or about 15
percent of Salem's population, a higher proportion than ever.[4]

White Brethren's immersion in slaveholding reflected change within
their communities and the United States at large. But their experience also
encapsulated a larger debate within the worldwide Unity over slavery and
racial identity, a debate church leaders were extremely reluctant to face. In
the 1820s, North Carolina Brethren were not alone in their discomfort with
worshiping and learning beside blacks. When "colored children" asked permission to attend a Moravian school in the German congregation town of
Neuwied in 1825, church directors squirmed and called the request "awkward." When English Brethren criticized the ownership of slaves by Moravian missionaries in the West Indies, Unity leaders defensively replied that
slaves were indispensable to the missionaries' support and were treated
more like "servants and maids" than as slaves. Besides, churchmen added,
missionaries were concerned only with converting blacks, not "political disputes" regarding their freedom.[5]

The Unity was finally forced to free its slaves in the British West Indies

3. Another significant change was that after 1856 church records were kept in English rather
than German. On these controversies and other aspects of antebellum Salem, see Jerry L.
Surratt, "The Role of Dissent in Community Evolution among Moravians in Salem, 1772–
1860," NCHR, LII (1975), 235–255 (quotation on 254); Michael Shirley, From Congregation
Town to Industrial City: Culture and Social Change in a Southern Community (New York, 1994).

4. Census Returns, Salem, 1858. The white population included 215 female students at
Salem Academy.

5. Protokoll des Synodus, 1825, Archiv der Brüder-Unität, Herrnhut, Germany, 266, 284.
Along with the racial distinctions creeping into Moravian worship and education practices
comes evidence of dismay over potential class divisions. Lamenting the "Introduction of Pews
into the galleries of chapels," English Brethren predicted the "Distinction which would naturally ensue between rich and poor, and which would not only destroy that peculiar beauty of
our mode of worship which allows no such distinction between them in the house of God; but
also produces much offense, which at the same time it appeared to be in direct exposition to the
rule laid down by James 2:1–4"; see Minutes of Provincial Conference, Fairfield, 1824, Archiv
der Brüder-Unität, Herrnhut, Germany, 74.

when slavery ended in those colonies in 1833. A similar general emancipation ended Moravian slaveholding in the Danish West Indies in 1848. That left the North Carolina Brethren as the last remaining Moravian slaveholders, making them the target of a harsh rebuke by English Brethren. A synod in Fulneck, England, in 1853 expressed its "utter repugnance to this great evil," and it "affectionately but earnestly" urged "brethren in the American Province who are implicated in the practice of slaveholding, to adopt measures for freeing themselves from all connexion with a system so dishonouring to the cause of Christ, and which is absolutely injuring us in public opinion in this Province, and consequently injuring our usefulness as a church." The English complained to the church synod in Herrnhut in 1857, but, still unable to condemn human bondage, Unity directors advised them to express their objections privately to the North Carolinians.[6]

In the United States, the church's Northern Province refrained from criticizing southern Brethren's slaveholding until October 1861, and even then the Pennsylvanians' complaint was timid. North Carolina Brethren rejected all such criticism and eagerly embraced the Confederate cause. Having long since abandoned their pacifist stance, northern and white southern Brethren bore arms on opposite sides during the Civil War.[7]

As white Brethren wrestled with competing definitions of morality, African Americans demonstrated the formidable staying power of the Afro-Moravian tradition. The black congregation remained fairly small during the antebellum years as Methodist churches, with their more openly emotional appeal, proved increasingly attractive to slaves. But large gatherings of a hundred or more continued to fill the church on special festival occasions. In 1860, Unity officials decided to finance the larger brick church for the congregation, ostensibly to provide more space, though it is also possible they intended the church as a gesture to encourage loyalty in the slave population as secession loomed.

During the war and after emancipation, the church provided a crucial anchor of stability and organization for the African-American community. The church continued to function in the late 1860s and early 1870s largely under the care of unordained black lay leaders, though congregants often

6. Letter from B. Seiffert to Rev. John G. Herman, Sept. 29, 1853; Protokolle der General-Synodus, 1857, Archiv der Brüder-Unität, Herrnhut, Germany, II, 185.

7. Richmond E. Myers, "The Moravian Church and the Civil War," *TMHS*, XX (1965), 226–248; Douglas Letell Rights, "Salem in the War between the States," *NCHR*, XXVII (1950), 277–288; Shirley, *From Congregation Town to Industrial City*, chap. 5.

clashed with white officials over the direction of the church. In the last quarter of the nineteenth century, Winston's black population swelled with migrants eager for work in the booming R. J. Reynolds tobacco factories. A surge in independent new churches of several denominations accompanied this influx, and, through the leadership of ordained African-American ministers, their membership swelled. Salem's black congregation was still controlled by the Moravian Church, which made little effort to train and ordain black ministers to serve its Southern Province. Under the guidance of white pastors, the membership remained relatively modest, numbering fifty-four communicants by the turn of the century. The church's rich liturgical and social life nonetheless continued to serve the expanding African-American neighborhoods around the old Moravian core of Salem well into the twentieth century.[8]

In 1914, shortly after Winston and Salem merged to form the new town of Winston-Salem, Moravian ministers gave the black congregation a formal name: Saint Philip's Moravian Church. New generations continued to worship at Saint Philip's, and, though the old brick church was closed in 1949, the congregation survived in other locations, gained its first African American minister in 1966, and remains one of the oldest black churches in continuous existence in the South. Overshadowed by the Baptist and Methodist Churches, the Moravian Church claims a relatively small number of African-American adherents and a handful of black congregations in North America. In the Caribbean and Africa, however, the Unity's early foothold in the mission field was decisive and enduring. Of the approximately half-million Moravians worldwide, three quarters are of African descent.

8. Rohrer, "Freedman of the Lord," chaps. 2–4, esp. 46, and "A Mission among the People: The World of St. Philip's Church from 1890 to 1952," Old Salem, Inc., 1993; and Bertha Hampton Miller, "Blacks in Winston-Salem, North Carolina, 1895–1920: Community Development in an Era of Benevolent Paternalism" (Ph.D. diss., Duke University, 1981). On black church development in the South, see William E. Montgomery, *Under Their Own Vine and Fig Tree: The African-American Church in the South, 1865–1900* (Baton Rouge, La., 1993); Evelyn Brooks Higginbotham, *Righteous Discontent: The Women's Movement in the Black Baptist Church, 1880–1920* (Cambridge, Mass., 1993).

. . . .

Biographies of African Americans in the Moravian Records

THE FOLLOWING figure prominently in the Moravian records (prebaptismal names are in parentheses where applicable).

ABRAHAM (Sambo), circa 1730–1797. A Mandingo from West Africa, he was bought by the Moravian Church in 1771 to work in the tannery. His escape attempt in 1775 failed. Baptized and christened Abraham in 1780, he was a member of the Salem Single Brothers' Choir until his marriage to Sarah in 1785. A communicant Moravian, Abraham was buried in the Salem God's Acre.

ANNA (Patty; also called Nancy), ?–1829. A West African, she was bought by the Salem congregation in 1781 to work in the Salem tavern. She was baptized and christened Anna in 1783, married Christian, and later became a communicant. She spent many years working in the Bethabara store, but after falling out of favor she was banished from the Bethabara congregation and was resettled in Hope and then on the Salem plantation. She became a communicant of the black congregation and was buried in the church graveyard in 1829.

BODNEY, circa 1756–1829. With his wife, Phoebe, and family, he was a member of the Bethania congregation early in the nineteenth century until Moravian slaveholder George Hauser sold the family to the Salem congregation. Bodney was overseer of the Salem plantation. He and Phoebe became communicants in the Salem congregation and later in the black congregation.

CATHY, 1761–1777. The daughter of Caesar and Susy, she worked first in the Bethabara tavern, then in the Salem tavern. She expressed occasional interest in the Moravian Church, converted on her deathbed, and was buried in the Single Sisters' plot of the Salem God's Acre.

CHRISTIAN (Frank), ?–1789. A West African, Frank was bought by the Moravian Church from Rowan County slaveowner William Gilbert in 1771. He worked for years in the Bethabara store, joined the church in 1780, and was christened Christian. He married Anna in 1783, worked for a few years at the Salem tavern, then moved back to Bethabara, where he and Anna were members of the Married Men's and Women's Choirs. He died from an injury in 1789 and was buried in the Bethabara God's Acre.

DAVID, ?–1838(?). A slave of Bethanian Solomon Transou, he was to be sold to the Deep South but apparently escaped. Recaptured and held in the Germanton jail, he and a free black inmate set fire to the jail and tried unsuccessfully to flee. He was convicted of arson and presumed executed.

DAVID, CHRISTIAN (Davy), circa 1780–1839. He was bought by the church from Stokes County slaveholder James Barham in 1805 to work in the Bethabara distillery. Later he was transferred to the Salem plantation and then became a personal servant and gardener to the Unity administrator in Salem. He joined the black congregation in 1824, was christened Christian David, and became a communicant. His wife, Rose, who lived apart from him, was a Methodist but worshiped with the congregation on occasion. David was appointed sexton in the early 1830s.

IMMANUEL, JOHN (Jack), 1775–1835. Born in Amelia County, Virginia, he was sold to Bethanian Christian Conrad and learned to speak German better than English. He was baptized in 1804, joining the Bethania congregation, and was later sold to the Salem congregation. He worked in the Salem tannery but was nearly sold after an alleged romance with Christine Oliver. In the 1820s, Immanuel became a communicant and sexton of the black congregation, served as godfather to many children, and was buried in the black congregational graveyard.

JACOB, ?. A member of the Salem congregation, he lived in Salem between 1773 and 1779. Baptized in 1775, he worked as a hostler in the Salem tavern and then as a teamster for the Single Brothers. He was a member of the Single Brothers' Choir until he fell out of favor and was sold out of the community.

MOSES, ?. Bought as a youth by the church in 1779, he worked for many years on the Bethabara farm. He rejected efforts to convert him, and, "by his own request," he was sold in 1794.

OLIVER, CHRISTINE, ?. A free black woman, she worked in domestic service for various Moravians early in the nineteenth century until her marriage to Peter Oliver. She was baptized and joined the Salem congregation. After Peter's death, she was accused of an illicit romance with the enslaved brother John Immanuel and was evicted from her property near Salem. The courts assumed custody of her children, and she disappeared from the records.

OLIVER, PETER (Oliver), 1766–1810. Born in King and Queen County, Virginia, he was known as Oliver when bought by the Moravian Church in 1785. Baptized and christened Peter Oliver in 1786, he apparently lived in the Single Brothers' House for several years before moving to Bethabara to learn pottery. He later moved back to Salem and bought his freedom in the late 1790s. He married a free black woman, Christine, and lived outside of Salem, supporting himself through farming and ceramic work until his death in 1810. Peter Oliver was the last African American to be buried in the Salem God's Acre.

PAUL (Jupiter), ?. A West African, reportedly the son of a king, who arrived with Abraham (Sambo) in 1771, he was bought by English Moravian John Douthit in Hope. He was baptized and joined the Hope congregation in 1780 (his sponsors were John Samuel and Abraham), married Emma, a non-Moravian, and raised a large family. He was sold away from the Moravian community sometime in the early nineteenth century and disappeared from the records.

PHOEBE, circa 1770–1860. Along with her husband, Bodney, and family, she was sold from Bethania to Salem in 1809, joined the Salem congregation, and lived on the Salem plantation. She was one of the earliest communicants in the new black congregation.

PRISCILLA, 1748–1834. Born in Maryland and baptized in the Anglican Church, she migrated to North Carolina in 1775 with her English Moravian owners, the Peddycords, settling in Hope. She was formally received into the church in 1783. A longtime communicant member of the Hope congregation, she sponsored dozens of baptisms for black adults and children and was buried in the Hope God's Acre in 1834.

SAM, ?. A free black, he rented land from the Moravians and lived near Salem for many years, hiring his labor out to them. He fell into debt and was forced to flee the area in 1803.

SAMUEL, ANNA, 1792–?. Daughter of Johann and Maria Samuel, she was raised and schooled in the Bethabara congregation. Later, unlike her surviving brothers, she seems not to have taken an active role in the African-American congregation.

SAMUEL, ANNA MARIA, 1781–1798. The first daughter of Johann and Maria Samuel, she was raised and educated in the Moravian Church. As a member of the Older Girls' Choir, she lived in the Single Sisters' House in Salem between 1793 and 1795. She gained her freedom when her mother was emancipated in 1795 and moved back to Bethabara. After her death from illness, she was buried in the Bethabara God's Acre.

SAMUEL, CHRISTIAN, 1797–1826. Free black son of Johann and Maria Samuel, he was raised in Moravian schools and later served as violinist for the black congregation.

SAMUEL, JACOB, 1801–1833. Free black son of Johann and Maria Samuel, he was raised in Moravian schools and later served as sexton and musician for the black congregation. He fell out of favor after selling liquor to slaves, lost his post, and later died of illness.

SAMUEL, JOHANN (Sam), circa 1750–1821. Initially known as Sam, he was the first black Moravian in North Carolina. He worked as a hired cattle hand in the early Bethabara settlement and in 1769 became the first slave bought by the Brethren in North Carolina. He learned German and attended a Moravian school. Baptized and christened Johann Samuel in 1771, he worked as a supervisor of the Bethabara farm and married Maria in 1780. Emancipated in 1800, he rented a farm near Bethabara, but, when his family fell into poverty, Samuel was arrested for theft and was banished from the church in 1813. He and Maria died near Bethania in 1821.

SAMUEL, JOHN, 1788–1825. Like his brothers and sisters, he attended Moravian schools in Bethabara in his childhood and later was a musician for the black congregation in Salem.

SAMUEL, MARIA (Ida, Idy), ?–1821. Bought by the Moravian Church in 1778 to work in the Salem tavern, she was baptized as Maria in 1780. She married Johann Samuel soon thereafter, moved to Bethabara, served as cook for the congregation, and raised a large family. She was emancipated in 1795, and, when Johann gained his freedom five years later, they set up their own farm. After Johann was arrested for theft, the family was banished from the Bethabara congregation and evicted from church land. She and Johann died within three weeks of each other in 1821.

. . . .

Memoir of Abraham

Translated by Erika Huber

OUR DEAR BROTHER ABRAHAM, otherwise called Sambo, a Negro from the Mandingo Nation on the coast of African Guinea, was born about the year 1730. It appears that his father was a respected man among his country-men. Through diligent praying he established a religious way of thinking himself, though this was mixed with heathen superstition. When he grew up and was already father of several children, he went to war like others in the frequent hostilities with the neighboring tribes. In one of those wars he was wounded severely in head and face and was taken prisoner, and then sent back to his father with mutilated ears. He, the father, became so angry about this that he stirred the inhabitants of the community to another war to get his revenge. They started at once, and Sambo, wounded though he was, did not let them keep him from following them. Now he was taken prisoner for the second time and sold to European slave traders, who brought him to the West Indies and sold him on a French island. He was there for several years. Later he was brought to Virginia. In August of 1770 his master (H. Lyon)[1] intended to sell him again and brought him with two other Negroes to Brother Herbst (tanner here). For several days they stayed under his supervision. One of them was sold to Hope not far from here, was baptized and called Paul. In the beginning Brother Herbst was not willing to keep one of them, because at that time already there were important reasons for not keeping any Negroes in the Salem Community. However, his atten-

---

1. Identified as Edmund Lyne in a bill of sale from Aug. 24, 1771. See Bills of Sale file, Slavery box.

tion was called mainly to Sambo, who seemed to be of good humor, and who perhaps could be won for the Lord, and he could not get rid of this thought. Therefore he decided to pay the price for him and to keep him here for a time on approval. At that time Sambo suffered severely from the Guinea worm on his big toe, which had to be taken off. For quite a while he stayed in his former heathen ways and mores. We could not give him the right instruction because he understood only his native language and a little French. After he had been here for three years, he ran away from his master quite unexpectedly, but was, however, returned to Salem, after he had suffered much from hunger, and of his own free will he admitted that he ought to be punished. Since that time he started to think about the status of his soul, attended diligently the Congregation meetings, and was eager to learn German and verses. He asked the Brethren *how* one can become happy eternally, and his attention was called to the Gospel, that a poor and oppressed sinner through faith in Jesus Christ can be relieved from the burden of sins and sinning. Still some time passed until he learned to see himself as the poorest sinner and to realize this evil. Finally, however, he came to the thorough perception of his lost condition, and admitted openheartedly and repentantly to a Brother what a slave of sin he had been up to now and how much he would like to be saved and become happy. It was a comforting word for him that Jesus Christ had come into this world to make sinners happy. He prayed to the Lord for mercy and pardon. We took special care of him, and he paid attention to the exhortations of the Brethren. Since we noted distinctly that his heart had truly changed and that he was longing for the washing of his sins with the blood of Christ, he received holy baptism through our dear Brother Graff on December 26, 1780, and afterwards we saw with joy that he had not received the mercy of God in vain. In June of 1787 he received the Holy Communion, and he received it in the perception of Jesus Christ and himself. Simple like a child, he kept to the Lord and he testified daily that he would always ask that the Lord would cleanse him now with his blood. He had some weaknesses in his character, which required the patience of his master and all those who were around him. On the whole he was loved by the congregation and recognized as a special example of the mercy of Jesus Christ. He enjoyed the news from our missions in the West Indies very much, thought of it daily in his prayer, and also contributed his part.

On July 30, 1785, he married Sarah, at present his widow, about whose soul he was very troubled, and he often mentioned his concern about her unhappy state of heart. Though he could hardly express himself in matters concerning his soul, he used opportunities to announce to other Negroes the truths of the Gospel.

On March 27 he became sick and showed at once that at this time he would go to the Lord, to which he was looking forward. It was really edifying to see him with his pains which he felt mainly in his abdomen, so quiet, patient, and free from all fright of death, yea, the calmness and the well-being of his soul sparkled in his countenance. When he was asked what would be mainly comforting to him, he prayed like a child the verse: The blood and righteousness of Christ are my adornment and dress of honor.

He asked to be blessed before his death, which happened on April 6, 1797, and on the 7th he passed away calmly, at the age of about 60 years.

SELECTED BIBLIOGRAPHY

. . . .

Unpublished Primary Sources

Archiv der Brüder-Unität, Herrnhut, Germany
  Bericht der Provinzial-Conferenz in der Wachau zur Vorbereitung für den Synoden der
    Brüder-Unität, 1824.
  Fairfield Provincial Conference, 1824.
  Protokolle des General-Synodus, 1857.
  Protokolle des Synodus.
Duke University Manuscript Collection, Durham, North Carolina
  Conrad Family Papers.
Library of Congress, Manuscripts Division, Washington, D.C.
  European Photostats, Germany, Herrnhut, Archiv der Brüder-Unität.
Moravian Archives, Northern Province, Bethlehem, Pennsylvania
  Aeltesten Conferenz.
  Bethlehem Aufseher Collegium.
  Personal Memoir File.
  Wachovia-Bethlehem Correspondence. Microfilm.
Moravian Archives, Southern Province, Winston-Salem, North Carolina
  Aeltesten Conferenz.
  Aufseher Collegium.
  Bethabara Committee.
  Bethabara Diacony Journal.
  Bethabara Diacony Ledger.
  Bethabara Diarium [Bethabara Diary].
  Bethabara Hausvater-Conferenz [Housefathers' Conference].
  Bethabara Kirchen-Buch [Church-Book].
  Bethabara Livestock Inventory.
  Bethabara Wirtschafts-Conferenz [Economic Conference].
  Bethania Committee.
  Bethania Diarium [Bethania Diary].
  Bethania Hausvater-Versammlung [Housefathers' Conference].
  Bethania Kirchen-Buch [Church-Book].
  Brotherly Agreement of Evangelical *Gemeine* of Brethren at Salem.
  Brotherly Agreement on the Rules and Orders for the Brethren's Congregation in and
    about Hope Settlement.
  Census Returns, Salem, 1858.
  Church-Book for the People of Color in and about Salem.
  Correspondence File.

Diarium der led. Brn. in Salem [Single Brothers' Diary].
Diarium der led. Schw. in Salem [Single Sisters' Diary].
Diary of the Small Negro Congregation in and around Salem.
European Unity Directorate. Annual Reports.
Female Mission Society.
Frederic Marshall Papers.
Friedberg Church Register.
Friedberg Committee.
Grosse Helfer Conferenz [Greater Helpers' Conference].
Haus-Conferenz der led. Brn. in Salem [House-Conference of the Single Brothers].
Helfer Conferenz [Helpers' Conference].
Helfer Conferenz fürs Ganze [Helpers' Conference for Wachovia].
Hope Church Register.
Hope Committee.
Landarbeiter Conferenz [Conference of Country Congregation Ministers]. Minutes and
    Reports.
Memorandum concerning Chimney Sweeps.
Personal Memoir File.
Salem Diarium [Salem Diary].
Salem Gemein Rath [Salem Congregational Council].
Salem Tavern Inventories.
Slave Bills of Sale.
Societät zu Ausbreitung des Evangelii unter den Heiden in Nord-America [Society for the
    Propagation of the Gospel among the Heathen in North America].
North Carolina Department of Archives and History, Raleigh, North Carolina
Stokes County Court of Pleas and Quarter Sessions. Minutes.
Stokes County List of Taxables.
Stokes County Patrol Records.
Stokes County Slave Records.
Stokes County Superior Court. Minute Dockets.
Old Salem, Inc., Winston-Salem, North Carolina
Bahnson, George F. Journal.
Leinbach, John Henry. Journal.
Map Files.
Personal Files.
Schober, Gottlieb. Papers.
Wolle, Peter. Diary.
Southern Historical Collection, University of North Carolina at Chapel Hill
Conner, Juliana Margaret. Diary.
Conrad Family Papers.
Stokes County Courthouse, Danbury, North Carolina
Will Books.

Published Primary Sources

Absher, Mrs. W. O. *Stokes County Wills*, Vols. I–IV, *1790–1864.* Easley, S.C., 1985.
"At the Baptism of Adults from among the Heathen." In *Liturgic Hymns of the United
    Brethren.* London, 1793.

"Autobiography of Omar ibn Said, Slave in North Carolina, 1831." *American Historical Review,* XXX (1925), 787–795.

Butler, Lindley S., and Alan D. Watson, eds. *The North Carolina Experience: An Interpretive and Documentary History.* Chapel Hill, N.C., 1984.

Clark, Walter, ed. *The State Records of North Carolina.* 22 vols. Winston and Goldsboro, N.C., 1895–1907.

Curtin, Philip D., ed. *Africa Remembered: Narratives by West Africans from the Era of the Slave Trade.* Madison, Wis., 1967.

Equiano, Olaudah. *The Interesting Narrative of the Life of Olaudah Equiano, or Gustavas Vassa, the African. . . .* London, 1789. In Henry Louis Gates, Jr., ed., *The Classic Slave Narratives,* 1–182. New York, 1987.

Fries, Adelaide L., et al., eds. *Records of the Moravians in North Carolina.* 11 vols. Raleigh, N.C., 1922–1969.

Greene, Jack P., ed. *The Diary of Colonel Landon Carter of Sabine Hall, 1752–1778.* 2 vols. Charlottesville, Va., 1965.

Hamer, Philip M., et al., eds. *The Papers of Henry Laurens.* 14 vols. Columbia, S.C., 1968–.

Hamilton, Kenneth G., ed. and trans. *The Bethlehem Diary, 1742–1744.* Bethlehem, Pa., 1971.

Jobson, Richard. *The Golden Trade; or, A Discovery of the River Gambia, and the Golden Trade of Aethiopians.* London, 1623.

Jones, George Fenwick, ed. *Detailed Reports on the Salzburger Emigrants Who Settled in America. . . . Edited by Samuel Urlsperger.* Trans. Hermann J. Lacher. 17 vols. Athens, Ga., 1966–.

Labaree, Leonard W., et al., eds. *The Papers of Benjamin Franklin.* Vol. IV. New Haven, Conn., 1959.

"Letter from the County of Surry, N.C., to a Gentleman in Halifax" (Feb. 20, 1793). *The North Carolina Journal of Halifax.* Reprinted in *Old Salem Gleaner,* XVI, no. 1 (Summer–Fall 1972).

Moore, Francis. *Travels into the Inland Parts of Africa. . . .* London, 1738.

Muhlenberg, Henry Melchior. *The Journals of Henry Melchior Muhlenberg.* Trans. Theodore G. Tappert and John W. Doberstein. 3 vols. Philadelphia, 1942–1958.

Oldendorp, C.G.A. *History of the Mission of the Evangelical Brethren on the Caribbean Islands of St. Thomas, St. Croix, and St. John.* Ed. and trans. Arnold R. Highfield and Vladimir Barac. 1770; reprint, Ann Arbor, Mich., 1987.

Park, Mungo. *The Life and Travels of Mungo Park.* Edinburgh, 1864. Orig. publ. as *Travels in the Interior Districts of Africa,* 1799.

Prince, Mary. *History of Mary Prince, a West Indian Slave.* London, 1831. In Henry Louis Gates, Jr., ed., *The Classic Slave Narratives,* 183–238. New York, 1987.

Rawick, George P., ed. *The American Slave: A Composite Autobiography.* Vol. XIV. North Carolina Narratives, pt. 1. Contributions in Afro-American and African Studies, no. 11. Westport, Conn., 1972.

"Report of the Managers to the American Colonization Society, at Its Twenty-first Annual Meeting." *The African Repository and Colonial Journal,* XIV, no. 1 (January 1938), 1–15.

Saint-Mery, Mederic-Louis-Élie Moreau de. *Description topographique, physique, civile, politique, et historique de la Partie Française de l'Isle Saint Domingue.* 1797; reprint, Paris, 1958.

Saunders, William L., ed. *The Colonial Records of North Carolina.* 10 vols. Raleigh, N.C., 1886–1890.

Spangenberg, August Gottlieb. *An Exposition of Christian Doctrine as Taught in the Protes-tant Church of the United Brethren or Unitas Fratrum*. Ed. and trans. J. Kenneth Pfohl and Edmund Schwarze. 1778; reprint, Winston-Salem, N.C., 1959.

"Statutes of the Congregation at Herrnhut, in the year 1727." In *The Memorial Days of the Renewed Church of the Brethren*, 106–109. Ashton-under-Lyne, 1822.

"Twenty-third Annual Meeting of the American Colonization Society." *The African Reposi-tory and Colonial Journal*, XVI, no. 5 (March 1840), 65–77.

Wilson, George Follett. *Journal, April 27, 1828–September 30, 1830*. Ed. Evelyn H. Wilson. Greenville, S.C., 1984.

Zinzendorf, Nikolaus Ludwig von. *Texte zur Mission*. 1748; reprint, Hamburg, 1979.

Published Secondary Works

Abraham, W. E. "The Life and Times of Anton Wilhelm Amo." Historical Society of Ghana, *Transactions*, VII (1964), 60–81.

Abrahams, Roger D. *Singing the Master: The Emergence of African American Culture in the Plantation South*. New York, 1992.

Africa, Philip. "Slaveholding in the Salem Community, 1771–1851." *North Carolina Histor-ical Review*, LIV (1977), 271–307.

Andrews, William L. *To Tell a Free Story: The First Century of Afro-American Autobiogra-phy, 1760–1865*. Urbana, Ill., 1986.

Aptheker, Herbert. *American Negro Slave Revolts*. 2d ed. New York, 1987.

Bailyn, Bernard, and Philip D. Morgan, eds. *Strangers within the Realm: Cultural Margins of the First British Empire*. Chapel Hill, N.C., 1991.

Bassett, John Spencer. *Slavery and Servitude in the Colony of North Carolina*. Johns Hopkins University Studies in Historical and Political Science, 14th Ser., nos. IV-V. Bal-timore, 1896.

Beck, Herbert H. "Town Regulations of Lititz, 1959." Moravian Historical Society, *Transac-tions*, XI (1936), 158–173.

Berdahl, Robert M. *The Politics of the Prussian Nobility: The Development of a Conserva-tive Ideology, 1770–1848*. Princeton, N.J., 1988.

Berlin, Ira. "From Creole to African: Atlantic Creoles and the Origins of African-American Society in Mainland North America." *William and Mary Quarterly*, 3d Ser., LIII (1996), 251–288.

——. *Slaves without Masters: The Free Negro in the Antebellum South*. New York, 1974.

——. "Time, Space, and the Evolution of Afro-American Society on British Mainland North America." *American Historical Review*, LXXXV (1980), 44–78.

Berlin, Ira, and Herbert G. Gutman. "Natives and Immigrants, Free Men and Slaves: Urban Workingmen in the Antebellum American South." *American Historical Review*, LXXXVIII (1983), 1175–1200.

Berlin, Ira, and Philip D. Morgan, eds. *Cultivation and Culture: Labor and the Shaping of Slave Life in the Americas*. Charlottesville, Va., 1993.

——. *The Slaves' Economy: Independent Production by Slaves in the Americas*. London, 1991.

Berlin, Ira, and Ronald Hoffman, eds. *Slavery and Freedom in the Age of the American Rev-olution*. Charlotteville, Va., 1983.

Bernheim, G. D. *History of the German Settlements and of the Lutheran Church in North and South Carolina*. 1872; reprint, Baltimore, 1975.

Bird, Charles S. "The Development of Mandekan (Manding): A Study of the Role of Extra-linguistic Factors in Linguistic Change." In David Dalby, ed., *Language and History in Africa: A Volume of Collected Papers Presented to the London Seminar on Language and History in Africa (Held at the School of Oriental and African Studies, 1967–69,* 146–159. New York, 1970.

Bireley, Robert. *Religion and Politics in the Age of the Counterreformation: Emperor Ferdinand II, William Lamormaini, S. J., and the Formation of Imperial Policy.* Chapel Hill, N.C., 1981.

Bishir, Catherine W. "A Proper, Good, and Nice Workmanlike Manner: A Century of Traditional Building Practice, 1730–1830." In Catherine W. Bishir, Charlotte V. Brown, Carl R. Lounsbury, and Ernest H. Wood III, *Architects and Builders in North Carolina: A History of the Practice of Building,* 48–129. Chapel Hill, N.C., 1990.

Bivins, John, Jr. *The Moravian Potters in North Carolina.* Chapel Hill, N.C., 1972.

Bivins, John, Jr., and Paula Welshimer. *Moravian Decorative Arts in North Carolina: An Introduction to the Old Salem Collection.* Winston-Salem, N.C., 1981.

Blackburn, Robin. *The Making of New World Slavery: From the Baroque to the Modern, 1492–1800.* New York, 1997.

Blackwelder, Ruth. "The Attitude of the North Carolina Moravians toward the American Revolution." *North Carolina Historical Review,* IX (1932), 1–21.

Blassingame, John W. *The Slave Community: Plantation Life in the Antebellum South.* New York, 1972.

Boles, John B. *Masters and Slaves in the House of the Lord: Race and Religion in the American South, 1740–1870.* Lexington, Ky., 1988.

Bossy, John. "Blood and Baptism: Kinship, Community, and Christianity in Western Europe from the Fourteenth to the Seventeenth Centuries." In Derek Baker, ed., *Sanctity and Secularity: The Church and the World,* 129–143. Studies in Church History, X. Oxford, 1973.

——. *Christianity in the West, 1400–1700.* New York, 1985.

Bowman, Shearer Davis. *Masters and Lords: Mid-Nineteenth Century U.S. Planters and Prussian Junkers.* New York, 1993.

Braude, Benjamin. "The Sons of Noah and the Construction of Ethnic and Geographical Identities in the Medieval and Early Modern Periods." *William and Mary Quarterly,* 3d Ser., LIV (1997), 103–142.

Brewer, James. "Legislation Designed to Control Slavery in Wilmington and Fayetteville." *North Carolina Historical Review,* XXX (1953), 155–166.

Bridenbaugh, Carl. *The Colonial Craftsman.* New York, 1950.

——. *Myths and Realities: Societies of the Colonial South.* New York, 1965.

Brock, Peter. *The Political and Social Doctrines of the Unity of Czech Brethren in the Fifteenth and Early Sixteenth Centuries.* London, 1957.

Buchner, J. H. *The Moravians in Jamaica: History of the Mission of the United Brethren's Church to the Negroes in the Island of Jamaica, from the Year 1754 to 1854.* London, 1854.

Bugner, Ladislas, ed. *The Image of the Black in Western Art,* 4 vols. Lausanne and Cambridge, Mass., 1979–1989.

Butner, Jo Conrad. "A New Town in Wachovia." In *Three Forks of Muddy Creek,* VI, 1–11. Winston-Salem, N.C., 1978.

Caldwell, Alice M. "Liturgical and Social Change in Moravian Communities, 1750–1823." *Communal Societies,* IX (1989), 23–38.

Cassell, Frank A. "Slaves of the Chesapeake Bay Area and the War of 1812." *Journal of Negro History,* LVII (1972), 144–155.

Cimbala, Paul A. "Fortunate Bondsmen: Black 'Musicianers' and Their Role as an Antebellum Southern Plantation Slave Elite." *Southern Studies*, XVIII (1979), 291–303.

Clark, Ernest James, Jr. "Aspects of the North Carolina Slave Code, 1715–1860." *North Carolina Historical Review*, XXXIX (1962), 148–164.

Clasen, Claus-Peter. *Anabaptism: A Social History, 1525–1618*. Ithaca, N.Y., 1972.

Cornelius, Janet Duitsman. *"When I Can Read My Title Clear": Literacy, Slavery, and Religion in the Antebellum South*. Columbia, S.C., 1991.

Creel, Margaret Washington. *"A Peculiar People": Slave Religion and Community-Culture among the Gullahs*. New York, 1988.

Crittenden, Charles Christopher. *Commerce of North Carolina, 1763–1789*. New Haven, Conn., 1936.

Crow, Jeffrey J. *The Black Experience in Revolutionary North Carolina*. Raleigh, N.C., 1977.

——. "Liberty Men and Loyalists: Disorder and Disaffection in the North Carolina Backcountry." In Ronald Hoffman, Thad W. Tate, and Peter J. Albert, eds., *An Uncivil War: The Southern Backcountry in the American Revolution*, 125–178. Charlottesville, Va., 1985.

——. "Slave Rebelliousness and Social Conflict in North Carolina, 1775 to 1802." *William and Mary Quarterly*, 3d Ser., XXXVII (1980), 79–102.

Crow, Jeffrey J., and Larry E. Tise, eds. *The Southern Experience in the American Revolution*. Chapel Hill, N.C., 1978.

Curtin, Philip, D. *The Atlantic Slave Trade: A Census*. Madison, Wis., 1969.

——. *Economic Change in Precolonial Africa: Senegambia in the Era of the Slave Trade*. Madison, Wis., 1975.

Daniel, W. Harrison. "North Carolina Moravians and the Negro, 1760–1820." *Virginia Social Science Journal*, XII (1977), 23–31.

——. "Virginia Baptists and the Negro in the Early Republic." *Virginia Magazine of History and Biography*, LXXX (1972), 60–69.

Davidson, Basil. *The African Slave Trade: Precolonial History, 1450–1850*. Boston, 1961.

Davis, David Brion. *The Problem of Slavery in the Age of Revolution, 1770–1823*. Ithaca, N.Y., 1975.

——. *The Problem of Slavery in Western Culture*. Ithaca, N.Y., 1966.

Debrunner, Hans Werner. *Presence and Prestige, Africans in Europe: A History of Africans in Europe before 1918*. Basel, 1979.

Devisse, Jean. *From the Demonic Threat to the Incarnation of Sainthood*. Cambridge, Mass., 1979.

Devisse, Jean, and Michel Mollat. *Africans in the Christian Ordinance of the World (Fourteenth to Sixteenth Century)*. Cambridge, Mass., 1979.

Dillard, J. L. *Black English: Its History and Usage in the United States*. New York, 1972.

Du Bois, W.E.B. *The Souls of Black Folk*. 1903; reprint, New York, 1961.

Eaton, Clement. "Slave-Hiring in the Upper South: A Step Toward Freedom." *Mississippi Valley Historical Review*, LXVI (1959–1960), 663–678.

Egerton, Douglas R. " 'Fly across the River': The Easter Slave Conspiracy of 1802." *North Carolina Historical Review*, LXVIII (1991), 87–110.

——. *Gabriel's Rebellion: The Virginia Slave Conspiracies of 1800 and 1802*. Chapel Hill, N.C., 1993.

Ekirch, Roger A[rthur]. *"Poor Carolina": Politics and Society in Colonial North Carolina, 1729–1776*. Chapel Hill, N.C., 1981.

Eltis, David. "Free and Coerced Transatlantic Migrations: Some Comparisons." *American Historical Review*, LXXXVIII (1983), 251–280.

Epstein, Dena J. *Sinful Tunes and Spirituals: Black Folk Music to the Civil War*. Urbana, Ill., 1977.

Faust, Albert Bernhardt. *The German Element in the United States.* . . . 2 vols. New York, 1927.

Ferguson, Leland. *Uncommon Ground: Archaeology and Early African America, 1650– 1800*. Washington, D.C., 1992.

Fields, Barbara. "Ideology and Race in American History." In J. Morgan Kousser and James M. McPherson, eds., *Region, Race, and Reconstruction: Essays in Honor of C. Vann Woodward*, 143–177. New York, 1977.

Fisher, Elizabeth W. " 'Prophesies and Revelations': German Cabbalists in Early Pennsylvania." *Pennsylvania Magazine of History and Biography*, CIX (1985), 299–333.

Fogleman, Aaron Spencer. *Hopeful Journeys: German Immigration, Settlement, and Political Culture in Colonial America, 1717–1775*. Philadelphia, 1996.

Fousek, Marianka S. "On Secular Authority and Military Service among the Bohemian Brethren in the Sixteenth and Seventeenth Centuries." In Bela K. Kiraly, ed., *Tolerance and Movements of Religious Dissent in Eastern Europe*, 53–64. New York, 1975.

———. "The Perfectionism of the Early Unitas Fratrum." *Church History*, XXX (1961), 396– 413.

———. "Spiritual Direction and Discipline: A Key to the Flowering and Decay of the Sixteenth Century Unitas Fratrum." *Archive for Reformation History*, LXII (1971), 207–224.

Franklin, John Hope. *The Free Negro in North Carolina, 1790–1860*. Chapel Hill, N.C., 1943.

———. *From Slavery to Freedom: A History of African Americans*. 7th ed. New York, 1994.

Frazier, E. Franklin / C. Eric Lincoln. *The Negro Church in America / The Black Church since Frazier*. Sourcebooks in Negro History. New York, 1974.

Frey, Sylvia R. "Shaking the Dry Bones: The Dialectic of Conversion." In Ted Ownby, ed., *Black and White Cultural Interaction in the Antebellum South*, 23–54. Jackson, Miss., 1993.

———. *Water from the Rock: Black Resistance in a Revolutionary Age*. Princeton, N.J., 1991.

———. " 'The Year of Jubilee Is Come': Black Christianity in the Plantation South in Post-Revolutionary America." In Ronald Hoffman and Peter J. Albert, eds., *Religion in a Revolutionary Age*, 87–124. Charlottesville, Va., 1994.

Fries, Adelaide L. "An Early Fourth of July Celebration." *Journal of American History*, IX (1915), 469–474.

———. "Moravian Customs: Our Inheritance." Moravian Historical Society, *Transactions*, XI (1936), 215–274.

———. *The Moravians in Georgia, 1735–40*. Raleigh, N.C., 1905.

Frijhoff, Willem. "The Kiss Sacred and Profane: Reflections on a Cross-Cultural Confrontation." In Jan N. Bremmer and Herman Roodenburg, eds., *A Cultural History of Gesture*, 210–236. Ithaca, N.Y., 1992.

Fulbrook, Mary. *Piety and Politics: Religion and the Rise of Absolutism in England, Württemberg, and Prussia*. New York, 1983.

Fulop, Timothy E., and Albert J. Raboteau, eds. *African American Religion: Interpretive Essays in History and Culture*. New York, 1997.

Furley, Oliver W. "Moravian Missionaries and Slaves in the West Indies." *Caribbean Studies*, V, no. 2 (July 1965), 3–16.

Gagliardo, John G. *From Pariah to Patriot: The Changing Image of the German Peasant, 1770–1840*. Lexington, Ky., 1969.

Gallay, Allan. "The Origins of Slaveholders' Paternalism: George Whitefield, the Bryan

Family, and the Great Awakening in the South." *Journal of Southern History*, LIII (1987), 369–394.

Garrett, Clarke. *Spirit Possession and Popular Religion: From the Camisards to the Shakers*. Baltimore, 1987.

Gaspar, David Barry. "Slavery, Amelioration, and Sunday Markets in Antigua, 1823–1831." *Slavery and Abolition*, IX (1989), 1–28.

Geggus, David. "Sugar and Coffee Cultivation in Saint Domingue and the Shaping of the Slave Labor Force." In Ira Berlin and Philip D. Morgan, eds., *Cultivation and Culture: Labor and the Shaping of Slave Life in the Americas*, 73–98. Charlottesville, Va., 1993.

Gehrke, William H. "Negro Slavery among the Germans in North Carolina." *North Carolina Historical Review*, XIV (1937), 307–324.

——. "The Transition from the German to the English Language in North Carolina." *North Carolina Historical Review*, XII (1935), 1–19.

Genovese, Eugene D. *From Rebellion to Revolution: Afro-American Slave Revolts in the Making of the Modern World*. Baton Rouge, La., 1979.

——. *Roll, Jordan, Roll: The World the Slaves Made*. New York, 1974.

Georgia Writers' Project. *Drums and Shadows: Survival Studies among the Georgia Coastal Negroes*. 1940; reprint, Athens, Ga., 1986.

Gilman, Sander L. *On Blackness without Blacks: Essays on the Image of the Black in Germany*. Boston, 1982.

Gollin, Gillian Lindt. *Moravians in Two Worlds: A Study of Changing Communities*. New York, 1967.

Gomez, Michael A. "Muslims in Early America." *Journal of Southern History*, LX (1994), 671–710.

Grant, Douglas. *The Fortunate Slave: An Illustration of African Slavery in the Early Eighteenth Century*. London, 1968.

Gravely, Will B. "The Rise of African Churches in America (1786–1822): Re-examining the Contexts." In Gayraud S. Wilmore, ed., *African American Religious Studies: An Interdisciplinary Anthology*, 301–317. Durham, N.C., 1989.

Griffin, Frances. "The English Settlement." In *Three Forks of Muddy Creek*, VI, 1–12. Winston-Salem, N.C., 1979.

——. "Land of Peace." In *Three Forks of Muddy Creek*, VII, 1–12. Winston-Salem, N.C., 1980.

——. *Less Time for Meddling: A History of Salem Academy and College, 1772–1866*. Winston-Salem, N.C., 1979.

Gudeman, Stephen. "Spiritual Relationships and Selecting a Godparent." *Man*, X (1975), 221–237.

Gudeman, Stephen, and Stuart B. Schwartz. "Cleansing Original Sin: Godparenthood and the Baptism of Slaves in Eighteenth-Century Bahia." In Raymond T. Smith, ed., *Kinship Ideology and Practice in Latin America*, 35–56. Chapel Hill, N.C., 1984.

Gutman, Herbert G. *The Black Family in Slavery and Freedom, 1750–1925*. New York, 1976.

Hall, N.A.T. "Maritime Maroons: *Grand Marronage* from the Danish West Indies." *William and Mary Quarterly*, 3d Ser., LXII (1985), 476–498.

Hamilton, J. Taylor. *A History of the Missions of the Moravian Church during the Eighteenth and Nineteenth Centuries*. Bethlehem, Pa., 1901.

Hamilton, Kenneth G., and J. Taylor Hamilton. *History of the Moravian Church: The Renewed Unitas Fratrum, 1722–1957*. Bethlehem, Pa., 1967.

Hannaford, Ivan. *Race: The History of an Idea in the West*. Baltimore, 1996.

Harding, Vincent. *There Is a River: The Black Struggle for Freedom in America*. New York, 1981.

——. "The Uses of the Afro-American Past." In Donald R. Cutler, ed., *The Religious Situation: 1969*, 829–840. Boston, 1969.

Harris, W. T., and Harry Sawyerr. *The Springs of Mende Belief and Conduct: A Discussion of the Influence of the Belief in the Supernatural among the Mende*. Freetown, Sierra Leone, 1968.

Harris-Schenz, Beverly. *Black Images in Eighteenth-Century German Literature*. Stuttgart, 1981.

Hastings, S. U., and B. L. MacLeavy. *Seedtime and Harvest: A Brief History of the Moravian Church in Jamaica, 1754–1979*. Bridgetown, Barbados, 1979.

Haupert, Thomas J. "Apprenticeship in the Moravian Settlement of Salem, North Carolina, 1766–1786." *Communal Societies*, IX (1989), 1–9.

Higginbotham, Don. *The War of American Independence: Military Attitudes, Policies, and Practice, 1763–1789*. New York, 1971.

Hoffman, Ronald. "The 'Disaffected' in the Revolutionary South." In Alfred F. Young, ed., *The American Revolution: Explorations in the History of American Radicalism*, 275–316. Dekalb, Ill., 1976.

Hoffman, Ronald, Thad W. Tate, and Peter J. Albert, eds. *An Uncivil War: The Southern Backcountry during the American Revolution*. Charlottesville, Va., 1985.

Hopkins, Leroy T. "The Germantown Protest and Afro-German Relations in Pennsylvania and Maryland before the Civil War." *The Report: A Journal of German-American History*, IV (1990), 23–31.

Hopkins, Nicholas S. "Maninka Social Organization." In Carleton T. Hodge, ed., *Papers on the Manding*, 99–117. Bloomington, Ind., 1971.

Hsia, R. Po-chia. *Social Discipline in the Reformation: Central Europe, 1550–1750*. London, 1989.

Huggins, Nathan Irvin. *Black Odyssey: The African-American Ordeal in Slavery*. New York, 1990.

Hughes, Sarah S. "Slaves for Hire: The Allocation of Black Labor in Elizabeth City County, Virginia, 1782 to 1810." *William and Mary Quarterly*, 3d Ser., XXXV (1978), 260–286.

Ingram, Jeannine S. "Music in American Moravian Communities: Transplanted Traditions in Indigenous Practices." *Communal Societies*, II (1982), 39–52.

Inikori, J. E. *Forced Migration: The Impact of the Export Slave Trade on African Societies*. New York, 1982.

Inikori, Joseph E., and Stanley L. Engerman, eds. *The Atlantic Slave Trade: Effects on Economies, Societies, and Peoples in Africa, the Americas, and Europe*. Durham, N.C., 1992.

James, Hunter. "Friedberg: The Early Years." In *Three Forks of Muddy Creek*, III, 11–24. Winston-Salem, N.C., 1976.

——. *The Quiet People of the Land: A Story of the North Carolina Moravians in Revolutionary Times*. Chapel Hill, N.C., 1976.

Johnson, Clifton H., ed. *God Struck Me Dead: Religious Conversion Experiences of Negro Ex-Slaves*. Philadelphia, 1969.

Johnson, Guion Griffis. *Ante-Bellum North Carolina: A Social History*. Chapel Hill, N.C., 1937.

Jones, Jacqueline. "Race, Sex, and Self-Evident Truths: The Status of Slave Women during the Era of the American Revolution." In Ronald Hoffman and Peter J. Albert, eds., *Women in the Age of the American Revolution*, 297–337. Charlottesville, Va., 1989.

Jordan, Winthrop D. *White over Black: American Attitudes toward the Negro, 1550–1812*. Chapel Hill, N.C., 1968.

Kaiser, Gerhard. *Pietismus und Patriotismus im literarischen Deutschland*. . . . Wiesbaden, 1961.

Kaminsky, Howard. *A History of the Hussite Revolution*. Berkeley, Calif., 1967.

———. "Peter Chelciky: Treatises on Christianity and the Social Order." *Studies in Medieval and Renaissance History*, I (1964), 107–179.

———. "The Religion of Hussite Tabor." In Miloslav Rechcigl, ed., *The Czechoslovak Contribution to World Culture*, 210–223. The Hague, 1964.

Kay, Marvin L. Michael, and Lorin Lee Cary. "Class, Mobility, and Conflict in North Carolina on the Eve of the Revolution." In Jeffrey J. Crow and Larry E. Tise, eds., *The Southern Experience in the American Revolution*, 109–151. Chapel Hill, N.C., 1978.

———. "A Demographic Analysis of Colonial North Carolina, with Special Emphasis upon the Slave and Black Populations." In Jeffrey J. Crow and Flora J. Hatley, eds., *Black Americans in North Carolina and the South*, 71–121. Chapel Hill, N.C., 1984.

———. "Slave Runaways in Colonial North Carolina, 1748–1775." *North Carolina Historical Review*, LXIII (1986), 1–39.

———. *Slavery in North Carolina, 1748–1775*. Chapel Hill, N.C., 1995.

Klein, Rachel N. *Unification of a Slave State: The Rise of the Planter Class in the South Carolina Backcountry, 1760–1808*. Chapel Hill, N.C., 1990.

Kolchin, Peter. "Reevaluating the Antebellum Slave Community: A Comparative Perspective." *Journal of American History*, LXX (1983–1984), 579–601.

———. *Unfree Labor: American Slavery and Russian Serfdom*. Cambridge, Mass., 1987.

Kulikoff, Allan. *The Agrarian Origins of American Capitalism*. Charlottesville, Va., 1992.

———. "The Origins of Afro-American Society in Tidewater Maryland and Virginia, 1700 to 1790." *William and Mary Quarterly*, 3d Ser., XXXV (1978), 226–259.

———. "Uprooted Peoples: Black Migrants in the Age of the American Revolution, 1790–1820." In Ira Berlin and Ronald Hoffman, eds., *Slavery and Freedom in the Age of the American Revolution*, 143–171. Charlottesville, Va., 1983.

Landers, Jane. "Gracia Real de Santa Teresa de Mose: A Free Black Town in Spanish Colonial Florida." *American Historical Review*, XCV (1990), 9–30.

Lefler, Hugh T., and William S. Powell. *Colonial North Carolina: A History*. New York, 1973.

Lefler, Hugh Talmage, and Albert Ray Newsome. *North Carolina: The History of a Southern State*. Chapel Hill, N.C., 1954.

Lemmon, Sarah McCulloh. *Frustrated Patriots: North Carolina and the War of 1812*. Chapel Hill, N.C., 1973.

Levering, Joseph Mortimer. *A History of Bethlehem, Pennsylvania, 1741–1892, with Some Account of Its Founders and Their Early Activity*. Bethlehem, Pa., 1903.

Levine, Lawrence W. *Black Culture and Black Consciousness: Afro-American Folk Thought from Slavery to Freedom*. New York, 1977.

Lewis, Arthur James. *Zinzendorf, the Ecumenical Pioneer: A Study in the Moravian Contribution to Christian Mission and Unity*. Philadelphia, 1962.

Lewis, Johanna Miller. *Artisans in the North Carolina Backcountry*. Lexington, Ky., 1995.

Lincoln, C. Eric. "Black Religion in North Carolina: From Colonial Times to 1900." In Jeffrey J. Crow and Robert E. Winters, Jr., eds., *The Black Presence in North Carolina*, 9–24. Raleigh, N.C., 1978.

Lincoln, C. Eric, and Lawrence H. Mamiya. *The Black Church in the African-American Experience*. Durham, N.C., 1990.

Locklair, Paula W. "The Moravian Craftsman in Eighteenth-Century North Carolina." In Ian M. G. Quimby, ed., *The Craftsman in Early America,* 273–298. New York, 1984.

Mainwaring, W. Thomas. "Communal Ideals, Worldly Concerns, and the Moravians in North Carolina." *Journal of Communal Societies,* VI (1986), 138–162.

Manning, Patrick. *Slavery and African Life: Occidental, Oriental, and African Slave Trades.* Cambridge, 1990.

Martin, Dale B. *Slavery as Salvation: The Metaphor of Slavery in Pauline Christianity.* New Haven, Conn., 1990.

Martin, Peter. *Schwarze Teufel, edle Mohren.* Hamburg, 1993.

Mathews, Donald G. "Charles Colcock Jones and the Southern Evangelical Crusade to Form a Biracial Community." In *Journal of Southern History,* XLI (1975), 299–320.

——. *Religion in the Old South.* Chicago, 1977.

Maurer, Maurer. "Music in Wachovia, 1753–1800." *William and Mary Quarterly,* 3d Ser., VIII (1951), 214–227.

Mbiti, John S. *African Religion and Philosophy.* New York, 1969.

Meier, Gudrun. "Preliminary Remarks on the Oldendorp Manuscripts and Their History." In Stephan Palmié, ed., *Slave Cultures and the Cultures of Slavery,* 67–77. Knoxville, Tenn., 1996.

Merrens, H. Roy. *Colonial North Carolina in the Eighteenth Century: A Study in Historical Geography.* Chapel Hill, N.C., 1964.

Merrill, Michael. "Putting 'Capitalism' in Its Place: A Review of Recent Literature." *William and Mary Quarterly,* 3d Ser., LII (1995), 315–326.

Miller, Perry. *Errand into the Wilderness.* 1956; reprint, New York, 1964.

Miller, Randall M., ed. *States of Progress: Germans and Blacks in America over Three Hundred Years.* Philadelphia, 1989.

Mintz, Sidney, and Richard Price. *The Birth of African-American Culture: An Anthropological Perspective.* 1976; reprint, Boston, 1992.

Mintz, Sidney W., and Eric R. Wolf. "An Analysis of Ritual Co-Parenthood (Compadrazgo)." *Southwestern Journal of Anthropology,* VI (1950), 341–367.

Morgan, Philip D. "British Encounters with Africans and African-Americans, circa 1600–1780." In Bernard Bailyn and Philip D. Morgan, eds., *Strangers within the Realm: Cultural Margins of the First British Empire,* 157–219. Chapel Hill, N.C., 1991.

——. "Slave Life in Piedmont Virginia, 1720–1800." In Lois Green Carr, Philip D. Morgan, and Jean B. Russo, eds., *Colonial Chesapeake Society,* 433–484. Chapel Hill, N.C., 1988.

Morgan, Philip D., and Michael L. Nicholls. "Slaves in Piedmont Virginia, 1720–1790." *William and Mary Quarterly,* 3d Ser., XLVI (1989), 211–251.

Morris, Charles Edward. "Panic and Reprisal: Reaction in North Carolina to the Nat Turner Insurrection, 1831." *North Carolina Historical Review,* LXII (1985), 29–52.

Myers, Richmond E. "The Moravian Church and the Civil War." Moravian Historical Society, *Transactions,* XX (1965), 226–248.

Nelson, Vernon H. "Samuel Isles, First Moravian Missionary in Antigua." Moravian Historical Society, *Transactions,* XXI (1966), 3–27.

Niemeyer, Otto. "Deutsche Sklavenhalter und Germanisierte Neger." *Deutsche Pioneer,* II (1870–1871), 280–284.

North, Alice Henderson. "New Minister at Bethania." In *Three Forks of Muddy Creek,* 23–24. Winston-Salem, N.C., 1974.

Norton, Mary Beth, Herbert G. Gutman, and Ira Berlin. "The Afro-American Family in the

Age of Revolution." In Ira Berlin and Ronald Hoffman, eds., *Slavery and Freedom in the Age of the American Revolution*, 175–191. Charlottesville, Va., 1983.

O'Brien, Susan. "A Transatlantic Community of Saints: The Great Awakening and the First Evangelical Network, 1735–1755." *American Historical Review*, XCI (1986), 811–832.

Olwig, Karen Fog. "African Cultural Principles in Caribbean Slave Societies: A View from the Danish West Indies." In Stephan Palmié, ed., *Slave Cultures and the Cultures of Slavery*, 23–39. Knoxville, Tenn., 1996.

——. *Cultural Adaptation and Resistance on St. John: Three Centuries of Afro-Caribbean Life*. Gainesville, Fla., 1985.

Ownby, Ted, ed. *Black and White Cultural Interaction in the Antebellum South*. Jackson, Miss., 1993.

Ozment, Steven. *The Age of Reform, 1250–1550: An Intellectual and Religious History of Late Medieval and Reformation Europe*. New Haven, Conn., 1980.

Palmié, Stephan. *Slave Cultures and the Cultures of Slavery*. Knoxville, Tenn., 1995.

Parramore, Thomas C. "Aborted Takeoff: A Critique of 'Fly across the River.' " *North Carolina Historical Review*, LXVIII (1991), 111–121.

——. "Conspiracy and Revivalism in 1802: A Direful Symbiosis." *Negro History Bulletin*, II (1980), 28–31.

Parrinder, Geoffrey. *African Traditional Religion*. London, 1962.

Patterson, Orlando. *Slavery and Social Death: A Comparative Study*. Cambridge, Mass., 1982.

Perella, Nicolas James. *The Kiss Sacred and Profane: An Interpretive History of Kiss Symbolism and Related Religio-Erotic Themes*. Berkeley, Calif., 1969.

Piersen, William D. *Black Legacy: America's Hidden Heritage*. Amherst, Mass., 1993.

Pinson, Koppel S. *Pietism as a Factor in the Rise of German Nationalism*. New York, 1934.

Pollak, Otto. "German Immigrant Problems in Eighteenth-Century Pennsylvania as Reflected in Trouble Advertisements." *American Sociological Review*, VIII (1943), 674–684.

Powell, William S., ed. "Tryon's 'Book' on North Carolina." *North Carolina Historical Review*, XXXIV (1957), 406–415.

Price, Richard. *Alabi's World*. Baltimore, 1990.

Quarles, Benjamin. *The Negro in the American Revolution*. 1961; reprint, Chapel Hill, N.C., 1996.

——. "The Revolutionary War as a Black Declaration of Independence." In Ira Berlin and Ronald Hoffman, eds., *Slavery and Freedom in the Age of the American Revolution*, 283–301. Charlottesville, Va., 1983.

Quinn, Charlotte A. *Mandingo Kingdoms of the Senegambia: Traditionalism, Islam, and European Expansion*. Evanston, Ill., 1972.

Raboteau, Albert J. "African-Americans, Exodus, and the American Israel." In Albert J. Raboteau, *A Fire in the Bones: Reflections on African-American Religious History*, 17–36. Boston, 1995.

——. *A Fire in the Bones: Reflections on African-American Religious History*. Boston, 1995.

——. *Slave Religion: The "Invisible Institution" in the Antebellum South*. New York, 1978.

Radcliffe-Brown, A. R., and Daryll Forde, eds. *African Systems of Kinship and Marriage*. London, 1950.

Ramsey, Robert W. *Carolina Cradle: Settlement of the Northwest Carolina Frontier, 1747–1762*. Chapel Hill, N.C., 1964.

Rawley, James A. *The Transatlantic Slave Trade: A History*. New York, 1981.

Ray, Benjamin C. *African Religions: Symbol, Ritual, and Community*. Englewood Cliffs, N.J., 1976.

Rights, Douglas Letell. "Salem in the War between the States." *North Carolina Historical Review,* XXVII (1950), 277–288.

Rodney, Walter. *History of the Upper Guinea Coast, 1545–1800.* Oxford, 1970.

Roeber, A. G. "In German Ways? Problems and Potentials of Eighteenth-Century German Social and Emigration History." *William and Mary Quarterly,* 3d Ser., XLIV (1987), 750–774.

——. " 'The Origin of Whatever Is Not English among Us': The Dutch-speaking and the German-speaking Peoples of Colonial British America." In Bernard Bailyn and Philip D. Morgan, eds., *Strangers within the Realm: Cultural Margins of the First British Empire,* 220–283. Chapel Hill, N.C., 1991.

——. *Palatines, Liberty, and Property: German Lutherans in Colonial British America.* Baltimore, 1993.

Roediger, David R. "And Die in Dixie: Funerals, Death, and Heaven in the Slave Community, 1700–1865." *Massachusetts Review,* XXII (1981), 163–183.

Sabean, David. "Aspects of Kinship Behavior and Property in Rural Western Europe before 1800." In Jack Goody, Joan Thirsk, and E. P. Thompson, eds., *Family and Inheritance: Rural Society in Western Europe, 1200–1800,* 96–111. New York, 1976.

——. *Power in the Blood: Popular Culture and Village Discourse in Early Modern Germany.* New York, 1984.

Sachse, Julius F. *The German Pietists of Provincial Pennsylvania.* Philadelphia, 1895.

Salinger, Sharon V. *"To Serve Well and Faithfully": Labor and Indentured Servitude in Pennsylvania, 1682–1800.* New York, 1987.

Scott, James C. *Domination and the Arts of Resistance: Hidden Transcripts.* New Haven, Conn., 1990.

Sensbach, Jon F. *African-Americans in Salem.* Winston-Salem, N.C., 1992.

——. "Charting a Course in Early African-American History." *William and Mary Quarterly,* 3d Ser., L (1993), 394–405.

——. "Culture and Conflict in the Early Black Church: A Moravian Mission Congregation in Antebellum North Carolina." *North Carolina Historical Review,* LXXI (1994), 401–429.

——. "Interracial Sects: Race, Gender, and the Moravian Church in Early North Carolina." In Catherine Clinton and Michele Gillespie, eds., *The Devil's Lane: Sex and Race in the Early South,* 154–167. New York, 1997.

Sessler, Jacob John. *Communal Pietism among Early American Moravians.* New York, 1933.

Shirley, Michael. *From Congregation Town to Industrial City: Culture and Social Change in a Southern Community.* New York, 1994.

——. "The Market and Community Culture in Antebellum Salem, North Carolina." *Journal of the Early Republic,* XI (1991), 219–248.

Smaby, Beverly Prior. *The Transformation of Moravian Bethlehem: From Communal Mission to Family Economy.* Philadelphia, 1988.

Smith, H. Shelton. *In His Image, But . . . : Racism in Southern Religion, 1780–1910.* Durham, N.C., 1972.

Smith, James Wesley. *Sojourners in Search of Freedom: The Settlement of Liberia by Black Americans.* Lanham, Md., 1987.

Smith, Theophus H. *Conjuring Culture: Biblical Formations of Black America.* New York, 1994.

Sobel, Mechal. *Trabelin' On: The Slave Journey to an Afro-Baptist Faith.* 2d ed. Princeton, N.J., 1988.

——. *The World They Made Together: Black and White Values in Eighteenth-Century Virginia.* Princeton, N.J., 1987.

Sommer, Elisabeth. "A Different Kind of Freedom? Order and Discipline among the Moravian Brethren in Germany and Salem, North Carolina, 1771–1801." *Church History,* LXIII (1994), 221–234.

Southern, Eileen. *Music of Black Americans: A History.* New York, 1971.

Spindel, Donna J. *Crime and Society in North Carolina, 1663–1776.* Baton Rouge, La., 1989.

Stoeffler, F. Ernest. *German Pietism during the Eighteenth Century.* Leiden, 1973.

Strickland, John Scott. "The Great Revival and Insurrectionary Fears in North Carolina: An Examination of Antebellum Southern Society and Slave Revolt Panics." In Orville Vernon Burton and Robert C. McMath, Jr., eds., *Class, Conflict, and Consensus: Antebellum Southern Community Studies,* 57–95. Westport, Conn., 1982.

Stroupe, Henry S. " 'Cite Them Both to Attend the Next Church Conference': Social Control by North Carolina Baptist Churches, 1772–1908." *North Carolina Historical Review,* LII (1975), 156–170.

Stuckey, Sterling. *Slave Culture: Nationalist Theory and the Foundations of Black America.* New York, 1988.

Surratt, Jerry L. *Gottlieb Schober of Salem: Discipleship and Ecumenical Vision in an Early Moravian Town.* Macon, Ga., 1983.

——. "The Role of Dissent in Community Evolution among Moravians in Salem, 1772–1860." *North Carolina Historical Review,* LII (1975), 235–255.

Sweet, William W. "The Churches as Moral Courts of the Frontier." *Church History,* II (1933), 3–21.

Tadman, Michael. *Speculators and Slaves: Masters, Traders, and Slaves in the Old South.* Madison, Wis., 1989.

Taylor, Rosser Howard. "Slave Conspiracies in North Carolina." *North Carolina Historical Review,* V (1928), 20–34.

——. *Slaveholding in North Carolina: An Economic View.* The James Sprunt Historical Publications, XVIII. Chapel Hill, N.C., 1926.

Thompson, Robert Farris. *Flash of the Spirit: African and Afro-American Art and Philosophy.* New York, 1983.

Thornton, John. *Africa and Africans in the Making of the Atlantic World, 1400–1680.* New York, 1992.

Thorp, Daniel B. "Assimilation in North Carolina's Moravian Community." *Journal of Southern History,* LII (1986), 19–42.

——. "Chattel with a Soul: The Autobiography of a Moravian Slave." *Pennsylvania Magazine of History and Biography,* CXII (1988), 433–451.

——. "The City That Never Was: Count von Zinzendorf's Original Plan for Salem." *North Carolina Historical Review,* LXI (1984), 36–58.

——. *The Moravian Community in Colonial North Carolina: Pluralism on the Southern Frontier.* Knoxville, Tenn., 1989.

——. "Taverns and Tavern Culture on the Southern Colonial Frontier: Rowan County, North Carolina, 1753–1776." *Journal of Southern History,* LXII (1996), 661–688.

Three Forks of Muddy Creek. 14 vols. Winston-Salem, N.C., 1974–.

Thurman, Howard. *Jesus and the Disinherited.* 2d ed. Richmond, Ind., 1976.

Tise, Larry E. *The Yadkin Melting Pot: Methodism and Moravians in the Yadkin Valley, 1750–1950, and Mt. Tabor Church, 1845–1966.* Winston-Salem, N.C., 1967.

Towlson, Clifford W. *Moravian and Methodist: Relationships and Influences in the Eighteenth Century.* London, 1957.

Trommler, Frank, and Joseph McVeigh, eds. *America and the Germans: An Assessment of a Three-Hundred-Year History.* 2 vols. Philadelphia, 1985.

Turner, Mary, ed. *From Chattel Slaves to Wage Slaves: The Dynamics of Labour Bargaining in the Americas.* Bloomington, Ind., 1996.

Uttendörfer, Otto. *Zinzendorfs Weltbetrachtung: eine systematische Darstellung der Gedankenwelt des Begrunders der Brüdergemeine.* Berlin, 1929.

Veazie, Isabel. "Master and Apprentice." In *Three Forks of Muddy Creek,* III, 49–57. Winston-Salem, N.C., 1976.

Vlach, John Michael. *The Afro-American Tradition in Decorative Arts.* 1978; reprint, Athens, Ga., 1990.

——. "Graveyards and Afro-American Art." *Southern Exposure,* V (1977), 161–165.

Wagner, Murray L. *Petr Chelčický, a Radical Separatist in Hussite Bohemia.* Scottdale, Pa., 1983.

Ward, W. R. *The Protestant Evangelical Awakening.* New York, 1992.

Watson, Alan D. "Impulse toward Independence: Resistance and Rebellion among North Carolina Slaves, 1750–1775." *Journal of Negro History,* LXIII (1978), 317–328.

——. "North Carolina Slave Courts, 1715–1785." *North Carolina Historical Review,* LX (1983), 24–36.

Weinlick, John R. *Count Zinzendorf.* New York, 1956.

Wellenreuther, Herman. "Image and Counterimage, Tradition and Expectation: The German Immigrants in English Colonial Society in Pennsylvania, 1700–1765." In Frank Trommler and Joseph McVeigh, eds., *America and the Germans: An Assessment of a Three-Hundred-Year History,* 85–105. 2 vols. Philadelphia, 1985.

Westergaard, Waldemar. *The Danish West Indies under Company Rule, 1671–1754.* New York, 1917.

White, Deborah Gray. *Ar'n't I a Woman? Female Slaves in the Plantation South.* New York, 1985.

Wiecek, William M. "The Statutory Law of Slavery and Race in the Thirteen Mainland Colonies of British America." *William and Mary Quarterly,* 3d Ser., XXXIV (1977), 258–280.

Wiesner, Merry E. "Guilds, Male Bonding, and Women's Work in Early Modern Germany." *Gender and History,* I (1989), 125–137.

Wokeck, Marianne. "Harnessing the Lure of the 'Best Poor Man's Country': The Dynamics of German-Speaking Immigration to British North America, 1683–1783." In Ida Altman and James Horn, eds., *"To Make America": European Emigration in the Early Modern Period,* 204–243. Berkeley, Calif., 1991.

Wood, Forrest G. *The Arrogance of Faith: Christianity and Race in America from the Colonial Era to the Twentieth Century.* New York, 1990.

Wood, Peter H. *Black Majority: Negroes in Colonial South Carolina from 1670 through the Stono Rebellion.* New York, 1974.

——. "The Changing Population of the Colonial South: An Overview by Race and Region, 1685–1790." In Peter H. Wood, Gregory A. Waselkov, and M. Thomas Hatley, eds., *Powhatan's Mantle: Indians in the Colonial Southeast,* 35–103. Lincoln, Nebr., 1989.

——. " 'I Did the Best I Could for My Day': The Study of Early Black History during the Second Reconstruction, 1960 to 1976." *William and Mary Quarterly,* 3d Ser., XXXV (1978), 185–225.

——. " 'Liberty Is Sweet': African American Freedom Struggles in the Years before White Independence." In Alfred F. Young, ed., *Beyond the American Revolution: Explorations in the History of American Radicalism,* 149–184. Dekalb, Ill., 1993.

——. "Nat Turner: The Unknown Slave as Visionary Leader." In Leon Litwack and August Meier, eds., *Black Leaders of the Nineteenth Century,* 21–40. Urbana, Ill., 1988.

Woodson, Carter G. *The History of the Negro Church.* 2d ed. Washington, D.C., 1921.

Young, Alfred F., ed. *Beyond the American Revolution: Explorations in the History of American Radicalism.* DeKalb, Ill., 1993.

Zahan, Dominique. *The Religion, Spirituality, and Thought of Traditional Africa.* Chicago, 1970.

Zeman, Jarold Knox. *The Anabaptists and the Czech Brethren in Moravia, 1526–1628: A Study of Origins and Contacts.* The Hague, 1969.

Unpublished Secondary Works

Ferguson, Leland. "Hidden Testimony: A Perspective from Historical Archaeology on African Americans and Cemeteries in Old Salem." Winston-Salem, Forsyth County, Kernersville Preservation Council, 1994.

——. "A Report on Archaeological Testing of the St. Philips Moravian Church and Parish Graveyard." Winston-Salem, Forsyth County, Kernersville Preservation Council, 1992.

Hartley, Michael O. "Bethania in Wachovia." Bethania Historical Society, Winston-Salem, N.C., 1989.

Hartley, Michael O., and Martha Brown Boxley. "Wachovia in Forsyth." Wachovia Historical Society, Winston-Salem, N.C., 1987.

Hendricks, Wanda. "St. Philips Moravian Church of Salem, North Carolina, Its Past and Future." Master's thesis, Wake Forest University, 1984.

Lenius, Susan. "Slavery and the Moravian Church in North Carolina." Honors thesis, Moravian College, 1974.

Miller, Bertha Hampton. "Blacks in Winston-Salem, North Carolina, 1895-1920: Community Development in an Era of Benevolent Paternalism." Ph.D. diss., Duke University, 1981.

Mitchell, Norma Taylor. "Freedom and Authority in the Moravian Community of North Carolina, 1753–1837." Master's thesis, Duke University, 1962.

Rogers, Ellin Lee. "History of the Paper Mill at Salem, North Carolina, 1789–1873." Master's thesis, Wake Forest University, 1982.

Rohrer, S. Scott. "Freedman of the Lord: The Black Moravian Congregation of Salem, N.C., and Its Struggle for Survival, 1856–1890." Research report, Old Salem, Inc., 1993.

——. "Friedrich Schuman and His Slaves: Portrait of a Plantation." Research report, Old Salem, Inc., 1990.

——. "A Mission among the People: The World of St. Philip's Church from 1890 to 1952." Research report, Old Salem, Inc., 1993.

Sommer, Elisabeth W. "Serving Two Masters: Authority, Faith, and Community among the Moravian Brethren in Germany and North Carolina in the Eighteenth Century." Ph.D. diss., University of Virginia, 1991.

Surratt, Jerry L. "From Theocracy to Voluntary Church and Secularized Community: A

Study of the Moravians in Salem, North Carolina, 1772–1860." Ph.D. diss., Emory University, 1968.

Thorp, Daniel B. "Buying Men and Saving Souls: The Moravians' Response to Slavery in Eighteenth-Century North Carolina." Unpublished paper, n.d.

——. "Moravian Colonization of Wachovia, 1753–1772: The Maintenance of Community in Late Colonial North Carolina." Ph.D. diss., Johns Hopkins University, 1982.

Willis, Raymond F., and R. Jackson Marshall III. "Archaeological and Archival Studies at Historic Bethabara Park: Proposed Visitor Center Site." Report, Wake Forest University Archaeology Laboratory, Winston-Salem, N.C., 1985.

Zogry, Kenneth J. "A Research Report and Historic Furnishings Plan for the Salem Tavern." Old Salem, Inc., 1991.

INDEX

• • • • • • • • • • • • • • • • •

Abendmahl. See Communion
Abraham (brother of Anthony), 30
Abraham (preacher on Saint Thomas), 38
Abraham (Sambo), 99, 105, 109, 132, 135, 139, 163, 296; purchase of, by Moravians, 1–2, 17–18, 68; *Lebenslauf* (memoir) of, 2–3, 11, 12, 16, 152, 172, 178; Mandingo culture of, 3–9; capture of, 11; and French West Indies, 13, 15–16; and Virginia, 16–17; relationship of, to Paul (Jupiter), 17–18, 109, 139–140; resistance of, against slavery, 87, 90–91; attempted escape and punishment of, 89–90; beating of, 94; conversion of, 107–108, 112; as baptismal sponsor, 109, 139–140; in Hourly Intercession Society, 122; as informal preacher, 122–123, 146, 265–266; as Single Brother, 125–126; discipline of, by elders, 129; marriage of, 133; work relations of, with white Moravians, 151–154; will of, 153–154; death of, 178–179, 222
Abraham (son of Paul and Emma), 140
Adam, 288–289
Aeltesten Conferenz. See Elders' Conference
African Americans. See Afro-Christianity; Afro-Moravians; Church, African-American; Interracial activity; Non-Moravians, African-American; Rebellion, slave; Resistance, slave; Slavery; Work
Afro-Christianity, 16, 75, 112–113, 116–117, 122–124, 126, 138–143, 178–179, 218–219, 230–231, 240, 242, 245–248, 280–282, 291–293. See also Afro-Moravians; Church, African-American

Afro-Moravians: in Saint Thomas mission, 33–41, 115, 134, 139, 195; in transatlantic black evangelicalism, 39–41, 265–266, 302; participation of, in church ritual and congregational life, 74, 83–84, 104–105, 113–117, 120–146, 296–297; conversions of, in early Wachovia, 82–84, 97, 105–117; meaning of conversion for, 105–106, 110–113, 115–117, 144, 146; in choir system, 125–126, 136–137; in disciplinary system, 125–130, 205–206; marriage and families of, 130–143; baptismal sponsorship and extended kinship of, 138–143; as workers in Moravian economy, 147–159, 171–173, 176–177; work relations of, with whites, 147–159, 171–172, 177; and mission, 195–197; response of, to white separatism, 200–206, 214–215; exclusion of, from integrated churches, 211–215, 252; participation of, in black church, 222–223; in modern era, 301–302
Agriculture: African-American workers in, 62–65, 69, 72–73, 170–176, 273–275, 277–285; importance of, in Moravian economy, 170–176, 191; and Moravian religion, 279–280
Alabama, 251, 294
Amish, 56
Amo, Anton Wilhelm, 31
Anabaptists, 22
Andrew (Bethlehem), 111–112
Anna (Patty; also Nancy), 121, 135, 172, 173; conversion of, 108; marriage of, 108, 132–133; as spiritual elder, 142; as tavern worker, 150–151; work relations of, with whites, 150–151, 205; participation of,